FRAMING PUBLIC LIFE

Perspectives on Media and Our
Understanding of the Social World

FRAMING PUBLIC LIFE

Perspectives on Media and Our
Understanding of the Social World

Edited by

STEPHEN D. REESE
University of Texas at Austin

OSCAR H. GANDY, JR.
University of Pennsylvania

AUGUST E. GRANT
Focus 25 Research & Consulting
Columbia, South Carolina

2001

LAWRENCE ERLBAUM ASSOCIATES, PUBLISHERS
Mahwah, New Jersey   London

Lawrence Erlbaum Associates, Inc., Publishers
10 Industrial Avenue
Mahwah, NJ 07430

Cover design by Kathryn Houghtaling Lacey

Library of Congress Cataloging-in-Publication Data

Framing public life: Perspectives on media and our understanding
of the social world / edited by Stephen D. Reese, Oscar H. Gandy, Jr.,
August E. Grant.
p. cm.
Includes bibliographical references and index.
ISBN 0-8058-3653-5 (cloth : alk. paper)
ISBN 0-8058-4926-2 (pbk. : alk. paper)
1. Journalism—Objectivity. 2. Journalism—Social aspects.
3. Reporters and reporting. I. Reese, Stephen D. II. Gandy, Oscar H.
III. Grant, August E., 1956–

PN4784. O4 F69 2003
302.23—dc21   2001023611
                                                          CIP

Books published by Lawrence Erlbaum Associates are printed on acid-
free paper, and their bindings are chosen for strength and durability.

Printed in the United States of America
10 9 8 7 6 5 4 3 2

Contents

CONTENTS

Foreword

William A. Gamson
Boston College

This collection provides a picture of the multidisciplinary field of frame analysis as it presently exists. Don't look for a portrait with a unified understanding of the framing process; a collage is a better metaphor—a series of Images connected by certain common themes. What does it tell us about the state of the art?

Oscar Grandy, in the concluding chapter, does a fine job of answering this question from the standpoint of a scholar working in the field of communications. Whereas I agree with many of his observations, they made me sharply aware of our disciplinary differences. I am a visitor from the neighboring field of political sociology. Although I am pretty familiar with this communication neighborhood and visit it often, I am also struck by ways in which it is subtly different from my home turf.

Drawing on the sociology of culture, I am accustomed to thinking of a full-fledged frame analysis as having three components. First, there is attention to the production process—the ways in which carriers of particular frames engage in activities to produce and reproduce them. A focus on the production process alerts us to issues of power and resources, to the framing process as a struggle over meaning that is ultimately expressed through texts.

There are many studies of more overt forms of sponsorship in which actors engage in identifiable activities to further the career of preferred frames. These studies are a constant reminder that frame contests do not take place on a level playing field. They highlight the central importance of the relationship between journalists and sources and the process of selecting sources to quote. But attention to the production process also alerts us to less visible uses of power, those that exclude certain sponsors or marginalize their preferred frames. It leads us to attend to absences and silences in a discourse as well as what is there.

Power, contention, hegemony, are the names of the main thoroughfares in my neighborhood; they seem more like side streets in the communications neighborhood. Concerns with the production process are not absent in this volume—they are implied, for example, in the concept of a "web of subsidies"—but taken as a whole, they are quite muted. Many of the analyses begin with the characteristics of texts and move to their effects on the audience. The operation of power in their production is not examined directly.

The second part of a frame analysis involves the examination of texts, and here the neighborhoods don't seem that different. We all struggle with the same issues, particularly the vexing problem of the level of analysis. There are event frames, issue frames, master frames, and worldviews—frames within frames within frames. Even within an agreed level of analysis (e.g., frames about abortion policy), two independent investigators will inevitably slice up the discourse in different ways.

Is there any use for a concept that every investigator ends up applying in a different fashion? I have gradually come to the conclusion that this level of analysis problem has no solution but may be less of a problem than it first appears. Suppose we simply define a frame as a central organizing principle that holds together and gives coherence to a diverse array of symbols or idea elements. That different investigators may construct frames at various levels of abstraction to illuminate different aspects of texts does not imply that the locus of the frames is in the minds of the investigators—that these frames are pure social constructions. The frames are a property of texts and the analyst is attempting to identify a coherence and infrastructure that is contained in texts.

Inasmuch as I have recently completed a coauthored book on abortion discourse (Ferree, Gamson, Gerhards, & Rucht, 2001) I will stick to this example for illustration. For some questions, we want to contrast different policy frames. Hence, we show that Women's Self-Determination is used more by abortion rights advocates in Germany whereas a Right to Privacy frame is used more by such advocates in the United States. For other questions, we slice things up differently by contrasting frames that emphasize rights relative to those that emphasize needs. For still other questions, we ask how collective identities are framed on the abortion issue—who are "we" and "they" or whether the frames being used present women as clients in need of protection or as independent moral agents. These alternative ways of extracting frames from the same discourse are complementary rather than mutually exclusive alternatives—each useful for answering different questions.

Finally, a framing analysis needs to address the complex interaction of texts with an active audience engaged in negotiating meaning, doing what Elihu Katz (1990) has called "viewer's work." Again, my neighborhood looks different from the communications neighborhood as represented in this collection. Stuart Hall and the tradition of British cultural studies and audience ethnography seem much more part of my home turf, making me aware again of my visitor status.

Influenced by the media effects tradition, communication scholars seem much more likely to put their emphasis on the content of texts and how they influence a relatively passive audience. Perhaps this is most strongly represented in the debate over whether framing effects can be reduced to a second-order form of agenda setting, focusing on certain attributes of objects and actors. Both the power issues raised in examining production and the meaning issues raised by an audience capable of oppositional and negotiated readings of texts seem to get left out. In this context, the argument that framing can be usefully treated as a secondary component of agenda setting seems too reductionist. As argued in this volume, it seems to sap from this rich concept most of its vitality and capacity for producing insight.

In my neighborhood, the framing issues that people are grappling with these days concern the connection between narrative analysis and framing and the role of emotions in forms of framing analysis that seem overly cognitive. Again, although some of these issues are addressed in chapters in this volume, they are less central than in the discourse on framing in which I am embedded.

But travel broadens and I found many of the chapters in this collection insightful and refreshing. Many offer new ideas and techniques for carrying out systematic framing analysis, with particularly strong emphasis on framing as contained and revealed in media texts. I am happy to bring home the news that framing analysis is alive and thriving in communications land. Visitors and residents alike will find in this volume a valuable guide to the images and themes in the framing collage.

REFERENCES

Ferree, M. M., Gamson, W. A., Gerhards, J., & Rucht, D. (2001). *Shaping abortion discourse: Democracy and the public sphere in Germany and the United States.* New York: Cambridge University Press.
Katz, E. (1990). *"Viewer's work."* Wilbur Schramm Memorial Lecture, University of Illinois, Urbana.

Preface

In writing and editing this book, we are responding to the growing interest in understanding media power using the concept of framing. Whether called a theory, paradigm, model, or perspective, "framing's" appeal is growing. The popularity of the framing perspective is readily seen in the conference programs of groups like the Association for Education in Journalism and Mass Communication, the International Communication Association, and others. The concept is gaining strength, as scholars talk about framing issues across disciplinary lines, and increasingly across national boundaries. European researchers are just as likely to pose framing questions as North American scholars. Thus, framing appears to be a crossover perspective, appealing to scholars around the world and to working media professionals as well. The looseness with which scholars use framing suggests an important value for a volume like this one, to begin to clarify and organize this wide ranging area of research.

This volume began as a conference, although we have developed it far beyond that starting point. Augie Grant organized the conference Framing in the New Media Landscape at the University of South Carolina, held in October of 1997, and enlisted the services of the other two editors, Stephen Reese and Oscar Gandy, to deliver keynote and postnote addresses, respectively. The conference attracted strong interest, paper submissions, and attendance, confirming our notion that there was a need for organizing this emerging paradigm in communication. After the conference, the editors identified the significant contributions from the program that would be appropriate for a coherent book project, and then we proceeded to commission other contributions to generate as comprehensive a list of chapters as possible. We further elaborated our own contributions to reflect further thinking and reaction to the various submissions.

The overall plan of the book began with the conference structure. Stephen Reese provides a "keynote" opening chapter, the prologue, which attempts to organize the critical issues in framing research and present some of the more often cited and exemplary citations to the literature. In Part I, a section of chapters follows that focuses on theoretical and methodological issues; Durham (chap. 6) was newly commissioned and the others chapters were greatly expanded and revised from their original form. A number of empirical applications of framing were presented at the conference, from which we selected a set. These chapters were further developed in consultation with the editors, in an effort to bring out interesting case-study issues and relate them to the framing perspective. In Part II, chapters by Hertog and McLeod, and Nelson and Willey, were commissioned from scholars who had previously published framing research. These chapters go into somewhat more depth to develop those authors' special perspective, with some exemplary empirical findings. In Part III, the final group of chapters retains the name of the original conference, and emphasizes new media issues. Finally, in the epilogue, Oscar Gandy wraps up, as he did at the conference, with a "post keynote," now expanded and revised to reflect the final line-up of chapters.

We should emphasize that although the book's genesis was in the conference, this is far from a loosely organized proceedings. (Indeed, we regret that space and thematic requirements did not allow us to include other provocative and excellent papers from that meeting.) Rather, as we view it, the conference allowed the editors a chance to monitor some of the key issues in current framing research, by reviewing the paper submissions and making their selections. Preparing keynote addresses provided for Reese and Gandy a further impetus to come to conceptual terms with this field—a daunting task as it turned out, given the fragmented and burgeoning research efforts in the area. Finally, the project provided a means for the contributors to clarify their own thinking, in preparing their original research, revising it after editorial comments, and, a platform for the other contributors who responded to our commissions.

We recognize that some redundancy across chapters is inevitable in a project like this. We have tried to avoid needless duplication of material, but the authors all have their own perspective on framing, which often requires them to take a running start at their projects by covering similar research literature. Indeed, most of the chapters are capable of standing alone. The contributors in the Cases section were provided the prologue and asked to avoid taking up space with reviewing similar literature. Other contributors were provided a plan of the book and asked to advance their own take on framing, their jumping off point. So we envision many of the theoretical chapters, as well as those in the other two sections, to be useful as stand-alone pieces, even though taken together we hope to provide an interrelated set of themes and observations.

One of the primary motivators for this book and the conference that preceded it is the changing nature of the media itself. The organizational structure and ownership of media have been dynamic since the study of media processes began, but the beginning of the new millennium is marked by significant changes in the media themselves. The Internet offers a wealth of new opportunities to communicate news and information to both existing media organizations and new entrants. The degree of user control and speed of Internet communication challenges these media outlets' ability to retain the same degree of editorial control—and power—over the public that they have in the past. Thus, we question whether this power will be ceded by news organizations and their agents to the public or to the newsmakers, public relations personnel, and others with a stake in news coverage.

We believe that changes in the media will challenge existing notions of framing. At the same time, a more thorough understanding of the framing process helps us understand how both existing and new media constrain and enhance interpretations of events. The primary objectives of this volume, therefore, are to lay a solid theoretical and methodological foundation for the study of framing and to look forward to how the paradigm can be applied to the study of the new media landscape.

Nevertheless, the focus of this project inevitably reflects our scholarly interests and background. Each of us has been involved in framing research over the years, although we may not have formally located ourselves within that terminology. Although framing is a broad topic, applicable to many social settings, here we use it specifically to understand mediated communication, especially through television and print media. More narrowly, we restrict the emphasis in many chapters to news and the coverage of political issues. Although many of our contributors share our journalism and communication background (Nelson and Willey are the avowed political scientists in the group), we have made efforts to be as interdisciplinary as possible.

We don't expect that this is the definitive word on framing, or the most comprehensive, although until another volume comes along we may modestly claim that it is both. Realistically, though, this emerging, "fractured" paradigm has already become too diverse to lay claim to that goal. We do hope that the volume will help to identify the key theoretical and methodological issues, suggest some exemplary case studies, pose some questions pertaining to the new media, in their emerging technological and global forms, and generally stimulate productive future research. We hope the book will be useful for both classroom and scholarly purposes, not only in journalism and communication, but also in sociology, political science, anthropology, and other fields. Clearly, the interdisciplinary quality of framing is among its attractive features and must be a part of future research.

We would like to thank the College of Mass Communication at the University of South Carolina for hosting the original conference, and the chapter contributors for their patience in this long process. We thank also the other conference presenters, who we were not able to include, for their provocative papers and participation. Linda Bathgate provided the commitment to this project from Lawrence Erlbaum Associates and believes, as we do, that we are helping to define a new frontier in the field. We are grateful for supporting reviewer comments, especially from Jennings Bryant and Stanley Baran, who, along with Dennis Davis, has found the framing concept useful in his own book projects. We hope that this volume will stimulate further research in this provocative paradigm, and fruitful perspective on media power in public life.

Stephen D. Reese
Oscar H. Gandy, Jr.
August E. Grant

Introduction

In devising a coherent structure for a diverse approach to framing, we bookend this volume with two synthesis review chapters by Reese and Gandy, as prologue and epilogue, respectively. Reese presents his own organizing "framework" for framing research and provides an illustrative case analysis. Gandy uses the chapters in this volume and others in the literature to provide a synthetic overview and launch his critique of the subfield, in addition to offering some challenges for future efforts. Between these offerings we present three collections of chapters: the first includes a diverse set of theoretical and methodological perspectives on framing; the second emphasizes specific cases and empirical efforts by framing analysts, many of whom have extensive research programs in the area; and the third takes the framing paradigm into innovative subjects areas—exploring the implications of framing for visual issues, international news flow, and the new media technology.

PART I: THEORETICAL AND MEASUREMENT APPROACHES

Zhongdang Pan and Gerald Kosicki here further explicate the framing paradigm, an effort begun in their often-cited 1993 article in *Political Communication*. They consider framing within the larger context of public discourse, political "talk," including an extensive case study analysis of the national health care debate to exemplify their approach to framing as a strategic resource.

Other chapters in this section illustrate how framing is appropriated within an existing theoretical traditions, agenda setting, and how others—supporting its value as a distinct approach unto itself—may resist such absorption. We necessarily must here leave open the question of whether framing occupies its own domain or is more profitably subsumed under a broader umbrella, but the question itself is illustrative.

Maxwell McCombs is widely known for his work in public opinion and the media's agenda-setting role. Here with Salma Ghanem he makes the case that framing occupies a space within that domain, as a "second level." Arguing that framing essentially constitutes a more fully elaborated description of issue aspects, the second level of agenda setting, allows them to organize it within a larger theoretical system—bringing order to the "fractured" paradigm.

Mike Maher takes issue with this "theoretical imperialism" and reviews the autonomous aspects and overlap of the framing tradition relative to the agenda-setting paradigm. In explicating these areas, his chapter illustrates the dynamic tensions that shape how emerging subfields are appropriated, and tend to resist, more established perspectives. Although parsimony is desirable in our theoretical formulations, damage may be done to the framing perspective if it subsumed elsewhere.

James Tankard approaches framing from a content-analytic empirical tradition, providing a perspective that is in many ways, as he acknowledges, sympathetic to the agenda-setting tradition. Although yet unpublished, the 1991 conference paper Tankard wrote with four Texas coauthors has been frequently cited by others who find useful its early attempt to wrestle with definitional and measurement issues. Here he advocates a clear and empirically reliable way to identify frames in media content, and he reviews a number of quantitatively oriented examples from his own research and that of his colleagues. Given the slippery quality of many approaches to describing frames, Tankard considers how frames may be usefully described, measured, and summarized.

Consistent with Tankard's approach, Mark Miller has developed an empirically grounded approach to framing that lends itself to quantitatively mapping frames. With Bonnie Riechart he shows how these mapping procedures allow him to apply data-reduction techniques to great amounts of content. In their chapter, they defend the use of this approach against more qualitative and interpretive methods and illustrate its application.

Frank Durham provides perhaps the most different perspective in this section, in considering framing from a postmodern, interpretive angle. His 1998 article in the *Journal of Communication* showed how journalists and sources framed a major plane crash. He explicates the theoretical perspective on which that study was based and considers what gets left out when we construct social narratives to explain the world. For the modernist practice of journalism he asks about the implications of thinking we have successfully described, or framed, the social world, when ultimately we have not and can not.

SECTION II: CASES: OBSERVATIONS FROM THE FIELD

The relevance of the framing paradigm to the larger body of research in mass communication would be limited without a body of evidence to support the underlying theories and processes. A great deal of the evidence that has been amassed has been referenced in chapters in the preceding section. The goal of this section is to help advance the framing paradigm by providing examples of research that test, validate, and extend the theories and processes addressed in the preceding section.

It is beyond the scope of this volume to present virtually every approach to research on framing. Rather, this section presents case studies that help to illustrate the range of methods and phenomena that can be addressed to extend our understanding of framing. The methods used in the individual cases include quantitative and qualitative analysis, with a few combining the two. Although the set of methods used is not comprehensive, it does serve to illustrate a range of techniques for systematic analysis of framing processes. In addition, the cases included in this section were selected for the range of phenomena they analyze.

One thing that is notably absent from this section is a comprehensive study that applies a broad range of methods and perspectives in a unified research program. Such a study might include measures of media coverage, its effects, and the forces shaping that coverage. A study this comprehensive is well beyond the scope of this text, but we hope that the presentation of the range of elements encourages researchers to consider a more comprehensive approach to the framing analysis, developing research designs that cut across the elements presented. Readers are therefore encouraged to develop future research projects that build upon the lessons and methods presented in this section and to fill in the missing elements so that our understanding of the framing process will be more complete.

To introduce this section, James Hertog and Douglas McLeod report on their multiperspectival approach to framing, with an emphasis on their cultural aspects and role in the treatment of social movements. Their previous published work on the anarchist march in Minneapolis is a good example of multimethod analysis of media framing of deviance, observations with renewed currency given the renewed social protests—including anarchists—surrounding the World Trade Organization demonstrations in Seattle in 1999. They provide a useful guide for conducting framing research based for the prospective analyst.

Donna Dickerson takes a qualitative approach to examining news texts. She uses a comparative approach to gauge how ostensibly equivalent news subjects—controversial professors, one White and one Black—are treated differently. News framing is thus tied to larger racial stereotyping in society.

Philemon Bantimaroudis and Hyun Ban take a somewhat more traditional approach to media content analysis. In their comparative approach, they examine both the *New York Times* and the *Manchester Guardian*. They develop an issue-based quantitative and qualitative analysis of the U.S. military mission to Somalia, using Tankard's key word approach combined with textual analysis.

Ross Fuglsang examines the evolution of the motorcycle outlaw media image over a 50-year period. He considers the role of the mainstream media in upholding social norms and deviance from them, by incorporating myth and outlaw imagery into a meaningful framework that continually redefines the line between good and evil, right and wrong, citizen and noncitizen.

Lynn Zoch takes a different perspective, considering how the media, specifically state newspapers in South Carolina, covered the media's framing of their own participation in a news feeding frenzy in a local and national story.

Ernest Wiggins focuses on an unusual source of framing evidence: letters to the editor. He considers how news coverage of a minority social practice, a controversial lesbian wedding ceremony, generated reader response and revealed community norms in reaction to media frames.

Messaris and Abraham argue that the use of visuals allows the producers of television news to *show* what they are afraid to *say* more directly. In suggesting that the "indexicality of visual propositions" supports the delivery of subtle, but unavoidably racist cues, which will activate or evoke traditional stereotypes of African Americans, Messaris and Abraham challenge us to pay more attention to the use of visuals as framing resources in the news.

Dhavan Shah, David Domke, and Daniel Wackman report on their extensive program of framing research, which focuses on audience responses and decision making as a function of message framing. They provide an empirical example from their recent experimental research on different groups' voting decisions as a response to framing of political information.

Thomas Nelson and Elaine Willey provide a perspective from political science, reviewing the research in public cognitive processes in forming political judgments. They present research from their efforts and consider how frames relate to values as they conduct a new examination of subject responses to a complex issue of community redlining.

SECTION III: THE NEW MEDIA LANDSCAPE

Understanding the nature and impact of framing in the new media environment will depend to a large extent on the breadth and depth of our understanding of just what the topography of this landscape will ultimately become. There is already considerable uncertainty about the media environment because of our confusion about just where cyberspace is. The uncertainty about locale is heightened by concerns about who will draw the borders that will define both the markets and the regulatory regimes that will emerge to govern them.

The six chapters we have included in this section make an important contribution to this mission. Four of the chapters deal explicitly with the Internet, but each brings a unique perspective to bear on the relations between the present and the intermediate future.

Eric Fredin's chapter emphasizes an important aspect of the emerging network environment. The expanded use of hypermedia links within news stories accessed through the Web raises a challenge to the ways we have traditionally thought about the balance of power between journalists and the consumers of news. Fredin helps us to think about hyperlinks as supporting "digressions" that make the composition of the whole, which each person consumes very much far from certain. The "hyperstory interaction cycles" that each person goes through will reflect their quite different levels of knowledge, interest, and skill in navigating the Web. Although journalists can help shape this experience by virtue of the links and cues that are provided within a "frame database," individual differences, perhaps linked to locations within the social structure, will still play a critical role in shaping the frames of understanding that survive the experience.

Eric Engel's analysis of advertisements within magazines devoted to the emerging media helps us to see the ways in which the "rhetoric of the page" is being transformed by the very medium they are trying to sell. The rapid evolution of the multimedia pages of the World Wide Web (Web) has clearly transformed the ways in which print media are expressing the essence of connectivity and continuity across media. The ways in which visual rhetoric helps us to navigate the links between time and space has to be seen as a core question for us to explore as the Internet continues to reveal its shape and function.

John Pavlik's engagement with news on the Web emphasizes the ways in which the technology of gathering images might help news consumers resist the tyranny of perspective that selectivity represents for some. "Omnidirectional imaging" and "object-oriented video" are two emerging tools within the reach of electronic journalists that would allow consumers to select their own point of view. The ability to tilt, pan, and zoom a remote camera could provide each member of the audience with a unique vantage point from which to understand a demonstration or other event unfolding before their "eyes."

Ed Mabry's chapter helps us to understand how groups of "news junkies" or other virtual communities might come together and make sense of news events. However, Mabry's focus is on the ways in which the technology of computer mediated communication shapes the quality and character of the interaction between the members of this community, rather than on the ways in which they access the event directly. The "communication ecology" of online groups is shaped in a variety of ways by the enablements and constraints that a text-based form of interaction presents. The "cut-and-paste" character of thematic strings in news group discourse is seen to temper the emotional tone of discussions in ways that might conflict with the normative expectations of some of the participants. Mabry's examination of the distinguishing attributes of on-line groups and the relations between framing resources and emotion helps us to chart a course for further study of interaction within virtual communities.

Although the chapter provided by Chris Paterson is focused primarily on more traditional versions of television news, he raises critical issues and offers novel insights that will also help us understand some of the mysteries of the Web and the new globalized media world. He calls our attention to the structural influences that both limit what we see and shape what we might take away from our engagement with television news.

Paterson's chapter should be seen as a timely update of the classic studies of gatekeeping that demonstrate that editorial autonomy is more illusory than real. As globalization of media becomes more of a reality, the homogenizing influence of a dominant source, or sources of visual images seems all the more certain. Paterson supports the assessments he derives from content analysis of satellite news feeds from the major supplier of news video with ethnographic interviews of the professionals who supply the images they believe the editors have in mind. The emergence of a common global standard for framing a broad variety of news stories is an inescapable conclusion from his work.

Each of these chapters pushes us toward the horizons of scholarship in media framing. Each of them also provides us with explicit, and quite useful guidelines, resources, and support for our own journeys along these routes, a theme Gandy more fully explores in his epilogue chapter.

Stephen D. Reese
Oscar H. Gandy, Jr.
August E. Grant

Prologue—Framing Public Life: A Bridging Model for Media Research

Stephen D. Reese

Within the last several years, the concept of framing has become increasingly attractive in media research, finding its way into a number of related fields—including communication, sociology, and political science. Framing refers to the way events and issues are organized and made sense of, especially by media, media professionals, and their audiences. Sociologist Erving Goffman (1974) is often credited with introducing the framing approach, along with the anthropologist–psychologist Gregory Bateson (1972), whom Goffman credited with originating the metaphor. Within their social–psychological perspective we consider how people rely on expectations to make sense of their everyday social experience. A similar but more sociological approach has been more typically applied to questions of framing in media and communication research and opened an important field of analysis: Precisely how are issues constructed, discourse structured, and meanings developed? (e.g., Gamson, 1989, 1992).[1]

Framing has been particularly useful in understanding the media's role in political life. Although it need not be restricted this way, I adopt this focus in later discussion. Under this approach issues are not unproblematic; labeling, classifying, and reducing them to a simple theme is not the straightforward task performed elsewhere in studies of news content. As both a noun and a verb, the word *frame* suggests an active process and a result.

---

[1]Framing has begun to find its way into the textbooks of the field, including volumes by Stanley Baran and Dennis Davis which devote considerable attention to its theoretical value (Baran & Davis, 2000; Davis & Baran, 1981).

Entman (1993a) refers to framing as a fractured paradigm, but like the communication field itself its interdisciplinary nature makes it attractive. When viewed as the interplay of media practices, culture, audiences, and producers, the framing approach guards against unduly compartmentalizing components of communication (sender, content, audience). As with any theoretical formulation, we must consider what aspects of the social world are better explained with it, and which are obscured.

The framing approach bridges the competing tendencies of social analysis toward closure and openness and may be regarded as one of its strengths. On one hand, traditional behavioral social science strives for data reduction and parsimony, measuring the accumulation of emphasis in the observed and explicit. Quantification's precise measurement makes it preferred by many scholars, but the most important frame may not be the most frequent. On the other hand, the qualitative turn of much framing analysis helps resist the reductionistic urge to sort media texts and discourse into containers and count their size or frequency. Indeed, some define frames as an inherently qualitative construct. In this case, one must capture the meanings embedded in the internal relations within texts, which collapsing into reductive measures would obscure. The positivist, behavioral measures of frames based on manifest content do not capture the tensions among expressed elements of meaning, or between what is said and what is left unsaid.

The tendency, for example, to classify issues into categories, such as "the economy" and "crime," obscures the important questions of how they are defined in the first place. As Kosicki (1993) noted, the agenda-setting approach to issues, emphasizing the salience of topics, misses a "real focus on the nature of the disagreement between the parties and the essence of the controversy. In short, a great deal of valuable contextual information about the issue would be lost" (p. 116). Thus, the traditional topical agenda approach doesn't reveal much about what makes issues interesting: the way they're defined. McCombs and colleagues have responded in part by incorporating frames as a different level of agenda-setting (e.g., McCombs & Ghanem, chap. 2, this volume; McCombs, Shaw, & Weaver, 1997). More critical, qualitative and interpretive approaches allow for ambiguity, historical contingency, the implicit, and emphasize how meaning is signified. In the first case, the danger is oversimplification, reducing a complex structure to a set of classifying measures. In the second case, however, thick description can go on and on without producing patterns that transcend the particulars. Qualitative description may produce a thorough treatment of a given issue but not help reduce the mass of information to meaningful and readily demonstrable themes.

In spite of a more nuanced approach than traditional content analysis, framing research slips just as easily into the effects paradigm. Within this audience-centered, social–psychological approach, one can demonstrate, for example, that how a social problem is cast makes a big difference in how one responds to it. Two equivalent risk scenarios, in one often repeated example, receive vastly different support from subjects depending on whether they are phrased in terms of saving lives or causing deaths (Kahneman & Tversky, 1984). This approach leads one to ask how readily the audience adopts the framing presented through the media? Pan and Kosicki (1993), for example, showed how the matrix of signifying elements is linked to audience interpretations, recognizing that the text alone does not determine the meaning but interacts with audience memory. The audience is similarly important for Entman (1993b), who considered how it engages in "counterframing" against the dominant meanings in texts. (These questions resemble those asked in the "reception analysis" strand of cultural studies and its "oppositional readings.") Scheufele (1999) organized framing within a "theory of media effects," although allowing frames to be considered as dependent as well as independent variables.

Unquestionably, the way information is structured affects cognitive processing, and audience schemata interact with texts to determine the ultimate meaning derived from them (e.g., Iorio & Huxman, 1996). Indeed, I am willing to grant the agenda-setting hypothesis as a basic premise—that media structure, if not dictate, the way the public thinks about its second-hand reality. Therefore, I place greater emphasis here on how issues are framed as a result of social and institutional interests. Interest in framing responds to Hackett's (1984) recommendation that media studies move beyond a narrow concern with bias—deviation from an objective standard—to a more fruitful view of the ideological character of news, thoroughly structured in its content, practices and relations with society. I argue that plugging in framing as just one more content element, against which to measure effects, risks continuing to ignore basic power questions.

Within this ideological realm, careful framing studies have the potential to help clean up some of the problems with cultural studies, identified by Schudson (1997). Although the British strand is closely linked with sociology and empirically rooted in "lived social experience," he argued that American-style cultural studies, more influenced by French structuralism, has become unhinged from any connection to real social interaction. Claiming that all knowledge is in the service of power wrongly becomes the end of the inquiry. This insight should rather be the beginning of our attempt to understand how human knowledge relates to the world. Framing helps provide tools for examining these knowledge structures, or, as Tucker (1998) suggested, empirically measuring the construction of common sense. This must in turn be carefully tied to frame sources and sponsors, social practices, and interests. With ties, then, to both the critical, qualitative, and ideological perspective and the behavioral content, audience, and effects tradition, framing provides an important bridge between them. It opens up connections among areas that for too long have been unduly compartmentalized.

Purpose

My purpose here is to consider the framing perspective's value for social analysis, and review its crucial definitional components. I present framing as an exercise in power, particularly as it affects our understanding of the political world. I do not attempt the impractical task of making an exhaustive inventory of the burgeoning research literature (other than to identify the most frequently cited, useful, and exemplary works). I will try to make sense of some of the different ways others have used framing and derive appropriate research questions using a definition and model. I explore also a case of framing in perhaps an unusual location: a new museum in Washington, DC, called the "Newseum," sponsored by The Freedom Forum. Presenting the newsgathering enterprise in museum form carries important structured meanings, especially in obscuring the very framing that is built into news.

MAPPING THE FRAMING TRADITION

A number of definitions have been proposed to refine the framing concept. According to Entman (1993a), a frame is determined in large part by its outcome or effect:

> To frame is to select some aspects of a perceived reality and make them more salient in a communicating text, in such a way as to promote a particular problem definition, causal interpretation, moral evaluation, and/or treatment recommendation. (p. 52)

Similarly, Tankard, Hendrickson, Silberman, Bliss, and Ghanem (1991) said:

> A frame is a central organizing idea for news content that supplies a context and suggests what the issue is through the use of selection, emphasis, exclusion, and elaboration. (p. 11)

Iyengar (1991) made more modest claims for his definition: ". . . the concept of framing refers to subtle alterations in the statement or presentation of . . . problems" (p. 11).

Morley (1976) said it's important to examine the "basic conceptual and ideological 'framework' through which events are presented and as a result of which they come to be given one dominant/primary meaning rather than another" (p. 246). Accordingly, other definitions move beyond an emphasis on selection to capture a more active generation of meaning. I would regard framing as similar to Hall's (1982) idea of defining the situation, which if compellingly presented "provides the criteria by which all subsequent contributions are labeled as relevant or irrelevant—beside the point" (p. 59). Gamson and Modigliani (1989) defined frame as a "central organizing idea . . . for making sense of relevant events, suggesting what is at issue" (p. 3). And it causes other events to be noticed out of "happenings." This core frame is suggested by the "media package" of metaphors and other devices. Goffman (1974) noted that frames help classify, allowing users to "locate, perceive, identify, and label a seemingly infinite number of concrete occurrences defined in its limits" (p. 21). Similarly, Edelman (1993) said frames exert their power "especially in how observations are classified . . . and categorized" (p. 232). Hertog and McLeod (1995) noted that framing defines the context for an occurrence: "The frame used to interpret an event determines what available information is relevant (and thereby what is irrelevant)" (p. 4). If a protest march, for instance, is framed as a confrontation between police and marchers, the protesters' critique of society may not be part of the story—not because there wasn't room for it, but because it was not defined as relevant.

In one of the most common citations, Gitlin (1980) viewed frames as "persistent patterns of cognition, interpretation, and presentation, of selection, emphasis, and exclusion, by which symbol-handlers routinely organize discourse . . ." (p. 7). His definition lays the emphasis on the routine organization that transcends any given story and is "persistent" over time (resistant to change). In dealing with information, frames enable journalists to "recognize it as information, to assign it to cognitive categories . . ." (p. 21). This gives frames a power, actively to bring otherwise amorphous reality into a meaningful structure, making it more than the simple inclusion or exclusion of information. Thus, frames are active, information generating, as well as screening devices.

A Working Definition

Framing is concerned with the way interests, communicators, sources, and culture combine to yield coherent ways of understanding the world, which are developed using all of the available verbal and visual symbolic resources. Before proceeding further, it will be helpful to propose my own working definition of framing, one that suggests a series of research questions out of its components.

> Frames are *organizing principles* that are socially *shared* and *persistent* over time, that work *symbolically* to meaningfully *structure* the social world.

- *Organizing*: Framing varies in how successfully, comprehensively, or completely it organizes information.

- *Principles*: The frame is based on an abstract principle and is not the same as the texts through which it manifests itself.
- *Shared*: The frame must be shared on some level for it to be significant and communicable.
- *Persistent*: The significance of frames lies in their durability, their persistent and routine use over time.
- *Symbolically*: The frame is revealed in symbolic forms of expression.
- *Structure*: Frames organize by providing identifiable patterns or structures, which can vary in their complexity.

Organizing

To say that frames organize suggests the active work that goes on in generating meaning. We may ask how much meaning frames—some more ambitious than others—attempts to organize. How successful is a frame in accounting for the social reality it tries to explain? In an interactive process, journalists are said to routinely seek the best narrative fit between incoming information and existing frames (Wolfsfeld, 1997).

Framing "organizes" in a number of ways, but two major ways of thinking about this can be identified: cognitively and culturally. Cognitively organizing frames invite us to think about social phenomena in a certain way, often by appealing to basic psychological biases. Studies have examined, for example, the effects of information that emphasizes positive or negative aspects, the individual or the collective, and the episodic or the thematic. Reporting on racial issues has been examined for its emphasis on winners or losers (Goshorn & Gandy, 1995). In another example, Davis (1995) experimented with changes to environmental stories, producing the best result with a message emphasizing the negative results of the public's own inaction to themselves or their current generation. This "tactical" framing suggests a specific arrangement or pattern of information, with a scope limited to that message (even if such a pattern, e.g., "horse race" political coverage, is pervasive).

This framing organization may be limited to casting a problem in terms of either saving lives or certain deaths, as in the often cited Kahneman and Tversky (1984) example, or in Iyengar's (1991) comparison of issues based on episodic or thematic treatment. The episodic, or "anecdotal," story offers compelling stories of concrete events and individuals, which find a more ready cognitive reception than the more accurate, perhaps, but duller thematic, "baseline" story. In studies like these the specific content of the frame is usually less important than the effects question: How does one way or another of presenting a story affect audience response? Although their impact may be important, they do not have the same dynamic quality of organizing a broader cultural terrain.

Other, more "cultural" frames don't stop with organizing one story, but invite us to marshal a cultural understanding and keep on doing so beyond the immediate information. These are the "strategic" frames that speak to a broader way to account for social reality. Wolfsfeld (1997), for example, adopted Gamson's notion of frame "depth," ranging from *deep* (older, more taken for granted, more general) to *shallow* (recent, specific). In Vietnam frames, for example, "Peace through strength" and "Cold War" are deeper than "falling domino" and "unprovoked attack." Indeed, the culturally wide ranging Cold War frame contained within it a vast array of deeply rooted assumptions, and ways of understanding and depicting global relations.

In a more recent example, the "War on Drugs" frame used military imagery to explain the nation's illegal drug problem in a way that organizes a broad swath of events and issues (e.g., McCauley & Frederick, 1993). Or consider the affirmative action debate within higher education. The frames of "equal treatment" and "merit-based admissions" have a vast apparatus behind them, and are based on a set of assumptions, evidence, and world view. The more elaborated and purposive political efforts of social movements exploit these frames when they seek to organize meaning for their supporters by diagnosing problems and proposing solutions (Snow & Benford, 1988). Examining coverage of the Palestinian *intifada* uprising reveals two basic "metaframes"—"law and order" and "injustice and defiance"—which are historically preferred by the powerful and weaker antagonists, respectively (Wolfsfeld, 1997). Thus, these frames distill and call up a larger world of meaning. When these frames are picked up without their supporting apparatus, made implicit and naturalized, they gain organizing power.

We must trace then the scope of frames, to evaluate the sweep of social reality they propose to explain and organize—considering their restrictiveness, openness, coherence, and comprehensiveness. All frames are not equal in their ability to cause information to cohere, making sense out of the world. We should ask how much "framing" is going on? How adequate is the frame to contain the elements it proposes to embrace? How close is the frame to that promoted by sources or indicated by an event? Is the frame convincing in accounting for reality?

Ultimately, frames are of greatest interest to the extent they add up to something bigger than an individual story. In that respect, we gain little from the concept if a frame is reduced to a "stance" or position on an issue, or "dominant theme," as do, for example, Friedland and Mengbai (1996). Pan and Kosicki (1993) even have said that, because of its structuring function, a theme is a frame. Thus, the theme identified in an article about a Wichita antiabortion rally—"Abortion debate is a conflict and confrontation"—comes closer to being frame-like because it organizes a way of viewing the issue (with greater "depth"), compared to one of the subthemes: "antiabortion protesters want to change the established law" (p. 67). This theme/frame simply describes their actual stance as reported in the story and does not organize meaning much beyond that basic chunk of social reality.[2] The dynamic nature of framing is better captured if we presume that the reporter understood the rally through the confrontation frame, causing the gathering to be linked to a previous violent episode.

Principles

In referring to a frame as an organizing "principle," I emphasize its abstract quality. The frame is not the same as its symbolic manifestation, which means we must get behind surface features to the generating principle that produced one way of framing a story, but is at work in many others as well. This suggests that we must often infer the organizing principle from media discourse, which is a conglomeration of interlocking and competing organizing ideas. Or we must ask what principles are held by journalists or frame sponsors that give rise to certain ways of expressing them.

Ultimately, frames may best be viewed as an abstract principle, tool, or "schemata" of interpretation that works through media texts to structure social meaning. Gamson and Modigliani (1989), for example, referred to a frame as an "organizing idea." These interpretive principles are made manifest in discourse; symbolic devices making up media texts constitute the epiphenomena of the underlying principle. Entman (1993a) suggested that frames can be located in the communicator, the text, the receiver, and the culture. More accurately perhaps we should say that frames are principles of organizing information, clues to which may be found in the media discourse, within individuals, and within social and cultural practices. Although we may consider whether information is in or out of a text, we need also to consider the principles that naturally lead to it being excluded or included, such that one may not even notice the exclusion. In Gitlin's (1980) view, for example, frames are inevitably part of a much larger set of structures, or societal ideology, that finds its manifestation in the text. To ignore the principle that gives rise to the frame is to take media texts at face value, and to be misled by manifest content.

A focus on the organizing principle should caution us that what is seen in media texts is often the result of many interrelated, competing principles from contending sources and media professionals themselves. The framing principle may generate a coverage blackout, yielding little discourse to analyze. This is the case, for example, with stories identified by Project Censored in both the United States and Canada (1996), watchdog groups that look for issues not getting the coverage their importance deserved. Thus, we may ask whose principle was dominant in producing the observed cov-

---

[2]A framing analysis of Operation Rescue abortion protest was carried out by Bergen, Reese, and Mueller, 1994.

erage? How did the principles brought to bear by journalists interact with those promoted by their sources? These questions require looking behind the scenes and making inferences from the symbolic patterns in news texts.

Thus, a frame is a moment in a chain of signification. As sources promote "occurrences" into "events," as journalists define and seek out information that fits their organizing ideas, frames can help designate any number of moments when we can say that a certain organizing principle was operating to shape social reality. These moments being fluid makes it risky for us to fix one point in time that happens to be most visible, such as in a news story. As discussed earlier, when issues are analyzed, we tend to prematurely think of their definition as self-evident. It is, of course, useful to partition off a set of concerns and call it, for example, the "drug issue," but framing reminds us that the way issues are defined is itself problematic. How much does this issue definition embrace, and when does it transition into another?

Shared

Given that frames must be shared in order to be useful and noteworthy organizing devices, we must question the extent to which they are shared. Asking this may help us determine whether they are personal and idiosyncratic, social and shared, or, if broadly and deeply shared, cultural. Frames may be considered as always in the process of gaining or losing organizing value—and are adopted or abandoned accordingly. Thus, frames vary at any given time in the number of people who may find them useful and share them. Neuman, Just, and Crigler (1992), for example, found that news media used the tactical frames of "conflict" and "powerlessness" most of the time, whereas audience members relied on such frames as "human impact" and "moral values." Frame sponsors, thus, must capitalize on shared frames.

Of course, this leads us to the next question for framing study: What makes a satisfactory, and thus readily embraced, frame? What makes a frame "work"? When is it successful in providing a useful and coherent way of accounting for social reality? Of course, frames are never imposed directly on media audiences. The acceptance and sharing of a media frame depends on what understandings the "reader" brings to the text to produce negotiated meaning.

Persistent

By frames I presume we are talking about those patterns that are important enough to warrant our study—either that they are connected to some more important cause, or that they persist over time and over instances. Unless frames endure over time they have relatively little importance for analysis.

This leads us to question what factors account for one frame's persistence over another. Gamson and Modigliani (1989), for example, traced the "interpretive packages" in news coverage of nuclear power over 40 years, showing how media discourse could be characterized by three major phases. Taking this constructionist view shows how long frames persist before evolving into different forms.

As mentioned earlier, Gitlin defines a frame as a persistent and routine way of handling information, suggesting tendencies that are resistant to change. Routinization suggests that a frame has become second-nature, well entrenched, and built into the way of doing things. This embedding of frames within organizational practices can be seen in, for example, local television coverage of domestic war protest (Reese & Buckalew, 1994). This resistance to change, indicated by such a routine, suggests in functional terms that we've stumbled upon a structure that is satisfying some important need. The more persistent the frame, the more likely it deserves examination.

Symbolic

To say that frames work symbolically refers to how they are manifested and communicated in their various forms, through any combination of symbolic devices. This area has accounted for the most research and leads one to ask what kinds of symbolic elements work together to constitute a frame. The framing approach enlivens the study of media discourse, taking it seriously enough to rigorously examine its symbolic organization. In this respect, it is closely related to such European efforts as the Glasgow Media Group (1995), Fowler (1991), and van Dijk (1993).

Miller and his colleagues, for example, stick close to the symbolic level as they seek to identify and compare competing frames by examining specific vocabularies (e.g., Miller, 1997; Miller & Riechart, chap. 5, this volume). Certainly, media texts represent the most readily available evidence of frames, and creating an inventory of verbal and visual features can be useful. We still need, however, to figure out how those features are woven together to signify a frame. Pan and Kosicki (1993), for example, elaborated framing in news discourse to include four structures: syntactical, script, thematic, and rhetorical. Gamson and Modigliani (1989) measured framing "devices"—metaphors, catchprases, exemplars, depictions, and visual images.

Although framing's symbolic aspect is important, equating it with the text unduly narrows the focus. In community power research, for example, focusing on only overt political decision has caused analysts to underestimate the underlying power that can prevent some issues from ever coming up. Just because issues make the agenda, doesn't mean they are necessarily the key issues—they may just be the only ones on which elites disagree. As Lukes (1974) argued, the most effective power prevents conflicts (and perhaps manifested frames) from arising in the first place. Of course, we can

most easily measure what is visible and available, and from there we take the
"highlighted," "noticeable," and most "salient" features. We shouldn't over-
sell this aspect, however, just because it is most manifest. Framing should
remind us that content is only the tip of a very big iceberg.

Entman (1993a) said framing offers a way to "describe the power of a
communicating text" and "the transfer of information from one location . . .
to that consciousness" (pp. 51–52). Of course, the symbolic aspect of framing must be described, but it leads easily into a transmission model, as in
the work of Pan and Kosicki (1993), who place the frame between producers
and audiences, yielding another content measure to represent a source of
effects. Even their approach to coding stories is based on how a reader
would consume them—story by story, sentence by sentence. Indeed, we
must question whether this is the way frames add up, with the shear weight
of accumulated sentences. A frame may be distributed across a number of
stories in its symbolic terrain.

Miller (1997), Tankard et al. (1991), and others treat media as a symbolic
site, on which various stakeholders contend. They might ask, for example, if
a story is better characterized as pro-life or pro-choice? This, however, may
fix the terrain prematurely—viewing news stories as neutral vessels, holding
various pro and con positions. But what were the choices available for the
story, what were the structured tendencies to produce stories containing a
balance of certain views? What were the rules working to screen out particular perspectives? Of course, the media structure creates certain kinds of
frames routinely and exclude much of what doesn't fit. Thus, the way we
emphasize symbolic content and handle its measurement structures the
conclusions we may reach about framing.

Structure

Frames structure. That is, they impose a pattern on the social world, a pattern constituted by any number of symbolic devices. Early in the life of an issue, for example, a dominant frame may not have taken hold but may gain in
the complexity and coherence of its structure over time. The frame metaphor draws our attention to this structure—how the principles of organization create a coherent "package" by combining symbols, giving them relative
emphasis, and attaching them to larger cultural ideas (Gamson, 1992). By definition, then, it should not be possible to reduce a frame to single indicator, or
"topic." This structure may be manifest and explicit, or embedded and implicit. Some frames can be easily defined: lives lost or lives saved, positive or
negative. Others depend on more complex and implicit structures that are not
as easily classified and manipulated in, for example, an experimental setting.

Our libel laws are based on explicit and manifest expressions of framing
inclusion and exclusion. In a recent case in Philadelphia, a man sued a television station for libel for a story that depicted him as a child kidnapper.

The anchor (with an over-the-shoulder graphic of a close-up face and the words "A mother's anguish") introduced the story as follows: "Can you imagine the anguish of a mother who finds her *missing* child, only to live in fear he will *disappear* again? (our reporter) has one such story . . ." (Emphasis added; WCAU-TV, May 29, 1996). The station, in its defense, correctly stated that the man had been arrested in Texas. The arrest, however, came as a result of his wife falsely accusing him of abducting their child. The more implicit and deeply structured bias of the story was found in the frame of "a mother's suffering." The reporter criminalized the father, who had legal custody of the child under Mexican law, and cast him in opposition to the heroic mother. The president of the Center for Missing Children was interviewed to further reinforce the criminal frame:

> We *broke the case*. We got *a lead*, which led us to believe that the *abducting parent* and (son) were going to be coming in to Houston Intercontinental Airport.

This less explicit and manifest frame made it more difficult for the plaintiff to build a successful case.[3]

To say, as in some "minimalist" definitions, that frames call attention to certain aspects of reality, makes no claim greater than for any other act of communication. Texts always include some ideas and leave out others. The definition proposed earlier gets at a more active structuring job that frames perform in conveying meaning, and moves beyond the presence or absence, or mere emphasis of information. The simple notion of inclusion and exclusion at least reminds us that a method must be found to evaluate it. That requires being in a position to know what could have been included that was not. These frames can be seen as having a deep and implicit symbolic structure, which suggests strongly rooted assumptions and rules for making sense of the world, or they may be more manifest, surface structures, which may be more objectively determined by the presence or exclusion of information. Both need to be taken into account to gain a complete picture of framing.

Agenda setting uses Entman's language of exclusion/inclusion in identifying the kinds of attributes selected to describe a particular subject (object), with emphasis serving as the primary determinant of framing power. Although McCombs, Shaw, and Weaver (1997) acknowledge that a "rich variety of frames" affects the details of what we get from the news, there is many a slip between agenda object and picture in our head, and it is pre-

---

[3]I obtained these materials when approached by the father's lawyer about serving as an expert witness. The background details, legal maneuverings, and questioning by the station's lawyers made the case illustrative to me of many of the issues discussed here.

cisely these details that concern us here. Thus, the structuring of meaning must go beyond inclusion or exclusion. If a frame produces "omission," we ask how that omission is naturalized, made to seem as a logical exclusion or common-sensical irrelevancy.

On the most basic level, frame structure calls attention to the internal organization within news stories. Tankard's (chap. 4, this volume) "list of frames" approach doesn't as directly tackle this structuring dynamic (Tankard et al., 1991). For example, choosing an issue like abortion immediately brings with it a polarized way of thinking of the subject. I might be surprised if a story could be reliably categorized using only one pole of the debate, such as pro-life. Instead the frame of such a story would more likely tend to a metastructure, an accepted, "on one hand versus the other hand," way of organizing the discussion.

Coverage of the Holocaust revisionist movement shows a similar media tendency to seek a misguided form of "balance," even when dealing with incredible claims. The inclusion of a revisionist position in coverage shifts the frame to a "two sides to every story," "the truth must lie somewhere in between" kind of judgment. Indeed, the presence of two competing sponsored frames creates a larger and self-justifying metaframe structure, which implies its own success in accounting for the defined "positions" on the issue.[4] This surface structure, however, may not reveal the complete picture, given that the most dominant position often need not enter the fray, but needs to be taken into account. By tackling the question of how meaning is structured, framing relates closely to ideological analysis, but it places greater emphasis on the nature of the organizing structures and how they get established.

The Framing Model

Using the definition proposed earlier helps pose a number of research questions raised by the framing perspective. Another way to look at it is to consider what makes framing problematic? In my view, the territory marked out by framing can best be described by the following question model:

> What power relationships and institutional arrangements support certain routine and persistent ways of making sense of the social world, as found through specific and significant frames, influential information organizing principles that are manifested in identifiable moments of structured meaning and become especially important to the extent they find their way into media discourse, and are thus available to guide public life.

---

[4]Elsewhere, I have explored how source arrangements, or "networks," within television news programs acts to provide a "framework" for points of view (Reese, Grant, & Danielian, 1994).

In this more politically pointed approach, frames are connected to asymmetric interests. The power to frame depends on access to resources, a store of knowledge, and strategic alliances. Alternatively, some have depicted media as upholding a natural order. Ericson, Baranek, and Chan (1991), for example, viewed news as a "daily barometer" of how society works. Bird and Dardenne (1988) claimed that news "creates order out of disorder—provides answers to baffling questions . . ." (p. 67). Of course, as the framing model suggests, there is no unproblematic natural order not developed through ongoing contestation.

This notion of framing contestation draws attention to how journalists organize information as the outcome of their interaction with their sources promoting their various perspectives. Entman and Rojecki (1993) considered how journalists exercise "framing judgments" that filter into the news. On a specific level, these include evaluations of groups' rationality, expertise, public support, partisanship, unity, extremism, and power—and are influenced by elite sources and professional ideology. In another source-oriented approach, Snow and Benford (1988) treated framing as something social movements do—it is the result of their activities, with their success depending largely on the result of their framing success efforts. The critiques of the public relations industry, for example, are full of these success stories, which help explain why certain sources are so successful in convincing journalists that their frame is the most useful way or organizing an issue.

In a more ideological sense, news frames can support interests even if not intentionally. An analysis of a General Motors plant closing argues that the "lean and mean" frame, accepted uncritically by the media, supported core capitalist values (Martin & Oshagan, 1997). In international news, U.S. policy in El Salvador is framed as honorable (Solomon, 1992), and the *New York Times* used frames undermining the viability of the West German Green party (Carragee, 1991).

News Framing and the Growth Issue

One short example illustrates these links between frames, sources, and interests. In reporting on growth issues in communities, the media frequently resort to the frame of "the team" or "the game." This approach locates the local media as a member of the community team as they compete with other cities to acquire highly sought after business (often high technology). This frame is persistent, widely shared, and clearly promoted by the sponsors.

For example, high tech initiatives in Austin, Texas, have been presented as being beneficial for local citizens, as they have elsewhere. Programs like Microelectronics and Computer Consortium (MCC), Sematech, and U.S.

Memories, were promoted in the 1980s by a coalition of local business, governmental, and media leaders, but the entire community has not benefited. Studies show that unemployment is no lower in communities that are growing, and, in fact, crime, congestion, and other problems typically ensue (Molotch, 1993). While the city has grown rapidly, so have environmental problems and the difficulty finding affordable housing.

In an analysis of local television news several years ago, I found a number of framing examples supporting local economic interests.[5]

- At the successful attraction of Sematech to town in 1988, the newscast banner read: "We Win!" An anchor claimed: "We can expect long term benefits." (Note the word "we.") The organizing idea of an entire town winning turned up frequently. The governor called it a "home run."
- Over time, as the "winning" frame gained strength, reporter estimates of city benefit escalated from "$80 to 100 million" in one story, to "100 million" in another, to finally "at least a 100 million."
- As to the impact of Sematech on neighborhoods, a reporter said, "All of Austin is anxious to get Sematech here," especially, it was reported, in one high unemployment area. Later it was acknowledged that local residents wouldn't qualify for the hi-tech jobs in question.
- Later, conflict emerged over Sematech as the "winning" frame weakened, allowing another view to creep in. The county appraisal review board said the consortium was not tax exempt. A Sematech executive, persisting with the original "everybody wins" frame, raised a warning about losing firms like his: "I don't think that sends the kind of signal that we in Texas are proud of sending."
- In 1989 U.S. Memories was visiting Austin to scout locations. A reporter said that Austin may win with its "people package and attitude." A local leader of the effort said, "We know we can do it again." When Austin made the short list for the company, the mayor said, "The entire Austin community made it possible."

These frames were powerful, well-structured, and widely shared, especially among the business and media community, but based on key political interests, not the overall welfare of the community as implied.

---

[5]This is perhaps a classic case of one's research interests tracking life issues. Shortly after moving to Austin in 1982 I was warned to buy a house as quickly as possible for fear that prices would soar out of reach (as they were beginning to do). Not long after heeding that advice, the market collapsed leaving me and many others holding our real estate "bags." This rather helpless feeling set my professional curiosities to understanding how this had come about. One of my graduate seminars in 1990 tackled the growth and environment issue and reviewed local news coverage.

FRAMING CASE STUDY: THE NEWSEUM

Much of the framing research reviewed earlier has examined media coverage of issues. Given the symbolic quality of frames, they may be found
across many settings and not limited to written texts. Like the news media,
museums are often presented as objective containers of our history, physical world, and accomplishments as a society, but they have their own structured meaning, or "frames." Donna Haraway (1989), for example, has analyzed the politics of culture of New York's American Museum of Natural
History. Australian scholar Tony Bennett (e.g., 1992) has carried out similar
work in considering how museums ought best to handle the Aboriginal culture and experience. I am also influenced by recent analyses of Disney's
parks, and others like Sea World, which consider the powerful frames generated by the interlocking symbolic machinery of these attractions as tied
to marketing and media operations (e.g., Davis, 1997; Fjellman, 1992; Giroux,
1999). Structured meaning must be understood across the entirety of these
settings, not just in the viewing of a particular show or buying a certain
product.

That museums, some more directly than others, are tied to interests is
not always self-evident. Even the National Park Service has allowed commercial intrusion in some of its locations. In the visitor's center for Old Iron-
sides, the U.S.S. Constitution ship in Boston, for example, the defense con-
tractor Raytheon has placed several posters depicting the uniforms of the
armed forces over the years, complete with patriotic slogans. Thus, a commercial firm appropriates Americans' affection for historic sites, while establishing an implicit promilitary frame within an ostensibly noncommer-
cial and neutral setting.

Newseum Background

One of the most recent and heavily promoted museums in the United States
is privately financed and—officially autonomous of its corporate origins—
was created by the foundation originating from the Gannett newspaper
chain, the nation's largest. Espousing nonpartisan devotion to "free press,
free speech, and free spirit," The Freedom Forum, supported by a just over
one billion dollar endowment (as of 1999), opened "The Newseum" in April
of 1997. Presented as the only interactive museum of news, the Newseum
contains a history gallery, an interactive newsroom, an auditorium for broadcasting interviews with newsmakers and journalists, a video news wall, a
movie theater, and the inevitable gift shop. Adjacent to the Newseum is
Freedom Park, which memorializes slain journalists. Museum designer
Ralph Appelbaum oversaw the project, which followed his acclaimed
United States Holocaust Memorial in Washington, DC. A news story about

his work questioned whether objects had "communicative power without clever packaging," concerning which Appelbaum said, "Objects need to be contextualized . . . People want stories" (Solomon, 1999, p. 12).

The Freedom Forum grew out of the Gannett Foundation Media Studies Center and operates the Media Studies Center in New York, the First Amendment Center at Vanderbilt University in Nashville, and now the Newseum at its World Center headquarters in Arlington, Virginia.[6] Examining this impressive 50-million dollar museum investment calls for a case-study, multimethod approach that suits framing studies. My analysis is based on my visits to the Newseum in July 1997 and again in April 1998, where I took notes and gathered the available printed material. The case is particularly interesting for a number of reasons. Although ostensibly autonomous, The Freedom Forum has close corporate ties to Gannett. Forum founder and chairman, former Gannett head Al Neuharth, was succeeded by former Gannett vice-president Charles Overby, with former *USA Today* editor Peter Prichard serving as Forum President. Two other former Gannett paper editors, John Seigenthaler and John Quinn, are also trustees.

In recent years, the Forum's Media Studies Center has moved from an academic setting at Columbia University to midtown Manhattan, to better reflect its mission shift from a media think tank with a scholarly emphasis to a decidedly industry-oriented public outreach. Thus, while it does contain a fascinating array of historical materials devoted to news, I would argue that the Newseum is, from a framing standpoint, a public showcase for how American corporate media would want the public to perceive their work.[7]

Newseum Framing

Ironically, the Newseum's frame suggests that there is no frame for news, deflecting attention from the way news is structured in support of organizational and societal interests. Following, I suggest a number of ways the Newseum strives to present a view of the news product as an unproblematic commodity. The possibility of news resulting from powerful and contending views of reality is effectively denied by this "antiframe."

The Freedom Forum says that "by taking visitors behind the scenes we hope to forge a deeper public understanding about why and how news is reported . . . and remind the public . . . of the great risks many journalists take to bring us the news" (1996 Annual Report, p. 7). Elsewhere, the Forum provides a Newseum Education Center, which makes teaching materials available for schools to help "students become better informed news con-

---

[6]For a further analysis of the Forum's efforts in journalism education, see Reese (1999).

[7]In the absence of illustrations here, the obligatory web site has extensive information and supporting visuals of the Newseum and other programs: *www.freedomforum.org*.

sumers" (p. 4). Although admirable in one respect, such education efforts can be faulted for preparing the public to accept news the way it is, with little critique of how it relates to the larger society or admission of any shortcomings.

The Eternal News Cycle

Upon entering the Newseum, one is invited to view a short film, "What's News." The introduction says, "We are all reporters: look to the left and right. One of you may be a reporter. Be careful what you say!" Presented in an IMAX style spherical theater, with dramatic sound and visual effects, the film depicts news as part of the never-ending cycles of war and peace, love and hate, life and death: "The world comes to you. We call it news. From tranquility base to Kitty Hawk, news is 'firsts.' History starts as news. . . . Life is news. Where there's life there's news."

By inviting the viewer to regard news within a context of natural cycles, news becomes an organically necessary and unproblematic feature of society—as natural as life and death and the basis for all else. Indeed, the brochure distributed at the Newseum makes the argument directly: "From its birth as shared stories, news has fulfilled a fundamental human need—the need to know. . . . First come facts, then ideas, then ideals." As the brochure explains, "News is as old as human history—and as new as a digital image flashing halfway around the world." This "natural news" frame presents news as the very basis for society, the fact gathering function on which ideals are based, an eternal cycle that equates early oral storytelling with modern, global, corporate media. This universalism is underscored: "News tells a compelling, universal story. It binds us together to share moments of joy and tragedy."

On the 126-foot-long Video News Wall, news from around the world is presented. An inscription on a nearby wall tells visitors that

> This is the news stream—the endless flow of fresh data, events, issues, and ideas that give us our picture of the world. In the digital age, the news stream is growing beyond measures—News comes faster from all directions.

This view of news as raw empiricism again diverts attention from the social judgments and arrangements of power that go into framing that stream of information into meaningful stories and routine patterns.

News and Freedom

The Newseum further shapes its view of news by connecting it to freedom. If news is unframed, then the only distortion arises from hampering its dissemination. As stated in its materials, "The Newseum focuses on the inseparable link between news and freedom." Although freedom is an important value in American society, the Newseum privileges this one over others and suggests that more freedom (and not greater responsibility or public involvement) is the main solution to any concerns with the news media. If the news is a natural and universal need, then any attempts to impede it and threaten the freedom of those who produce it is, of course, unacceptable. One Forum program, for example, was said to "give industry leaders a better understanding of the rights inherent in the First Amendment." A Forum newsletter column argues that "At a time of growing public dissatisfaction with the press, a little James Madison may go a long way" (Paulson, 1997, p. 8). This emphasis on rights versus responsibilities for news producers combines easily with the preference for consumer appreciation for news over public critique.

News is further bound to core values with Freedom Park, and its Journalists Memorial. A nearby sign carries the following inscription:

> Freedom Forum journalists memorial honors reporters, editors, photographers, and broadcasters who gave their lives reporting the news. Around the world journalists have placed themselves in peril. Thousands simply disappeared, the victims of cruel regimes. Their names lost to history. Those named here intone their collective legacy: They fought and died in the battle to report the truth.

This public listing of journalists' names resembles the Vietnam memorial and invites visitors to attribute to them the same heroic qualities evoked by the nation's military tradition. The emphasis on fallen journalists as "martyrs," to use Al Neuharth's phrase, and to attribute heroic qualities to them in the memorial, purposefully borrows the meaning of these terms—to show courage and die on behalf of a noble calling and great principle. In one of the news releases for the memorial, the journalists were said to have given their lives to "get the truth."

Through the memorialized journalists, news takes on mythic and idealized proportions. Although sympathetic to those who have lost their lives and shown genuine courage, the effect of giving news and the profession of journalism such heroic overtones is to give it to their employers as well. This hagiography further roots news within an individual context, casting journalists as the ones responsible for the news we get. One would feel terribly ungrateful in criticizing the news media if to do so is to dishonor the unfortunate individuals who were killed while gathering its raw material. Collapsing all of the practices and institutional arrangements used to produce the news commodity into a powerfully framed heroic monument obliterates more critical questions.

News as Individual Effort

Indeed, the individualistic nature of journalism permeates the Newseum. Visitors are invited to "interview a journalist" by selecting options on a computer monitor. In the interactive newsroom, visitors are invited to test their "news judgment" and "Be a Reporter." The computerized guide urges participants to "dig for the truth." Another station invites visitors to "Be an Editor: print fair news, be accurate, consider news value, confirm your facts, meet your deadline." The implicit message here is that a fixed standard governs news decisions, and the visitor should strive to follow the suggested framework in making the correct judgments. The further implication is that the individual news professional, who one is emulating interactively, is in control of the relevant news shaping decisions. The practical requirements of rendering a more efficient handling of visitors lead to the interactive questions being strictly formatted, and the do-it-yourself news "anchors" encouraged to stick to a prepared script. As Friedman (1998) pointed out, this limited framework ironically approximates the way actual journalists' autonomy is institutionally constrained.[8]

These interactive stations further advance the frame that news is a natural product, prepared by professionals who are given the power to make the appropriate decisions. Locating this power at the journalist level leaves little of it for outside sources, sponsors of frames, or corporate influence. It is the corollary of the Right-Wing critique of the biased liberal journalist, a critique favored by journalists themselves for granting them more autonomy than the liberal countercritique centering on corporate influence. At worse, the journalist may be accused of liberal bias, at best one may aspire to be memorialized in Freedom Park. In either case, the frame hides the larger forces at work behind the news product.

As a monument to the profession, the overall project is actually in odd tension with journalists' view of themselves; in a *New York Times* article the writer said the Newseum is making every effort to "demystify a process that often mystifies its practitioners." Tacitly accepting the antiframe, she claimed that "Reporters are players, but bit players" in a larger historical show (Barringer, 1998).

Audience Response

The Polling Place invites visitors to register their opinions about news and see the results displayed after they respond. Given that the museum goers

---

[8]I was intrigued to find that independently I had reached impressions similar to those of Ted Friedman (1998), who following his deconstruction of Atlanta's World of Coca-Cola Museum (1992), prepared a review of the Newseum. Comparing our efforts shows that I gravitated toward a more "seamless" framing, while his considered the elements in tension embedded in "heroic objectivity."

would likely have more interest in news than the public at large, it is perhaps not surprising to see generally favorable responses. When asked to rate the job the news media are doing, 13% said *excellent* and 52% said *good*. Rating the overall quality of news received every day, 15% again said *excellent* and 53% said *good*. (These figures were from July 10th, and are updated cumulatively with each additional visitor voting. They had not changed appreciably as of April 2000, with 25,372 voting.) Of course, after being treated to a free admission, it may seem churlish for a visitor to respond otherwise. When asked to respond to more specific criticisms of news, visitors were more troubled: 63% said *it was a problem that news was manipulated by special interests*, 58% said *bias was a major problem*, 57% that *it was superficial*, and 72% that *it was sensationalized*. The Newseum, however, is not designed to tackle these issues.

Visitors are also asked how concerned they are that news "covers the liberal point of view?": 27% said *a great deal*, 22% *some*, and 12% *a little*. The matching question regarding the "conservative point of view" is not asked, but that is in keeping with the nature of the "liberal bias" critique—that the source of the bias is located with the individual journalist, attributing to them the kind of power underscored by the Newseum.

SUMMARY AND CONCLUSION

The case of the Newseum usefully illustrates the definition of framing proposed earlier. The museum displays, programs, and commentary organize a wide range of history, professional practices, and technological trends under the naturalized news "antiframe." The principle guiding these presentations must in part be derived from what we know of Gannet and other media corporation objectives, that how news is conceived must support the modern commercial system of newsgathering, not calling into question the basic rightness of this arrangement for American society. (Much of the Freedom Park exhibit is devoted to symbols of threats to freedom from outside this country: the Berlin Wall, South Africa, Cuba, and so forth.)

The frame is clearly shared, given the popularity of the exhibits and the uncritical reception that the Newseum has received. The persistence of this frame is strong, given its connection to enduring American values such as freedom. The symbolic aspects of the frame are seen in the entire experience that visitors are given, from the moment they enter the building to exiting through the gift shop with their souvenir T-shirts and coffee mugs. The frame is clearly well-structured, especially given that it is under the control of a single sponsor, the Forum. Competing frames are not available, so this one is well-integrated. Although my analysis is designed to be more provocative than comprehensive, the Newseum case suggests the value of the framing model for understanding media. Of course, my approach here resembles an ideological analysis, but the framing approach helps further point to a body of questions that organize our thinking.

I have attempted to suggest through definitions, model, and illustrative cases such framing questions that commend themselves to media analysis. Of course, posing the questions is always much easier than answering them, with specific methods, measurements, and research strategies. My working definition suggests a number of possibilities, but certainly examining framing requires that we do comparative work. Given that the naturalistic nature of much of the framing process makes it tough to identify, research would benefit from observations over time to examine emerging frames, and cross-cultural work to compare the framing process under different societal conditions and with other indicators of social reality. This means not confining ourselves to media materials, but interviewing journalists, sources, and audience members.

By bridging the behavioral and critical, the quantitative and qualitative, the framing paradigm has potential for informing and enriching these approaches. It's not enough to say either that knowledge is in the service of power or that knowledge emerges naturally through the pluralistic interplay of forces. Framing suggests that we specifically study how our social understanding is structured and how these understandings are tied to interests. Thus, to study framing means we must address normative issues. Although social science research has not emphasized explicit value judgments in analysis of press coverage, framing can't help but suggest them. How well did the press frame do justice to the issue? Why were journalists so willing to adopt the frame of a special interest group, when another would have been closer to the truth?

These are questions that academic analysts can easily share with media professionals. In his review of press coverage of China, for example, journalist James Mann (1999) considered the frame concept: "the single story, image, or concept" (p. 103) that governs the reporting in the media, affects editors mindsets, and sets the context against which journalists contend. Specifically, he warned against reducing China to a one dimensional, and distorting, frame. Editor Frank Denton (1998) cited framing research he found useful in understanding how journalists and readers approach stories from different perspectives.

The growing and powerful media watchdog industry, especially well-funded on the Right, has been doing this kind of framing research for years without exactly calling it that (e.g., Accuracy in Media, Media Research Institute, Fairness & Accuracy in Reporting). And critical analyses have been emerging recently of the important framing role played by the public relations industry (Ewen, 1996; Nelson, 1989; Stauber & Rampton, 1995). Even if academic media researchers do not share the political spin of such groups, it is important that they be aware of the concerns that animate them—that the media are powerful, economic concerns, often distant from the audiences they serve, producing news as a commodity, generating frames that may distort as much as they illuminate our social world. The framing model comes closer than many research areas in our field to posing important, intelligible questions of common concern to scholars, press watchdogs, and ultimately the public as well.

REFERENCES

Baran, S., & Davis, D. (2000). *Mass communication theory: Foundations, ferment, and future.* Belmont, CA: Wadsworth.
Barringer, F. (1998). Media: Press, a look back at reporting in 1968 yields a mixed lesson. *New York Times*, May 4, p. D8.
Bateson, G. (1972). *Steps to an ecology of mind: Collected essays in anthropology, psychiatry, evolution, and epistemology.* New York: Ballantine.
Bennett, T. (1992). Putting policy into cultural studies. In L. Grossberg, C. Nelson, & P. Treichler (Eds.), *Cultural studies* (pp. 23–37). London: Routledge.
Bergen, L., Reese, S., & Mueller, J. (1994). *Constructing the abortion controversy on local television: Operation Rescue's Summer of Mercy in Wichita.* Paper presented to the International Communication Association, Sydney, Australia.
Bird, E., & Dardenne, R. (1988). Myth, chronicle, and story: Exploring the narrative quality of news. In J. Carey (Ed.), *Media, myths and narratives* (pp. 67–86). Thousand Oaks, CA: Sage.
Carragee, K. (1991). News and ideology: An analysis of coverage of the West German Green Party in the New York Times. *Journalism monographs*, 128.
Davis, D., & Baran, S. (1981). *Mass communication and everyday life: A perspective on theory and effects.* Belmont, CA: Wadsworth.
Davis, J. (1995). The effects of message framing on response to environmental communications. *Journalism & Mass Communication Quarterly, 72*(2), 285–299.
Davis, S. (1997). *Spectacular nature: Corporate culture and the Sea World experience.* Berkeley: University of California Press.
Denton, F. (1998). Cracking the spiral of silence, empowering people. *Civic catalyst: Pew Center for civic journalism* (summer), pp. 14–15.
Edelman, M. (1993). Contestable categories and public opinion. *Political Communication, 10*(3), 231–242.
Entman, R. (1993a). Framing toward clarification of a fractured paradigm. *Journal of Communication, 43*(4), 51–58.
Entman, R. (1993b). Freezing out the public: Elite and media framing of the U.S. anti-nuclear movement. *Political Communication, 10*, 155–173.
Entman, R., & Rojecki, A. (1993). Freezing out the public: Elite and media framing of the U.S. anti-nuclear movement. *Political Communication, 10*(2), 151–167.
Erickson, R., Baranek, P., & Chan, J. (1991). *Representing order: Crime, law, and justice in the news media.* Toronto: University of Toronto Press.
Ewen, S. (1996). *PR! A social history of spin.* New York: Basic Books.
Fjellman, S. (1992). *Vinyl leaves Walt Disney World and America.* Boulder: Westview.
Fowler, R. (1991). *Language in the news: Discourse and ideology in the press.* New York: Routledge.
Friedland, L., & Mengbai, Z. (1996, April). International television coverage of Beijing spring 1989: A comparative approach. *Journalism & Mass Communication Monographs*, 156.

Friedman, T. (1998). From heroic objectivity to the news stream: The Newseum's strategies for relegitimizing journalism in the information age. *Critical studies in mass communication, 15*(3), 325–335.

Friedman, T. (1992). The world of the world of Coca-Cola. *Communication research, 19*(5), 642–662.

Gamson, W. (1989). News as framing. *American behavioral scientist, 33*(2), 157–161.

Gamson, W. (1992). *Talking politics*. New York: Cambridge University Press.

Gamson, W., & Modigliani, A. (1989). Media discourse and public opinion on nuclear power: A constructionist approach. *American Journal of Sociology, 95*, 1–37.

Giroux, H. (1999). *The mouse that roared: Disney and the end of innocence*. New York: Rowman & Littlefield.

Gitlin, T. (1980). *The whole world is watching*. Berkeley: University of California Press.

Glasgow Media Group (1995). *Reader, Vol. 2: Industry, economy, war and politics*. G. Philo (Ed.). New York: Routledge.

Goffman, E. (1974). *Frame analysis: An essay on the organization of experience*. Boston: Northeastern University Press.

Goshorn, K., & Gandy, O. (1995). Race, risk and responsibility: Editorial constraint in the framing of inequality. *Journal of communication, 45*(2), 133–151.

Hackett, R. (1984). Decline of a paradigm? Bias and objectivity in news media studies. *Critical Studies in Mass Communication, 1*(3), 229–259.

Hall, S. (1982). The rediscovery of 'ideology': Return of the repressed in media studies. In M. Gurevitch, T. Bennett, J. Curran, & J. Wollacott (Eds.), *Culture, society and the media* (pp. 56–90). London: Metheun.

Haraway, D. (1989). *Primate visions: Gender, race, and nature in the world of modern science*. New York: Routledge.

Hertog, J., & McLeod, D. (1995). Anarchists wreak havoc in downtown Minneapolis: A multi-level study of media coverage of radical protest. *Journalism Monographs, 151*, June.

Iorio, S., & Huxman, S. (1996). Media coverage of political issues and the framing of personal concerns. *Journal of communication, 46*(4), 97–115.

Iyengar, S. (1991). *Is anyone responsible?* Chicago: University of Chicago Press.

Kahneman, D., & Tversky, A. (1984). Choices, values and frames. *American psychologist, 39*, 341–350.

Kosicki, G. (1993). Problems and opportunities in agenda-setting research. *Journal of Communication, 43*(2), 100–127.

Lukes, S. (1974). *Power: A radical view*. London: MacMillan.

Mann, J. (1999). Framing China: A complex country cannot be explained with simplistic formulas. *Media studies journal*. Winter, pp. 102–107.

Martin, C., & Oshagan, H. (1997). Disciplining the workforce: The news media frame a General Motors plant closing. *Communication research, 24*(6), 669–697.

McCauley, M., & Frederick, E. (1993). *The war on drugs: A constructionist view*. Paper presented to the Association for Education in Journalism and Mass Communication, Kansas City.

McCombs, M., Shaw, D., & Weaver, D. (1997). *Communication and democracy: Exploring the intellectual frontiers in agenda-setting*. Mahwah, NJ: Lawrence Erlbaum Associates.

Miller, M. (1997). Frame mapping and analysis of news coverage of contentious issues. *Social Science Computer Review, 15*(4), 367–378.

Molotch, H. (1993). The political economy of growth machines. *Journal of Urban Affairs, 15*(1), 29–53.

Morley, D. (1976). Industrial conflict and the mass media. *Sociological Review, 24*, 245–268.

Nelson, J. (1989). *Sultans of sleaze: Public relations and the media*. Monroe, MA: Common Courage Press.

Neuman, R., & Just, M., & Crigler, A. (1992). *Common knowledge: News and the construction of political meaning*. Chicago: University of Chicago Press.

Pan, Z., & Kosicki, G. (1993). Framing analysis: An approach to news discourse. *Political Communication, 10*, 55–75.

Paulson, K. (1997, September). Editors, executives need First Amendment primer. *Freedom Forum and Newseum News, 4*(12), 8.

Project Censored Canada Yearbook (1996). Blindspots in the news agenda? In M. Lowes, R. Hackett, J. Winter, D. Gutstein, & R. Gruneau (Eds.). Burnaby, BC, Canada: Simon Fraser University.

Reese, S. (1999). Progressive potential of journalism education: Recasting the academic vs. professional debate. *Harvard International Journal of Press/Politics, 4*(4), 70–94.

Reese, S., & Buckalew, B. (1994). The militarism of local television: The routine framing of the Persian Gulf war. *Critical Studies in Mass Communication, 12*(1), 40–59.

Reese, S., Grant, A., & Danielian, L. (1994). The structure of news sources on television: A network analysis of *CBS News, Nightline, McNeil-Lehrer* and *This Week with David Brinkley. Journal of Communication, 44*(2), 84–107.

Scheufele, D. (1999). Framing as a theory of media effects. *Journal of Communication, 49*(1), 103–122.

Schudson, M. (1997). Paper tigers: A sociologist follows cultural studies into the wilderness. *Lingua Franca* (August), pp. 49–56.

Snow, D., & Benford, R. (1988). Ideology, frame resonance, and participant mobilization. *International Social Movement Research, 1*, 197–217.

Solomon, D. (1999, April 21). He turns the past into stories, and the galleries fill up. *New York Times*, p. 12.

Solomon, W. S. (1992). News frames and media packages: Covering El Salvador. *Critical Studies in Mass Communication, 9*, 56–74.

Stauber, J., & Rampton, S. (1995). *Toxic sludge is good for you! Lies, damn lies and the public relations industry*. Monroe, MA: Common Courage Press.

Tankard, J., Hendrickson, L., Silberman, J., Bliss, K., & Ghanem, S. (1991). *Media frames: Approaches to conceptualization and measurement.* Paper presented to the Association for Education in Journalism and Mass Communication, Boston.

Tucker, L. (1998). The framing of Calvin Klein: A frame analysis of media discourse about the August 1995 Calvin Klein jeans advertising campaign. *Critical Studies in Mass Communication, 15*, 141–157.

Van Dijk, T. (1993). *Elite discourse and racism*. Newbury Park, CA: Sage.

Wolfsfeld, G. (1997). *Media and political conflict: News from the Middle East.* New York: Cambridge University Press.

THEORETICAL AND
MEASUREMENT APPROACHES

1

Framing as a Strategic Action in Public Deliberation

Zhongdang Pan
Gerald M. Kosicki

We are in the age of "talk." With the proliferation of interactive electronic media including radio and television talk shows, Internet chat rooms, news groups and other new media forms, talk as a mode of communication, rooted in dialogue or conversation, is changing not only the political process but also how we communicate in society. These changes are visibly blurring the traditional boundaries between communicators and audiences, news and entertainment, information and opinion, journalists and talking heads, political and nonpolitical issues, interpersonal and mass communication, as well as political communication, mobilization, and participation (e.g., Gamson, 1992; Jamieson, Cappella, & Turow, 1998; Livingstone & Lunt, 1994; Munson, 1993; Owen, 1995; Verba, 1993).

With the increasing high volume and widespread nature of such "talk," there emerges "an imaginary and discursive space where issues 'sizzle' and political 'bashing' can happen" (Munson, 1993, p. 4). Such talk is said to provide a necessary venue for the public, under specific conditions, to overcome or correct the unrepresentative opinions of their "surrogate deliberators," that is, political elites (Page & Tannenbaum, 1996). In essence, the normative idea of "deliberative democracy" (see Bohman, 1996; Bohman & Rehg, 1997; Calhoun, 1992; Elster, 1998) is slowly becoming a genuine empirical phenomenon with which to reckon (see Gamson, 1992; Katz, 1995; Kim, Wyatt, & Katz, 1999; Page, 1996; Verba, 1993).

Such talk also has structural underpinnings. The public arena that serves as the infrastructure for public deliberation is structurally arranged

(Dahlgren, 1991; Hillgartner & Bosk, 1988). In addition, such structuring is also enforced discursively through political actors manipulating symbols to "spin" issues or events. In other words, political actors skew the flow of information and opinions in public deliberation toward their advantage by using discursive means (see Maltese, 1994; Zaller, 1992). News media, operating in terms of their professional ideology and established work ways (Price & Tewksbury, 1997), more often than not are found to be collaborating with the ruling elite in weaving this discursive order (e.g., Bennett, 1990; Gitlin, 1980; Page & Tannenbaum, 1996; Zaller & Chiu, 1996). Public deliberation, therefore, is not a harmonious process but an ideological contest and political struggle. Actors in the public arena struggle over the right to define and shape issues, as well as the discourse surrounding these issues. Sometimes, actors struggle mightily to keep important issues off the public agenda (Cobb & Ross, 1997).

Gamson (1996) described framing as a discursive process of strategic actors utilizing symbolic resources to participate in collective sense-making about public policy issues. Thus, we have argued that framing is an essential part of public deliberation (Pan & Kosicki, 1997). With this re-situation of the key problems of framing analysis, we advanced a perspective that helps connect various conceptions of framing (e.g., Cappella & Jamieson, 1997; Entman, 1993; Gamson, 1981; Ghanem, 1997; Iyengar, 1991; Price & Tewksbury, 1997). We argued that framing analysis connects the normative propositions of "deliberative democracy" and the empirical questions of collective decision making (see Baumgartner & Jones, 1993; Kingdon, 1984) and helps understand the operation of American democracy (Cobb & Elder, 1983).

In this chapter, we extend this earlier conceptualization and discuss framing as "strategic actions" in public deliberation. We then explicate two key concepts that can be applied to analyze such strategic actions, "discursive communities," and "web of subsidies," and show their application with one illustrative case.[1]

TO PARTICIPATE IS TO FRAME

Although its exact nature and practical feasibility remain to be debated, public deliberation is generally understood as a process of collective and open reasoning, and discussion about the merits of public policy (Bohman & Rehg, 1997; Elster, 1998; Page, 1996). Two propositions make the idea fundamental for political communication research. One is that, as a normative ideal, public deliberation is the essence of democracy. Deliberation has a long intellectual as well as political tradition from which American democ-

---

[1]The authors wish to thank Stephen D. Reese for his detailed and insightful comments on an earlier version of this chapter.

racy developed (Bohman 1996; Habermas, 1989; Page, 1996; Page & Shapiro, 1992).[2] Second, political communication increasingly is being democratized. Opportunities for public participation in producing political discourse have proliferated not only in the media but also in deliberating institutions such as Congress (Cook, 1989; Frantzich & Sullivan, 1996; Livingstone & Lunt, 1994; Munson, 1993; Page & Tannenbaum, 1996; Verba, 1993).

Such participation is potentially transforming the public's role from that of mere spectators of political sports (Edelman, 1988) or targets of elite manipulation (Zaller, 1992) into that of actors or citizens in the American political process. Meaningful participation opens up public deliberation and makes it more inclusive. Members of the public develop their own interpretations of media messages but also incorporate these meanings into their store of everyday common-sense knowledge (Neuman, Just, & Crigler, 1992). They talk about public policy issues by making use of the symbolic resources available to them, originating with media discourse, personal experiences, and popular wisdom (Gamson, 1992). Such discussion in the public arena constitutes not only the "public mood" or "public sentiment" that is closely monitored by public officials and media, but also the texture of policy discourse (Gamson & Modigliani, 1989; Page, 1996; Stimson, 1991; Verba, 1993).

Therefore, we argue that participating in public deliberation inevitably involves the discursive practices of framing an issue, which is *not* the exclusive province of political elites or media. However, this observation takes us only so far toward our goal of conducting framing analysis. At this point, we must consider two questions that lie at the heart of the framing process. First, how do people develop the terms, that is, the *frames and signification devices* of the frames that they use in the deliberation process? Second, how are different perspectives or points of view, that is frames, contested or struggled over in the public arena?

FRAMING IN PUBLIC DELIBERATION

In his widely cited book, Goffman (1974) defines frames as "schemata of interpretation" that enable individuals "to locate, perceive, identify, and label" occurrences or life experiences (p. 21).[3] He proceeds to show how our

---

[2]There are different views on this historical lineage. For example, Schudson (1992, 1997) explicitly rejects the deliberative basis of this kind in American democracy.

[3]Over the years, scholars have offered numerous definitions of frames or framing (see Cappella & Jamieson, 1997; Entman, 1993; Gamson & Modigliani, 1989; Gitlin, 1980; Iyengar, 1991; Kahneman & Tversky, 1984; Minsky, 1975; Price & Tewksbury, 1997; Snow et al., 1986; Tuchman, 1978). We will not get into the tedious task of listing all the definitions. Suffice to say that almost all these definitions, in one way or another, make reference to Goffman's seminal work.

common sense knowledge performs its constructive role in our everyday life and how such schemata of interpretation are "acted out." Following this tradition, framing analysis is concerned with how various social actors act and interact "to yield organized ways of understanding the world" (Reese, see prologue, this volume). Such understandings are developed *via* symbolic means, including language, which in Berger and Luckmann's (1967) terms is capable of both objectifying and typifying our experiences. Frames are the "central organizing ideas" to achieve such understanding and to organize political reality (Gamson & Modigliani, 1989, p. 3).[4]

Framing as a process has its cognitive underpinnings, which many scholars have made attempts to articulate. For example, Price and Tewksbury (1997) argued that the three major media effects hypotheses, agenda-setting, priming, and framing all address the issue of "knowledge activation and use" (p. 184). Thus they attempt to account for such effects by applying the associative network model of memory structure and related concepts, such as accessibility and spread of activation. According to them, framing effects result from the salient attributes of a media message changing the applicability of particular thoughts, resulting in their activation and use in evaluations. Their work represents a formal statement of the cognitive view of the framing effect and how it takes place (see also Higgins, 1996; Kahneman & Tversky, 1984).[5] Incorporating both cognitive processes and discourse analysis of news text, Rhee (1997) showed that audiences frequently use the thoughts associated with the frame made salient in media coverage to talk about an

---

[4]While gaining rapid currency in our field, frame remains an ill-defined concept. Some researchers define it by referring to social actors' practices in "acting out" a frame, that is, selection, emphasis, and exclusion in message presentation (Entman, 1993). Some define it by referring to a narrative form or a (relatively) nonsubstantive template, for example, episodic *vs.* thematic (Iyengar, 1991), issue *versus* strategic (Cappella & Jamieson, 1997). For the definitions or actual uses consistent with our definition, see Gamson and Modigliani (1987, 1989), Gamson (1992), Kinder and Sanders (1990), Pan and Kosicki (1993), Snow and Benford (1988, 1992). The major difference here is that this latter group of researchers sees frames to be more substantive. A frame reveals a persistent point of view, which is shared on some level and communicable. It organizes our experiences and renders meaning to such organized information. It both motivates and is signified by paradigmatic choices as well as syntagmatic arrangements (see Pan & Kosicki, 1993; Reese, see prologue, this volume).

[5]Using less formal terms, other scholars have articulated similar ideas. For example, Entman (1993) argued that framing involves "selection and highlighting, and use of the highlighted elements to construct an argument about problems and their causation, evaluation" (p. 53). McCombs and Shaw (1993) argued that agenda setting "is a theory about the transfer of salience, both the salience of objects and the salience of their attributes (p. 62)." The latter is expanded into what is now called "second level agenda setting" (McCombs & Ghanem, chap. 2, this volume). Cappella and Jamieson (1997) offered a somewhat different version of the cognitive account, relying similarly on the concepts of associative network, accessibility, and spread of activation. They argued that "(p)riming and the spread of activation are the mechanisms through which news frames stimulate thought processes and emotional reactions" (p. 59).

election campaign (see also Kintsch, 1988; Pan & Kosicki, 1993; van Dijk, 1988). In sum, framing effects result from schema activation or modification and can be found in how information is processed and made sense of, how people talk about an issue, and how they form political evaluations.

Demonstrating the nature and process of framing *effects* is an important area of research (Cappella & Jamieson, 1997; Iyengar, 1991; Kinder & Sanders, 1990; Scheufele, 1999). However, the effects paradigm is limited for framing analysis. First, as Gamson (1992, 1996) demonstrated, people *construct* their understanding of issues (see also Crigler, 1996; Neuman et al., 1992). They do so by tapping into the symbolic resources that are available to them in their everyday lives, as conveyed through their experiential knowledge, popular wisdom, and media discourse. They combine such symbolic resources differently across varying situations. In other words, individuals *strategically* maneuver to "tame the information tide" (Graber, 1988) and to communicate with others. For example, Iorio and Huxman (1996) showed that voters from Wichita, Kansas, employed linking, collapsing, and colorizing strategies in making use of various resources to talk about their concerns. The question raised by this line of reasoning, to paraphrase Katz (1959), is not what media discourse does to people but what people do with media discourse?

Second, talking about public issues is not limited to people's leisure time. Very often, such talk takes place in public arenas for specific political objectives (Page, 1996; Verba, 1993). Such talk is, using Katz's (1995, p. xxi) characterization, "the elementary building block" of political participation. A frame is an idea through which political debate unfolds, and political alignment and collective actions take place (see Snow & Benford, 1988; Snow, Rochford, Worden, & Benford, 1986; Zald, 1996). In public deliberations, the rise and fall in the prevalence of a frame, and consequently, a particular policy option, clearly involve debates among people who sponsor or align with different frames (Gamson & Modigliani, 1989; Snow & Benford, 1988). Which frame to sponsor, how to sponsor it, and how to expand its appeal are strategic issues to participants (Ryan, 1991). The infamous political campaign against Robert Bork's nomination to the U.S. Supreme Court is an example (Pertschuk & Schaetzel, 1989). These should also be issues to address in framing analysis.

In sum, framing an issue is to participate in public deliberation strategically, both for one's own sense making and for contesting the frames of others. Thus, limiting ourselves to the effects paradigm prevents us from analyzing the strategic contests in framing processes.

We need to say a little more about the linkage between framing and frame contestation. In "public deliberation," a frame also functions as a key idea to animate and sustain individual participation in collective actions, a necessary part of the policy making process (Snow & Benford, 1992; Zald,

1996). It also offers an organizing schema for policy making or implementing an agency's organizational mission (Moore, 1993).

Adopting a certain frame is manifested in paradigmatic choices from the existing cultural repertoire of symbolic resources (Gamson & Modigliani, 1987, 1989; Hartley, 1988; Pan & Kosicki, 1993). Such choices often are imparted by and resonate with some broader ideological perspective (Snow & Benford, 1988, 1992). Therefore, framing is an ideological contest over not only the scope of an issue, but also over matters such as who is responsible and who is affected, which ideological principles or enduring values are relevant, and where the issue should be addressed (Cobb & Elder, 1983; Hilgartner & Bosk, 1988).

In such a contest, participants maneuver strategically to achieve their political and communicative objectives. Each actor needs to take strategic steps to "get messages across" and win arguments. A step toward framing is strategic if it makes one's message meet the epistemic standards of "good arguments" and achieve "cultural resonance" (Gamson & Modigliani, 1987; Snow & Benford, 1988). Such a step is also strategic if it leads to a desirable configuration of social and political forces. Frames may be differentiated in terms of the strengths of their political and cultural appeals (Snow & Benford, 1988, 1992). Similarly, framing actions differ in their potential for achieving the desired political and discursive goals. Framing an issue is therefore a strategic means to attract more supporters, to mobilize collective actions, to expand actors' realm of influences, and to increase their chances of winning (Snow & Benford, 1988, 1992; Zald, 1996).

Framing is also part of constructing "political spectacle" (Edelman, 1988). First, framing involves elite manipulations and performances (Kinder & Herzog, 1993), although not necessarily to the exclusion of citizen participation. The venues of the public sphere can then be viewed as "stages" for performances by elites. Although such stages may have privileged access by elites, they may also be constructed and used by grassroots and/or dissenting groups (Benford & Hunt, 1992; Page, 1996; Ryan, 1991). Second, framing involves interpreting political activities and statements to construct the factuality of the political world. Their degrees of empirical credibility vary in their degrees of conformity to the prescribed conventions shared by the participants and their roles in the political world (Blumler & Gurevitch, 1980; Edelman, 1988, pp. 94–97). Consequently, framing involves political drama and theater (Benford & Hunt, 1992; Cobb & Elder, 1983; Esherick & Wasserstrom, 1990; Gamson, 1988; Gitlin, 1980; Ryan, 1991). It also involves personalities, characters, scripts, conflicts, dramas, emotions, symbols, and expressive activities consisting of both "real" and "pseudo-events" (Boorstin, 1971/1992).

The Persian Gulf conflict in 1990 and 1991 was a good case in point. Elite debate and the antiwar protests at the margin were conducted on a stage designed for and by the media, especially television. Remarkably, diplomatic exchanges between the hostile parties were carried through the same venue (see Kellner, 1992). Historical icons of Hitler and Vietnam were invoked. Metaphorical depictions such as American flags, yellow ribbons, "line in the sand," and "surgical strike" became condensed expressions of a patriotic hype, justice, and determination. With these symbolic devices, the public discourse depicted a drama of confrontation between a determined leader of the "free world" and a villain from the authoritarian underworld, the spectacle of the U.S. high-tech weaponry crushing ruthless but powerless Iraqi "Republican Guards," and a timid antiwar protest.[6] Public deliberation thus includes political performances in all the venues of the "public arena." Many examples of recent large-scale, well-developed public policy controversies—such as the "gays in the military" issue, the Lani Guinier nomination, health care reform, the various "-gates" involving Bill Clinton, and the bitter impeachment battle—all illustrate such attribute of the framing process.

FRAMING BOUNDARIES AND BUILDING
DISCURSIVE COMMUNITIES

Frames provide labels to typify social conditions and policy concerns (Best, 1995) and thus allow us to choose from a "repertoire of interpretations" (Mooney & Hunt, 1996). But which sector of this repertoire of interpretation would we tap into? How is the choice of political vocabulary related to our conceptions of the actors, their relationships, and their actions? To answer these questions, we begin with the point that frames define the boundaries of the discourse concerning an issue and categorize the relevant actors based on some established scheme of social taxonomy. In this way, framing can be seen as a means for community building, although the nature of the resulting community is hardly traditional. We do not mean a sociologically close-knit unit in a confined geographic area but a transitory and discursively bound aggregate, capable of collective action in deliberative politics.

What goes into an issue and how a given issue is related to others are not as ontologically obvious as the concept of agenda setting would lead us to believe. Heated political fighting is involved over an acceptable definition and thus the social and cultural boundaries of each issue, as several

---

[6]The antiwar activists got their message blurred because they failed to place their opposition to the war and their "support for our troops" in one coherent frame. This failure had its roots in the political culture at the time, which was dominated by the frequent associations of the historical images of antiwar protests, social unrest, and military failure during the Vietnam War.

studies have demonstrated in journalistic work (e.g., Ericson, Baranek, & Chan, 1989; Gans, 1980; Gitlin, 1980; Tuchman, 1978). In the more general setting of public deliberation, several researchers have argued for the political and ideological nature of the process of classifying social conditions into issue categories and policy making venues (Best, 1995; Cobb & Elder, 1983; Hilgartner & Bosk, 1988; Kingdon, 1984). Political actors use language to express and "signal" as well as to "objectivate" the conceptual boundaries in the adopted classification scheme (Berger & Luckmann, 1967). Framing, therefore, is also a process for strategic actors to (re)negotiate such boundaries as well as the relative degrees of extendibility and openness of various frames (Snow et al., 1986).

We can see this boundary-defining function of framing in a variety of examples. In the public deliberation concerning the Persian Gulf conflict, political elites close to the Bush administration made a successful effort to frame, or to "confine," the debate over the appropriate option to "punish" Iraq and right the wrong of Iraqi aggression within a narrow range of the discourse (Bennett & Paletz, 1994; Kellner, 1992). Antiwar protests, in comparison, were not very successful in redrawing what they considered to be the appropriate boundaries of the issue. As a result, they fell into the administration conceptual categories and consequently were not effective in influencing the policy debate. Similarly, in the public discourse on nuclear weapons, much of the elite discourse confined the talk to the frameworks of national security and conflict between rival superpowers with opposing ideologies. By designing its discourse in these frames, the Reagan administration was able to sell its policy of achieving a nuclear freeze through overpowering the rival militarily (Meyer, 1995).

The boundary-defining function of framing takes place at different levels, which we address as more than a levels-of-abstraction attribute. Although frames do vary in abstraction, our concern is how framing, by activating the conventions and tacit rules of interpretation and text construction shared by participants, differentiates categories of actors, types of actions, and kinds of action settings. Those who share such conventions and tacit rules are said to be in the same "discursive community," a historical moment of a social aggregate, which functions as a basis for collective action (Wuthnow, 1989).[7] In framing an issue, each social aggregate "acts out" its discursive as well as sociological binding.

This proposition is shown in the differentiation among categories of discourse based on the "actors–speakers" in public deliberation. For example,

---

[7]Similar conceptual elements are found in the discussions of the concept of "interpretive community" (e.g., Fish, 1980; Radway, 1984; Schroder, 1994; Zelizer, 1993). However, we choose the term *discursive community* to emphasize the sociological and historically situated binding, as well as the constructive forces of the shared talk and its conventions (Lincoln, 1989).

Meyer (1995) differentiated political, strategic expert, scientific expert, and challenger discourses in his study of public discourse on nuclear weapons. Similarly, Gamson and Modigliani (1989) differentiated specialist, official, and challenger discourses in their study of media nuclear power discourse. Different actors–speakers in public deliberation develop their own frames of an issue based on their own ideological principles and institutionally specified roles. For example, in their study, Terkildsen, Schnell, and Ling (1998) showed that while media incorporated interest groups' frames in reporting the abortion debate, they also created their own based on their professional ideology of objectivity and balance. Others have also argued that U.S. media, driven by their commitment to journalistic professional values, often end up covering policy debate in a strategy frame (e.g., Cappella & Jamieson, 1997; Patterson, 1993; Price & Tewksbury, 1997).

These studies demonstrate that each category of actors in public deliberation employs the established and shared conventions and norms. As a result, their framing efforts reproduce themselves as a "discursive community." Some of those norms and conventions are found in the well-understood work routines of a profession or community, as shown, for example, for journalists (Fishman, 1980; Gans, 1980; Gitlin, 1980; Tuchman, 1978). Whereas some of those norms and conventions may be stabilized as formal, even codified bureaucratic procedures and rules, others may exist as tacit expectations, which in some communities may be repeatedly discussed or "talked about" (Zelizer, 1993). This creates an expectation of not only how but also in what terms an actor talks about a public policy issue. Social groups develop a shared discursive field to enable them to engage in an orderly deliberation (Wuthnow, 1989). For example, journalists and politicians, despite their differences, are able to understand each other's role and to follow workable routines governing their interactions (Blumler & Gurevitch, 1980).[8] This boundary notion of discursive community yields the possibility of discursive political alignment. That is, actors in different categories may be bound into a shared policy position through what is called "frame alignment" (Snow et al., 1986), a process of essentially redrawing boundaries.

Framing then involves defining and redefining the actors–speakers themselves. For example, in the U.S. peace movement, different frames of the peace movement were associated with different types of actors (Marullo, Pagnucco, & Smith, 1996). Although some of the actors acquired the image of "moderates," others acquired the image of "radicals." Acquiring such an identity and projecting such images are part of the actor–speaker's strate-

---

[8] Where there has long been tension and conflict in the relationships between journalists and official sources. The shared culture of these actors is being eroded by mutual mistrust and escalating cynicism and blame (Kurtz, 1998; Walsh, 1996).

gic choice of framing tactics. As a result, we find that framing and social movement identities are closely related. Successful framing requires making clear boundaries separating one from others. We can see numerous examples showing the importance of framing such sociological and cultural boundaries of actors. Framing public policies designed to address race relations in terms of "reverse discrimination" clearly points to racial division and the emphasis on "equal opportunity" being measured at the aggregate level of racial groups (Gamson & Modigliani, 1987). Similarly, framing the "gays in the military" issue in terms of "minority rights" is clearly aimed at weakening the boundaries between social categories based on sexual orientations and expanding the boundaries of the sociological concept of "minority."

In brief, framing not only frames an issue but also frames social groups. In other words, frames of an issue also frame framers. They define not only the categories of social groups. They shape not only the public discourse concerning an issue but also the discursive communities involved. Through framing, cultural categories are reproduced and enriched and the sociological boundaries of these physical units are also reinforced or remapped. It is in this sense that discourse helps construct the very social structure that serves as its physical support and political alignment that supports it (Lincoln, 1989).

WEB OF SUBSIDIES AND FRAME SPONSORSHIP

Framing thus places social actors' strategic choices at the analytical center. In this "framework," winnowing issue candidates and policy alternatives in issue evolution (Carmines & Stimson, 1989; Kingdon, 1984) is not a process of natural selection but is driven by strategic actors (Gamson & Meyer, 1996; Zald, 1996). At the same time, framing analysis recognizes that social actors differ in their framing power. The question is how to conceptualize such power and its use. Here, we argue that framing potency comes from three sources: access to and control of material resources, strategic alliances, and stock of knowledge of and skills in frame sponsorship (Gamson, 1988). By combining these resources, we argue, political actors weave a "web of subsidies" to privilege the dissemination and packaging of information to their advantage.

What constitutes vital resources for different actors in a framing contest? By definition, resources here refer to the material, social structural, institutional, and cultural means that are available to an actor to promote his or her frame and to influence the language, context, and atmosphere of public deliberation concerning an issue. Put simply, resources are things that would win a political actor a spoken role in a public performance.

Different actors have different resources. For elected officials, resources include positions in the authority hierarchy, standings in opinion polls, and the ability to stage newsworthy events. For appointed officials of the executive branch, relationships with the elected official who appointed them, standings in the policymaking community, relationships with other strategic actors (including the expert or scientific community, media, and the activist community) are among the most important resources. For experts and research specialists, academic standing, relationships with key members of the other communities, and skills in interaction with the media are among the resources. For activists, their organization, standing in the network of policy making, research, and journalistic communities, and their ability to stage newsworthy events are among their resources. For the public, their claim of the legitimacy of their voices, ability to communicate concerns to policy and journalistic communities, stake in a policy issue, influence on outcome of an opinion poll and an election, and access to various communication channels in the public arena are among their resources (Cobb & Elder, 1983; Hilgartner & Bosk, 1988; Kingdon, 1984; Knoke, 1993).

Mass media are also important political actors in public deliberation (Cook, 1998), not just neutral conduits. As we pointed out in the previous section, media frame issues and public deliberation in particular ways. Although lacking the information dissemination capacity of the mainstream media, some interactive media, especially radio talk shows, can draw their resources from their ideological and financial backing, from the charisma of the hosts, and from the shows mobilization as well as organizational capacity (Jamieson et al., 1998).

Resources are not distributed equally. Actors strategically cultivate their resources and translate them into framing power, a process Gamson (1988) called "frame sponsorship." With this concept, Gamson suggested a particular dynamic interface between resources that an actor utilizes and the ideational dimension of the frame that the actor sponsors. As a conceptual tool to analyze this interface, we use the concept of the "web of subsidies," which refers to both institutionally structured and strategically cultivated networks through which resources for influence in public deliberation flow. With the concept of "subsidies," we are arguing that cost reduction is a basic mechanism for enhancing framing potency. Gaining subsidies in the form of information, potent frames and their signification devices, as well as influential carriers of these ideational elements is the way to reduce costs in political actors' framing efforts.

The concept of "web of subsidies" is rooted in the political economic analysis of information and influence flow between sources and news media (Gandy, 1982) as well as the phenomenological analysis of how journalists' news net becomes the sociological basis of journalistic epistemology and determines the facticity of the news reality (Tuchman, 1978). Focusing on the economic and information dimensions of communication, Gandy (1982) examined the relationship between sources and media organizations as an economic transaction. Sources influence media content by raising or reducing the cost of (or "subsidizing") news production, including news gathering and packaging. Through such subsidies, sources control the "access to and use of information" in news production (p. 61). Similarly, "news net" is a type of social network through which information comprising news flows.

These ideas provide more specific explication of Gamson's notion of "package sponsorship." Using our terminology, political actors "sponsor" a frame by adjusting the ratio of the value of their information to the cost for another actor to use the information. For example, staging an event that fits journalists' professional standards of news values may increase the value of an actor's information (Cobb & Elder, 1983, pp. 95–140; Hilgartner & Bosk, 1988, pp. 61–66; Price & Tewksbury, 1997). Scheduling such an event to fit media deadlines and providing copies of press kits with prepackaged images and texts would be among the techniques to reduce the cost for media organizations (Ryan, 1991).

Strategic framing involves both weaving and mobilizing such webs of subsidies. Issue entrepreneurs may subsidize public deliberation through three routes. First, they may subsidize the news media, thus influencing media discourse, by (a) lowering the cost of information gathering and (b) generating cultural resonance of their frame with the news values held by journalists. Second, they may subsidize the policymakers, thus influencing elite discourse, by (a) reducing the cost for policymakers to garner and process information and (b) reducing the (perceived) political risks for policymakers to take a public stand on an issue. Third, issue entrepreneurs may subsidize the public, thus influencing public opinion, by (a) creating ideologically toned and emotionally charged catchphrases, labels (e.g., pro-life vs. pro-choice) or exemplars and (b) linking a position to a political icon, figure, or group.

Three examples would help illustrate the presence and mobilization of the "web of subsidies." The first is Eliasoph's (1988) study of the organizational and cultural contexts of producing "oppositional news" in a radio station. She showed that the ideological positioning of the radio station and its lack of financial resources and stable and experienced "professional journalists" made its news reportage quite different from that of the "mainstream" media outlets. The station's journalists followed the mainstream definition and conventions of news, but related differently to the potential sources and audiences. The informal network of potential sources for leads and quotes and the close proximity to protesting movements, ideologically and physically, privileged "oppositional" framing of issues reported by the station.

The second example is Valocchi's (1996) study of the U.S. civil rights movement. He showed that historically, the integrationist ideology, the idea system emphasizing dismantling segregation and enforcing integration with the means of the federal government, won the contest within the movement against alternative ideologies. It did so primarily through its leading proponents' strategic skills, their access to and maintenance of financial support from White liberal funders, their institutional ties with the Roosevelt Administration, and the within-movement struggle to brand those holding alternative ideologies as "radicals." In our terminology, these factors influenced the likelihood of success of the integrationist ideology by reducing the relative cost of its adoption and promotion.

The third example is an historical study of the first White House press corps (Ponder, 1994). Of course, based on our experiences with the contemporary media world, it is not surprising that President McKinley, by allowing closer physical proximity with reporters, having regular press briefings, preparing advanced copies of his statements, and so forth, was successful in winning favorable press coverage. By making reporters' jobs easier, a form of information subsidy, the White House (or a source in general) could more easily win a framing contest (see Hertsgaard, 1988; Kurtz, 1998; Maltese, 1994). At a certain historical moment, we can see that certain "information subsidy" activities may have far-reaching institutional and structural implications.[9]

Building upon these cases, we see that framing cannot be a one-way street in which political elites manipulate the public's evaluations of political leaders or their policy preferences. Rather, framing is a multifaceted process in which influences travel in different directions. For example, Page and Tannenbaum (1996) showed that in the case of Zoe Baird's nomination, the public succeeded in framing the issue in terms of class division and respect for rule of law. Such success was possible because these frames met the standards of empirical credibility, experiential commensurability, and narrative fidelity (Snow & Benford, 1988). No less important are the social networks formed around key radio talk shows, which provide the basis for a discursive community to be formed and mobilized (Jamieson et al., 1998; Munson, 1993).

---

[9]We can list at least three significant changes triggered by McKinley's information subsidy activities. First, the journalistic "news net" was reconfigured as indicated by the creation of a regular White House beat. Second, the power relationship between the Congress and the White House was reshaped, with the White House becoming increasingly more visible in policy making. Third, the pathway of policy making was modified. With the press being so close to certain policy makers, policy making is increasingly intertwined with newsmaking (Cook, 1989). As a result, policymakers are divided into "visible" and "hidden" actors (Kingdon, 1984). Related to this role division is that political resources available to policy makers also became diversified. For example, lawmakers might play a successful "outside" game by appearing frequently on selected media. Making news becomes a governing tool (Cook, 1998).

THEORETICAL PROPOSITIONS AND ANALYTICAL APPROACH

Clearly, public deliberation over an issue involves contests among multiple narratives. Each narrative is sponsored by a group of actors, based on some overarching ideological principles and cultural resonance. Plurality of public discourse is both the defining feature and prerequisite of public deliberation. Indeed, public deliberation may sometimes be frustratingly "hyperplural," but it is nevertheless a significant part of American political life, which we celebrate as realizations of the democratic ideal (e.g., Page & Tannenbaum, 1996).

Thus, it would be inadequate to limit our inquiry on framing as media stimuli affecting audiences. Nor would it be politically realistic to consider framing exclusively as elite manipulation of public opinion. Rather, frames and their signification devices result from and are means for strategic actions of political actors in public deliberation.

We can summarize the foregoing analysis in the following propositions.

1. Framing is an integral part of public deliberation and it is a strategic action by all participants.

2. Framing initiatives may come from any participant at any stage of the process, which is essentially a contest involving different actors with competing goals, interests, or messages.

3. Participants' political goals dictate their communication objectives in public deliberation, which are essentially "getting the message across" and "winning the argument." Framing an issue is a strategic means to realize such communication objectives.

4. Participants vary in their "framing potency," which is influenced by discursive factors, including the cultural attributes of the frames that they sponsor and the symbolic devices used to signify such frames (see Cobb & Elder, 1983 and Hillgartner & Bosk, 1988 for a list of attributes).

5. The combination of a frame and its symbolic devices functions as a narrative "package" which may resonate in the mind of other actors if it meets the standards of empirical credibility, experiential commensurability, and narrative fidelity (Snow & Benford, 1988). Such resonance is the basis of frame alignment (Snow et al., 1986).

6. Framing potency is also determined by sociological factors, including the size and depth of the actor's web of subsidies and the actor's ability to cultivate and mobilize such web of subsidies with strategic targeting.

7. "Frame alignment" and the web of subsidies may reinforce each other to enhance an actor's framing potency. Framing an issue defines an actor's identity, interests, and images. It also redefines the boundaries negotiated in

forming political realignment. The need for forming such an alignment provides in turn the incentive for a strategic actor to increase frame flexibility.

8. The interaction between frame alignment and the web of subsidies binds interests into a "discursive community," making collective action possible. Such collective action in turn strengthens the discursive and sociological binding of the community.

9. Political actors may achieve "frame alignment" by linking their frames to some enduring values in the society, thus subsidizing the other actors in processing and packaging information concerning an issue.

10. Political actors may increase their framing potency by influencing the frames of news coverage. This is achieved by linking their frames to some enduring value *and* the news values in the society, thus subsidizing the media.

11. Political actors may increase their framing potency by influencing frames adopted by key members of the policymaking community. This is achieved by linking their frames to some enduring value *and* by reducing the associated political risks, thus subsidizing the policymakers in adopting the sponsored frames.

12. The broader a "discursive community" and the clearer its identity, the greater are its chances for being influential.

Empirically examining these propositions calls for some analytical strategies different from those in framing effects research and must address the dynamics of public deliberation. These propositions specify two important dynamic interfaces: between the ideational and the sociological dimensions of the framing process, and between and among various actors, as well as their narratives. To fully demonstrate these two dynamics we find the case history approach promising (e.g., Gamson & Modigliani, 1987, 1989; Gitlin, 1980; Marullo et al., 1996; Mooney & Hunt, 1996; Valocchi, 1996). One may examine either the evolution of an issue or the development of a particular social movement by analyzing the discourse of each political actor in context. This in-depth contextual and historical view cuts across different levels of analysis and is both discursive and sociological, requiring multiple methods.

HEALTH CARE REFORM: 1993–1994

As a demonstration of our approach, we analyze the 1993–1994 health care reform case, one of the most intensively debated domestic policy issues in recent history. The case has already generated numerous studies from different disciplines, which differ in their theoretical approaches. From an institutional analysis perspective, Steinmo and Watts (1995) argued that comprehensive national health insurance is doomed to fail. The checks and balances of the American system allot enormous power to intransigent interest groups, making it impossible to form a working coalition of majorities, the necessary condition for any reform measure to be adopted. Many do agree that the fragmentation of the policymaking institutions makes "outside strategies," or "government by publicity" (Cook, 1998; Kernell, 1993), a key feature of the deliberation over health care reform (e.g., West, Heith, & Goodwin, 1996). However, they argued that such institutional arrangements and modes of operation per se are not the direct causes of its failure. They cite instead the success of certain interest groups in creating the impression of public opinion shift in the mind of key policymakers and determining the terms with which health care reform debate was conducted, and the Clinton administration's failure to cultivate the right "discursive community" to act as a potent framing actor. Thus, the failure lay in discursive strategies.

This illustrates a framing process as simultaneously discursive, political, and sociological. While the public and the political elite were bound by the talk of "health care crisis," there was no politically functioning "discursive community" on *what* and *how* to carry out the reform. The public was ambivalent. The administration failed to build a political alignment for its plan, and its opponents never attempted to build their political alignment based on reform discourse (Johnson & Broder, 1996). The case, therefore, is not only about how the issue was framed but about how public deliberation disintegrated through such framing. Understanding how the framing process failed sheds light on how public deliberation may be conducted to advance a policy agenda.

The Case: Opportunities for the Clinton Administration

On September 22, 1993, President Clinton formally unveiled his 1,364-page American Health Security Act. Addressing the joint session of the Congress in prime time, Clinton framed the plan in terms of providing health coverage to everyone, while curtailing the rise of the health care cost. This definition of the terms of public deliberation contained the seeds of the demise of Clinton's plan.[10] Its master frame for the proposed reform, "health security," is signified by the historical exemplar of the social security system. Clinton attempted to crystallize it into the image of a "health security card" that he waved to the lawmakers and the prime time audience during his address.

---

[10] The initial reception of Clinton's plan was positive and even enthusiastic. For example, *The Washington Post* observed that the Clinton plan is "a liberal's passion to help the needy, a conservative's faith in free market, and a politician's focus on the middle class" (cited in Center for Public Integrity, 1995a, p. 441). We should also note here that the demise of the Clinton plan is not equal to the end of the reform. Some researchers have noted that many of the ideas appearing in Clinton's plan have started being implemented by the health insurance industry (Mintz, 1998).

Other devices include widely circulated but hardly explicated jargon, such as "universal coverage," "cost containment," "portability," and so on (Jamieson & Cappella, 1998).

Health care reform registered on top of Clinton's agenda first as a political opportunity (Center for Public Integrity, 1995a; Skocpol, 1995, 1997). Heightened by the economic recession in 1990 and 1991, polls showed that concerns over health care coverage were at an all-time high. Such concerns were further focused by the improbable triumph of Harris Wofford in the 1991 special U.S. Senatorial election in Pennsylvania. By the 1992 presidential election, all candidates were under pressure to include health care in their campaign agenda. Whereas the Democratic candidates, most notably Bill Clinton, seized the issue as a key agenda item, the Republicans, as well as opponents of government reform initiatives, acknowledged the need to reform and were ready to work *with* the new administration (see also Wilson, 1996). A window of opportunity for major policy initiatives seemed clearly present (Kingdon, 1984). Congress was greatly interested (Jones & Hall, 1995, p. 197) as were staffs of health care associations (Baumgartner & Talbert, 1995, p. 106).

The escalating cost of health care in the nation and the lack of security and universal coverage were haunting the recession-weary public, thus uniting political players of different ideological stands and interests into a "discursive community" to acknowledge a "health care crisis." Political actors actively cultivated such discursive binding, and the election campaign was an ideal venue to push the issue to the top of the agenda (see Dearing & Rogers, 1996), leading to real political consequences. The candidate who pledged to keep health care reform on the top of his domestic agenda was swept into the White House and the Democratic Party maintained a sufficient working majority in both House and Senate. Hidden behind this seeming unity of public concern, however, were the real ideological divisions and clashes of interests. Although there was a shared frame of the problem, there was no shared frame for how to address it. Although candidate Clinton powerfully articulated the public's concerns over this issue, he offered no central frame for his policy measures (Johnson & Broder, 1996). As one scholar pointed out, "neither the magnitude of the issue nor the public scrutiny of a weakened system was sufficient to carry the reform effort" (Mintz, 1998, p. 210).

The Problem: Framing "Out" Important Actors

Candidate Clinton actively cultivated and broadened the opportunity to enact a major health care reform by finding experts with a broad range of interests and policy proposals (Center for Public Integrity, 1995a; Wilson, 1996). However, right from the beginning, he framed out some legitimate policy ideas, along with some important actors who were carriers of these ideas.

Determined to take a "New Democrat's" position, Clinton took his initial position near the center and rejected the Canadian-style, single-payer system and possible payroll tax for health care. In doing so, he unwittingly made certain that his proposed plan would be on the left of the ideological spectrum (Mintz, 1998). His goal—as one of his campaign documents called it, "National Health Care Insurance Reform to Cut Costs and Cover Everybody" (Center for Public Integrity, 1995a, p. 431)—had a broad appeal, but was not easily translated into a call for action (Heclo, 1995). When the administration adopted specific measures to achieve these goals, their premises, rationale, and real-world implications, both financial and political, had not been well deliberated, not to mention accepted among the elites or general public. In other words, there was no ready political alignment of actors bound by the same discourse of solutions for the widely acknowledged problems.

Clinton's strategy in devising his own plan also made it impossible to develop such an action-generating discursive community, despite the administration's intention of doing just that (Johnson & Broder, 1996). From the published studies, we can see at least four elements of the Clinton strategy relevant to our discussion here.

First, by naming his wife and a personal friend to head the high-profile health care task force, Clinton framed health care reform to be an issue *owned* by the New Democrats as well as a political device for rebuilding the Democratic majority (see Heclo, 1995; Weir, 1995). This institutional arrangement represented a significant inhibition to those who had been interested in working with the new administration on health care reform. While these tactics succeeded in framing the administration's commitment to addressing the issue, it also succeeded in framing the issue as a highly partisan one, creating an opportunity for the subsequent bitter partisan battle (Skocpol, 1995, 1997).[11]

Second, although the task force began its work by consulting a wide spectrum of opinions and expertise, the secrecy of its operation actually framed the "ins" and "outs" of the deliberation process. By setting up such a task force to develop a bill that was later to be negotiated and passed in Congress, the Clintons created a politically as well as discursively exclusive venue for policy innovation. Those who were not in the Clinton's inner circle became mere "consultants," not stakeholders in political bargaining

---

[11]Johnson and Broder (1996) reported that while the Task Force was formed with the explicit intention to be "inclusive," Clinton made it clear that the congressional aids to Republican members of Congress were not allowed to participate, aggravating the feeling among Republican lawmakers of being excluded.

(Skocpol, 1995, 1997). Consequently, the groups who had not been "consulted" felt left out. However, even those who had been consulted at the task force hearings or who had met with top task force people still felt that they were not given an adequate chance to influence the policy outcome (Wilson, 1996).

Third, while intentionally incorporating the representatives of big businesses and their ideas (Center for Public Integrity, 1995a; Mintz, 1998) and anticipating some of the existing political obstacles, the administration created a situation where opportunities to participate in policy formation were not evenly distributed (Wilson, 1996). This situation was aggravated by the administration's political rhetoric against some villains (Center for Public Integrity, 1995a, 1996; Wilson, 1996) rather than to articulate the specific measures in terms of broadly shared principles. The political strategy of building a broad political coalition led to the exact opposite, alienation and exclusion.

Fourth, and finally, the Clinton health care team did not devise a coherent strategy to package its plan in discursively resonant terms. The Clinton campaign did recognize the need for a "simple, core idea" as a device to capture the whole reform plan (Johnson & Broder, 1996, p. 17), but its master frame could not coherently dissolve the attacking frames such as "big government." Mindful of the public's distaste for big government, the administration equivocated on the exact nature of the proposed "health care alliance," the key mechanism to curtail the rise of premiums (Skocpol, 1995, p. 74), thus losing the credibility to claim that the Clinton plan would not involve major government interventions. Given such equivocation, there was no discursive basis for Clinton supporters to mount a coherent, sharply focused, and energized campaign. As a result, they lost frame potency when confronted with major opposition.

In summary, Clinton's political strategies had the discursive function of hardening the boundaries between "us" and "them," thus preventing a discursive community from materializing in support of Clinton's plan, a vital step for any health care reform. As a "consolidating" reform (Heclo, 1995),[12] formulating the content of the health care reform policy is a *political* rather than a technical struggle. This suggests that it is vital for the administration to build a discursive community that shares the same scheme for weighing

---

[12] The Center for Public Integrity (1995b) notes that health care is an industry generating $800 billion a year in business. In this industry, "the positions of the various special interests regarding the government's proper role in health care were staked out years ago" (p. 593). However, this is not inconsistent with the observation that interest groups do not have fixed or established positions on all policy matters. Very often, their positions are formed during the process of policy deliberation and in this process, a group's ideology is only one, albeit an important one, of the factors (Wilson, 1996). The gradual hardening of interest groups' positions on Clinton's health care plan was a case in point (see also Mintz, 1998).

the pros and cons of specific policy components. Such a scheme needs to be articulated through a fair participation of all parties and reframing the relationships between losses and gains. In light of this logic, the administration's strategy clearly involved "owning" the reform and thus "framing out" important players. Many examples can be cited for this exclusive framing. The Republican representative at that time, Julie Kosterlitz (1996) complained that although she was among those moderate Republicans ready to work with the administration, she found that they were "prematurely excluded from the early planning stages." She attributed the Republicans' decision to launch an all-out campaign to destroy Clinton's plan to the "resentment at being shut out of the process" (p. 136). Thus, when one of Clinton's fellow Democrats, Jim Cooper packaged his own plan as the only bill with "significant bipartisan support," his claim received immediate media acceptance despite the contrary evidence (Jamieson & Cappella, 1998; Lieberman, 1994).

Heclo (1995) pointed out another institutional process required for a major reform of this type to succeed, a process that he calls "gestation." Basically, this is a process of careful deliberation, clarifying the lines of dissent, testing factual claims and alternative policy options. He argued that "the Clinton project falls into the unfortunate category of poorly gestated initiatives envisioned by the textbook presidency" (p. 95). Without the thorough "gestation" of various policy proposals, candidate Clinton went through several permutations in a health care reform that he could support (see also Center for Public Integrity, 1995a; Skocpol, 1995, 1997). As a result, some of the key elements of the Clinton plan, such as "employer mandate," "health care alliance," "premium cap," and so on, were not fully tested and deliberated. Framing out other actors only short-circuited the necessary public deliberation about these measures.

To some extent, this heavy-handed, campaign mode of operation also allowed the quality of public deliberation to deteriorate from the fall of 1993 to the summer of 1994 (Jamieson & Cappella, 1998; Patterson, 1993). The jargon-filled media coverage of the debate was filled with leaks from the task force, which were often blown out of proportion or mis-characterized (Johnson & Broder, 1996). Distortions, misstatements, and factual errors characterized the interest-group sponsored ads and talk radio. Members of the public were confused, irritated, and frustrated (see Jamieson & Cappella, 1998).

The Tide Turns: The Development
of an Oppositional Discursive Community

Although the administration lost its framing initiatives soon after Clinton's televised address, the opposition started to pick up momentum, even before the plan was formally introduced to Congress (Center for Public Integrity, 1995a, 1995b). Leaks from the secretive task force were keeping many interest groups on edge and increasingly pushing them into an antagonistic position (Johnson & Broder, 1996; Wilson, 1996). In the last 3 months of 1993, a concerted oppositional campaign was locked into place. By the spring of 1994, the White House was further distracted from its attempt to sell its plan by journalists' increasing interest in the Whitewater investigation (Jamieson & Cappella, 1998).

To say that the oppositional campaign was concerted is to say that some major interest groups, conservatives in Congress, and the energized and mobilized conservative members of the public were "locked into" a coherent oppositional discourse. The basic terms that functioned as frames to "bind" them into a unified actor were clearly articulated by the leading voices of the conservative camp. Public support for the Clinton plan had begun to erode since September, William Kristol pointed out, and "an aggressive and uncompromising counterstrategy" by the Republicans could ultimately kill the plan, if it could convince middle-class Americans that *there really was no national health care crisis* after all (quoted in Skocpol, 1995, pp. 75–76). A letter from Rep. Richard K. Armey in *The Wall Street Journal* on October 13, 1993, claimed that "the Clinton health plan could create 59 new federal programs or bureaucracies, expand 20 others, impose 79 new federal mandates and make major changes in the tax code." He illustrated his points with a "flow chart" and "Clinton plan glossary" allegedly showing the administrative excesses that would tower over hapless "patients" should the Clinton plan be enacted (quoted in Skocpol, 1995, p. 75). Thus, the frames of "no health care crisis" and "big government bureaucratic monster" became the cornerstones for the oppositional discourse. Many middle-class citizens—Independent, moderate Democrats and Republicans, and former Perot supporters—had come to perceive the Clinton plan as a misconceived "big-government" effort that might threaten the quality of their health care (Skocpol, 1995, p. 76). Then, not only the Senate Republican Minority Leader, Bob Dole, but also the Democratic Chairman of the Senate Finance Committee, Daniel Patrick Moynihan, declared publicly that there was no health care crisis, taking away the basic tenet of Clinton's domestic agenda.

With a unified message, the conservatives brought to bear enormous resources, "subsidizing" the debate toward the direction of rejecting the Clinton plan. Many published studies detail the patterns of such resource allocation and the processes of the mobilization of what we call "the web of subsidies" (see Center for Public Integrity, 1995a, 1995b, 1996; Mintz, 1998; Wilson, 1996). We can differentiate three categories of the resource mobilization efforts: weaving and mobilizing the web of subsidies, creating a unified "oppositional discourse," and combining the insider and outsider strategies.

The reform opposition devoted major efforts to weave and mobilize the web of subsidies, known in the literature as "web of interests" (Center for Public Integrity, 1995b, p. 596). A major component of weaving this web is to hire lobbyists with either work experience and thus connections in Congress; specialties in media and grass-roots campaign operations; or who are authorities in the health care area. A number of large insurance companies formed the Alliance for Managed Competition, a "loose association" whose "only purpose is to work on health care reform" (Center for Public Integrity, 1995b, p. 602). In 1993 the Health Care Leadership Council, made up of the CEOs of 55 insurance, hospital, pharmaceutical and other companies, hired former Democratic presidential candidate Paul Tsongas to campaign for a less restricted form of managed competition. In January 1993, the Health Insurance Association of America (HIAA) lured Bill Gradison, the ranking Republican member of the House Ways and Means Health Subcommittee, to be its head. He brought not only stature to the organization but the intimate knowledge of Congress as well as crucial congressional connections.

The various opponents of Clinton's plan opposed different provisions in the overall bill. For example, the largest insurance companies opposed the premium caps while the medium and small insurance companies represented by HIAA opposed "employer mandates." With the Clinton plan as the target, however, the attacks on different components of the plan were "united" discursively in opposition, without the need to offer any constructive alternative. At least that was the case in the attack ads, which increasingly came to constitute a key element of the discourse (Jamieson & Cappella, 1998). In addition, the opponents of Clinton's plan created and spread a variety of ideologically intoned labels that would color and even distort the measures in Clinton's plan, thus generating fear and misunderstanding (Jamieson & Cappella, 1998). Similarly, the Clinton camp tried to use less threatening and possibly less accurate labels to further equivocate its messages. For example, while the opponents characterized "premium cap" as "price control," supporters of the Clinton plan objected and called it "budget constraint" (Center for Public Integrity, 1995b, pp. 600–601). While Clinton likened his plan to Social Security by labeling it the Health Security Act and displaying a "health security card," this analogy only invoked the images of "entitlement" and "big government" that were exploited effectively in the oppositional discourse (Jamieson & Cappella, 1998; Skocpol, 1995, 1997).

A clear example of strategically combining the insider and outsider strategies is the now famous "Harry and Louise" television commercial series sponsored by HIAA. Although many credited the commercials with being a major force to shift public opinion on Clinton's health care plan, Cappella and Jamieson (1997) showed that viewers who had watched the commercials learned little about the health care issue and experienced little attitude change as a result of viewing. Rather, researchers pointed out that the airing of the commercials was combined with the inside game of (a) directly influencing key lawmakers (Jamieson & Cappella, 1998; Wilson, 1996) and (b) using the commercials as political leverage to negotiate with the White House and its supporters in Congress (Center for Public Integrity, 1995b). While the White House "framed out" potentially collaborating actors such as HIAA, conservative lawmakers were collaborating with those interest groups that opposed certain provisions in Clinton's plan. In addition to the usual practice of interest groups gaining access by contributing to the lawmakers' campaigns or PACs, the union between interest groups and lawmakers was also held together by some interest groups taking cues from the opponents of Clinton's plan in Congress, an example of the so-called "backward lobbying" (Skocpol, 1995).

Throughout the debate, media played more than the role of a neutral observer and chronicler. Media covering the health care debate also contributed their own frames to the public discourse on health care reform. Rooted in the ideology of news values (Price & Tewksbury, 1997), the most significant media frames are those of conflict between supporters and opponents of the Clinton plan and the strategies of each side (Jamieson & Cappella, 1998). Media coverage depicted critics of the Clinton plan as the President's "enemies," dramatizing their divisions and reducing the differences concerning the complex issue into two sides. This made it discursively as well as politically more difficult for the administration to negotiate and bargain with various groups. Playing into the media logic, the Clinton administration targeted the insurance industry and pharmaceutical companies as villains, lending credibility to the "conflict" frame. By focusing on strategies of each side, the media also depicted the health care debate as a sport, with Clinton's attempts to stay "on message" by packaging and selling his health reform plan, while journalists were more interested in the Whitewater investigation. Media coverage depicted Clinton as a cynical manipulator who was using the health care debate to divert public attention from the scandal, further eroding the public's trust in the Clinton administration and depriving the public opportunities to learn the substance of the policy debate (Jamieson & Cappella, 1998).

In frequently reporting opinion poll results, media not only dramatized the political conflict in the health care debate, but also personalized the debate as a matter of Clinton struggling to maintain his popularity. This Clinton popularity frame played a significant role in influencing the debate discourse. First, this frame continuously reinforces the conventional wisdom that the president's power resides in his approval ratings: Clinton's sliding popularity was a cue for his opponents to attack rather than to cooperate. Second, this frame gives "empirical credibility" and "narrative fidelity" to the idea that Clinton was manipulating the health care debate for his own political gain.

Media also incorporated the frames of various political opponents. Right after Clinton's health care address to Congress, media mostly had adopted his frame of universal coverage with contained cost. Very soon, however, the conflict frame and strategy frame made media vulnerable to oppositional efforts. For example, reporters bought into Rep. Cooper's claim that his plan was the only one with bipartisan support (Jamieson & Cappella, 1998, pp. 114–115; Lieberman, 1994). When the HIAA started airing its "Harry and Louise" commercials, media saw them as indicating an escalation of the political conflict and rushed to report them, not only on their themes but also on their presumed impact on public opinion. The media obsession with these ads not only further exacerbated the elite's perception that public opinion was shifting against Clinton's plan but more importantly, legitimized HIAA as a key player in the health care debate. This helped shift the debate from providing coverage to everyone to maintaining the quality of the existing system that the middle class were enjoying (Lo, 1998).

Summary

We offer a discursive explanation of health care reform failure by focusing on how Clinton and his opponents framed the debate: including the issue, the arguments, and the actors who carried the arguments. We must recognize that the Health Security Act 1993 was one of the most comprehensive domestic policy proposals made by an American president in this century. Due to its scope, and the suspense and drama that incubated Clinton's bill, the reform issue unleashed unprecedented coverage of a policy issue by the media and political mobilization at all levels (West et al., 1996). In addition, the President positioned himself as a Washington outsider, contributing to the unprecedented adoption of "outsider strategies" by various players. Despite the Administration's decisive failure to achieve its reform goal, health care became nevertheless an unprecedented case of broad participation. But the quality of the public deliberation was much less than to be desired.

Our explanation for such poor quality lies in the actors' framing strategies. Whether or not media are a suitable stage for policy deliberation, they did perform such a role in the health care debate. One may criticize the media for the quality of public deliberation, but to blame open and free public deliberation—a large part of which must and does take place through media—would be misguided. The real threat to public deliberation lies in the mutual suspicion of each actor's intention and ever-escalating effort based on such suspicion to "spin" an occurrence, an actor's statement, or a particular headline (Kurtz, 1998). This prevents different actors in the public debate from operating in the same "discursive community" with the shared ground rules (conventions) and expectations.

CONCLUSION AND DISCUSSION

This chapter began with the basic premise that public deliberation is a democratic ideal for which the proliferating talks involving policymakers, political activists, talk show hosts, and members of the general public have created a new landscape. Here, the mode of policy deliberation and the constitution of public discourse are increasingly democratized, allowing a proliferation of frames and framing actors, and thus creating an ideal site for framing analysis.

Thus, we argue that framing is a strategic action in a discursive form. It involves political actors making sense of an issue and participating in public deliberation. In this process, political actors frame themselves, their relationships with other actors, and the meaning of their actions. Framing in a real political process is never limited to influencing news coverage or diffusely defined "public opinion," as many studies seem to imply, with their exclusive focus on either news text or on framing effects. Rather, framing is a discursive means to achieve political potency in influencing public deliberation. It is an integral part of the process of building political alignments. Achieving such political goals through framing involves weaving a web of subsidies and building a "discursive community." Framing thus integrates the discursive, political, and sociological subprocesses in public deliberation.

In our illustrative case analysis of health care reform, we attribute the demise of Clinton's health care reform plan to the actions and strategies of political actors framing the debate at the discursive level. This failure of the activist and reform-minded Clinton presidency to frame the proper role of the federal government in American society, more importantly, is a failure of public deliberation in America. Although the administration failed to build the necessary discursive community to support and enact the proposed reform, the antireform campaign succeeded in derailing not only Clinton's proposal but also reform itself (Johnson & Broder, 1996).

In today's age of talk, framing a policy debate and thus the public discourse, requires great political skills. While playing the "outside game" sometimes might give the President certain leverage, it also carries great risks and uncertainties (Kernell, 1993). Many political decisions become publicly expressive and thus have framing consequences. Thus, they should be approached in such light. Political skills in cultivating a discursive community are thus necessary for any real public policy measure to be adopted and implemented. Building such discursive community requires searching for and creating a frame that binds diverse interests and actors together. As part of the political strategies of today's leaders, framing ought to be examined as part of the public deliberation process.

While the proliferation of talk provides more opportunities for elite manipulation of public opinion, it also constrains elites by subjecting them to the frustrating process of public deliberation. As the health care reform case shows, participation in public deliberation came not only in the form of opinion poll data, but also in talk on radio, faxes, letters, and email messages to lawmakers. Although the failure of the reform is frustrating, the debate heightened public's concern over the issue, brought to the public arena many difficulties in reforming the system, and caused the American public to examine once again the role of the government in American society. It changed the political landscape in the immediate aftermath of the debacle, casting a long shadow in American political life.

The case thus illustrates some of the general theoretical propositions on framing in public deliberation, which brings together institutional, sociocultural, and discourse analyses. We want to broaden framing analysis with this theoretical integration and to bring it to the real political process. This addresses a system-level question confronting scholars, political commentators, and the general public: What is wrong in public deliberation in today's America? We would argue that framing an issue should not be dismissed as cynical political spin. Such a view of framing in the political process grows in part from and further exacerbates the present cynical political climate (Cappella & Jamieson, 1997). If participants hold such a cynical view of one another, it will make it exceedingly difficult to build a unified discursive community for a major constructive political action. This "spiral of cynicism" is largely responsible for the deteriorating quality of public deliberation. Rather, we would argue for returning to Goffman (1974) and Berger and Luckmann (1967) to view framing as an inevitable way for human actors to make sense of our experiences and engage in social interactions. Framing is a way to discursively organize public deliberation, allowing political actors to present their arguments and for others to understand and evaluate these arguments. That is the essence of public deliberation.

We recognize that framing potency in public deliberation is not evenly distributed in a system that privileges those with more economic, political, and media resources. We also recognize that framing an issue is *not* always based on noble motives and in a deliberative spirit. More often, self-interests and prejudice or passion become most potent causes of framing choices. This reality renders greater significance to openness of and patience with public deliberation, with which not only the merit of ideas may be evaluated but also the web of subsidies that may emerge for the ideas that resonate in society.

This argument calls for a broader and longer view of framing than it is generally the case in the present literature. Strategic framing is not just for gaining immediate political advantage or for building temporary political alignments, but also for building a discursive community, which constitutes the fabric of deliberative democracy. To operate well, public deliberation needs the participants to share not only the values for policy judgments and evaluations but also the principles, conventions, and norms for articulating these values. With that, political contentions become occasions for acting out genuine differences in perceptions and opinions as well as such shared culture, thus reproducing the community binding. Such normative ideas must be the guide for participants in public deliberation to devise their framing strategies and for scholars of public deliberation to analyze and critique political actors' framing actions. Framing analysis must allow for such linkages between the domains of research and the practical, the normative and the empirical.

REFERENCES

Baumgartner, F. R., & Jones, B. D. (1993). *Agendas and instability in American politics.* Illinois: University of Chicago Press.

Baumgartner, F. R, & Talbert, J. C. (1995). Interest groups and political change. In B. D. Jones (Ed.), *The new American politics: Reflections on political change in the Clinton administration* (pp. 93–108). Boulder, CO: Westview.

Benford, R. D., & Hunt, S. A. (1992). Dramaturgy and social movements: The social construction and communication of power. *Sociological Inquiry, 62,* 36–55.

Bennett, W. L. (1990). Toward a theory of press-state relations in the United States. *Journal of Communication, 40,* 103–125.

Bennett, W. L., & Paletz, D. L. (Eds.). (1994). *Taken by storm: The media, public opinion, and U.S. foreign policy in the Gulf War.* Illinois: University of Chicago Press.

Berger, P. L., & Luckmann, T. (1967). *The social construction of reality.* New York: Anchor Books.

Best, J. (1995). *Images of issues: Typifying social problems* (2nd ed.). Hawthorne, NY: Aldine de Gruyter.

Blumler, J. G., & Gurevitch, M. (1980). Politicians and the press: An essay on role relationships. In D. D. Nimmo & K. R. Sanders (Eds.), *Handbook of political communication* (pp. 467–493). Beverly Hills, CA: Sage.

Bohman, J. (1996). *Public deliberation.* Cambridge, MA: MIT Press.

Bohman, J., & Rehg, W. (Eds.). (1997). *Deliberative democracy: Essays on reason and politics.* Cambridge, MA: MIT Press.

Boorstin, D. (1971/1992). *The image.* New York: Vintage.

Calhoun, C. (Ed.). (1992). *Habermas and the public sphere.* Cambridge, MA: MIT Press.

Cappella, J. N., & Jamieson, K. H. (1997). *Spiral of cynicism: The press and the public good.* Oxford, England: Oxford University Press.

Carmines, E. G., & Stimson, J. A. (1989). *Issue evolution.* Princeton, NJ: Princeton University Press.

Center for Public Integrity (1995a). Well-healed: Inside lobbying for health care reform, Part I. *International Journal of Health Services, 25,* 411–453.

Center for Public Integrity (1995b). Well-healed: Inside lobbying for health care reform, Part II. *International Journal of Health Services, 25,* 593–632.

Center for Public Integrity (1996). Well-healed: Inside lobbying for health care reform, Part III. *International Journal of Health Services, 26,* 19–46.

Cobb, R. W., & Elder, C. D. (1983). *Participation in American politics: The dynamics of agenda-building*. Baltimore, MD: Johns Hopkins University Press.

Cobb, R. W., & Ross, M. H. (1997). *Cultural strategies of agenda denial: Avoidance, attack and redefinition*. Lawrence: University of Kansas Press.

Cook, T. E. (1989). *Making laws and making news*. Washington, DC: Brookings Institute.

Cook, T. E. (1998). *Governing with the news: The news media as a political institution*. Illinois: The University of Chicago Press.

Crigler, A. N. (1996). Introduction: Making sense of politics; constructing political messages and meanings. In A. N. Crigler (Ed.), *The psychology of political communication* (pp. 1–10). Ann Arbor: The University of Michigan Press.

Dahlgren, P. (1991). Introduction. In P. Dahlgren and C. Sparks (Eds.), *Communication and citizenship: Journalism and the public sphere* (pp. 1–24). London: Routledge.

Dearing, J. W., & Rogers, E. M. (1996). *Communication concepts 6: Agenda-setting*. Thousand Oaks, CA: Sage.

Edelman, M. (1988). *Constructing the political spectacle*. Illinois: The University of Chicago Press.

Eliasoph, N. (1988). Routines and the making of oppositional news. *Critical Studies in Mass Communication, 5*, 313–334.

Elster, J. (Ed.). (1998). *Deliberative democracy*. Cambridge, England: Cambridge University Press.

Entman, R. M. (1993). Framing: Toward clarification of a fractured paradigm. *Journal of Communication, 43*, 51–68.

Ericson, R. V., Baranek, P., & Chan, J. B. L. (1989). *Negotiating control: A study of news sources*. Toronto: University of Toronto Press.

Esherick, J. W., & Wasserstrom, J. N. (1990). Acting out democracy: Political theater in modern China. *Journal of Asian Studies, 49*, 835–865.

Fish, S. E. (1980). *Is there a text in this class? The authority of interpretive communities*. Cambridge, MA: Harvard University Press.

Fishman, M. (1980). *Manufacturing the news*. Austin: University of Texas Press.

Frantzich, S., & Sullivan, J. (1996). *The C-span revolution*. Norman: University of Oklahoma Press.

Gamson, W. A. (1981). The political culture of Arab-Israeli conflict. *Conflict and Management Science, 5*, 79–93.

Gamson, W. A. (1988). A constructionist approach to mass media and public opinion. *Symbolic Interaction, 11*, 161–174.

Gamson, W. A. (1992). *Talking politics*. Cambridge, England: Cambridge University Press.

Gamson, W. A. (1996). Media discourse as a framing resource. In A. N. Crigler (Ed.), *The psychology of political communication* (pp. 111–132). Ann Arbor: The University of Michigan Press.

Gamson, W. A., & Meyer, D. S. (1996). Framing political opportunity. In D. McAdam, J. D. McCarthy, & M. N. Zald (Eds.), *Comparative perspectives on social movements* (pp. 275–290). New York: Cambridge University Press.

Gamson, W. A., & Modigliani, A. (1987). The changing culture of affirmative action. In R. G. Braungart & M. M. Braungart (Eds.), *Research in political sociology* (Vol. 3, pp. 137–177). Greenwich, CT: JAI Press.

Gamson, W. A., & Modigliani, A. (1989). Media discourse and public opinion on nuclear power: A constructionist approach. *American Journal of Sociology, 95*, 1–37.

Gandy, O. H. Jr. (1982). *Beyond agenda setting: Information subsidies and public policy*. Norwood, NJ: Ablex.

Gans, H. J. (1980). *Deciding what's news: A study of CBS Evening News, NBC Nightly News, Newsweek and Time*. New York: Vintage.

Ghanem, S. (1997). Filling in the tapestry: The second level of agenda setting. In M. McCombs, D. L. Shaw, & D. Weaver (Eds.), *Communication and democracy* (pp. 3–15). Mahwah, NJ: Lawrence Erlbaum Associates.

Gitlin, T. (1980). *The whole world is watching*. Berkeley: University of California Press.

Goffman, E. (1974). *Frame analysis*. New York: Harper & Row.

Graber, D. A. (1988). *Processing the news: How people tame the information tide* (2nd ed.). New York: Longman.

Habermas, J. (1989). *The structural transformation of the public sphere.* Cambridge, MA: The MIT Press.

Hartley, J. (1982). *Understanding news.* London: Routledge.

Heclo, H. (1995). The Clinton health plan: Historical perspective. *Health Affairs, 14,* 86–98.

Hertsgaard, M. (1988). *On bended knee: The press and the Reagan presidency.* New York: Farrar, Straus, Giroux.

Higgins, E. T. (1996). Knowledge activation: Accessibility, applicability, and salience. In E. T. Higgins & A. W. Kruglanski (Eds.), *Social psychology: Handbook of basic principles* (pp. 133–168). New York: Guilford.

Hilgartner, S., & Bosk, C. L. (1988). The rise and fall of social problems: A public arenas model. *American Journal of Sociology, 94,* 53–78.

Iorio, S. H., & Huxman, S. S. (1996). Media coverage of political issues and the framing of personal concerns. *Journal of Communication, 46,* 97–115.

Iyengar, S. (1991). *Is anyone responsible? How television frames political issues.* Illinois: University of Chicago Press.

Jamieson, K. H., & Cappella, J. N. (1998). The role of the press in the health care reform debate of 1993-1994. In D. Graber, D. McQuail, & P. Norris (Eds.), *The politics of news, the news of politics* (pp. 110–131). Washington, DC: CQ Press.

Jamieson, K. H., Cappella, J. N., & Turow, J. (1998). Limbaugh: The fusion of party leader and partisan mass medium. *Political Communication:* Special Electronic Issue.

Johnson, H., & Broder, D. S. (1996). *The system: The American way of politics at the breaking point.* Boston, MA: Little, Brown.

Jones, B. D., & Hall, B. (1995). Issue expansion in the early Clinton administration. In B. D. Jones (Ed.), *The new American politics: Reflections on political change in the Clinton administration* (pp. 191–211). Boulder, CO: Westview.

Kahneman, D., & Tverski, A. (1984). Choices, values, and frames. *American Psychologist, 39,* 341–350.

Katz, E. (1959). Mass communication research and the study of culture. *Studies in Public Communication, 2,* 1–16.

Katz, E. (1995). Introduction: The state of the art. In T. L. Glasser & C. T. Salmon (Eds.), *Public opinion and the communication of consent* (pp. xxi–xxxiv). New York: Guilford.

Kellner, D. (1992). *The Persian Gulf TV war.* Boulder, CO: Westview Press.

Kernell, S. (1993). *Going public: New strategies of presidential leadership* (2nd ed.). Washington, DC: CQ Press.

Kim, J., Wyatt, R. O., & Katz, E. (1999). News, talk, opinion, participation: The part played by conversation in deliberative democracy. *Political Communication, 16,* 361–386.

Kinder, D. R., & Herzog, D. (1993). Democratic discussion. In G. E. Marcus & R. L. Hanson (Eds.), *Reconsidering the democratic public* (pp. 347–377). University Park: Pennsylvania State University Press.

Kinder, D. R., & Sanders, L. M. (1990). Mimicking political debate with survey questions: The case of White opinion on affirmative action for Blacks. *Social Cognition, 8,* 73–103.

Kingdon, J. W. (1984). *Agendas, alternatives, and public policies.* New York: HarperCollins.

Kintsch, W. (1988). The role of knowledge in discourse comprehension: A construction-integration model. *Psychological Review, 95,* 163–182.

Knoke, D. (1993). Networks as political glues: Explaining public policy-making. In W. J. Wilson (Ed.), *Sociology and the public agenda* (pp. 165–184). Newbury Park, CA: Sage.

Kosterlitz, J. (1996). Comments. In H. Aaron (Ed.), *Problem that won't go away: Reforming US health care financing* (pp. 130–135). Washington, DC: Brookings Institute.

Kurtz, H. (1998). *Spin cycle: How the White House and the media manipulate the news.* New York: Simon & Schuster.

Lieberman, T. (1994). The selling of "Clinton Lite." *Columbia Journalism Review* (March/April), 20–22.

Lincoln, B. (1989). *Discourse and the social construction of reality.* New York: Oxford University Press.

Livingstone, S. M., & Lunt, P. (1994). *Talk on television: Audience participation and public debate.* London: Routledge.

Lo, C. Y. H. (1998). The malignant masses on CNN: Media use of public opinion polls to fabricate the "conservative majority" against health-care reform. In C. Y. H. Lo & M. Schwartz (Eds.), *Social policy and the conservative agenda* (pp. 227–244). Malden, MA: Blackwell.

Maltese, J. A. (1994). *Spin control: The White House Office of Communication and the management of presidential news* (2nd ed.). Chapel Hill: University of North Carolina Press.

Marullo, S., Pagnucco, R., & Smith, J. (1996). Frame changes and social movement contraction: U.S. peace movement framing after the Cold War. *Sociological Inquiry, 66*, 1–28.

McCombs, M. E., & Shaw, D. L. (1993). The evolution of agenda-setting research: Twenty-five years in the marketplace of ideas. *Journal of Communication, 43*, 58–67.

Meyer, D. S. (1995). Framing national security: Elite public discourse on nuclear weapons during the Cold War. *Political Communication, 12*, 173–192.

Minsky, M. (1975). A framework for representing knowledge. In P. H. Winston (Ed.), *The psychology of computer vision* (pp. 211–277). New York: McGraw-Hill.

Mintz, B. (1998). The failure of health-care reform: The role of big business in policy formation. In C. Y. H. Lo & M. Schwartz (Eds.), *Social policy and the conservative agenda* (pp. 210–224). Malden, MA: Blackwell.

Moony, P. H., & Hunt, S. A. (1996). A repertoire of interpretations: Master frames and ideological continuity in U.S. agrarian mobilization. *The Sociological Quarterly, 37*, 177–197.

Moore, M. (1993). What sort of ideas become public ideas? In R. B. Reich (Ed.), *The power of public ideas* (pp. 55–84). Cambridge, MA: Harvard University Press.

Munson, W. (1993). *All talk: The talk show in media culture.* Philadelphia: University of Pennsylvania Press.

Neuman, W. R., Just, M. R., & Crigler, A. N. (1992). *Common knowledge.* Illinois: University of Chicago Press.

Owen, D. (1995). Who talking? Who listening? The new politics of radio and television talk shows. In S. C. Craig (Ed.), *Broken contract: Changing relationships between citizens and their government in the United States.* Boulder, CO: Westview.

Page, B. (1996). *Who deliberates? Mass media in modern democracy.* Illinois: University of Chicago Press.

Page, B., & Shapiro, R. (1992). *The rational public.* Illinois: The University of Chicago Press.

Page, B. I. & Tannenbaum, J. (1996). Populistic deliberation and talk radio. *Journal of Communication, 46*, 33–54.

Pan, Z., & Kosicki, G. M. (1993). Framing analysis: An approach to news discourse. *Political Communication, 10*(1), 55–75.

Pan, Z., & Kosicki, G. M. (1997, July 29). *Framing public discourse: Another take on a theoretical perspective.* Paper presented at the 80th annual conference of the Association for Education in Journalism and Mass Communication, Chicago, IL.

Patterson, T. (1993). *Out of order.* New York: Alfred Knopf.

Pertschuk, M., & Schaetzel, W. (1989). *The people rising.* New York: Thunder's Mouth Press.

Ponder, S. (1994). The President makes news: William McKinley and the first presidential press corps, 1897-1901. *Presidential Studies Quarterly, 24*, 823–836.

Price, V., & Tewksbury, D. (1997). News values and public opinion: A theoretical account of media priming and framing. In G. A. Barnett & F. J. Boster (Eds.), *Progress in communication sciences* (Vol. 13, pp. 173–212). Greenwich, CT: Ablex.

Radway, J. (1984). *Reading the romance.* Chapel Hill: University of North Carolina Press.

Rhee, J. W. (1997). Strategy and issue frames in election campaign coverage: A social cognitive account of framing effects. *Journal of Communication, 47*, 26–48.

Ryan, C. (1991). *Prime time activism: Media strategies for grassroots organizing.* Boston, MA: South End Press.

Scheufele, D. A. (1999). Framing as a theory of media effects. *Journal of Communication, 49*, 103–122.

Schroder, K. C. (1994). Audience semiotics, interpretive communities, and the "ethnographic turn" in media research. *Media, Culture and Society, 16*, 337–347.

Schudson, M. (1992). Was there a public sphere? If so, when? In C. Calhoun (Ed.), *Habermas and the public sphere* (pp. 143–163). Cambridge, MA: MIT Press.

Schudson, M. (1997). Why conversation is not the soul of democracy. *Critical Studies in Mass Communication, 14*, 297–309.

Skocpol, T. (1995). The rise and resounding demise of the Clinton Plan. *Health Affairs, 14*, 66–85.

Skocpol, T. (1997). *Boomerang: Health care reform and the turn against government.* New York: Norton.

Snow, D. A., & Benford, R. D. (1988). Ideology, frame resonance, and participant mobilization. In B. Klandermans, H. Kriesi, & S. Tarrow (Eds.), *From structure to action: Comparing social movement research across countries* (pp. 197–217). Greenwich, CT: JAI Press.

Snow, D. A., & Benford, R. D. (1992). Master frames and cycles of protest. In A. D. Morris & C. M. Mueller (Eds.), *Frontiers in social movement theory* (pp. 133–155). New Haven, CT: Yale University Press.

Snow, D. A., Rochford, E. B., Worden, S. K., & Benford, R. D. (1986). Frame alignment processes: Micromobilization and movement participation. *American Sociological Review, 51*, 464–481.

Steinmo, S., & Watts, J. (1995). It's the institutions, stupid! Why comprehensive national health insurance always fails in America. *Journal of Health Politics, Policy and Law, 20*, 329–371.

Stimson, J. A. (1991). *Public opinion in America: Moods, cycles, and swings.* Boulder, CO: Westview Press.

Terkildsen, N., Schnell, F. I., & Ling, C. (1998). Interest groups, the media, and policy debate formation: An analysis of message structure, rhetoric, and source cues. *Political Communication, 15*, 45–62.

Tuchman, G. (1978). *Making news.* New York: Free Press.

Valocchi, S. (1996). The emergence of the integrationist ideology in the civil rights movements. *Social Problems, 43*, 116–130.

Van Dijk, T. A. (1988). *News as discourse.* Hillsdale, NJ: Lawrence Erlbaum Associates.

Verba, S. (1993). The 1993 James Madison Award Lecture: The voice of the people. *PS: Political Science & Politics, 26*, 677–686.

Walsh, K. T. (1996). *Feeding the beast: The White House and the press.* New York: Random House.

Weir, M. (1995). Institutional and political obstacles to reform. *Health Affairs, 14*, 102–104.

West, D., Heith, D., & Goodwin, C. (1996). Harry and Louise go to Washington: Political advertising and health care reform. *Journal of Health Politics, Policy, and Law, 21*, 35–68.

Wilson, G. K. (1996). Interest groups in the health care debate. In H. Aaron (Ed.), *Problem that won't go away: Reforming US health care financing* (pp. 110–130). Washington, DC: Brookings Institute.

Wuthnow, R. (1989). *Communities of discourse.* Cambridge, MA: Harvard University Press.

Zald, M. N. (1996). Culture, ideology, and strategic framing. In D. McAdam, J. D. McCarthy, & M. N. Zald (Eds.), *Comparative perspectives on social movements* (pp. 261–274). New York: Cambridge University Press.

Zaller, J. (1992). *The nature and origins of mass opinion.* Cambridge, England: Cambridge University Press.

Zaller, J., & Chiu, D. (1996). Government's little helper: U.S. press coverage of foreign policy crisis, 1945-1991. *Political Communication, 13*, 385–405.

Zelizer, B. (1993). Journalists as interpretive communities. *Critical Studies in Mass Communication, 10*, 219–237.

2

The Convergence of Agenda
Setting and Framing

Maxwell McCombs
Salma I. Ghanem

Early last century Walter Lippmann (1922) observed that much of the behavior underlying public opinion is a response to mental images of events,
an imagined pseudoenvironment that is treated as if it were the real environment. Those mental images are a key site where agenda setting and
framing converge. One result of the continuing explication of agenda-setting
theory over recent decades is that these two research traditions now share
considerable common ground.

Agenda setting is a theory about the transfer of salience from the mass
media's pictures of the world to those in our heads. Elaborating Lippmann's
perspective, the core idea is that elements prominent in the media's pictures become prominent in the audience's picture. In the metaphorical language of the theory, the media's agenda sets the public's agenda. Theoretically, these agendas could be composed of any set of elements. In
practice, the vast majority of the studies to date have examined an agenda
composed of public issues. For these studies the core theoretical assertion
is that the degree of emphasis placed on issues in the mass media influences the priority accorded these issues by the public. This proposition
has been supported in more than 200 studies over the past 25 years (Dearing & Rogers, 1996), both election and nonelection studies with considerable diversity in their geographic settings, time spans, news media, and
public issues studied.

This particular emphasis in the empirical research reflects the long-
dominant effects tradition in mass communication research, in general, and

the specific origins of agenda setting within the tradition of public opinion research. But just as agenda-setting research has grown beyond this particular point of origin to encompass a wide range of communication situations, including the shaping of the media agenda (Dearing & Rogers, 1996; McCombs, 1992), this chapter's discussion of the convergence of agenda setting and framing also is intended to reflect a breadth of research.

This convergence offers several theoretical advantages, because the traditional emphases of the framing and agenda-setting research traditions complement each other to a considerable degree. Within the agenda-setting tradition there is a vast wealth of research on the impact of mass media content on the public agenda and considerably less attention to the variety of influences shaping the media agenda. Within the framing tradition there has been considerable attention to the frames found in the media and sometimes the origins of those frames, with much less attention to the impact of those frames on the public. The convergence of these two research traditions will yield a greater unity in our knowledge of how the media's pictures of the world are constructed and, in turn, how the public responds to those pictures. More precisely, the outcome can be a unified theoretical framework linking communication settings, ranging from news sources and interest groups through the media to the public.

OBJECTS AND ATTRIBUTES

The metaphor of an agenda need not restrict us to a list of public issues, the approach taken in the majority of studies to date. Public issues are not the only objects that can be studied from the agenda-setting perspective. The objects defining an agenda can be political candidates, public institutions, or competing brands of goods, for example. Beyond the agenda of objects, there is another aspect to consider. Each of these objects has numerous attributes, those characteristics and properties that fill out the picture of each object.

Just as objects vary in salience, so do the attributes of each object. When journalists and, subsequently, members of the public think about and talk about various objects, some attributes have center stage. Others are relegated to lesser roles, and many are absent altogether. Just as there is an agenda of objects, there also is an agenda of attributes for each object that can be organized according to the relative salience of the attributes. Both the selection of objects for attention and the selection of attributes for thinking about these objects are important in the agenda-setting process (Shaw & McCombs, 1977). Although attribute agenda setting was touched upon in some of the earliest theoretical writings (McCombs & Masel-Walters, 1976) and explored in a handful of early studies, sustained interest in this second level of agenda setting emerged only recently (McCombs, 1994; McCombs & Evatt, 1995).

The first level of agenda setting is the transmission of object salience, and the second level is the transmission of attribute salience. Iyengar and Simon's (1993) analysis of the Persian Gulf crisis illustrates the difference between the two levels. When their survey respondents stated that the Gulf crisis was the most important problem facing the nation, we are dealing with the first level. When these respondents described the crisis in terms of diplomatic or military options, we are dealing with the second level. As this new research frontier expands our perspective on the agenda-setting role of mass communication to a new level, Bernard Cohen's (1963) famous dictum about media effects must be revised. Cohen noted that while the media may not tell us *what to think*, the media are stunningly successful in telling us *what to think about*. Explicit attention to the second level, attribute agenda setting, further suggests that the media also tell us *how to think* about some objects. It is here that agenda setting and framing share common ground.

CONCEPTUAL CONVERGENCE

One of the strengths of agenda-setting theory that has prompted its continuing growth for more than 30 years is its compatibility and complementarity with a variety of other concepts and theories. At various points, agenda setting has incorporated or converged with other mass communication subfields. Incorporated concepts include gatekeeping, now frequently referred to as intermedia agenda setting, and status conferral, the salience or perceived importance of persons, issues, and other objects. Conceptual complements include the "spiral of silence" theory of public opinion, which shares a common psychological explanation with agenda setting in their otherwise distinct and separate views of human phenomena.

The convergence of the basic agenda-setting idea and framing has long been recognized by scholars in many fields, including mass communication (Weaver, Graber, McCombs, & Eyal, 1981), political science (Iyengar & Simon, 1993), and rhetoric (Kuypers, 1997). Attribute agenda setting explicitly integrates the theory with framing research. The major focal points of framing research, *frames*, the *process of framing*, and *framing effects*, are, respectively, *attribute agendas*, the *dynamics of the agenda-setting process*, including its contingent conditions, and *agenda-setting influence*, or effects. The traditional diagram of agenda setting presented in Fig. 2.1 illustrates these distinctions and can be used for a preliminary sorting of the literature on both framing and second-level agenda setting.

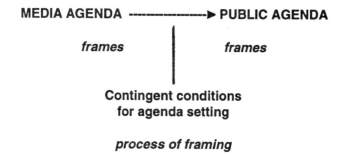

FIG. 2.1. Agenda setting effects described in the vocabulary of framing.

In a frequently cited definition, Tankard, Hendrickson, Silberman, Bliss, and Ghanem (1991) described a media frame as "the central organizing idea for news content that supplies a context and suggests what the issue is through the use of selection, emphasis, exclusion and elaboration" (p. 3). Specifically in terms of salience, Entman (1993) said:

> To frame is to select some aspects of a perceived reality and make them more salient in a communicating text, in such a way as to promote a particular problem definition, causal interpretation, moral evaluation and/or treatment recommendation for the item described. (p. 52)

To paraphrase these scholars in the language of attribute agenda setting, framing is the construction of an agenda with a restricted number of thematically related attributes in order to create a coherent picture of a particular object.

Although these two definitions of framing easily can be restated in the language of attribute agenda setting, this surface convergence only hints at the potential in the merged consideration of framing and agenda setting. In addition to providing a useful framework (no pun intended) for sorting out the many meanings and kinds of frames, agenda-setting theory also suggests a criterion for deciding which specific frames to study. Although omissions are sometimes significant, a sound general strategy for research in this area is to concentrate on the origins and transformations of frames that successfully move from agenda to agenda and to bypass those frames that became the dross of the communication process. Using successful agenda-setting outcomes as a criterion for the selection of research topics is underscored by the limited carrying capacity of agendas (Hilgartner & Bosk, 1988; McCombs & Zhu, 1995; Shaw & McCombs, 1977). The public agenda, for example, usually consists of five or fewer issues with significant constituencies, a constraint that almost certainly will be found at the second level of agenda setting as well.

DISTINGUISHING FORMAT AND CONTENT

Using agenda-setting theory to explicate the nature of frames, an initial distinction can be made between frames that are attributes of communication presentations and frames that are attributes of the objects being presented. This dichotomy, illustrated in Fig. 2.2, is similar to Gamson and Modigliani's (1989) distinction between framing devices and reasoning devices.

The origins of the term *framing* in the context of communication are in photography and cinematography, where framing refers to such variables as camera angle and perspective in the styling of a visual message. Although television news uses a wide variety of framing techniques to enhance news presentations, the concept of framing also is used in the production of print media. For example, Ghanem (1997) found that certain framing mechanisms used in the design of a daily newspaper, such as page placement, influenced the degree of concern expressed by Texans about crime. McCombs and Mauro (1977) found that page placement, story for-

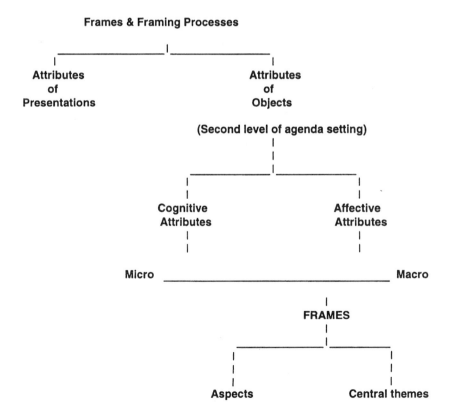

FIG. 2.2. A definition tree for frames and the framing process.

mat, and other framing mechanisms available to newspaper editors also influenced the level of readership for a specific news story among the audience. There is a considerable research literature on frames that are attributes of media products, the techniques used in the design of films, television news shows, newspapers, and magazines (e.g., Neuman, Just, & Crigler, 1992).

Although much of this work awaits systematic organization and explication—and there is much more to be done on the framing mechanisms relevant to message production that could be applied by mass media professionals—we shall concentrate on the content of news stories and people's thoughts. The attributes of objects are the properties and traits that fill out and detail the content of news stories and people's thoughts.

ATTRIBUTE AGENDA SETTING

The process of attribute agenda setting is most easily illustrated and understood when presented in terms of relatively simple attributes, such as the images of political candidates. Weaver et al. (1981), for example, found a high degree of correspondence between the agenda of attributes in the *Chicago Tribune* and the subsequent agenda of attributes in Illinois voters' descriptions of Jimmy Carter and Jerry Ford during the 1976 presidential election. In the 1976 presidential primaries, Becker and McCombs (1978) also found significant correspondence between the agenda of attributes in *Newsweek* and the agenda of attributes in New York Democrats' descriptions of the contenders for their party's presidential nomination. The attributes in these early studies included issue stands, personality traits, and perceptions of principled leadership, and competency. More recently, King (1997) documented the attribute agenda-setting influence of Taipei newspapers on voters' images of the three candidates for mayor.

The idea of attribute agenda setting also has been applied to more complex objects, such as public issues, which can be presented in many different ways. Benton and Frazier's (1976) analysis of a recurring major issue, the economy, identified agenda-setting effects involving such attributes as the specific problems, causes, and proposed solutions associated with the general topic of the economy, as well as the pro and con rationales for economic solutions.

In the first study to simultaneously examine both first and second level agenda setting, Takeshita and Mikami (1995) analyzed the issue of political reform during the 1993 general election in Japan. They found news media influence on the overall salience of political reform on the public agenda and at the second level on the salience of the system-related aspects of political reform. Both television and the newspapers mentioned system-related aspects of reform twice as often as ethics-related aspects.

COGNITIVE AND AFFECTIVE ATTRIBUTES

News stories, as well as people's personal descriptions, convey more than facts. They also convey feeling and tone (McCombs, 1992; Patterson, 1993). The distinction between cognitive and affective attributes of objects in Fig. 2.2 parallels the suggestion of Noelle-Neumann and Mathes (1987) that media coverage of public issues be considered in terms of:

- agenda-setting, which we have identified as first-level agenda setting;
- focusing, which deals with the definition of issues and is identified here as cognitive attributes at the second level; and
- evaluation, identified here as affective attributes at the second level.

Two studies of attribute agenda setting in the 1995 Spanish regional elections explicitly distinguished between the cognitive and affective attributes of the candidates' images.

McCombs, Llamas, Lopez-Escobar, and Rey (1997) examined the influence in Spain of two local newspapers, a regional television news program, and political advertising on Pamplona voters' cognitive and affective images of the candidates for mayor and leader of the provincial parliament. Three categories of cognitive attributes were analyzed: ideology and issue positions, qualifications and professional experience, and personal traits and personality. The affective attribute categories were positive, negative, and neutral. Although evidence of attribute agenda setting was found for both the substantive and affective dimensions, there was stronger evidence of affective effects among the audience. A second study based on these data found intermedia attribute agenda setting for cognitive, but not affective, attributes among the same three news media and political advertising (Lopez-Escobar, Llamas, McCombs, & Lennon, 1998).

Additional evidence of attribute agenda setting in the Spanish political setting comes from the 1996 national elections where McCombs, Lopez-Escobar, and Llamas (2000) analyzed detailed descriptive matrices defined by five cognitive categories and three affective categories. Three matrices constructed from Spanish voters' descriptions of each of the major candidates were compared with the presentations of those three candidates in two local newspapers, two national newspapers, two national television news services, and the television political ads. All 21 comparisons (3 candidates × 7 media) with the voters' descriptions showed a high degree of correspondence.

A RANGE OF ATTRIBUTES

Descriptions of objects can be simple and discrete, such as a person's age or marital status, or highly complex, such as fiscal conservative or national hero. This range from the micro-level to the macro-level for both cognitive and affective attributes is illustrated in Fig. 2.2. The cognitive and affective attributes of the political candidates examined in the three Spanish election studies are arrayed from the middle toward the micro end of this continuum. The aspects of public issues studied by Benton and Frazier (1976) and Takeshita and Mikami (1995) are more macro-attributes.

Broadbrush labels for the attributes of these issues and other objects are the stuff of headlines and news story leads. They also are shorthand labels for frames, the ideas used to organize both news presentations and personal thoughts about objects. Although frames can vary along a micro–macro continuum, most frames tend toward the complex because they encompass or imply a number of lower level attributes. Another way of putting it is that frames are organizing principles incorporating and emphasizing certain lower level attributes to the exclusion of many others. Frames serve as efficient bundling devices of micro-attributes and, in turn, can be thought of as macro-attributes. A stereotype is an example of a macro-attribute that bundles together a number of micro-attributes. From this perspective, not all attributes are frames, but all frames are attributes. All frames are attributes because they describe an object. An attribute is a frame only when it is a macro-attribute that subsumes other lower order attributes.

Distinguishing frames as a special class of attributes—complex attributes falling toward the macro end of the continuum—is a useful first step, but there is considerably more to explicate in terms of locating attributes and frames within the theoretical space defined by agenda-setting theory. To some degree any hierarchy of concepts under consideration can be repositioned as the focal point as the research emphasis varies. What is an object in one instance can become an attribute in another. For Benton and Frazier, the object was the economy, and they examined various attributes of that broad issue. But attributes of the economy, such as inflation or budget surpluses, could become the object of attention with their own sets of attributes. Recall that Benton and Frazier's title for their article was "The agenda-setting function of the mass media at three levels of information-holding." McCombs and Zhu (1995) faced a similar situation in grouping 179 unique categories into meaningful sets for an analysis of the public's agenda of the most important problems facing the country from 1954 to 1994. In the original 140 Gallup Polls, these 179 issues were the objects. In the set of 18 categories devised by McCombs and Zhu, these 179 issues are the attributes of 18 objects. Of course, in the original polls, the 179 categories are macrocategories subsuming individual responses. Despite its long history, public opinion research has never developed a nomenclature for dealing with issues at different levels of abstractness.

Similar variations in the focal point of research are reflected in discussions of framing. Although our earlier discussion located frames at the macro end of the continuum, it is possible to be more specific and to identify two distinct types of frames in the research literature: central themes and aspects. Both Tankard et al. (1991) and Gamson and Modigliani (1989) defined a frame as "a central organizing idea." But Tankard et al. also recognized that while some stories do have a single frame, many others have a multiplicity of frames. To characterize news stories only in terms of a single frame runs a substantial risk of overlooking a great deal of complexity and subtlety. They suggest that framing needs to be reconceptualized in terms of "degree of framing," which ties in with Entman's broader definition speaking of the agenda of attributes that highlight various aspects of the message's object of attention.

The fundamental difference among these definitions is central theme versus aspects, a difference that can be described in terms of Tankard et al.'s metaphor of a framed picture. In the case of the central theme, our concern is with the central focus of the picture. In the case of aspects, the frame distinguishes between the total set of attributes that the picture includes and what is left outside, a use of the term very similar to the original idea of framing in photography.

Operationally, recent articles in a variety of communication journals offer examples of this distinction in terms of the message units selected for attention: the central attributes of a news story versus a tally of various attributes appearing throughout the sentences and paragraphs of the story. McLeod and Detenber's (1999) experiment documents a variety of framing effects that result from news stories whose central theme is a narrative structure characterized as the protest paradigm. In other framing research, the focus is on the relative salience of various aspects of the topic rather than the dominant attributes defining the central theme of the news stories. Ashley and Olson's (1998) catalog of frames for the women's movement range from feminists' appearance (145 times in 499 stories) to the seldom mentioned goals of the movement (44 times in the 499 stories).

Comparing the framing in U.S. and Chinese newspapers of the 1995 United Nations Conference on Women, Akhavan-Majid and Ramaprasad (1998) noted the marginalization of the conference's 12 critical areas of concern, especially in the U.S. coverage. Out of 2,924 mentions of aspects of the conference in seven U.S. dailies, only 25% were about these 12 issues of critical concern. Among the 3,219 mentions in the Chinese newspaper, 46% described these critical areas of concern. To catalog the attributes of four GOP presidential candidates and their campaigns, Miller, Andsager, and Reichert (1998) used computerized content analysis to identify 28 frames defined by words that frequently co-occurred in 245 press releases and 296 news stories. This latter study also illustrates the convergence of framing and agenda setting. Although the focus of the study was identification of the frames defining the attribute agendas of the press releases and news stories, these data could be analyzed to determine the attribute agenda setting effect of the press releases on the news stories. This provided a sophisticated replication of Lopez-Escobar et al.'s (1998) examination of intermedia attribute agenda setting in a Spanish election.

Although the distinction between aspects and central themes is clear, conceptually and empirically, it is more useful to limit the concept of frame (and framing) to central themes. The distinction found in the current vocabulary of the literature between the generic concept of attributes and frames that are aspects is a distinction without a difference. The important distinction is between descriptive attributes that appear here and there and a descriptive attribute (or set of attributes) defining the central theme. Limiting the term *frame* to this latter special role of dominance brings useful parsimony to our work.

INHERENT DIFFERENCES AMONG ATTRIBUTES

To paraphrase George Orwell, some attributes are more equal than other attributes. In the encoding of messages, some attributes are more likely to be regularly included. In the decoding of messages, some attributes are more likely to be noticed and remembered. And in the interpretation of a message some attributes will be considered more pertinent than others. There are inherent differences in the salience of attributes.

For example, the narrative tradition and norms of journalism produce sets of attributes that differ from the general public's pictures of public affairs (Hofstetter, 1976; Neuman et al., 1992; Patterson, 1993). Examining the public's response to news reports about crime, Ghanem (1996) found that certain attributes of newspaper crime coverage exerted as much or more influence on the public's concern about crime as a social problem than did the overall volume of crime coverage. At the first level of agenda setting, there was a high degree of correspondence between the total pattern of crime coverage in the newspapers and Texan's concern about crime from 1992 to 1995. At the second level of agenda setting, the pattern of news coverage about crime that possessed certain attributes—such as a small psychological distance from the reader—showed similar, or even higher, levels of impact on the salience of crime among the public. Ghanem's research suggests that these crime stories possessing certain attributes are *compelling arguments* for the public about the importance of crime as an issue. Some ways of portraying an object resonate more than others with the public.

Jasperson, Shah, Watts, Faber, and Fan (1998) demonstrated both the value of compelling arguments (that is, attributes that have a particularly strong impact on the perceived salience of an object) and the value of combining first and second level agenda-setting analysis to explain public opinion. The total pattern of news coverage during the mid-1990s had strong explanatory power in predicting public concern about the federal budget. Further examination of four specific frames in the news coverage—nonconfrontational talks, conflict and clashes, impasse, and crisis—identified the first two of these frames as compelling arguments. The addition of these two frames as predictors significantly increased the amount of variance explained. The pattern of news coverage containing the other two frames did not have any relationship with the salience of this issue among the public. For issues other than crime and the federal budget, other attributes are likely to be compelling, sometimes early in the communication process at the level of attention, sometimes further on at the point of comprehension (McGuire, 1989).

At the level of general encoding behavior, McCombs and Smith (1969) found striking similarity in the pattern of attributes used by laboratory subjects to describe ordinary photographs and by journalists to describe New Orleans' Mardi Gras. For example, such attributes as color or size not only differ in their absolute salience—color was cited far more frequently than size by both—they are virtually identical in their relative ranking among the attributes cited by the journalists and laboratory subjects. These cultural differences in the salience of various attributes offer tantalizing cues and hypotheses about which attributes might function as "compelling arguments" in the flow of communication.

BEYOND SALIENCE

Attribute agenda setting has consequences beyond the pictures in our heads. Frames do more than bundle descriptive attributes. The mosaic or gestalt resulting from a frame can predispose the recipient of the framed message toward a particular line of reasoning or outcome (see Maher, chap. 3, this volume). This is agenda setting with major behavioral consequences. There are many other examples of attribute agendas' consequences:

- Media reports on social problems that use episodic versus thematic frames predispose the audience to attribute the responsibility for those problems very differently. Episodic frames suggest individual responsibility while thematic frames suggest systemic causes (Iyengar, 1991).
- Tulis (1987) asserted that many of the excesses of Cold War anticommunism can be traced to a single presidential appeal, the Truman Doctrine speech. This particular framing of East–West relations by President Truman, argues Tulis, shaped subsequent elite debate, news coverage, and congressional deliberation.
- Baumgartner and Jones (1993) hypothesized that major shifts in public opinion and public policy are preceded by significant shifts in the salient aspects of public issues. Their case studies include nuclear power, tobacco, pesticides, and auto safety.
- Entman's (1993) definition of framing identified four potential outcomes: defining problems, identifying causes, making moral judgments, and suggesting solutions.

In each of these examples framing has consequences for attitudes, private reasoning, and even public behavior. There is a certain irony here that these consequences of framing and attribute agenda setting bring us back to a consideration of the influence of mass communication on attitudes and opinions. That is where mass communication started in the 1940s and 1950s, and that is the area that was neglected after Klapper (1960) and others told us there were few significant effects. Indeed, agenda setting emerged as a response to that narrow judgment.

SUMMING UP

To clarify the diverse meanings of frames and to identify the conceptual connections between attributes and frames, this chapter first distinguished between frames that are attributes of communication presentations and frames that are attributes of the objects being presented in the content. Focusing on the characteristics of the objects that are the subject matter of mass media messages as well as individuals' thoughts and remarks, our explication noted that these object attributes can be identified as either cognitive or affective attributes and that both can be arrayed along a micro–macro continuum. Frames typically are macro-attributes, often containing a mix of cognitive and affective elements. Frames further can be distinguished as attributes that describe aspects of an object, or as attributes that characterize the dominant traits of an object and are the central theme of a particular message.

All these distinctions are useful steps in sorting out the many kinds of frames that exist in the research literature and have the potential to advance us beyond the *ad hoc* frames that are typical of the research literature. By *ad hoc* we mean frames defined specifically for a single study with little or no attention to explicating either their basic characteristics or theoretical context. Scholars need to elaborate in much more specific, but simultaneously generalizeable, terms the kinds of frames commonly found in the media and in public depictions of public issues, political candidates, and other topics.

The creation of specific categories that can be generalized across many different situations is, of course, the problem that content analysis has never solved. But we can identify several existing broad, exhaustive conceptual systems that are useful for sorting out message content in universal terms. Two of these systems are well-known, although seldom thought of as exhaustive category systems for attributes and frames: the Dewey decimal and Library of Congress systems for cataloging library materials. A third, potentially useful system for cataloging message content is Roget's thesaurus. Most people think of this as essentially a dictionary of synonyms and are unfamiliar with the underlying hierarchical set of categories. But this thesaurus system has proved useful in analyses of specific message content—and the theoretical and methodological leads of this approach to analyzing attributes appear promising.

The task before us is to move beyond the tangled plethora of meanings labeled frames and framing. Toward that goal, there is considerable promise in the theoretical and empirical contributions of attribute agenda setting, regarding both the content of attribute agendas and the connections between these agendas. Continuing accumulation of evidence on attribute agenda setting has created a convergence of interests among researchers with independent conceptual starting points in agenda setting and framing. Both communities could continue to launch their respective studies, but pursuit of isolated redundancy would be terribly wasteful. Both traditions can profit from the explication of a more general theoretical structure describing the frames and attributes that are important to the communication process. At present, a major weakness of communication research as a discipline is its highly fragmented state. There is much to gain from a cooperative effort.

REFERENCES

Akhavan-Majid, R., & Ramaprasad, J. (1998). Framing and ideology: A comparative analysis of U.S. and Chinese newspaper coverage of the Fourth United Nations Conference on Women and the NGO Forum. *Mass Communication & Society, 1*, 131–152.

Ashley, L., & Olson, B. (1998). Constructing reality: Print media's framing of the women's movement, 1966 to 1986. *Journalism & Mass Communication Quarterly, 75,* 263–277.

Baumgartner, F. R., & Jones, B. D. (1993). *Agendas and Instability in American Politics.* Chicago: University of Chicago Press.

Becker, L., & McCombs, M. (1978). The role of the press in determining voter reactions to presidential primaries. *Human Communication Research, 4,* 301–307.

Benton, M., & Frazier, P. J. (1976). The agenda-setting function of the mass media at three levels of information-holding. *Communication Research, 3,* 261–274.

Cohen, B. (1963). *The press and foreign policy.* Princeton, NJ: Princeton University Press.

Dearing, J. W., & Rogers, E. (1996). *Agenda setting.* Thousand Oaks, CA: Sage.

Entman, R. (1993). Framing: Toward clarification of a fractured paradigm. *Journal of Communication, 43*(3), 51–58.

Gamson, W. A., & Modigliani, A. (1989). Media discourse and public opinion on nuclear power: A constructionist approach. *American Journal of Sociology, 95,* 1–37.

Ghanem, S. (1996). *Media coverage of crime and public opinion: An exploration of the second level of agenda setting.* Unpublished doctoral dissertation, University of Texas at Austin.

Ghanem, S. (1997). Filling in the tapestry: The second level of agenda setting. In M. McCombs, D. Shaw, & D. Weaver (Eds.), *Communication and democracy: Exploring the intellectual frontiers in agenda-setting theory* (pp. 3–14). Mahwah, NJ: Lawrence Erlbaum Associates.

Hilgartner, S., & Bosk, C. (1988). The rise and fall of social problems: A public arenas model. *American Journal of Sociology, 94,* 53–78.

Hofstetter, C. R. (1976). *Bias in the News: Network television coverage of the 1972 election campaign.* Columbus: Ohio State University Press.

Iyengar, S. (1991). *Is anyone responsible? How television frames political issues.* Chicago: University of Chicago Press.

Iyengar, S., & Simon, A. (1993). News coverage of the Gulf crisis and public opinion: A study of agenda-setting, priming, and framing. *Communication Research, 20,* 365–383.

Jasperson, A. E., Shah, D. V., Watts, M., Faber, R. J., & Fan, D. P. (1998). Framing and the public agenda: Media effects on the importance of the federal budget deficit. *Political Communication, 15,* 205–224.

King, P. (1997). The press, candidate images, and voter perceptions. In M. McCombs, D. Shaw, & D. Weaver (Eds.), *Communication and democracy: Exploring the intellectual frontiers in agenda-setting theory* (pp. 29–40). Mahwah, NJ: Lawrence Erlbaum Associates.

Klapper, J. (1960). *The effects of mass communication.* New York: Free Press.

Kuypers, J. (1997). *Presidential crisis rhetoric and the press in the post-cold war world.* Westport, CT: Praeger.

Lippmann, W. (1922). *Public opinion.* New York: Macmillan.

Lopez-Escobar, E., Llamas, J. P., McCombs, M., & Lennon, F. (1998). Two levels of agenda setting among advertising and news in the 1995 Spanish elections. *Political Communication, 15,* 225–238.

McCombs, M. (1992). Explorers and surveyors: Expanding strategies for agenda setting research. *Journalism Quarterly, 69,* 813–824.

McCombs, M. (1994). The future agenda for agenda setting research. *Journal of Mass Communication Studies, 45,* 181–217 [Japan].

McCombs, M., & Evatt, D. (1995). Los temas y los aspectos: Explorando una nueva dimension de la agenda setting [Objects and attributes: Exploring a new dimension of agenda setting]. *Comunicacion y Sociedad, 8*(1), 7–32.

McCombs, M., Llamas, J. P., Lopez-Escobar, E., & Rey, F. (1997). Candidate images in Spanish elections: Second-level agenda setting effects. *Journalism & Mass Communication Quarterly, 74,* 703–717.

McCombs, M., Lopez-Escobar, E., & Llamas, J. P. (2000). Setting the agenda of attributes in the 1996 Spanish general election. *Journal of Communication, 50*(2), 77–92.

2. AGENDA SETTING AND FRAMING

McCombs, M., & Masel-Walters, L. (1976). Agenda setting: A new perspective on mass communication. *Mass Comm Review, 3*(2), 3–7.

McCombs, M., & Mauro, J. (1977). Predicting newspaper readership from content characteristics. *Journalism Quarterly, 54*, 3–7, 49.

McCombs, M., & Smith, J. (1969). Perceptual selection and communication. *Journalism Quarterly, 46*, 352–355.

McCombs, M., & Zhu, J. (1995). Capacity, diversity and volatility of the public agenda: Trends from 1954 to 1994. *Public Opinion Quarterly, 59*, 495–525.

McGuire, W. J. (1989). Theoretical foundations of campaigns. In R. E. Rice & C. K. Atkin (Eds.), *Public communication campaigns* (2nd ed., pp. 43–65). Newbury Park, CA: Sage.

McLeod, D., & Detenber, B. (1999). Framing effects of television news coverage of social protest. *Journal of Communication, 49*(3), 3–23.

Miller, M., Andsager, J., & Riechert, B. (1998). Framing the candidates in presidential primaries: Issues and images in press releases and news coverage. *Journalism & Mass Communication Quarterly, 75*, 312–324.

Neuman, W. R., Just, M., & Crigler, A. (1992). *Common knowledge: News and the construction of political meaning.* Chicago: University of Chicago Press.

Noelle-Neumann, E., & Mathes, R. (1987). The "event as event" and the "event as news": The significance of "consonance" for media effects research. *European Journal of Communication, 2*, 391–414.

Patterson, T. (1993). *Out of order.* New York: Random House Vintage Books.

Shaw, D., & McCombs, M. (Eds.). (1977). *The emergence of American political issues.* St. Paul, MN: West.

Takeshita, T., & Mikami, S. (1995). How did mass media influence the voters' choice in the 1993 general election in Japan?: A study of agenda-setting. *Keio Communication Review, 17*, 27–41.

Tankard, J., Hendrickson, L., Silberman, J., Bliss, K., & Ghanem, S. (1991, August). *Media frames: Approaches to conceptualization and measurement.* Paper presented to the Association for Education in Journalism and Mass Communication, Boston.

Tulis, J. (1987). *The rhetorical presidency.* Princeton, NJ: Princeton University Press.

Weaver, D., Graber, D., McCombs, M., & Eyal, C. (1981). *Media agenda setting in a presidential election: Issues, images and interest.* New York: Praeger.

3

Framing: An Emerging Paradigm or a Phase of Agenda Setting?

T. Michael Maher

Communication theory lacks a paradigm; we have only various scholarly fiefdoms, each claiming purview over some realm of the kingdom. Cultivation theorists have staked out entertainment television; Spiral of Silencers, fear of social isolation; Diffusion, the spread of innovation.

An interesting border dispute has disrupted the land of political communication. McCombs, one of the avatars of agenda setting, has argued that framing has become the second dimension of agenda-setting research (1995). Some scholars see this as a colonizing claim, and not everyone accepts it. For example, Kosicki (1993) has stated flatly that framing should not be viewed as an extension of agenda setting, because framing begins from an explicit cognitive perspective, and agenda setting does not. Iyengar and Simon (1993) have published research that measures framing and agenda setting as separate concepts. Entman (1993) has written that framing is now the overarching concept that could become a general theory of how communication texts work.

When scholars who are doing framing research disagree to this degree, we must then wonder if they mean the same thing when they use the word *framing*. Communication theory is Balkanized enough without having conceptual confusion in this growing area of study. Theory should organize knowledge and guide future research, but with competing claims about what framing means and where framing belongs among the panoply of communication theories, we wonder whether a fresh framing study advances agenda-setting theory, framing theory, or both.

To try to clarify distinctions and similarities between framing and agenda setting, this chapter examines the conceptual history and internal logic of both theories. This is not merely academic taxonomy; I seek to specify aspects of communication studies that are unique to each tradition, and also to suggest realms of research that future agenda setting and framing scholarship could address mutually. Historically, framing and agenda setting have had opposite trajectories. Agenda-setting began with valuable approaches to measurement, but lacked theoretical depth. By contrast, framing began with roots deep in cognitive psychology, but it has proved to be an elusive concept to measure.

McCombs and Shaw (1972) begat agenda setting with their oft-cited high correlations between the media agenda and the public agenda. And although they later acknowledged the influence of Lippmann's *Public Opinion* (1922) and Cohen's *The Press and Foreign Policy* (1963), they did not initially theorize deeply about *why* the media agenda should set the public's agenda. The first major theoretical statements came with *The Emergence of American Political Issues*. Here Shaw and McCombs (1977) reaffirmed the core idea of agenda setting as the transfer of issue salience from the media to the public. However, in describing agenda-setting conceptually, they extended its boundaries beyond the transfer of issue salience, suggesting that media messages contain an agenda of both objects and attributes. Objects are typically equivalent to issues or candidates. Attributes are properties associated with the objects and have saliences that can also be transferred from the media to the public.

More recently, McCombs (1995), McCombs and Evatt (1995), and Ghanem (1997) have written that the agenda of attributes subsumes framing, and that both constitute a second dimension (or level) of agenda setting. Therefore, it is important to look closely at how the agenda of attributes has been defined and operationalized, vis-à-vis the concept of framing. McCombs and Shaw (1977) offered as examples of attributes "(topics, issues, persons, or whatever) reported in the media" (p. 12). However, in this study they did not attempt to measure the transfer of an agenda of attributes. But in a subsequent book, which McCombs and Evatt (1995, p. 12) have called "the preface to the 'second dimension' of agenda-setting," Weaver, Graber, McCombs, and Eyal (1981) explored the agenda of attributes.

This study operationalized the agenda of attributes in terms of the presidential candidates' affective qualities: *man of principles, inspires confidence, competent, versatile,* and so forth. The researchers found that these attributes had various saliences in media coverage, and that those saliences were transmissible to the voters. This was an important discovery, particularly in view of the finding that most campaign coverage has little to do with issues (Buchanan, 1991; McCombs & Shaw, 1972; Robinson & Sheehan, 1983). However, as McCombs (1992) noted, few subsequent studies continued this approach to the agenda of attributes.

One study that did continue this approach was done by McCombs, Llamas, Lopez-Escobar, and Rey (1997). They investigated the transfer of attribute salience in the 1995 elections in Spain. They found that both substantive and affective qualities of the candidates transferred from media messages to the public, particularly when the messages came from print media. As this study acknowledged, "How news frames impact the public agenda is the emerging second level of agenda setting" (p. 704). It identified itself as "one of the first studies to explore second-level agenda-setting effects" (p. 709). It configured a frame as an attribute of an object, which in this case was a candidate.

These studies have treated the concept of framing differently from the way it is described by most other theorists. The relationship between attributes (which include frames) and objects (e.g., issues, candidates) seems similar to the grammatical relationship between adjectives and nouns. The noun comes first and without it, the adjective would have no meaning. As Weaver et al. (1981) operationalized these agendas, the noun (object) might be *Jimmy Carter*, and the adjective (attribute) might be *forthright* or *appealing manner*. The Spanish election study (McCombs et al., 1997) identified both substantive and affective dimensions of the candidates, the latter of which were simply *positive, negative*, or *neutral*. However, even the substantive dimension of the candidates was operationalized in terms of adjectives like "left-wing," and in terms of the candidates' charisma and moral standing, as well as their qualifications.

This implies a researcher-specified relationship in which the agenda of objects is considered as a given starting point, and the attributes—even frames—are considered a dependent subset of the objects. The researchers do not consider where the attributes came from, nor why journalists chose those attributes over others. Further, the candidate image attributes measured—even those labeled substantive—are primarily affective rather than cognitive. This suggests that agenda-of-attributes researchers consider a frame as something *they* specify, rather than the framer of the message under study. Further, agenda-setting researchers assume that frames are dependent on whatever objects (e.g., candidates, issues) the researcher is interested in studying.

DISTINGUISHING FRAMING FROM AGENDA SETTING

Systems theory can help distinguish framing from agenda setting, for agenda-setting theorists' terms, *objects* and *attributes,* are identical to terms used by systems theorists.[1] In systems theory, objects and attributes are considered to be two of the four basic elements of all systems (Hall & Fagen, 1968; Littlejohn, 1989). The other two basic elements, *relationships* and the *environment* outside the system (Hall & Fagen, 1968), have been conceptually equivalent to key concepts in framing theory, but not in agenda setting.

Relationships

In systems theory, relationships tie a system together and distinguish it from the environment that lies outside. "It is, in fact, those relationships that make the notion of 'system' useful," according to Hall and Fagen (1968, p. 82; see FN[1]). Similarly, framing implies relationships among elements in a message, because those elements have been organized by a communicator (rather than by a communication researcher). Framing theorists Gamson and Modigliani (1989) call a frame "a central organizing idea . . . for making sense of relevant events, suggesting what is at issue" (p. 3). Cognitive psychologist Friedman (1979) defines framing as "a function that specifies the relations that hold among the arguments comprising a particular conceptual bundle at a particular level of abstraction" (p. 321). Agenda setting has typically not considered the relationships of elements within a text, as they are organized by the text's author. Rather, researchers have usually specified their own categories of objects or attributes, taking these as a starting point for research.

By contrast, framing theorists have consistently postulated a relationship between the microcosmic elements in a given message and a macrocosmic worldview of the communicator. Bateson (1972) stressed that framing implies sender-organized relationships among elements in a message, which reminds the receiver, "these messages are mutually relevant and the messages outside the frame may be ignored" (p. 188).

This early formulation of framing is closely tied to cognitive science. Indeed, the subtitle of Bateson's book, *Steps to an Ecology of Mind*, reads, "The new information sciences can lead to a new understanding of man." Bateson (1972), whose ideas imply a logical, information-processing approach to human understanding, described framing as "a certain set of rules for the making and understanding of messages" (p. 191). In his overview of the development of cognitive science, Gardner (1987) listed frames among the many vocabularies that psychologists have developed to describe cognitive representation.

---

[1]This similarity in terms between agenda-setting and systems theories is apparently fortuitous, as McCombs and Shaw did not derive the terms *objects* and *attributes* from systems theory. According to McCombs, they were using basic descriptors of social science in order to state agenda-setting theory in its most general form. (McCombs, personal communication, March 1998.)

Some communication scholars have faulted agenda-setting studies for not developing closer ties to cognitive psychology (Kosicki, 1993; Rogers & Dearing, 1988). By contrast, all the early definers of framing (e.g., Gitlin, 1980; Goffman, 1974; Tuchman, 1978) continued Bateson's thought by emphasizing framing as a process by which potential elements are either included or excluded from a message or its interpretation by virtue of a communicator's organizing principles. The communicator's act of inclusion implies relationships among those elements.

Environment

The systems theory concept of the *environment* further distinguishes framing from agenda setting. The environment lies outside the system, but interacts with it. As Hall and Fagen (1968) put it, "In a sense, a system together with its environment makes up the universe of all things of interest in a given context" (p. 83). If we think of news as a system, and the universe of reality that news stories *could* describe (but don't) as the environment outside the system, we see another key difference between framing and agenda setting. Framing theorists have often studied the environment that lies outside reporters' message system; agenda-setting researchers have not.

Like the arbitrary boundary between system and environment, the constructed nature of journalists' news decisions is the central point of many framing studies. An oft-cited example is Gitlin's (1980) discussion of UPI photos that the *New York Times* editors chose *not* to use, and his comparison of *New York Times* coverage of an antiwar protest with more extensive coverage by the *National Guardian*. In both examples Gitlin demonstrated that what *Times* journalists chose to leave outside the story frame made considerable difference in how the story could be interpreted.

Basic studies in message framing (e.g., Tversky & Kahneman, 1981) have shown that excluding information from a message frame can have considerable effect on how people interpret the message. One study of the women's movement has shown that media stories excluded the concerns that undergird the movement, while covering only events (Ashley & Olson, 1998). Similarly, Norris and Carroll (1997) used exit poll data and statistics on the number of women candidates and officeholders as a real-world benchmark to show how media framing distorted political reality. Studies of this nature, which compare media messages to the wider, excluded information environment, further distinguish framing from agenda setting.

Causal Reasoning

Framing also differs from agenda setting with its stronger emphasis on causal reasoning. Entman (1993) suggested four functions of framing: defining problems, diagnosing causes, making moral judgments, and suggesting remedies. Pan and Kosicki (1993) noted, "Within the realm of news discourse, causal reasoning is often present, including causal attributions of the roots of a problem" (p. 64). Iyengar and Simon (1993) wrote, "Attributions of responsibility (in framing) are generally divided into causal and treatment dimensions" (p. 369). Political scientists Schön and Rein (1994) have suggested that the perennial debate about root-level causality in human behavior—nature versus nurture—is a kind of metacultural frame that in turn determines how individuals frame many different political issues. Other writers on framing (Gamson & Modigliani, 1989; Iyengar, 1991) have also tied framing to causal reasoning.

Agenda-setting research has shown less interest in media portrayals of how social problems are caused. In positioning framing as a second phase of agenda setting McCombs' (1992) wrote that through agenda setting, the media tell us *what to think about*, whereas through framing the media tell us *how to think about it*. However, in studies explicitly identified as agenda-of-attributes research, "how to think about it" has usually been operationalized in terms of candidate images, for example, whether candidates project integrity and virtue (Weaver et al., 1981). A framing approach to "how to think about it" would instead focus on how and why journalists present (or ignore) competing explanations of what factors are causing a problem, and what solutions might be possible.

The most basic conceptual rift between agenda setting and framing is how researchers conceptualize the source of frames in the studied communication content. Agenda-setting scholars see a frame as an attribute of an object (Ghanem, 1997; McCombs, 1995; McCombs & Evatt, 1995). This assumes that the researcher-specified object (e.g., issue or candidate) is the starting point, and that a frame is simply one of many kinds of attributes that a researcher might attach to the object. In this tradition the communication researcher specifies the studied frames, and the chief goal seems to be statistically significant correlations between the media's attribute agenda and public understanding. But this approach ignores the context of the story and minimizes or ignores the role of the journalist as framer of the studied media content.

Framing scholarship instead emphasizes the constructed nature of media messages, and often examines media portrayals of issues as clues to journalists' framing decisions. These framing decisions, in turn, provide important evidence about the flow of power in society. To those working within the framing tradition, it seems counterintuitive to suggest that a frame is a mere attribute of an issue or a candidate. To framing researchers, journalists' framing organizes the meaning of issues, and not vice versa, as suggested by agenda-setting researchers.

Scholars in the two research traditions are using the term *framing* differently, and they vary chiefly in where they derive the source of the studied frames. Recall Entman's (1993) point that frames have at least four locations in the communication process: the communicator, the text, the receiver, and the culture. Framing scholarship typically concentrates on the communicator's framing, that is, the journalist's framing. Agenda-setting research typically examines the transfer of framing salience between the text (as interpreted by the researcher) and the receiver (public).

Much of the imprecision and misunderstanding in framing scholarship arise from the polysemic nature of the word *framing*. In past studies scholars have not clarified which source of frames they're discussing, and much conceptual work remains to give researchers a common vocabulary that will enable us to distinguish what source of frames we're discussing. If by *frame* we mean a communicator's frame, such a frame could hardly be an attribute of an object, for that would imply that the creation (the news story) organizes the creator (the journalist). But a textual or cultural frame could be considered an attribute of an object, for such a frame could arguably exist independent of the journalists who create the news. Examples of cultural frames could be the "media packages" suggested by Gamson and Modigliani (1989) for the nuclear power issue (e.g., progress, energy independence, devil's bargain, etc.), or the frames suggested by Norris and Carroll (1997) for the women's movement (gender gap, soccer moms, year of the angry White male).

For our purposes it is important to realize that agenda-setting scholars use the term *framing* in a narrow, restrictive sense when they discuss frames as attributes of objects (McCombs, 1995). On the other hand, the affective attributes of candidates or issues, as operationalized in several agenda-setting studies, seem beyond the purview of framing theory, because these attributes are specified by the researcher, rather than by the journalist whose work is under study. Further, these attributes are affective rather than cognitive. We illustrate the points of overlap and underlap in Fig. 3.1.

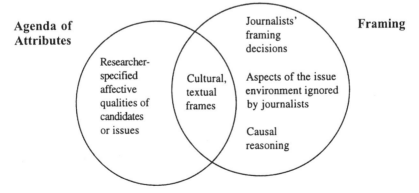

FIG. 3.1. The points of overlap and underlap.

Some have read agenda-setting scholars' claim that framing is a dimension of agenda-setting as an attempt to colonize framing theory. A different reading follows from the preceding discussion. Agenda-setting theorists are borrowing a limited subset from the overall concept of framing. Additional borrowing in the future is not merely likely but inevitable, as agenda setting and framing coalesce.

Similarities and Coalescence

In *The Sociological Imagination,* C. Wright Mills (1959) chastised the apostles of abstracted empiricism for measuring without theoretical guidance, for placing higher premium on statistical significance than on social significance, and for failing to examine the Big Questions. Similar criticisms have been leveled at agenda setting. For example, in their review of the first 15 years of agenda-setting research, Rogers and Dearing (1988) lamented that researchers had devoted much more effort to refining empirical measures of media and public agendas than they had to furthering theoretical development.

Mills' criticisms of sociological grand theory apply equally well to the framing literature. Mills faulted the grand theorists for their unintelligible writing and for their unwillingness to test their abstract ideas. Anyone who has waded through the discursive, rambling writings of Bateson or Goffman will acknowledge a similar weakness in these early formulations of framing theory. Framing is so broad a concept that it lacks the focus, predictive value, and testability of a more focused midrange theory. And until recently few studies have successfully quantified framing. Indeed, one study concluded that news framing was difficult to measure (Tankard, Henrickson, Silberman, Bliss, & Ghanem, 1991).

Studies from both theoretical traditions have been moving toward common ground, as well they should. Agenda setting needs the conceptual finer mesh of framing if future studies are to dispel what we might call the "Kosicki Curse," Kosicki's observation (1993) that agenda-setting research typically "strips away almost everything worth knowing about how the media cover an issue and leaves only the shell of the *topic*" (p. 112). Taking a cue from framing theory, agenda-setting studies have begun to acknowledge the controversy within individual issues and measure the effects of the media's role in framing contested definitions of problems. Takeshita (1997), writing within the agenda-setting tradition, noted a direction for future agenda-of-attributes research: "As a research strategy, I would like to recommend that we should first focus on problem definition and causes" (p. 25). That should sound familiar to framing scholars.

Framing studies, on the other hand, have begun to adopt the greater empirical sophistication of agenda-setting research. As Ghanem (1997) noted, most framing studies focus on the frames themselves, whereas agenda setting considers the impact of framing on the public. But some framing studies have begun to measure, rather than assume, that a given media frame will have an effect on audiences.

Both camps have produced crossover studies. Within the agenda-setting tradition, Benton and Frazier (1976) examined media coverage for its portrayal of the proposed solutions to issues, as well as for rationales for the proposed solutions. They termed this "information holding" rather than framing, but with its attention to causes and solutions, this study was about the transfer of framing salience. Williams, Shapiro, and Cutbirth (1983) studied framing as a contingent factor that could heighten an agenda-setting effect. Takeshita and Mikami (1995) continued Benton and Frazier's portrayal in measuring what they called "subissue salience" in the 1993 Japanese general elections. Their work tested the transfer from media to the public of proposed solutions to the issue of political corruption, essentially the transfer of framing salience.

Scholars within the framing tradition have begun to measure the transfer of salience from media to public, which has hitherto been the domain of agenda setting. Among these are Iyengar's 1991 book, *Is Anyone Responsible?*, which showed that media attributions of responsibility could influence how people think about the causality of social problems. My own study of media framing and public perception of causality in an environmental controversy showed that the most oft-mentioned media explanations for the causes of urban sprawl in Austin, Texas, became the causes given most frequently by a surveyed sample of Austinites (Maher, 1995). Miller, Andsager, and Riechert (1998) measured the transfer of framing salience, but in this study the transfer was from candidates to media, rather than from media to public. Iyengar and Simon's (1993) study of the Gulf War crisis is a complete hybrid, measuring agenda setting, priming, and framing (while saying nothing about objects and attributes). Shah, Domke, and Wackman (1996) also produced a hybrid study, measuring both the transfer of framing from media to public, and the priming effect of framing as it affected individuals' evaluation of related issues.

As the two trends coalesce, agenda-setting studies will continue to measure the transfer of attribute salience, while framing scholarship will increasingly measure audience effects. Both paths lead to the same communication phenomena-the media-public interaction in portrayals and understanding of elections or contested issues. Because scholars from both camps are marching toward the same realm of political communication, this returns us to the question posed in the opening paragraph of this chapter: Will scholars accept framing as a phase of agenda setting? Or, as Entman predicted, will framing become the paradigm for communication studies?

I think that neither agenda setting nor framing will outflank and envelop the other. Although framing offers a broader grounding in cognitive psychology and a finer conceptual mesh, agenda setting is more advantageous to studying how the affective components of a candidate or issue transfer from media to public. And agenda-setting has the scholarly momentum of having amassed more than 300 published studies. But there is also too much scholarly interest in framing studies, and too many excellent studies in framing, for it to be marginalized as a phase of agenda setting. Framing differs from an agenda of attributes sufficiently that the two should not be used interchangeably.

Despite their differences, the two theoretical perspectives have converged in recent years, and while neither will subsume the other, both will likely orbit within each other's gravity field as binary stars do. Many framing studies will remain qualitative, but we will increasingly see quantitative approaches to the process and effects of news framing. And although framing is too conceptually broad to be considered a mere attribute of an object, that should not prevent agenda-setting scholars from examining the transfer of framing salience. The measurement of framing effects through either theoretical path will be important to creating a model that will span the gap between the news agenda, the public agenda, and the policy agenda, as first suggested by Rogers and Dearing (1988). More study is needed of the role of news framing in advancing or ignoring various causal interpretations of the nation's problems, in winnowing out a range of possible solutions, and in affecting policy.

Quantifying the policy power of the media will require us to measure such framing questions as whose problem definitions, causal interpretations, and proposed solutions get the most media attention? And why? And with what effect on voters and legislators? Does framing of an issue vary across time as Downs (1972) implied? If so, what causes this variation? Do major changes in news framing precede major shifts in public opinion and policy, as Baumgartner and Jones (1993) suggested?

The study of framing can also add a normative dimension to the role of news in political communication. Although many dozens of agenda-setting studies have shown that the media tell us what to think about, no one has systematically studied whether the media are telling us to think about *the right things*. What kinds of issues, causal interpretations, and potential solutions are the news media ignoring that they should not be ignoring? Where do frames originate and how do they spread? Why do reporters adopt a given frame for a social problem and ignore other frames? Which segments of society gain or lose from journalists' framing decisions? Why do different publics accept or reject journalists' frames?

These and many other important questions remain for future scholarship. To answer them, the ostensible border dispute with which I opened this chapter may become moot, if future scholars heed Donald Shaw's (1998) admonition "to use the conceptual frameworks we inherited as platforms rather than fences" (p. 696). Despite their differences, framing and agenda setting are coalescing and both will be important platforms to yield answers about the role of media in a republic.

REFERENCES

Ashley, L., & Olson, B. (1998). Constructing reality: Print media's framing of the women's movement, 1966 to 1986. *Journalism & Mass Communication Quarterly, 75*(2), 263–277.

Bateson, G. (1972). A theory of play and fantasy. *Steps to an ecology of mind: Collected essays in anthropology, psychiatry, evolution, and epistemology* (pp. 177–193). San Francisco: Chandler.

Baumgartner, F., & Jones, B. (1993). *Agendas and instability in American politics.* Chicago: University of Chicago Press.

Benton, M., & Frazier, P. J. (1976). The agenda-setting of the mass media at three levels of 'information-holding.' *Communication Research, 3*(3), 261–274.

Buchanan, B. (1991). *Electing a president.* Austin: University of Texas Press.

Cohen, B. (1963). *The press and foreign policy.* Princeton, NJ: Princeton University Press.

Downs, A. (1972). Up and down with ecology: The issue-attention cycle. *The Public Interest, 28*, 38–50.

Entman, R. (1993). Framing: Toward clarification of a fractured paradigm. *Journal of Communication, 43*(3), 51–58.

Friedman, A. (1979). Framing pictures: The role of knowledge in automatized encoding and memory for gist. *Journal of Experimental Psychology: General, 108*, 316–355.

Gamson, W. A., & Modigliani, A. (1989). Media discourse and public opinion on nuclear power: A constructionist approach. *American Journal of Sociology, 95*, 1–37.

Gardner, H. (1987). *The mind's new science: A history of the cognitive revolution.* New York: Basic Books.

Ghanem, S. (1997). Filling in the tapestry: The second level of agenda setting. In M. McCombs, D. Shaw, & D. Weaver (Eds.), *Communication and democracy: Exploring the intellectual frontiers in agenda-setting theory* (pp. 3–14). Mahwah, NJ: Lawrence Erlbaum Associates.

Gitlin, T. (1980). *The whole world is watching: Mass media in the making & unmaking of the new left.* Berkeley: University of California Press.

Goffman, E. (1974). *Frame analysis: An essay on the organization of experience.* Boston: Northeastern University Press.

Hall, A., & Fagen, R. (1968). Definition of system. In W. Buckley (Ed.), *Modern systems research for the behavioral scientist* (pp. 81–92). Chicago: Aldine.

Iyengar, S. (1991). *Is anyone responsible? How television frames political issues.* Chicago: University of Chicago Press.

Iyengar, S., & Simon, A. (1993). News coverage of the Gulf Crisis and public opinion: A study of agenda-setting, priming, and framing. *Communication Research, 20*(3), 365–383.

Kosicki, G. (1993). Problems and opportunities in agenda-setting research: A 20-year assessment. *Journal of Communication, 43*(2), 100–128.

Lippmann, W. (1922). *Public opinion.* New York: Macmillan.

Littlejohn, S. (1989). *Theories of human communication* (3rd ed.). Belmont, CA: Wadsworth.

Maher, T. M. (1995). Media framing and public perception of environmental causality. *Southwestern Mass Communication Journal, 12*(1), 61–73.

McCombs, M. (1992). Explorers and surveyors: Expanding strategies for agenda setting research. *Journalism & Mass Communication Quarterly, 69*, 813–824.

McCombs (1995, September). *The media outside and the pictures in our heads: Surveying the second dimension of agenda setting.* Paper presented at the "New Trends in Communication" conference, Rome, Italy.

McCombs, M., & Evatt, D. (1995). Los temas y los aspectos: Explorado una nueva dimension de la agenda setting. *Communicacion y Sociedad, 8*, 7–32.

McCombs, M., Llamas, J., Lopez-Escobar, E., & Rey, F. (1997, winter). Candidate images in Spanish elections: Second-level agenda-setting effects. *Journalism & Mass Communication Quarterly, 74*(4), 703–717.

McCombs, M., & Shaw, D. (1972). The agenda-setting function of mass media. *Public Opinion Quarterly, 36*, 176–185.

McCombs, M., & Shaw, D. (1977). The agenda-setting function of the press. In D. Shaw & M. McCombs (Eds.), *The emergence of American political issues: The agenda-setting function of the press* (pp. 1–18). St. Paul, MN: West.

Miller, M., Andsager, J., & Riechert, B. (1998). Framing the candidates in presidential primaries: Issues and images in press releases and news coverage. *Journalism & Mass Communication Quarterly, 75*(2), 312–324.

Mills, C. W. (1959). *The sociological imagination.* New York: Praeger.

Norris, P., & Carroll, S. (1997, November). *The dynamics of the news framing process: From Reagan's gender gap to Clinton's soccer moms.* Paper presented at the Annual Meeting of the Southern Political Science Association, Norfolk, VA.

Pan, Z., & Kosicki, G. (1993). Framing analysis: An approach to news discourse. *Political Communication, 10*(1), 55–75.

Robinson, M., & Sheehan, M. (1983). *Over the wire and on TV: CBS and UPI in the campaign '80.* New York: Russell Sage Foundation.

Rogers, E., & Dearing, J. (1988). Agenda-setting research: Where has it been, where is it going? In J. A. Anderson (Ed.), *Communication Yearbook 11* (pp. 555–594). Newbury Park, CA: Sage

Schön, D., & Rein, M. (1994). *Frame reflection: Toward the resolution of intractable policy controversies.* New York: Basic Books.

Shah, D., Domke, D., & Wackman, D. (1996). "To thine own self be true": Values, framing, and voter decision-making strategies. *Communication Research, 23*(5), 509–560.

Shaw, D. (1998). Transition and change. *Journalism & Mass Communication Quarterly, 75*(4), 694–696.

Shaw, D., & McCombs, M. (1977). *The emergence of American political issues: The agenda-setting function of the press.* St. Paul, MN: West.

Takeshita, T. (1997). Exploring the media's roles in defining reality: From issue-agenda setting to attribute-agenda setting. In M. McCombs, D. Shaw, & D. Weaver (Eds.), *Communication and democracy: Exploring the intellectual frontiers in agenda-setting theory* (pp. 15–27). Mahwah, NJ: Lawrence Erlbaum Associates.

Takeshita, T., & Mikami, S. (1995). How did mass media influence the voters' choice in the 1993 general election in Japan? A study of agenda-setting. *Keio Communication Review, 17*, 27–41.

Tankard, Jr., J., Hendrickson, L., Silberman, J., Bliss, K., & Ghanem, S. (1991, August). *Media frames: Approaches to conceptualization and measurement.* Paper presented at the Association for Education in Journalism and Mass Communication, Boston.

Tuchman, G. (1978). *Making news: A study in the construction of reality.* New York: The Free Press.

Tversky, A., & Kahneman, D. (1981, Jan. 30). The framing of decisions and the psychology of choice. *Science, 211*, 453–458.

Weaver, D., Graber, D., McCombs, M., & Eyal, C. (1981). *Media agenda-setting in a presidential election: Issues, images, and interest.* New York: Praeger.

Williams Jr., W., Shapiro, M., & Cutbirth, C. (1983). The impact of campaign agendas on perception of issues. *Journalism Quarterly, 60*, 226–232.

4

The Empirical Approach to the Study of Media Framing

James W. Tankard, Jr.

Like other concepts of mass communication research, the term *framing* has also appeared in popular discourse—particularly that of media critics, politicians, and campaign insiders. For instance, linguistics scholar and media critic Noam Chomsky used the term in an interview discussing *New York Times* coverage of the crisis in Kuwait prior to the Gulf War (Szykowny, 1990). Chomsky argued that the *Times* story framed an offer by Iraq to withdraw from Kuwait in a way that trivialized the offer. Media critic David Shaw of *The Los Angeles Times* used the word *frame* in a discussion of news coverage of abortion (Shaw, 1990). Shaw noted that "the very language used to frame the abortion debate in much of the media implicitly favors the abortion rights advocates" (p. C1).

Political poll watchers have long known that wording a question in a particular way can frame the issue in a specific way. Different polls about abortion, for instance, will often produce contrary results. Pollster Harrison Hickman argued that this kind of effect can extend even beyond the polls: "Just as the polls come out according to the way the question is asked, so will the outcome of elections depend on who is more successful in framing what the question is about" (Tumulty, 1990, p. A29). Politicians are also aware of the importance of framing. For instance, Rep. Lee Hamilton, chairman of the House Foreign Affairs Middle East Subcommittee, said at the beginning of the Kuwaiti crisis in 1990: "The United States must not go it alone. We must frame this confrontation as a confrontation between the international community, on the one hand, and Iraq, on the other" (Keen, 1990, pp. 1A, 2A).

These examples of the term *framing* from public discourse show its popularity, but they also reflect some perceptiveness about the way media framing works. They show understanding of some key points: that news framing can eliminate voices and weaken arguments, that the media can frame issues in ways that favor a particular side without showing an explicit bias, and that defining the terms of a debate takes one a long way toward winning it.

IMPORTANCE OF THE MEDIA FRAMING APPROACH

The concept of media framing is important because it offers an alternative to the old "objectivity and bias" paradigm, it helps us understand mass communication effects, and it offers valuable suggestions for communication practitioners.

The concept of framing can offer an alternative to the old objectivity and bias paradigm that was popular in mass communication research for years. Hackett (1984) has argued that researchers should shift their focus from the study of objectivity and bias to the study of ideology in the news. He suggested the concept of framing as one useful approach because it has the potential of getting beneath the surface of news coverage and exposing the hidden assumptions. According to Hackett, the concept of ideology transcends the concept of bias. He argues that ideology provides a framework through which the news media often present events. For instance, Hackett noted that the conflict in El Salvador during the Reagan administration was framed by the government, and subsequently by the news media, as a national security issue. It could, of course, have been framed in other ways—for example, as a conflict between a wealthy and powerful nation and a weak and poor nation.

Framing differs from bias in several important ways. First, it is a more sophisticated concept. It goes beyond notions of *pro* or *con*, *favorable* or *unfavorable*, *negative* or *positive*. Framing adds the possibilities of additional, more complex emotional responses and also adds a cognitive dimension (beliefs about objects as well as attitudes). Second, framing recognizes the ability of a text—or a media presentation—to define a situation, to define the issues, and to set the terms of a debate. For example, defining abortion as an issue primarily concerning the life of the unborn child brings to the forefront a whole set of strongly held values and powerful emotions. Defining it as an issue primarily concerned with the freedom of choice of the mother raises a drastically different set of values and emotions. Convincing others to accept one's framing means to a large extent winning the debate.

Framing also reflects the richness of media discourse and the subtle differences that are possible when a specific topic is presented in different ways. These fine points are often lost in a crude *pro-or-con* bias approach. But this very subtlety also makes framing difficult to define. The specifics of measurement will differ for each topic of discourse. In his article, Hackett offers an intriguing premise—that framing might give quantitative research- ers a way to approach ideology, a subject dealt with until now mostly by critical theorists. Although he did not propose a quantitative measurement of framing, it does not seem to be a great step beyond what he was suggest- ing. Framing may even give quantitative researchers a means to examine the hypothesis of media hegemony, one that has been difficult to validate empirically. Media hegemony can be viewed as a situation in which one frame is so dominant that people accept it without notice or question. Thinking in terms of framing might force researchers to be more specific about media hegemony and pose some testable hypotheses.

Media framing is important because it can have subtle but powerful ef- fects on the audience, even to the point of helping to overthrow a presi- dent. The study of media framing can help us identify and examine crucial points in the opinion change process where these powerful effects are tak- ing place. For instance, Lang and Lang's (1983) study of public opinion for- mation in the Watergate scandal during the early 1970s found an important shift away from support for President Nixon when the media changed their framing. The press originally used the belittling frame of the "Watergate ca- per." Public opinion began to change only after the frame changed to a na- tional political scandal at the highest level (p. 59).

Much of the power of framing comes from its ability to define the terms of a debate without the audience realizing it is taking place. Media framing can be likened to the magician's sleight of hand—attention is directed to one point so that people do not notice the manipulation that is going on at another point.

The concept of framing is also important because it offers new insights— and leverage points—for communication practitioners, including journalists, planners of communication campaigns, and social activists. Newspaper edi- tor Steve Smith has stated that choosing a frame for a story is the most im- portant decision a journalist makes (Smith, 1997). He argued that journalists often reflexively choose a *conflict frame*—who are the antagonists or oppos- ing forces in this situation? He links the concept of framing with civic jour- nalism and says journalists need to make more use of *civic framing*—framing that deals with public life and focuses on process.

In Boston, the Media Research and Action Project (MRAP) takes advan- tage of frame analysis to help social movements and community groups use the news media to advance their political goals (Carragee, 1997). MRAP has worked with more than 200 social movement groups, including the Massa- chusetts Union of Public Housing Tenants (focusing on public housing is- sues in the state), the Hispanic Office of Planning and Evaluation (focusing on voter registration), and Cooperative Economics for Women (focusing on welfare and immigration issues). One MRAP strategy is to help groups to develop frames that resonate with broader political or social tendencies within American society. MRAP also encourages social groups to provide frames that analyze the causes of the conditions they are experiencing, rather than leaving that analysis up to experts.

THE EMPIRICAL APPROACH TO FRAMING

In both everyday and scholarly use, the term *frame* is sometimes used in an imprecise way, mostly as a metaphor. Much of the early research on framing relied on a qualitative, text-analysis approach, with an individual researcher working alone, as the expert, to identify the frames in media content. This approach makes frame identification a rather subjective process. Does one reader saying a story is using a *conflict* frame make that really the case? Indeed, coming up with the names for frames itself involves a kind of framing.

There is a danger in this kind of lone-scholar analysis that the identification of a set of possible frames can be done arbitrarily. An unsystematic approach to defining frames could mean that the set of possible frames is not exhaustive, or that the frame categories are not mutually exclusive. Also, without a systematic approach to defining possible frames, researchers may tend to find the frames they are consciously or unconsciously looking for. Researchers might also tend to define frames in a stereotypical or conventional way. For instance, the abortion debate might be viewed as involving only two positions—*pro-choice* and *pro-life*.

This chapter argues for approaches to measuring media framing that are systematic and empirical, and presents one such approach—the "list of frames."

Framing Definitions and Measurement Issues

An analysis of previous conceptualizations of framing reveals three distinct ways that the framing metaphor had been used in looking at media content. A comprehensive theoretical definition should be broad enough to include all three uses.

Two of the ways that framing has been used relate to the metaphor of a picture frame. One of the functions of a picture frame is to isolate certain material and draw attention to it. Goffman (1974), in an early discussion of framing in everyday life, presented the concept of a *strip*—"any arbitrary slice of cut from the stream of ongoing activity" (p. 10). It can be argued that picture frames present just this kind of a strip. A frame placed around a picture—whether the picture is a painting, a photograph, or a real-world scene—cuts one particular "slice" from that picture and excludes other possible slices. Tuchman (1978) discussed media framing in terms borrowed from Goffman. She stated that "frames organize 'strips' of the everyday world" (p. 192). Gitlin's (1980) definition of framing also implies the picture frame metaphor with its emphasis on "selection, emphasis, and exclusion" (p. 7).

Another function of a picture frame can be to suggest a tone for viewing a picture. For instance, an elaborately carved, wooden frame provides a different feeling from a mass-produced, metal one. Similarly, the news media can set a tone for an event or issue by the choice of frames. Graber (1989) highlighted this aspect of framing when she stated that "framing supplies the interpretive background by which the story is judged" (p. 7). Gitlin also appears to be talking about this function when he says that frames are patterns of "interpretation, and presentation" (p. 7).

The third way that the term *frame* can be used as a metaphor relates to the frame of a house or other building. In architecture, the frame is the organizing structure used to construct a house. In newswork, a frame can be the organizing idea on which a story is built. Gamson (1989) suggested a similar idea when he said "a frame is a central organizing idea for making sense of relevant events and suggesting what is at issue" (p. 157).

The "Media Package" Approach

One approach to measuring media frames has been to develop a paragraph called a "media package" (Gamson & Modigliani, 1989). The media package presents the keywords and common language that would help identify a particular frame. The paragraph is made up of paraphrased material and direct quotes from a number of sources. For instance, in developing a media package for a frame that describes nuclear power in terms of progress, Gamson and Modigliani (1989) took language from pamphlets and other writings by advocates of nuclear power. They argued that this kind of package "offers a number of different condensing symbols that suggest the core frame and positions in shorthand, making it possible to display the package as a whole with a deft metaphor, catchphrase, or other symbolic device" (p. 3).

Gamson and Modigliani have applied their media package approach to an analysis of television news broadcasts and news magazines. Within the nuclear progress package, they identified such categories as "Underdeveloped nations can especially benefit from peaceful uses of nuclear energy" or "Nuclear power is necessary for maintaining economic growth and our way of life." The study's coders looked for these specific categories instead of making a more global determination based on the package. With this approach, they were able to achieve an acceptable level of coder agreement of 80%.

Framing as a Multidimensional Concept

Another approach to measuring media frames is to conceive of framing as involving various elements or dimensions of stories. In a study of coverage of abortion news, Swenson (1990) coded eight elements or dimensions that defined story framing:

1. Gender of the writer.
2. Placement of the article (front page, editorial page, first section but not page 1, other).
3. Terms used to refer to the pro-choice group (pro-choice, abortion rights, pro-abortion, antilife, combination, not applicable).
4. Terms used to refer to the pro-life group (pro-life, right-to-life, antiabortion, antichoice, combination, not applicable).
5. Whether the woman's rights or the fetus's rights are considered paramount.
6. The morality orientation of the article.
7. Discussion of when life begins.
8. Terms used to refer to the fetus.

Swenson measured her reliability with the test–retest method, with the same coder apparently coding the material at two different times. She reported that percentages of agreement were generally around 100%.

THE "LIST OF FRAMES" APPROACH

In the fall of 1990, I taught a research seminar that focused on the concept of framing and addressed the issues of conceptualization and measurement.[1] Drawing on previous writings about the concept of frame, the research group came up with its own theoretical definition of framing:

> A frame is a central organizing idea for news content that supplies a context and suggests what the issue is through the use of selection, emphasis, exclu-

---

[1]Seminar participants were Kris Bliss, Salma Ghanem, Laura Hendrickson, Jackie Silberman, and David Thompson. The unpublished but widely cited paper referenced here as Tankard, Hendrickson, Silberman, Bliss, and Ghanem (1991) developed from this class and was presented at the conference of the Association for Education in Journalism and Mass Communication convention in Boston in 1991.

sion, and elaboration (Tankard, Hendrickson, Silberman, Bliss, & Ghanem, 1991).

We added the idea of elaboration to include the function of building a frame.

We looked at some of the previous work that had been done using the framing concept and found that much of it used a qualitative or text-analysis approach. With this approach, typically one scholar becomes the "expert" at identifying frames. We proposed an approach to studying frames in which a vital first step would be to identify a list of frames for the particular domain under discussion. To assist coders with the content analysis, each frame would then be defined in terms of specific keywords, catchphrases, and images.

We also identified a list of 11 framing mechanisms, or focal points for identifying framing:

1. Headlines and kickers (small headlines over the main headlines).
2. Subheads.
3. Photographs.
4. Photo captions.
5. Leads (the beginnings of news stories).
6. Selection of sources or affiliations.
7. Selection of quotes.
8. Pull quotes (quotes that are blown up in size for emphasis).
9. Logos (graphic identification of the particular series an article belongs to).
10. Statistics, charts, and graphs.
11. Concluding statements or paragraphs of articles.

From the beginning, our measurement attempts were influenced by the research on agenda-setting done by McCombs and others (e.g., McCombs & Shaw, 1972; Shaw & McCombs, 1977). Just as those researchers had conceptualized agenda setting as a list of issues, we were thinking of framing as a list of frames. There were differences in the overall goals, though. While agenda setting had focused primarily on *which* issues were covered, we conceptualized framing research as dealing more with *how* an issue or event is portrayed in the news.

The three approaches to measuring frames—the "media package," the "multidimensional concept," and the "list of frames"—present different conceptualizations of media framing. The multidimensional concept approach combines traditional story-presentation variables that are typically looked at in content analysis studies, such as location in the newspaper, with story content variables such as the kind of terms that are used to refer to a fetus in abortion stories. The media package and list of frames approaches focus more on how the issue is defined by inclusion and exclusion of certain key terms. The two approaches differ primarily in the way these key terms are found, with the media package approach examining pamphlets and other materials prepared by advocacy groups, and the list of frames uncovering terms through an examination of media content. They also differ in the ways the key terms are given to coders, with the media package approach presenting them in an integrated paragraph and the list of frames approach presenting them in lists of indicators. The three approaches to measuring frames share the requirement that frames and frame indicators must be discovered and defined for each new topic under investigation. This step seems unavoidable, since framing deals fundamentally with the differences in the ways particular stories are presented.

We tested our approach with the topic of abortion by coming up with a list of six frames: *anti-abortion, anti-pro-abortion, pro-life, pro-abortion, anti-anti-abortion* (arguments presented to refute arguments against abortion), and *pro-choice*. We analyzed a sample of articles from newspapers and magazines dealing with abortions, using the story as the coding unit. Our procedures did not include either "neutral" or "mixed" coding categories. Neutral categories were more or less ruled out by one of the basic assumptions of media framing theory—that every story has a frame. The "mixed" category was not used because it could become an easy way for coders to avoid tough coding decisions and because it would not provide useful information about the frames being used. Overall, the coder reliability did not reach acceptable levels until we collapsed the frames to two—*generally favorable to abortion* and *generally unfavorable*—when the coding for the magazine sample reached an acceptable level of 89% agreement between coders.

In a sense, this procedure was not a radical departure from the thinking of Hackett and Lang and Lang. It differed mainly in attempting to be more precise about the definitions of frames and more systematic about the procedures to be followed in identifying them. In general, the list of frames approach recommends the following steps: (1) Make the range of possible frames explicit, (2) Put the various possible frames in a manifest list, (3) Develop keywords, catchphrases and symbols to help detect each frame, (4) Use the frames in the list as categories in a content analysis, and (5) Get coders to code articles or other kinds of content into these categories. This approach makes the rules for identifying frames explicit and takes the subjectivity out of frame identification.

Graduate students at the University of Texas have continued to explore the list of frames measurement approach. Hendrickson (1994), in her dissertation, looked at news media framing of child maltreatment. She drew upon the field of social work for a list of five frames dealing with the causes of social problems and applied them to the particular problem of child maltreatment. With the list of five frames, she achieved 69% coder agreement. When she collapsed them into two—a psychological frame and a sociological frame—she achieved 87% coder agreement. Her research suggests that one useful approach to coming up with a list of frames can be to draw upon the theoretical or research literature pertaining to a topic of discourse. Hendrickson's research provided evidence that frames can be coded reliably and expanded on the list-of-frames approach by acknowledging that particular news stories might incorporate elements of more than one frame.

In another example, Maher (1995) examined news media framing of the Barton Creek watershed in Austin. Maher argued that a key component of framing is often the assignment of the causes of social problems. In his study, he looked for four categories of framing of the causes of environmental problems involving Barton Creek: polluters, developers, growth (in terms of physical urban expansion, not people), and population growth. He obtained coder agreement of 94%, demonstrating a successful use of a modified list-of-frames approach.

More recently, Bill Israel and I took a computer database approach to the measurement of framing by using Lexis–Nexis searches to look for keywords identifying frames (Tankard & Israel, 1997). Our work investigated some of the possible causal influences on media framing, a relatively unexplored area of research. We were specifically interested in the role of public relations firms in influencing media framing of international crises. Major U.S. public relations firms, including Hill and Knowlton and Ruder-Finn, have recently been employed by foreign governments to help them present their cases in times of crises. We compared statements by these PR firms about what they were trying to do with media framing of the crises to see if they succeeded. In the case of the Bosnia war, for example, Bosnia and Croatia employed Ruder-Finn to put out messages linking the Serbs to "ethnic cleansing" and "concentration camps." Basically, they were presenting a *Holocaust* frame, a powerful cultural frame with a great deal of resonance. We did Lexis–Nexis searches in five major newspapers for "Serb" and various keywords that indicated the Holocaust frame. James Harff of Ruder-Finn identified August, 1992, as the beginning of the PR campaign. Our analysis showed the frequency of stories using the terms *concentration camp* and *Serb* together reached a dramatic peak in August.

This kind of approach to measuring framing utilizes content analysis—either with human coders through the list-of-frames approach or computer-based, with a Lexis–Nexis search for keywords. The approach is not necessarily heavily quantitative. Rather, it attempts to be systematic about frame identification and to show that there are defining characteristics of media frames that different observers can recognize and agree upon. The point is not to be quantitative for its own sake, but to take the subjectivity out of the identification of frames.

ADVANTAGES OF THE EMPIRICAL APPROACH

After a decade or so of research on media framing, many studies remain merely descriptive, without much effort directed at theory building. Some studies that appear to deal with framing are actually using the term as a synonym for media presentation. These studies are actually quite similar to the old bias studies in being descriptive rather than theoretical and being limited in generalizability. Some precise conceptualization and careful empirical measurement of framing will be necessary if we are to move beyond description and do any serious theory building. Research on important topics like the effects of media framing is unlikely to move forward without careful operationalization of the framing concept itself. The advantages of an empirical approach to the study of framing include many of the standard advantages of social science research:

1. The reliability of measurement can be determined.
2. Achieving an acceptable level of reliability means the subjectivity has been taken out of the identification of frames.
3. The results are replicable. Other researchers should be able to identify the same frames in the same way.
4. The power of theory building and theory testing is brought to research on framing.

This larger theoretical work would involve steps that Hage (1972) has identified: conceptualization in terms of general variables, creation of theoretical and operational definitions, development of testable theoretical statements, and so forth. The goal of such a process would be to develop a set of testable propositions concerning media framing. These propositions might take the Hage form of "The greater the X, the greater the Y." For instance, Snow, Rochford, Worden, and Benford (1986) discussed the important concept of *frame resonance* and have proposed that "The higher the degree of *frame resonance*, the greater the probability that the framing effect will be relatively successful" (p. 477).

Our work at the University of Texas on measuring framing suggests the following lessons:

1. It is difficult to measure framing through a quantitative content analysis approach, but some attempts have been successful.

2. A smaller number of frame categories can help to improve the reliability of coding. But the trade-off may be to sacrifice some of the actual complexity and diversity of framing in order to achieve coder reliability.
3. One useful source for categories for a list of frames can be the theoretical literature dealing with a particular topic of discourse. Lists of frames developed this way gain validity and coherence from the previous theoretical work.
4. Several approaches to framing that have achieved successful coder reliability have narrowed the conception of framing to one dimension, such as causation.

In short, the empirical approach to the measurement of media framing is producing dividends, and it is likely that it will continue to do so. Psychologist E. L. Thorndike (1921) wrote, "Whatever exists, exists in some amount. To measure it is simply to know its varying amounts" (p. 379). This statement can fruitfully be applied to the examination of media frames.

REFERENCES

Carragee, K. M. (1997). *Framing, the news media, and collective action.* Paper presented at the Framing in the New Media Landscape conference, Columbia, SC.
Gamson, W. A. (1989). News as framing: Comments on Graber. *American Behavioral Scientist, 33,* 157–161.
Gamson, W. A., & Modigliani, A. (1989). Media discourse and public opinion on nuclear power: A constructionist approach. *American Journal of Sociology, 95,* 1–37.
Gitlin, T. (1980). *The whole world is watching: Mass media in the making & unmaking of the New Left.* Berkeley: University of California Press.
Goffman, E. (1974). *Frame analysis: An essay on the organization of experience.* Boston: Northeastern University Press.
Graber, D. (1989). Content and meaning. What's it all about? *American Behavioral Scientist, 33,* 144–152.
Hackett, R. A. (1984). Decline of a paradigm? Bias and objectivity in news media studies. In M. Gurevitch & M. R. Levy (Eds.), *Mass communication review yearbook* (Vol. 5, pp. 251–274). Beverly Hills, CA: Sage.
Hage, J. (1972). *Techniques and problems of theory construction in sociology.* New York: Wiley.
Hendrickson, L. J. (1994). *Media framing of child maltreatment: Conceptualizing framing as a continuous variable.* Unpublished doctoral dissertation, The University of Texas, Austin, TX.
Keen, J. (1990, August 21). How long will U.S. stay in the gulf? *USA Today,* pp. 1A, 2A.
Lang, G. E., & Lang, K. (1983). *The battle for public opinion: The president, the press, and the polls during Watergate.* New York: Columbia University Press.
Maher, T. M. (1995). *Media framing and salience of the population issue: A multimethod approach.* Unpublished doctoral dissertation, The University of Texas, Austin, TX.
McCombs, M. E., & Shaw, D. L. (1972). The agenda-setting function of mass media. *Public Opinion Quarterly, 36,* 176–187.

Shaw, D. (1990, July 15). Choosing sides: Media abortion bias may taint coverage of news, study says. *Austin American-Statesman*, pp. C1, C9.

Shaw, D. L., & McCombs, M. E. (1977). *The emergence of American political issues: The agenda-setting function of the press*. St. Paul, MN: West.

Smith, S. (1997, March 15). *Developing new reflexes in framing stories*. Paper presented at the Pew Center/RTNDF workshop "Civic Journalism: Doing it Daily," Chicago. Available at: *http:// www.pewcenter.org/PUBLICATIONS/CATALYST/CCAPRIL97/reflexes.html*

Snow, D. A., Rochford, E. B., Worden, S. K., & Benford, R. D. (1986). Frame alignment processes, micromobilization, and movement participation. *American Sociological Review, 51*, 464–481.

Swenson, J. (1990, August). *News coverage of the abortion issue: Framing changes in the 1980s*. Paper presented to the Committee on the Status of Women, Association for Education in Journalism and Mass Communication, Minneapolis, MN.

Syzkowny, R. (1990, November/December). The humanist interview: Bewildering the herd. *The Humanist*, pp. 8–17.

Tankard, J. W., Hendrickson, L., Silberman, J., Bliss, K., & Ghanem, S. (1991). *Media frames: Approaches to conceptualization and measurement*. Paper presented to the annual meeting of the Association for Education in Journalism and Mass Communication, Boston, MA.

Tankard, J. W., & Israel, B. (1997). *PR goes to war: The effects of public relations campaigns on media framing of the Kuwaiti and Bosnian crises*. Paper presented to the Association for Education in Journalism and Mass Communication, Chicago.

Thorndike, E. L. (1921). Measurement in education. *Teachers College Record 22*, No. 5, 371–379.

Tuchman, G. (1978). *Making news: A study in the construction of reality*. New York: The Free Press.

Tumulty, K. (1990, September 3). Abortion polls yield contradictory results. *Austin American-Statesman*, p. A29.

5

The Spiral of Opportunity and Frame Resonance: Mapping the Issue Cycle in News and Public Discourse

M. Mark Miller
Bonnie Parnell Riechert

Physicists study the fundamental properties of matter by accelerating subatomic particles to the speed of light and colliding them from opposite directions. By examining the debris from these collisions at theoretically impossible speeds, physicists enhance their understanding of how the world works. Although social scientists can't manipulate the stuff of their field as precisely, they can examine the outcomes of social collisions that occur naturally. Such events are not rare. In fact, it might be argued that collision and conflict are natural parts of the social landscape, especially in the public issues that make their way to the news media.

We examine this news media framing of public life in the context of contentious issues where opposing interests and values collide. In policy debates, for example, different groups of people often stand to be affected in different ways by the decisions that are made. A complex issue usually involves many aspects, some of which are more salient or important to particular groups than to others. What is unimportant to one person may be a key concern to another. Economic, as well as ideological, stakes come into play, and stakeholders engage in policy debates on behalf of the issue aspects that are most salient to them.

We argue that opposing stakeholders try to gain public and policymaker support for their positions less by offering new facts or by changing their evaluations of those facts, and more by altering the frames or interpretive dimensions by which the facts are to be evaluated. That is, they attempt to frame the issue. Thus, there is much to be learned by studying these contentious stakeholders and the collisions of their competing frames. The debris from such collisions is manifest in news media content.

Cobb and Elder (1983) and Manheim (1987) described the progression of issues—from public discussion, to media discussion, to policy making—as agenda building. The framing of issues clearly is integral to this process (Hallahan, 1999). We are especially interested in the processes of mutual influence by which public opinion, special interest groups, news media, and government officials interact in the debating and development of public policy. Special interest groups engage in public relations efforts, such as distributing news releases to news media and planning special events designed to build supportive coalitions and gain public visibility for their views (cf. Hallahan, 1999). These tactics to increase awareness and support for a particular position play a key role in developing policies on the national agenda.

In this chapter we propose a new theoretical approach to conceptualizing the processes involved in competing efforts by stakeholders to define selectively the boundaries of public discourse on issues. We also describe ways these processes can be investigated using the precision of computer-assisted content analysis and multidimensional scaling.

The theoretic view and methodological approach described here address some major research challenges that have been suggested by several leading scholars. First, this explication of framing is compatible with, and will advance, studies of media content as dependent variable. Shoemaker and Reese (1996/1991) proposed a concentric circle model of influences on news media content, including influences within the media organization and influences outside the media. Examples of these sources of influence would include special interest groups and advocacy organizations that actively engage in public debate relating to contentious policy issues. Shoemaker and Reese (1996) urge that researchers, rather than studying media effects, investigate "why such effect-producing content exists to begin with" (p. 5). Second, the conceptual development offered should advance theory-driven studies of the phenomena involved in the processes of framing. These investigations will contribute to developing and refining our theoretic understanding of framing beyond its status as a "fractured" paradigm lacking satisfying conceptual definitions (Entman, 1993). Third, the computer-assisted content analysis methods discussed herein are well designed for the intensive investigation of media coverage, over time, on single issues as urged by Dearing and Rogers (1996) in their review of the status of agenda-setting research.

SPIRAL OF OPPORTUNITY THEORY AND FRAMING

Our main thesis is that stakeholder attempts to frame issues interact with fundamental human values in ways that affect the relative attractiveness of policy options to the public and policymakers. Stakeholders articulate their positions and then monitor public responses to those articulations. If a stakeholder's articulation resonates positively with the public, then that group will intensify its efforts. On the other hand when an articulation resonates negatively, the stakeholder group will change its articulation or withdraw from debate. We label our position "Spiral of Opportunity."

By now it is well established that framing provides a fruitful way of conceptualizing how media shape news and people's perceptions of it. But the area lacks precision and coherence. Therefore, we need a systematic method for thinking about framing processes and how to observe them—in a word, *theory*. We offer a systematic theory of framing that defines key concepts, their interrelationships, and how to observe them.

In addition to its everyday usage, framing has taken on a variety of technical meanings. Sociologists, psychologists, and communication scholars all have used the term in a variety of contexts that would be hard to capture in a single conceptualization. We use a restricted definition. We think of framing as an ongoing process by which ideological interpretive mechanisms are derived from competing stakeholder positions. These selectively representative frames are manifest in the choice and range of terms that provide the context in which issues are interpreted and discussed.

Tuchman (1976) noted that "framing implies identifying some items as facts, not others" (p. 1066). Gitlin (1980) observed that "frames are the principles of selection, emphasis, and presentation composed of tacit little theories about what exists, what happens, and what matters" (pp. 6–7). We agree with these authors and have demonstrated how frames can be discerned by quantitative examination of the terms stakeholders choose to articulate their positions on contentious issues.

For example, early discussions of the Clinton health care plan were framed as issues of equality of a citizen's right to quality health care, which was manifest in such words as "fairness" and "access." Opponents of the plan succeeded in changing the frame to one of citizens' right to choose health care providers and government intrusion, which was manifest in such words as "choice" and "bureaucracy." The means we have developed for such examination of stakeholder terms are described later in the section on testing stakeholder propositions.

Many scholars conceive of framing as being driven by unitary ideologies that force news into a single interpretive context that supports elite interests. Hallin (1987), for example, argued that "The Cold War" provided the frame for international news coverage for decades. Although we don't deny that elite ideologies can have profound influences on news, we see hegemony as the end state of a process in which a single perspective has driven others from view. We prefer to investigate the processes by which such states come into being.

Issues

Issues are topics for which policy decisions must be made (including the decision to retain the status quo). In general, issues revolve around proposals for governmental actions. Policy proposals can be vague, as in the assertion: "We should do something about guns," or specific, as in: "We need to do background checks on people who purchase handguns at gun shows." The term *issue* often is used loosely to describe any topic that captures public attention, such as presidential morality. We exclude such usage, however, because no specific policy is being proposed.

Our approach to defining issues owes much to classic work on public opinion (Blumer, 1946; Park, 1904/1972). The public, these authors argue, is created when significant numbers of people become actively engaged in debate about how society at large should respond to an issue. Like Blumer and Park, we look at an issue as arising when the public debates policy options. By definition, issues are contentious with individuals and groups taking opposing positions. Where there is no argument there is no issue. There may, of course, be powerful cultural norms that shape policy without debate, but it is not our intent to address these.

Stakeholders and Stakeholder Competition

We use the word *stakeholders* to refer to individuals and groups in the policymaking process that "stand to win or lose as a result of a policy decision" (Lyons, Scheb, & Richardson, 1995, p. 497). For any given policy issue, population segments have particular concerns at stake; naturally, people tend to selectively focus on the policy implications most salient to them.

The term *claimsmaker* also is appropriate for these stakeholder groups. Members of these competing public and private stakeholder groups become claimsmakers when they articulate their perspective. As people discuss their position, they are making claims about the issues. Often, these claims are explicit, but perhaps just as often they are implied. With regard to debate over the Clinton health care plan, for example, the insurance industry stressed problems of unwieldy bureaucracy, implying that administration should be in private hands—theirs. Also, involved stakeholders will exclude competing or contradictory viewpoints. It is important to note that stakeholders may be individuals, informal groups, or organized interest groups. All of these have important functions in the operation of our theory as described next.

The process of framing becomes more apparent when stakeholders compete for support. They do this by talking across each other, not by dialogue. Dialogue means that when one side raises a subject, the other side addresses it. When there is true dialogue, stakeholders bring facts to each other's attention and debate the value of these facts. But, as Schon and Rien (1994) have stated, controversies persist precisely because stakeholders martial different facts and different interpretations of the facts. In a word, they "frame" things differently.

The observation that contending parties talk across each other is not new. In fact, Kelley (1960) traced this observation to Bryce's writings on elections campaigns at the end of the 19th century. According to Bryce:

> Anyone who should read the campaign literature of the Republicans would fancy that they are opposed to the Democrats on many important points. When he took up the Democratic speeches and pamphlets he would again be struck by the serious divergence of the parties, which however would seem to arise, not on the points raised by the Republicans, but on other points the Republicans had not referred to. (Bryce, cited in Kelley, 1960, p. 61).

Berelson, Lazarsfeld, and McPhee (1954) observed the same thing in their classic study of the Dewey–Truman presidential election, and it appears to be applicable in contemporary campaigns.

To summarize, we are interested in the effects of framing—or selective issue representation—related to issues that involve interested stakeholders who are participating in public discourse. Conceptualizing frames in terms of key verbal components measurable in news releases and news stories allows us to examine how the dominance of competing frames can shift over time in public discourse and in the news media. As we study these shifts, we observe a pattern of phases in the effects of issue framing. The following section describes the four stages we have discerned in this framing cycle.

The Framing Cycle

Social scientists have described many processes as evolving in cycles. For example, Cobb and Elder (1983) described the process of policy agenda building as evolving to interest ever-widening publics. Downs (1972) described an issue-attention cycle relating to topics such as environmental conservation. The framing process evolves in phases marked by the nature of the persuasive efforts made by stakeholders and their effects.

The Emergence Phase. Journalists don't report issues; they report news. When journalists scrutinize the world looking for news they evaluate what they see according to news values, which are criteria for deciding what to report and what emphasis to provide. Nearly all beginning reporting textbooks contain lists of news values, such as consequence, timeliness, proximity, and human interest. Because issues often are not directly attached to news values, they can lie dormant until they are impelled onto the public agenda. Walter Lippmann (1922) said of news:

> There must be manifestation. The course of events must assume a certain de-
> finable shape, and until it is in a phase where some aspect is an accomplished
> fact, news does not separate itself from the ocean of possible truth. (p. 340)

Schramm (1949), in his classic essay, "The Nature of News," observed that news is not the event but is the report of the event (p. 288). The initial or emergence phase of framing can be triggered by such things as catastrophic events, policy initiatives by stakeholder groups, activities of celebrities, and shifts in the ideological balance of government due to elections. During this phase, news content focuses primarily on the mere existence of the event that triggered it.

Often topics remain on the news agenda for a continuing period, during which time reporters write additional news articles and include comments from people involved in the issue. As stakeholders find access to journalists, they may be able to win visibility for their selective issue definition by exposure in the mass media. Journalists, striving for objectivity, depend on spokespersons as sources for information and comments. This dependence would suggest a win–win situation in which reporters need a quote, and group representatives want to publicize their perspective. As issues become more complex they involve multiple stakeholders or claimsmakers who then compete for access to news reporters.

The Definition/Conflict Phase. Once events drive an issue onto the public agenda, stakeholders begin efforts to frame them. A stakeholder's primary goal here is to establish a specific point of view as the appropriate frame for the issue. This is done by highlighting certain aspects of the issue and downplaying others. Stakeholders seek to articulate their positions to accommodate journalistic norms and to win support, competing for news media attention. The more a particular stakeholder group is quoted in news articles, the more prominently their particular issue definition is represented in news coverage. In this process, news media content is a dependent variable, influenced by comments and activities of some stakeholders who are external to the news organization.

Conflict among competing stakeholders is a main driving force for news. Usual discussions of news values state that conflict provides the drama needed to attract audiences and that the level of conflict indicates the passions felt and therefore the importance of the story. Perhaps more important, conflict motivates stakeholders to increase their efforts to shape media content. Stakeholders make substantial efforts to have their points of view reflected in news media. The notion of "information subsidies" described by Gandy (1982) and extended by Turk (1986, 1988) reveals the extent to which public relations practitioners go to accommodate journalists.

The Resonance Phase. The frames of one or another stakeholder groups become ascendant when they resonate with the values and experiences of the public. What happens is a cyclical process similar to that described by Noelle-Neumann (1984) in her Spiral of Silence Theory. That is, as one side of an issue gains support, it gains potency to drive out advocacy for the opposing side. When groups see that one frame articulation is resonating they adjust their rhetoric. Groups that find their position enhanced by the resonant frame use its terminology to promote their point of view. Those whose side is diminished can find that they must use the resonant frame terminology if only to counter it, which diminishes the resources that they can allocate to their own frame terms.

Whereas Noelle-Neumann (1984) holds that fear of isolation is the motivating factor driving the spiraling process, we hold to a contrasting point of view; groups and individuals articulate their positions when they sense that they have a chance of winning converts, and they become reticent when they see that their message would fall on deaf ears. The spiral then is driven by positive motivations to effect change rather than negative emotions to avoid social isolation.

The U.S. Health Care Debate of 1992 provides an example of how this process operates. During the 1992 election campaign President Clinton appeared to gain support through advocacy of a National Health Care Plan, framed in terms of universal access. In 1994 when specific legislation was under consideration, however, opponents of the plan reframed it as an issue of meddlesome, big government and freedom of choice. The opponents' position resonated and drove competing frames from the public discourse.

The Equilibrium or Resolution Phase. When the resonance process is complete, one frame comes to dominate debate, and decision makers set public policy to conform to it. In this situation proponents of the losing frame see no opportunities to win converts under their old frame. In this case, they can either adjust their rhetoric to the new frame or concede and withdraw from the policy debate. The winning frame can so dominate that others are delegitimized and given no credence in the media and public discourse. When this occurs the dominant frame could be said to be acting hegemonically, rendering "natural" the prevailing definition of the situation.

Stilling debate, however, does not mean that opposition to the dominant position has ceased. In fact, there are a number of intractable policy issues that go through periods of quiet. As Schon and Rien (1994) stated, "When policy controversies are enduring and invulnerable to evidence, what tends to result is an institutionalized political contention leading either to stalemate or to pendulum swings from one extreme to the other" (p. 8). Events that bring new factual information to the fore can break the equilibrium and place an issue back on the policy agenda. This point is well illustrated by

the series of school murders in 1998 and 1999 that forced the gun control issue into public debate. The resulting demand for news coverage forced
news media to provide opportunities for proponents of gun control to articulate their position.

TESTING FRAMING PROPOSITIONS

Our approach to empirical examination of news framing is derived from traditional explications of the concept. Following Tuchman (1976), we hold
that stakeholders (and the news media) create frames by means of "identifying some items as facts" by choosing words that signify those items, and
that items are treated as "non-facts" when words signifying them are excluded from discourse. Following Gitlin (1980), we hold that the "principles
of selection, emphasis and presentation" are manifest in the words actors
use, and that these choices represent what he calls "tacit little theories
about what exists, what happens, and what matters."

Frame Terms

Frames are manifest in the patterns of symbols that people choose to argue
for their positions. As Entman (1993) said, frames can be detected by probing for "the presence or absence of certain key words" (p. 53). Of course,
these key words are not of themselves the frames. Rather, the words are indicative of perspectives, or points of view, by which issues and events can
be discussed and interpreted. A qualitative researcher investigates frames
in a variety of manifestations, including figures of speech, pictures, and
catch phrases. We focus on the choice of words used in news releases and
news content to determine how different groups selectively define an issue,
and to what degree they succeed in placing their definition discussed in the
media.

We have devised quantitative methods for determining and studying
framing by stakeholder groups articulating their positions on contentious
issues.[1] These methods generally begin with computerized content analysis
of partisan texts such as news releases from competing groups. We then
use multidimensional scaling and cluster analysis to ascertain "frame
terms" that tend to be associated exclusively with one or another of the
stakeholder groups, signifying the frames. These methods are described
more completely in Miller (1997) and in Miller and Riechert (in press). The
frame terms must be examined to assure that they form coherent patterns

---

[1]These methods are described more completely in Miller (1997) and in Miller and Riechert
(in press).

and are indicative of the values that underlie a stakeholder's point of view. In our research on the issue of wetlands preservation, for example, we found that property owners selected words to frame the issue as one of property rights. Conservationists discuss wetlands conservation in different terms, focusing instead on the aspects relating to wildlife habitat and habitat preservation or restoration (Riechert, 1996). Of course, some terms that are associated with a stakeholder group's texts are indicative of such things as spokespersons or organizations, which are not properly called frame terms.

Stakeholders can choose words for articulating their frames in several ways. These symbol choices can be based solely on the worldview of the people articulating them. For example, it may be that landowners articulate their position on wetlands conservation in terms of property rights solely because that's how conservation interest groups may see the issue. On the other hand, stakeholders' choice of frame terms could be sophisticated and based on assessments of what will capture news media and public attention. Such choice even could be based on focus group or survey research. For example, it appears that opponents of the Clinton health care plan chose to frame it in terms of burdensome bureaucracy and intrusion on patients' rights because research indicated that these frames would effectively undermine support.

Frame Mapping

Conceiving of these competing issues frames as being signified by the frame terms used by competing stakeholders allows us to investigate explicitly their existence in news coverage. The precise measurement capability of computer content analysis is ideally suited to compare their relative prominence. For several years we have been working on computer programs and procedures for analyzing public discourse, primarily news stories and news releases. Because our approach relies on multidimensional scaling techniques that result in spatial representations of issue frames, we call our approach "frame mapping." Our approach examines policy processes by comparing issue representations by different stakeholders using this frame mapping.

Our studies have employed stakeholder texts such as news releases that are available in full text from online information services and from the World Wide Web. Such texts reflect public discourse and are easily analyzed by computer. The methods are described in Riechert (1996), Miller (1997) and Miller and Riechert (in press). They have been used to study framing of a variety of issues including pesticides (Miller & Riechert, 1994), wetlands regulation (Riechert, 1996), hate speech (Miller & Andsager, 1997), and silicone breast implants (Andsager & Smiley, 1998).

The computer programs, called VBPro, distributed with user manuals at no charge, perform a number of routine content analysis functions, including counting and sorting words, tagging key works in context, and coding collections of texts for frequency of occurrence of words or phrases by sentence, paragraph, or user defined document. (The VBPro family of computer programs are available on the World Wide Web at: *http://excellent.com.utk.edu/~mmmiller/vbpro.html*). A specialized program, called VBMap, provides the coordinates for creating maps of the relative positions of concepts based on their frequency of co-occurrence within a defined unit. Although VBPro can be programmed to code for sentence or paragraphs, we typically use the news release or news story as the unit. On these maps, terms that tend to co-occur appear close together, whereas those that tend not to co-occur appear far apart. Such visual configurations present a convenient snapshot of the relationships among sets of terms.

The VBMap program begins by calculating a term-by-term matrix of cosine coefficients that are based on the frequencies of term co-occurrence within each coding unit, typically a news release or news story. The cosine coefficient, a cousin of the Pearson's r, is the sum of the frequency cross products for each pair of terms divided by the square the product of their sums of squares. The coefficient takes on its upper limit of 1 when the proportions of occurrence are identical in each unit and a lower limit of 0 when the terms never co-occur.

VBMap extracts the eigenvectors from the cosine coefficient matrix after it has been centered such that matrix row and column averages all equal 0. These eigenvectors can be used as coordinates to plot the positions of terms in a multidimensional space. Typically we extract only the first three eigenvectors, which is the maximum that can be plotted conveniently. Three eigenvectors usually account for only a small percentage of the available variance (usually in the teens). As shown in the examples presented shortly, however, this amount of variance is sufficient to provide results in terms of the ways words cluster together and separation between clusters. More empirical and analytic work is needed to determine the optimal number of eigenvecters. Also, we have had little success in providing meaningful labels for the dimensions, as is common practice in conventional factor analysis.

We cluster analyze the coordinates from the VBMap output to ascertain which sets of terms "belong together." By inserting pseudoterms or codes that identify the sources of a given text prior to the analysis, we are able to determine which terms tend to be uniquely associated with a source. Because source identifiers are exhaustive and mutually exclusive they can never co-occur. This means that they will not be joined together until later stages of the cluster analysis. Thus, the terms chosen to represent the frames of the differing sources will be those that cluster with their source identifiers early in the cluster analysis. After we use the techniques described earlier to derive lists of frame terms from advocacy group texts, they are used to investigate propositions about their presence in news. That is, the mean frequency of occurrence of terms in news stories is taken as the degree to which that story reflects the frame of the advocacy group from whose texts the terms were derived.

The usefulness of the frame mapping method in investigating stakeholder debates of policy issues is demonstrated in ongoing studies by the authors. Policy debates related to the conservation and regulation of wetlands are among topics examined. News releases from conservation advocacy groups (such as National Audubon Society) and property-owner advocacy groups (such as American Farm Bureau Federation) were subjected to the multidimensional scaling analysis procedures to identify the sets of terms unique to the issue discussion by each group. The hierarchical cluster analysis procedures specified two distinct sets of terms manifest as most representative of each stakeholder group's discussion.

For example, the terms *river, natural, wildlife, species, conservation, watershed,* and so on, representative of the conservation frame (listed in Table 5.1), indicate that conservation advocacy groups are interested in conservation of natural resources such as forests and rivers; they want to protect and restore diverse ecosystems serving as habitat for endangered species such as migratory birds and other wildlife. The terms selected by frame mapping as representative of the property-owner frame include *farm, farmers, property, rights, agriculture, regulations, private, regulatory,* and so forth (see Table 5.1), revealing a much different focus of the property-owner advocacy groups in the debates on wetlands policy. Not surprisingly these property-owner advocates are concerned with the rights of private property owners, particularly in the agricultural community; they promote legislative reform in wetlands definition and regulation, and they seek compensation to landowners such as farmers and ranchers.

These distinctive sets of terms representing the contrasting stakeholder frames become useful as variables in comparing frame representation in news media coverage. Computer-assisted content analysis allows for precise comparisons of the occurrence of the frame terms in hundreds or thousands of news articles. As argued by Entman (1991, p. 7), "frames can be detected by probing for particular words." Once these representative co-occurring sets of terms are identified for each frame, their occurrence can be measured and tracked precisely in enormous sets of text. In fact, this type of examination revealed that in news coverage of U.S. wetlands by the Associated Press (AP), the conservation frame dominated from 1984 until 1990, at which time the property-owner frame gained dominance. Relatively similar prominence for the two frames overall is seen in the 1,465 AP articles from 1984 to 1995, which contained a total of 13,052 occurrences of con-

TABLE 5.1
Frame Terms for Conservation and Property Owner Advocates in the
Wetlands Issue, Identified Through Frame Mapping Procedures
as Most Representative of the Group's Discussion in News Releases

Conservation Advocates	Property Owner Advocates
River	Farm
Natural	Farmers
Wildlife	Property
Species	Rights
Conservation	Agriculture
Watershed	Regulations
Everglades	Legislation
Endangered	Private
Society	Landowners
Project	Compensation
Protect	Agencies
Bird	Support
Bay	Legislative
Acres	Wetland
Threatened	Statewide
Birds	Definition
Habitat	Agricultural
Fish	Owners
Ecosystem	Ranchers
Migratory	Supports
Ecosystems	Lawmakers
Area	Balance
Rare	Court
Earth	Issue
Forests	State
Preserve	Congressional
Restore	Business
Research	Laws
Protected	Law

servation frame terms, compared to 13,622 occurrences of property-owner frame terms.

Examination of news coverage on wetlands by year reveals the stunning shift in frame dominance. In 1984 to 1985, for example, 43 wetlands news articles contained 350 conservation frame terms and 237 property-owner frame terms, for a mean of 8.14 and 5.51, respectively. Comparisons by year show a reverse of frame dominance in 1990 and 1991, continuing at least through 1994 and 1995, during which 169 AP articles on U.S. wetlands contained 1,323 conservation frame terms and 2,526 property-owner frame terms, for a mean of 7.83 and 14.94, respectively.

The influence of stakeholders on the content of news media is confirmed in examination of these same articles by source. When conservation advocacy groups were quoted as news source in the articles, whether directly or indirectly, their frame terms appeared more frequently, resulting in more prominent representation of their frame compared to the property owner frame. Similarly, and as would be expected, when the news articles gave attribution to the property-owner advocacy groups, the property owner frame terms appeared more frequently. This pattern was observed under three conditions: when stakeholders were quoted at all (even indirectly), when they were quoted directly, and when they were the first-quoted news source in the article. These kinds of relationships are easily studied using the frequency of occurrences of frame terms as variables in statistical tests.

The employment of frame terms to create variables in content analysis is equally useful in extracting articles from huge text sets, separating and ranking them by relative prominence of one or another frame. This kind of sorting, ranking, and reviewing of the articles indicates the validity of the procedures to discern the opposing frames. For example, the computer programs easily extract from the data set of 1,465 wetlands news articles the articles with the most frequent occurrence of terms representing the conservation frame. These include an April 8, 1992, article that begins,

> A conservation group says the Columbia and Snake River system is the most endangered in North America, with more than 200 species of fish imperiled by dams and development in Oregon, Washington and Idaho.

The article, datelined Washington, contains 45 conservation frame terms and 2 property owner frame terms.

Articles that most prominently represent the contrasting property owner frame are sorted with equal ease. These include a March 3, 1995, AP article that leads with this:

> Declaring an assault on arrogant government, the House approved a bill today requiring federal agencies to compensate landowners for restrictions that protect wetlands and endangered species.

Also datelined Washington, the article contains 53 property-owner frame terms and 16 conservation frame terms.

The content analysis programs allow for an enormous array of precise comparisons and statistical tests relating to frame prominence and shifts in frame dominance. We do not propose that these methods should replace other kinds of framing analysis; however, we have demonstrated that they can effectively compliment, and be incorporated with, other types of framing studies. Research to date has made us confident that frame mapping provides a reliable, rigorous, and precise method for investigating framing processes. The research also points to the general utility of the theory we have outlined. There is, of course, a need to test propositions derived directly from Spiral of Opportunity Theory. Examining the visibility of competing frames at various phases in the framing process could do this. Of course, additional propositions could be tested on such important phenomena as the impact of various public relations strategies on placement of frames in news, or the impact of frames on public opinion.

CONCLUSIONS

In this chapter we have addressed the need for a more integrative approach called for by Entman (1993) by proposing a set of identifiable stages in which framing can be investigated in public discourse and mass media content, in a process we call the Spiral of Opportunity. We conceptualize news media framing of issues as an ongoing process in which journalists and contending stakeholders interact. Thus we must examine the imperatives under which journalists operate and how stakeholders attempt to exploit these imperatives. Journalists in turn capitalize on conflict between stakeholders, which in turn motivates stakeholders to provide journalists with the grist for producing news in a manner that is economical and convenient.

We have addressed the need for more precise analytic methods by proposing Frame Mapping, a new computer assisted content analysis method that incorporates cluster analysis and multidimensional scaling. The method is well suited for identifying multiple coexisting frames and for comparing their prominence in texts, such as news releases and mass media content. This chapter, therefore, has built on the foundations of framing scholarship by offering a broad guiding theory with which communication scholars may continue their studies.

REFERENCES

Andsager, J. L., & Smiley, L. (1998). Evaluating public information: shaping news coverage of the silicone implant controversy. *Public Relations Review 24*(2), 183–201.

Berelson, B., Lazarsfeld, P., & McPhee, W. (1954). *Voting: A study of opinion formation in a presidential campaign*. Chicago: University of Chicago Press.

Blumer, H. (1946). Collective behavior. In A. M. Lee (Ed.), *New outlines of the principles of sociology*. New York: Barnes & Noble.

Cobb, R. W., & Elder, C. D. (1983). *Participation in American politics: The dynamics of agenda-building* (2nd ed.). Baltimore: The Johns Hopkins University Press.

Dearing, J. W., & Rogers, E. M. (1996). *Communication concepts 6: Agenda-setting*. Thousand Oaks, CA: Sage.

Downs, A. (1972). Up and down with ecology—The "issue-attention" cycle. *The Public Interest, 28,* 28–50.

Entman, R. M. (1991). Framing U.S. coverage of international news: Contrasts in narratives of the KAL and Iran Air incidents. *Journal of Communication, 41*(4), 6–27.

Entman, R. (1993). Framing: Toward clarification of a fractured paradigm. *Journal of Communication, 43*(3), 51–58.

Gandy, O. J., Jr. (1982). *Beyond agenda setting: Information subsidies and public policy.* Norwood, NJ: Ablex.

Gitlin, T. (1980). *The whole world is watching: Mass media and the making and unmaking of the new left.* Berkeley: University of California Press.

Hallahan, K. (1999). Seven models of framing: Implications for public relations. *Journal of Public Relations Research, 11*(3), 205–242.

Hallin, D. (1987). Hegemony: The American news media from Vietnam to El Salvador: A study in ideological change and its limits. In. D. Paletz (Ed.), *Political communication research: Approaches, studies, assessments.* Norwood, NJ: Ablex.

Kelley, S. (1960). *Political campaigning: Problems in creating an informed electorate.* Washington: Brookings Institute.

Lippmann, W. (1922). *Public opinion, the press, and public policy.* Westport, CT: Praeger.

Lyons, W., Scheb, J. M., III, & Richardson, L. E., Jr. (1995). *American government: Politics and political culture.* Minneapolis: MN: West.

Manheim, J. B. (1987). A model of agenda dynamics. In M. L. McLaughlin (Ed.), *Communication yearbook 10* (pp. 499–515). Newbury Park, CA: Sage.

Miller, M. M. (1997). Frame mapping and analysis of news coverage of contentious issues. *Social Science Computing Review 15*(4), 367–378.

Miller, M. M., & Andsager, J. L. (1997). Media framing of hate speech: From campus to the public sphere. *Newspaper Research Journal, 18*(3–4), 2–15.

Miller, M. M., & Riechert, B. P. (1994, August). *Identifying themes via concept mapping: A new method of content analysis.* Paper presented at the annual meeting of the Association for Education in Journalism and Mass Communication, Atlanta.

Miller, M. M., & Riechert, B. P. (in press). Frame mapping: A new method for investigating issues. In M. D. West (Ed.), *Computer content analysis: Theory, methods, applications.* Norwood, NJ: Ablex.

Noelle-Neumann, E. (1984). *Spiral of silence: Our social skin.* Chicago, University of Chicago Press.

Park R. E. (1972). *The crowd and the public and other essays.* Chicago: University of Chicago Press. (Originally published 1904).

Riechert, B. P. (1996). Advocacy group and news media framing of public policy issues: Frame mapping the wetlands debates. *Dissertation Abstracts International,* 57(07A), 2723. (University Microforms No. 9636566)

Schon, D.A., & Rien, M. (1994). *Frame reflection: Toward the resolution of intractable policy controversies.* New York: Basic Books.

Schramm, W. (1949). The nature of news. In W. Schramm (Ed.), *Mass communications.* Urbana: University of Illinois Press.

Shoemaker, P., & Reese, S. (1996). *Mediating the message: Theories of influence on mass media content.* White Plains, NY: Longman. (Original publication 1991)

Tuchman, G. (1976). The news' manufacture of sociological data. *American Sociological Review, 41*, 1065–1067.

Turk, J. V. (1986). Information subsidies and media content: A study of public relations influence on the news, *Journalism Monographs.* 100.

Turk, J. V. (1988). Public relations influence on the news. In R. E. Hebert (Ed.), *Precision public relations* (pp. 224–239). White Plains, NY: Longman.

6

Breaching Powerful Boundaries: A Postmodern Critique of Framing

Frank D. Durham

"What we 'know' about the nature of the social world depends upon how we frame and interpret the cues we receive about that world," according to Edelman (1993, p. 231). By treating news frames as evidence of a system that defines what we know and how we know it, it is possible to consider the mass mediated practice of framing as a social process that enables society to function. As an exercise in the construction of meaning, it codifies some social experiences or voices into discrete units of social meaning recognized as "frames." Prominent approaches to this phenomenon include work by Edelman (1993), Entman (1993), Gamson (1988), Gamson and Modigliani (1989), Gans (1979), Gitlin (1980), and Pan and Kosicki (1993), which I hereafter refer to as "the literature" on framing.

Although this process makes social interaction more likely, it comes at the expense of cultural and ideological diversity, the main point I address in this chapter. The early gatekeeping studies (Gieber, 1956; Glasgow Media Group, 1976; Hirsch, 1977; McQuail, 1977; White, 1950) first recognized that to define certain meanings others must be excluded. They approached this question in terms of how subjective are the decisions made by news editors in selecting news content. According to McQuail (1987), the consensus within that literature is that, although patterns exist in selecting what becomes news, the process is not a subjective one. In McQuail's judgment,

> The gate-keeping concept, despite its usefulness and its potential for dealing with many different media situations, has a built-in limitation in its implication

that news arrives in ready-made and unproblematic event-story form at the
"gates" of the media, where it is either admitted or excluded. (p. 163)

Instead of this rational model presumed by the gatekeeping concept,
McQuail (1987) suggested that the information that eventually becomes
"news" comes from diverse places and "in different forms." The diversity of
this raw information often means that the news must be constructed ". . .
according to schemes of interpretation and of relevance which are those of
the bureaucratic institutions that are sources of news or which process
events (police departments, court, welfare agencies, government commit-
tees, etc.)" (p. 163).

In McQuail's terms, the rationalization of the news-making process
comes not from gatekeepers but from their systemic interaction with other
rational institutions. As if to bridge Edelman's (1993) social meaning of framing to the journalistic practice of creating frames, McQuail quoted Fishman
(1982): "What is known and knowable by the media depends on the informa-
tion-gathering and information-processing resources' of these agencies" (p.
163). In a study that interpreted the conditions that make framing likely, I
concluded that framing the news depends on the ability of reporters and
sources to share ideological assumptions about what constitutes evidence
and how to construct a frame with it (Durham, 1998).

In this chapter, I explore the same conceptual trajectory but in terms
that go beyond those offered by the gatekeeping literature. Instead of
studying the working context of journalism, I take McQuail's critique of the
institutional system of journalism as a point of departure to consider the
underlying philosophical and ideological bases of news-making as a rational
process. By critiquing the production and meaning of frames, I propose to
learn more about the ideology that underpins journalism by interpreting
what journalism as a social practice actually means to questions of constructed reality, how it arrives at that meaning, and what the implications
are for alternative forms of journalism.

TRADITIONAL CONCEPTS OF FRAMING

In traditionally empirical terms, concepts of framing offer a dichotomous
way to sort experience into—and out of—social relevance and power. According to Entman (1993) in his summary of the field,

> To frame is to *select some aspects of a perceived reality and make them more sa-
> lient in a communicating text, in such a way as to promote a particular problem
> definition, causal interpretation, moral evaluation, and/or treatment recommen-
> dation* for the item described. (p. 52; italics in original)

In this sorting process, being able to designate "salience" reflects the social power of journalism, which lies precisely in the inclusion of certain voices in normative social discourse and the exclusion of others.

In their various analyses, Edelman (1993), Gamson (1988), Gamson and Modigliani (1989), Gans (1979), Pan and Kosicki (1993), and Snow and Benford (1988) focus on the ways in which frames work to support social interaction. Entman's (1993) reference to Goffman's (1974) molar concept of "primary frameworks" underscores this point. As it helps us to locate each other in time and space, journalism presents a rational pursuit used to make order out of disorder. As such, journalists depend on establishing categories of social experience through frames. Perhaps Edelman (1993) expressed the empirical basis of framing most elegantly, when he wrote, "Categorization is, in fact, the necessary condition of abstract thought and of the utilization of symbols" (p. 232).

In these terms, the framing process would operate as follows:

> *Communicators* make conscious or unconscious decisions in deciding what to say, guided by frames (often called schemata) that organize their belief systems. The text contains the frames, which are manifested by the presence or absence of certain keywords, stock phrases, stereotyped images, sources of information, and sentences that provide thematically reinforcing clusters of facts or judgments (Entman, 1993, p. 52; italics in the original).

Similarly, Pan and Kosicki (1993) have explained,

> [W]e may conceive a news media frame as a cognitive device used in information encoding, interpreting, and retrieving; it is communicable; and it is related to journalistic routines and conventions. Framing, therefore, may be studied as a strategy of constructing and processing news discourse or as a characteristic of the discourse itself. (p. 57)

In describing "issues cultures," "arenas," or "packages," Gamson (1988) has conceptualized the broader meaning systems within which frames function (pp. 221–222). As these concepts variously map the empirical process of framing, they explain its normative ideological process as one of disparities between social norms and efforts for change. As Gamson (1988) suggested, "It is useful to think of themes dialectically. There is no theme without a countertheme. The theme is conventional and normative; the countertheme is adversarial and contentious" (p. 221). As he conceptualized the production of social structure as one of conflict over meaning, Gamson (1988) described an empirically modernist approach to communication. Indeed, this conflict between the "normative" and the "contentious," or the dominant and the "adversarial," signals—but does explicate—a modernist power relation that is at the epistemological heart of framing, and, namely, of the preservation of dominant power.

As they focus on the meanings that are manifest in news texts, the framing concepts considered thus far consider neither the implications of such a closed meaning system nor the broader, nonbinary social positions of the meanings at play in the production, transmission, and reception of news messages. In another example, when Snow and Benford (1988) wrote that frames "assign meaning to and interpret relevant events and conditions" (p. 198), the authors do not reflect on the implications for framing as a statement of dominant social power through the exclusion of other, competing meanings.

Frames and Power

Even as his work primarily addresses the text-based analyses of frames represented (above), Entman (1993) expanded the level of his analysis to outline the powerful implications of this process: "Analysis of frames illuminates the precise way in which influence over a human consciousness is exerted by the transfer (or communication) of information from one location—such as a speech, utterance, news report, or novel—to that consciousness" (1993, pp. 51–52).

Still, it is Gitlin (1980), a sociologist, who best advanced the social problematic of framing through Gramsci's (1971) concept of "hegemony." As he explicated the embedded nature of ideology, he also implicitly explained framing:

> [T]hose who rule the dominant institutions secure their power in large measure directly *and indirectly,* by impressing their definitions of the situation upon those they rule, and, if not usurping the whole of ideological space, still significantly limiting what is thought throughout society. (p. 10; italics in original)

In his analysis of mainstream news coverage of the New Left and the student protest movement of the 1960s, Gitlin focuses on the frame as the site where dominant social power is produced. In those terms, he studies the contest for the frame in terms of how hegemony is reproduced through the media, and what that can mean to otherwise marginalized groups. In this, Gitlin takes the same approach as the more micro-level theorists discussed earlier by operationalizing construction of social reality as one of inclusion or exclusion—all within a closed system where power is either accessed or not.

In terms of the range of levels of analysis represented in the literature—from studying dimensions of the text's manifest meanings to analyzing the social implications of framing—Gitlin's work presents the most macro-level version of an empirical analysis of framing. As such, it gives this chapter a point of departure for considering other, nonempirical, or "interpretive," ways of knowing about social meanings, including concepts of framing.

Assuming that journalism is a rational pursuit born of the Enlightenment and predicated on the assumption of dichotomies—for example, between the quantitative and qualitative, the nomothetic and the idiographic, the included and the excluded—for the empirical construction of reality (Christians, 1995), then accounting for the social meaning of framing means examining the philosophy of positivism as the basis for the dominant social ideology represented in the framing literature. By critiquing the epistemological limitations of the empirical framing theories presented here, it becomes possible to interpret the broader, discontinuous qualities of the holistic social process that journalism helps to produce in the name of social "unity." It also means being able to depart from empiricism as the basis for understanding these questions, which I explain in the following section.

PROBLEMATIZING THE FRAME: JAMESON'S POSTMODERN THEORY

To go beyond previous considerations of what gets into the news and what gets left out, it is important to ask what it means that such rational dichotomies dominate the news-making process. This requires another way to know about news and the construction of social meaning. Using Jameson's (1984, 1991) concept of ideologically discrete "social narratives," I propose that all social meanings do not depend on their being included or excluded from an empirical meaning system or news frame. Conversely, while the literature on framing acknowledges the dichotomous nature of the framing process (cf. Edelman, 1993; Entman, 1993; Gamson, 1988; Gamson & Modigliani, 1989; Gans, 1979; Pan & Kosicki, 1993; Snow & Benford, 1988), nowhere is attention paid to the social meanings that do not survive as frames. Yet, these meanings are important, especially as understanding them can tell us more about how framing happens within an holistic context. Instead of being included or excluded, Jameson proposes that it is possible for meanings to exist apart from an empirically ordered universe.

The difference between the position represented in the literature, which represents an empirical perspective, and this Jamesonian critique of framing can be expressed as the difference between empirical reasoning descended from the Enlightenment and interpretive or "dialectical" thought descended from Marx (Jameson, 1971). For each position, the question is one of power over who gets to nominate—and, therefore, to control—social meaning. According to Jameson,

> The dominant ideology of the Western countries is clearly the Anglo-American empirical realism for which all dialectical thinking represents a

threat, and whose mission is essentially to serve as a check on social consciousness. . . . The method of such thinking, in its various forms and guises,
consists in separating reality into airtight compartments, carefully distinguishing the political from the economic, the sociological from the historical,
so that the full implications of any given problem can never come fully into
view; and limiting all statements to the discrete and immediately verifiable, in
order to rule out any speculative and totalizing thought which might lead to a
vision of life as a whole. (1971, pp. 367–368)

The power conflict for Jameson comes from his postmodern philosophical
notion that "the truth is the whole" and that the "airtight compartments"
that are frames make a complete social consciousness impossible (Gross,
1989, pp. 101–102).

To characterize the "postmodern" and the "modern" in this chapter, I define an epistemological distinction by comparing Jameson's theory to
Habermas (1984). The difference is one of either accepting the value of rationalism—of reifying frames as a fundamental method of social organization—or doubting it. What makes Jameson a postmodernist, in part, is his
skepticism of rationalism. This stand contrasts with the emancipatory optimism that Habermas finds in the same rationally defined and constructed
social order he lauds as the "project of modernity." According to Swinge-
wood (1998), far from limiting the possibilities of human knowledge and
understanding, for Habermas "the rationalisation and differentiation of
spheres, with their concomitant specialised culture, opens the way to the
production of knowledge, criticism and communication" (pp. 151–152).

In *The Theory of Communicative Action*, Habermas (1984) explained,
"[R]ationality has less to do with the possession of knowledge than with
how speaking and acting subjects *acquire and use knowledge*" (p. 8; italics in
the original). In the case of news framing, the divergence between the
postmodern and empirical positions represented by Jameson and
Habermas, respectively, centers on the organization of social meaning that
we have inherited from the Enlightenment. Specifically, the question becomes how to understand the powerful implications of frames and framing,
and how to imagine knowing more than such powerful boundaries allow.

JOURNALISM AND IDEOLOGY

Identifying the practice of journalism with the dominant ideology that Jameson (1971) called "empirical realism" requires proposing a couple of postu-
lates. First, as is consistently represented in the literature, journalism is an
inherently rationalizing practice, reifying social meanings into "frames,"
while excluding other meanings from the dominant discourse. In those
terms, journalism embodies the Enlightenment-based principles designed

to lend order to the world by constructing a reality that is empirically know-able. And it is the system-ness of the way that frames make the world know-able that signals observable power relations, according to whose meanings are included and whose are not.

In such a discussion of power and meaning—and, more specifically, of power *over* meaning—a formal concept of "ideology" becomes useful to track the social process in question. According to Foss (1996), the term, *ideology*, is understood to mean "a pattern or set of ideas, assumptions, beliefs, values, or interpretations of the world by which a culture or group operates" (p. 291). Because journalism depends on the use of logic and a quasi-empirical approach in constructing a totalized reality, examining the philosophy of positivism as its ideological basis makes sense (Bhaskar, 1989).

Positivism as the Ideology of Framing

To reserve the powerful social resource of communication, mass mediated frames limit the range of interpretable meanings by an audience, a point that speaks to the heart of Jameson's (1971) criticism of empirical reality. In this light, the philosophy of positivism becomes the ideology of journalism in the sense that the act of framing creates meaning with powerful effect (Bhaskar, 1989). If this method of definition by exclusion functions in fram-ing, then other, discarded "social narratives," or cultural meanings, must also lie beneath every successful frame. The concept of the social narrative indicates the multiplicity of culturally and ideologically distinct meanings that must be dominated by the rationalism of framing for journalists to make "sense of your world," as promotions for the nightly news promise.

Journalists approach the task of identifying the frame of a news story within this holistic social context to make sense of the disorderly world they encounter in their work. When successful, they accomplish this by im-posing static meanings—frames—on the changing world around it (Giddens, 1979). The definition of a "positive" or "successful" frame depends on inter-preting how the framing process works to accomplish closure of that mean-ing. As I demonstrated earlier (Durham, 1998) and discussed later in the case of *The New York Times'* coverage of the crash of Flight 800, the system of rationalism that produces frames as "news" sometimes fails, especially where the assumptions about rational categories are not shared between reporters and their sources.

Whether they succeed in framing a news story or not, journalists' efforts to codify social meanings manifest the ideology of positivism. Acknowl-edging this premise is ultimately important, for acknowledging the failure to frame a news story would expose a fatal gap in the ideological boundary that journalism exists to maintain between the known and the unknowable, the bound and the unbound, the modern and the postmodern.

FRAMED HISTORY AS A RATIONAL ILLUSION

Framing creates the illusion of a comprehensive history by limiting the universe of possible social meanings contained in each previous frame and, therefore, by limiting how they can be included in subsequent histories. Empirically, only what has been known within frames can stand as the official historical record. In these terms, Habermas' idea that "rationality has less to do with the possession of knowledge than with how speaking and acting subjects *acquire and use knowledge*" (1984, p. 8; italics in the original) becomes anything but "emancipatory." In his criticism of Marx's theory of history, historical materialism, Jameson (1984, 1991) referred to this use of history as "pastiche," whereby narratives of specific events, places, and moments in time lose their authentic meanings when they are invoked to frame contemporary meanings. In Jameson's view, history is not made but lost when frames are treated as if they were part of a continuously retrievable history.[1] For him, they are not. In effect, for Jameson, far from relying on any empirical truth found in "history," only the many social narratives of the present can be reconstructed as meaningful.

According to Jameson (1984), any reliance on "history" intended to be empirical is made false by the use of "de-historicized" references to a past being made to serve the present. He referred to this as "a new connotation of 'pastness' and pseudo-historical depth" (Jameson, 1984, pp. 65–71).[2] Although such social narratives both precede and follow frame formation, the difference is that their meanings are only socially potent *prior* to the definition of a news frame. Afterwards, they have been rendered invisible by framing and to those whose investment is in that dominant reality.

Frames as Pastiche

In my analysis of the *New York Times'* coverage of the TWA Flight 800 crash of 1996 (Durham, 1998), the reporters' coverage of the extended crash investigation—and, in particular, of their daily exchanges with their official sources, the investigators—provided the opportunity to observe journalists struggling to construct a frame of the cause of the crash by using previous frames as historical references.

Beginning on July 17, 1996, the date of the crash, all possible crash scenarios drew consideration for the investigators of the crash of Flight 800, and, thus, as well as for the journalists. Although many notions were con-

---

[1]In a comment that applies to framing and the effect the empiricism has on the construction of a history that it can refer to, Jameson (1984) noted, "In faithful conformity to poststructuralist linguistic theory, the past as 'referent' finds itself gradually bracketed, and then effaced altogether, leaving us nothing but texts" (p. 66).

[2]For an accessible discussion of the topic, see Dowling (1984) and Jameson (1981).

sidered, the effort by journalists seemed to fill the present need to know, more than to make valid comparisons. In effect, the frames that were applied from moment to moment were all playing the role of pastiche.

Aside from the three main possible causes—a bomb, a missile, or a mechanical failure—the FBI allowed that the crash might have been caused by a "suicide bomber," a "revenge attack," or an "insurance scheme" (Johnston, 1996). But the idea that was most salient to the investigators was that of a bomb. As Johnston of *The Times* reported on July 19th,

> In public, government officials were careful today to refer to the fiery plunge of TWA Flight 800 as an accident. But in private, law-enforcement officers said their investigation was by necessity premised on the worst-case scenario: that the downing was caused by a bomb or maybe even a terrorist's missile. (1996, p. B9)

For the journalists, invoking previous, historical news frames that matched the type of event they were considering represented a step toward validating the cause. Clearly, both the forensics experts and *The Times'* journalists were aware of possible, pre-existing frames represented by previously reported stories that had defined apparently comparable events. Prior to the crash, security tensions had been running high. The Olympic games were on in Atlanta, various domestic and international terrorists were on trial, and a Marine barracks had been bombed in Saudi Arabia (Kleinfield, 1996). To explain his personal suspicion that Flight 800 had been a terrorists' target, James K. Kallstrom, assistant director of the FBI's New York office, said, "It's just the tenor of the times" (Scott, 1996, p. A1). In *The Times'* coverage of Flight 800, attempts to frame the story according to bomb and missile frames began with comparisons to the 1988 crash of Pan Am Flight 103 at Lockerbie, Scotland.

As Giddens (1979) suggested, the act of trying to frame the story with reference to historical frames represents journalists' ideological assumptions about their own social position and power: First, that their position among world events was "synchronous," or "timeless," and, second, that their task was to impose order on the changing, or "diachronous," world around them by determining a dominant frame (p. 8). It is this second assumption that previous frames are also available either to be included or excluded into a new frame that leads to frames' being employed as pastiche. Accordingly, as information about the crash became available, the *Times'* reporters, as well as others, made historical comparisons with a litany of other crash stories from around the world.

On July 31, 1996, a round-up story on comparisons ran under the headline, "The fate of Flight 800: The history; Investigators see 'Eerie similarities' with other airliners that blew up" (Van Natta, 1996). As the reporter detailed

the circumstances and causes of other crashes—the Lockerbie crash, an Air
India 747 that was bombed off the Irish coast in 1985, a French DC-10 that ex-
ploded over the Sahara in 1989, the American Airlines 757 that crashed on its
approach to Cali, Columbia, and the ValuJet crash of 1997 in the Everglades—
each story provided support for one of the three potential explanatory
frames of the Flight 800 disaster (Van Natta, 1996; Wald, 1996a, 1996b). As
none of the circumstances reflected in those crash frames bore any relation
to the Flight 800 disaster, we are left with a view of nascent, or emergent,
frames being treated as pastiche within this formative process.

In the end, the failure to designate one of these previous frames as a
model for a present one does not matter here. Any one of these contending
social narratives could have become the dominant, or ultimate, frame, if the
reporters and their sources had been able to agree on how to treat evidence in the analysis of what happened. What does matter is the ideological conceit that previous events could compare so neatly and fit so empirically with the present. If one of the previous frames had been appropriated
as the basis for a frame for the Flight 800 crash, its original meaning would
have to have been so adapted to the contemporary need to explain the
case that it would no longer have represented that past. As things happened in the present case, we have only the opportunity to watch the pro-
tracted effort to frame and, thus, to see how frames become pastiche.

When the journalists in the Flight 800 case instantiated pre-existing news
frames, they were not engaging in simple story-making but, rather, working
within what Thompson (1990) called ideological "relations of domination."
Although the cause of the plane crash was unknown, journalists already
knew previously valid frames—those pre-existing frames as social narratives—that they could tell about why planes, in general, crash. By reaching
for empirical evidence, frames that were themselves a product of dominant
rationalism, journalists were drawing on historical evidence of what Reese
(1990) called their own power "to make sense" of a world that otherwise
might not conform. The idea that journalism instills order in the world from
a self-described, fixed position, while the rest of the world happens around
it, is key to my analysis. In Giddens' (1979) critique, this rationalist preroga-
tive demonstrated by journalists to "reify" social meaning stems from their
collective, ideological assumption that it is the rest of the world that is moving while they make sense of it from a stationary center.

Bhaskar's (1989) explanation of positivism further explained this ideological position as I apply it to framing: "[I]f particular knowledge consists only
of knowledge of atomistic events, then general knowledge can only consist
of a knowledge of their relationships, more particularly of co-existence in
space and succession over time, which must be assumed to be constant"
(p. 52). At the level of the individual frame, such a mechanism for gathering
and joining "atomistic events" into news stories presents a powerful device

for controlling social meaning (p. 52). At a social, historical level, building frames on the basis of other, constructed frames offers journalists a way to perpetually reconstruct journalism as a static institution in an otherwise changing world.

In this view, framing as the production of meaning remains an expression of dominant ideological power. According to Thompson (1990),

> [T]he concept of ideology can be used to refer to the ways in which meaning serves . . . to establish and sustain relations of power which are systematically asymmetrical—what I shall call 'relations of domination.' Ideology, broadly speaking, is *meaning in the service of power* (p. 7; italics in the original).

At the center of this analysis is what Reese (1990) called the "journalistic 'occupational ideology' of objectivity" to make sense of the world in a way that leaves the sense-makers in control of meaning-making. Because it focuses on the routinized control of social meaning, empirical framing theory does not ask about effects outside of its epistemological view. In a typical example, Gamson (1988) represented this ideological position by assuming a central tension between the "normative" and the "adversarial." In doing so, he treats journalism as a temporally static function that must dichotomize and unify the conflict into one or more normative definitions of social order.

Still, in contrast to the empiricized dominance of framing, it remains important to locate social narratives in a diverse social landscape without succumbing to the relativism associated with other postmodern theses. Notably, a concept of power is central to Jameson's (1984) argument. He wrote,

> I have felt . . . that it was only in the light of some conception of a dominant cultural logic or hegemonic norm that genuine difference could be measured and assessed. . . . The postmodern is . . . the force field in which very different kinds of cultural impulses—what Raymond Williams has usefully termed 'residual' and 'emergent' forms of cultural production—must make their way. (p. 57)

Unlike Baudrillard (1983) or Lyotard (1989), whose postmodern theories lack concepts of power, Jameson made the case for a concept of power in social analysis. He explained its necessity for understanding different social and cultural meanings: "If we do not achieve some general sense of the *cultural dominant*, then we fall back into a view of the present as sheer heterogeneity, random difference, a coexistence of a host of distinct forces whose effectivity is undecidable" (p. 57; italics added). Within the argument I am making here, it is essential to recognize that the ideology of journalism—which I have discussed as a modernist practice known by terms including *rationalism, empiricism,* and *positivism*—is the "cultural dominant" against which all other social narratives are interpreted.

If we follow the implications of Jameson's critique of history, then decoding frames as empirical historical records with an understanding of their ideological premises is necessary to understand *whose* particular meanings are included in a generalized version of history, whose are not, and on whose terms they are either included or excluded. By contrast, an empirical history could not be valid enough to represent the Marxian ideal of the Totality, or to know all social narratives, including those that have been excluded from previous frames (Jameson, 1981). Although total consciousness remains an ideal, the goal of journalism should be to allow us to know more than what is contained within the powerful boundaries of frames.

CONCLUSIONS

The point of this chapter has been to understand what journalists do when they make frames and what that process means. Beyond this inquiry, I have not specifically set out to prescribe a new kind of journalism. Still, it seems reasonable to ask what the concepts raised here might add to the contemporary practice of framing. Initially, instead of searching for previous frames as evidence needed to reclaim their power in the present, reporters would react to diversity as the "cultural dominant," instead of empiricism (Jameson, 1984). In that fashion, they would implicitly account for the multitude of social narratives competing for the frame. As a result, their journalism would contribute to a more comprehensive historical record by documenting the figurative "crowd," as well as the outcome of any given event. In this way, a postmodernized journalism would interrogate what Griffin (1992) called the "prismatic" meanings and contradictory meaning systems, or ideologies, that the framing process otherwise excludes. Jameson (1984) proposed just this point when he suggested something that is antithetical to the rational ideology of framing, namely a way to map cultural diversity, instead of quelling it by exclusion. At the end of his essay on the "cultural logic of late capitalism," he described such a process as "an aesthetic of cognitive mapping—a pedagogical political culture which seeks to endow the individual subject with some new heightened sense of its place in the global system . . ." (p. 92). That is what a postmodernized journalism would have to become to "embrace diversity," as institutional voices are so fond of—but so ideologically incapable of—doing.

Also, as Jameson (1984) emphasized in his discussion of the *cultural dominant,* relativism could not be an option in sorting out contending social narratives to identify the meanings for events. Rather than foregoing reportorial conventions, such as evaluating source credibility to determine which meanings matter more to a story, this enhanced journalism would address itself to a wider spectrum of stories and meanings—in effect to get more of the story and more stories. In that way, we could know more about the social world by asking questions of the various social narratives that represent underlying ideologies within the news process, *including* the modernist pattern that legitimates dominant frames. Certainly, contemporary concepts like "public" and "civic" journalism would benefit from an epistemology of social inclusion, especially given that the empirical norm I have described here implicitly mitigates against diversity.

At bottom, in this imagined reportorial method, knowing the frame as *the sole answer* would be anathema to journalists as cultural interpreters. Instead, with the ideological assumption of inclusion in mind, something like accounting for the actual competition of "cultural diversity" would be the norm, instead of reducing that "Total" experience to a single category to preserve the empirical way that Edelman (1993) describes as how "we 'know' about the nature of the social world" (p. 231).

Although creating social continuity may be the first prerequisite of the modernist practice of journalism—and although that continuity certainly functions within the bounds it establishes for itself—the downside of that journalism is that it excludes those social narratives that do not serve to unify that same empirical ideology. The problem is that the same power that forces the present to "make sense" leaves its representation of society incomplete. Because of this, I have challenged the "empirical realism" of framing (Jameson, 1984). The alternative I am proposing is a journalism that would set us free from the imperative to unify social meanings, making us better able to listen to the multitude of voices that such unity quells today.

REFERENCES

Baudrillard, J. (1983). *Simulations*. New York: Semiotext.

Bhaskar, R. (1989). *Reclaiming reality: A critical introduction to contemporary philosophy*. New York: Verso.

Christians, C. (1995). Communication ethics as the basis of genuine democracy. In P. Lee (Ed.), *The democratization of communication* (pp. 75–91). Cardiff: University of Wales Press.

Dowling, W. C. (1984). *Jameson, Althusser, Marx: An introduction to 'the political unconsciousness.'* Ithaca, NY: Cornell University Press.

Durham, F. (1998). News frames as social narratives: TWA Flight 800. *Journal of Communication, 48*(4), 100–117.

Edelman, M. (1993). Contestable categories and public opinion. *Political Communication, 10*(3), 231–242.

Entman, R. M. (1993). Framing: Toward a clarification of a fractured paradigm. *Journal of Communication, 43*(4), 51–58.

Fishman, M. (1982). News and non-events: Making the visible invisible. In J. Ettema & D. C. Whitney (Eds.), *Individuals in mass media organizations* (pp. 219–240). Beverly Hills, CA: Sage.

Gamson, W. (1988). The 1987 Distinguished Lecture: A constructionist approach to mass media and public opinion. *Symbolic Interaction 11*(2), 61–174.

Gamson, W., & Modigliani, A. (1989). Media discourse and public opinion on nuclear power: A constructionist approach. *American Journal of Sociology, 95*(1), 1–37.

Gans, H. J. (1979). *Deciding what's news: A study of the CBS Evening News, NBC Nightly News, Newsweek, and Time.* New York: Pantheon.

Gieber, W. (1956). Across the desk: A study of 16 telegraph operators. *Journalism Quarterly, 33,* 423–433.

Gitlin, T. (1980). *The whole world is watching.* Berkeley: University of California Press.

Glasgow Media Group. (1976). *Bad news.* London: Routledge and Kegan Paul.

Goffman, E. (1974). *Frame analysis: An essay on the organization of experience.* Cambridge, MA: Harvard University Press.

Gramsci, A. (1971). *Selections from the prison notebooks.* Edited and translated by Quintin Hoare and Geoffrey Nowell Smith. New York: International Publishers.

Gross, D. S. (1989). Marxism and resistance: Frederic Jameson and the moment of postmodernism. In D. Kellner (Ed.), *Postmodern Jameson critique* (pp. 96–116). Washington, DC: Institute for Advanced Cultural Studies.

Habermas, J. (1984). *The theory of communicative action* (T. McCarthy, Trans.). Boston: Beacon Press. (Original work published 1981).

Hirsch, P. M. (1977). Occupational, organizational and institutional models in mass communication. In P. M. Hirsch, P. Miller, & F. G. Kline (Eds.), *Strategies for communication research* (pp. 13–42). Beverly Hills: Sage.

Jameson, F. (1971). *Marxism and form: Twentieth century dialectical theories of literature.* Princeton, NJ: Princeton University Press.

Jameson, F. (1981). *The political unconscious: Narrative as a socially symbolic act.* Ithaca, NY: Cornell University Press.

Jameson, F. (1984). Postmodernism, or the cultural logic of late capitalism. *New Left Review, 146,* 53–92.

Jameson, F. (1991). *Postmodernism or, the cultural logic of late capitalism.* Durham, NC: Duke University Press.

Johnston, D. (1996, July 19). Explosion aboard TWA Flight 800: The theories: Multitude of ideas, but little evidence. *The New York Times,* p. B9.

Lyotard, J.-F. (1989). *The Lyotard reader* (A. Benjamin, Ed.). Oxford: Blackwell.

McQuail, D. (1977). *Analysis of newspaper content.* Royal Commission on the press, Research Series 4: HMSO.

McQuail, D. (1987). *Mass communication theory: An introduction.* Beverly Hills, CA: Sage.

Pan, Z., & Kosicki, G. M. (1993). Framing analysis: An approach to news discourse. *Political Communication, 10*(1), 55–73.

Reese, S. D. (1990). The news paradigm and the ideology of objectivity: A socialist at the Wall Street Journal. *Critical Studies in Mass Communication 7,* 390–409.

Scott, J. (1996, July 21). The crash of Flight 800: Looking back; backtracking to find reasons for a tragedy. *The New York Times,* p. A1.

Snow, D., & Benford, R. D. (1988). Ideology, frame resonance, and participant mobilization. *International Social Movement Research, 1,* 197–217.

Van Natta, D. (1996, July 31). The fate of Flight 800: The history; Investigators see 'eerie similarities' with other airliners that blew up. *The New York Times,* p. B5.

Wald, M. (1996a, July 22). The fate of Flight 800: The timetable; Length of crash inquiries varies based on time needed to recover evidence. *The New York Times,* p. B4.

Wald, M. (1996b, July 29). The fate of Flight 800: The search; crews, aided by robots, turn to focus on evidence. *The New York Times,* B5.

White, D. M. (1950). The gatekeeper: A case-study in the selection of the news. *Journalism Quarterly, 27,* 383–390.

PART

II

CASES—OBSERVATIONS
FROM THE FIELD

7

A Multiperspectival Approach to Framing Analysis: A Field Guide

James K. Hertog
Douglas M. McLeod

That framing analysis has risen to a place of prominence in political science, sociology, and media studies is demonstrated by the many and diverse researchers undertaking framing analyses, the wide array of theoretical approaches and methods employed, and the significant and expanding
framing literature—including this volume. It has not, however, settled on a
core theory or even a basic set of propositions, nor has a widely accepted
methodological approach emerged. The range of approaches political scientists, sociologists, media researchers, and others bring to the study of
frames and framing is both a blessing and a curse.

To bring some order to the study of framing, we outline our own developing approach to the study of frames and framing. First, we discuss our approach to frames, structures of meaning found in any culture, and framing,
the construction and use of frames within a society. An analysis of the importance of frames and framing in social process, especially in defining and
channeling social controversy, follows. Once we have outlined our approach, we discuss our method for studying frames and framing as they relate to specific social controversies. Finally, we illustrate our approach to
frames and framing in an exploratory case study of social framing of anarchist protests in Minneapolis during the period from 1986–1988.

FRAMES AND FRAMING

Researchers approach the study of frames and framing in a number of
ways. Such extreme conceptual openness is a blessing in that it allows for
some of the most creative analysis of media in current scholarship. It is a
curse in that findings, methodological insights and theoretical conclusions
don't "add up." The cumulative learning that is supposed to accompany
normal science is not possible. Given the diversity in definitions, theories,
and methods found in framing research, it is essential that researchers outline their own approaches to frame/framing study in detail. Only with such
clarity will it be possible for scholars to choose the best among the wide array of approaches and move toward a coherent set of practices and findings. We hope to contribute by providing an outline of our own approach in
its current stage of development.

The first step in the study of frames and framing is to define the phenomena of interest. Stephen Reese proposed a general definition of frames in
the prologue of this volume:

> Frames are *organizing principles* that are socially *shared* and *persistent* over
> time, that work *symbolically* to meaningfully *structure* the social world (italics
> in original).

Although we agree with much of Reese's definition, we begin our discussion
with a divergence. We view frames as relatively comprehensive structures
of meaning made up of a number of concepts and the relations among
those concepts. Although each frame provides principles for the organization of social reality, frames are more than just principles. Frames have
their own content, as well as a set of rules for the processing of new content.

A core set of concepts determines much of the meaning assigned to the
frame as a whole and, by extension, to all content relating to the frame.
Models of cognitive structure that envision large numbers of concepts
(nodes) grouped together and connected by perceived relationships (links)
can serve as an analogy. The most "important" concepts are linked directly
and strongly to many other concepts. These central concepts and links
form a dense cluster. Moving out from the central concepts in the cluster,
links among nodes are less densely packed and weaker. As one approaches
the periphery, links to other clusters become more common, and nodes act
as bridges to additional clusters. Excitement or activation of one node will
also activate a number of others, with those "closest" or most strongly
linked also most likely to be activated. The meaning generated is a function
of the nodes and links activated and the pattern of relations among them.

We approach frames as cultural rather than cognitive phenomena. Frames, in our analysis, are cultural structures with central ideas and more peripheral concepts—and a set of relations that vary in strength and kind among them. The core concepts at the heart of frames are abstract and general in nature, encompassing a wide array of phenomena. Peripheral concepts may be more concrete and specific but need not be. What is the nature of concepts central to the frame? Some of the most powerful are myths, narratives, and metaphors that resonate within the culture. As many rhetorical and cultural scholars have noted, these cultural phenomena carry extensive meaning to culturally articulate individuals. That is true in at least three ways.

First, they have tremendous symbolic power. Members of the culture have strong affective reactions to the activation of certain myths. These myths are ego-involving. As a member of the society, an individual identifies with the morals, ideals, stories, and definitions of her culture. Certain myths, metaphors, and narratives are deeply embedded within the fabric of the culture—consider narratives such as Washington's crossing of the Delaware, the assassination of President Lincoln, or the Cuban Missile Crisis.

A second source of the power of culturally privileged narratives, metaphors and myths is that they carry "excess meaning." That is, by mentioning one or more of these powerful concepts the array of related ideas, social history, policy choices, heroes, and villains may be activated. A news story defining a political election as a "horse race" implies a tremendous number of additional ideas, beliefs, experiences, and feelings members of society know are related to the term. Framing an election has powerful implications for the way individuals and organizations act toward the election and governance in general. The content of a "horse race" frame is widely divergent from content that would accompany discussion of an election as "elite control."

A third source of power for frames is their widespread recognition. Individuals, organizations, and institutions act in ways that presume members of the society share the frame. All communication is dependent upon shared meaning among communicators. The speaker and the audience must approach words, icons, ideas, gestures, and so on in an identical fashion in order to communicate. The greater the difference in their individual understanding of symbols, the less able they are to communicate. Frames, as part of the deep structure of a culture, provide a significant portion of the shared meaning among society's members. Frames provide the unexpressed but shared knowledge of communicators that allows each to engage in discussion that presumes a set of shared assumptions. At a social level, organizations and institutions can produce content that will be interpreted in the manner intended by their publics. One of the most significant tasks of socialization is to teach new members of society the significant frames employed within a culture to construct social reality. Althusser (1971) identified a number of "ideological state apparatuses" that maintain and reinforce the set of beliefs critical to the maintenance of society. Frames are part of that larger set of beliefs.

As Reese notes, frames are persistent over time. Constructing cultural frames occurs over long periods of time with input from a large number of social actors. Based on a large storehouse of social knowledge, new information is unlikely to significantly alter their meaning. Another reason for their stability is that their function of facilitating communication is dependent upon their stability—if they changed quickly, members of society could not depend on others knowing and acting in accord with frames. Finally, because they are intimately interrelated with social institutions and processes, the stability of institutions in society contributes to the stability of frames. Because frames are valuable for maintaining social order and facilitating interaction, they are taught to new members of society and reinforced among the community at large.

With repeated contact, the individual comes to absorb the frame employed by the organization and to see the world in terms of that frame. Organizational and institutional frames exist to order human behavior in ways that advance organizational goals including the reduction of uncertainty in inputs and outputs, organizational survival and growth, and efficiency in task completion. Organizations are relatively stable social structures, and so we would expect their sponsorship of frames to increase the stability of those cultural structures.

The discussion so far has assumed the symbolic nature of frames—as cultural structures they are conveyed in and through symbols. From birth to death, all members of a culture are confronted with symbolic representation of the culture's significant frames. Frames are not only found in political rhetoric or news coverage, where the greatest research attention has been, but also in entertainment programming, conversations among society's members, interoffice memos, advertising, popular music, even architecture. Culture in its broadest sense is permeated with frames. It is the ubiquitous nature of frame representations that makes them seem "natural" and "obvious" to members of the society.

Finally, Reese's point that frames meaningfully structure the social world also receives support from our earlier discussion. Frames structure our understanding of social phenomena in a number of significant ways.

First, frames determine what content is relevant to discussion of a social concern. The very categorization of individual phenomena, concepts, and ideas into a topic is a framing exercise. Although seemingly obvious, these groupings represent cultural choice-making. As an example, grouping a wide array of phenomena under the heading "economics" is at least partially arbitrary. Like academic gerrymandering, choosing to place one concept or idea within one field of study structures the meaning of that concept very differently than placing it in another field would have. By categorizing phenomena as "in" the frame, other phenomena are defined as "out." That is, phenomena that could potentially be thought of as related to the phenomenon under study are no longer *relevant* to the discussion. If drug-taking is framed as a crime-and-punishment topic, then the potency of the drugs is not an important consideration, nor are the varying effects of different substances, the diseases linked to their use, and so on. Under a public health frame these would be significant concerns.

A second way frames structure our understanding of social phenomena is by defining the roles varied individuals, groups, organizations, and institutions play. Under one frame, a particular group may be seen as an essential actor in resolving a social problem while in another the same group may be perceived as peripheral to its resolution or even a source of the problem itself. In a number of controversial topics government is portrayed in very different ways depending on the frame applied. One such portrayal defines out whole groups of people or organizations, marginalizing them and, by extension, their views. No one shows up at their door for a quote. They are not invited to closed-door policy discussions nor are they privately asked for advice by their neighbors.

Third, frames outline the ways that various beliefs, values, and actions are related. Certain kinds of relationships are privileged by the frame—presenting them as likely and appropriate, whereas others are portrayed as inappropriate, illegitimate, or impossible. That is, even among those concepts that are deemed relevant to a topic, certain kinds of relationships are more or less likely, more or less appropriate, more or less valued.

Fourth, the symbolic representation of a topic, including language use, sentence structure, "code" words, and modifiers is influenced by frame choice. A "Prolife" frame will use terms like baby, abortionist, pro-abortion forces, unborn, mother, murder, and so on whereas the "Prochoice" frame employs fetus, doctor, woman, freedom, etc.

Finally, frames outline the values and goals inherent in the structuring of a content area. Each frame will privilege a given set of goals and ethics over others. This does not mean that it exclusively focuses on one or two moral guides, but that one or a few are core concepts and others peripheral.

Two concepts prominent in the literature must be distinguished from our definition of frames: One is ideology and the other narrative format. A number of authors have treated narrative formats, journalistic story types, and so on as frames. For example, the inverted pyramid of news style has been called a frame (Altheide, 1979). Our approach defines frames as content-based rather than format-based. Formats constitute a set of rules for communicating about a frame, but are not themselves frames. Writing a foreign policy story in a hard news format is not "framing" the topic of that story. Placing it within a constellation of phenomena framed as "first world–third world conflict" would be an act of framing.

Separating ideology and framing is more difficult. Although Hall (1979, 1984) argued that ideology is one of the most important concepts in media studies and is the source of a Renaissance in media/culture studies, the term has fallen on hard times as it has eluded clear definition. Many approaches to ideology portray it is an overarching popular or naïve metaphysics. In each society there exists a dominant approach to the questions of the nature of reality and of the supernatural, the means by which we come to know that reality, and the place of human beings and nature in the world. The abstract and all-encompassing nature of ideology make it difficult to identify empirically and to isolate data that reflect ideology in action. As a result, research meant to determine the presence of ideology or to follow its workings within society seems to flow more from each individual author's worldview than from any agreed-upon research tradition or theoretical base. Hackett (1984) identified framing as one of three completely distinct applications of the term *ideology*: framing, naturalization, and interpellation. His analysis portrays framing as the application of "deep structure" by society's members—including journalists and other media workers. Deep structure includes the taken-for-granted beliefs about the nature of the world and society, the responsibilities and roles of individuals and groups, and the preconscious causal attributions inherent in a culture.

Although separate concepts, ideology and frames are related in important ways. Ideology, as noted earlier, structures the common understanding of the nature of the world that is shared by members of a society. In each society there is a dominant ideology that most members accept without reflection—it is the commonsense of the culture. Certain ways of thinking are taken for granted—"natural." Even so, not all groups within a society accept its dominant ideology, whether their opposition is conscious or not. Competing ideologies come from the society's own history, from contact with other cultures or from conflict within the social structure (Hall, 1984).

Some frames "fit" a given ideology better than others. They better connect with the beliefs about basic social relations, the nature of social organizations, and the engines of social change. The underlying presuppositions about the nature of reality, human agency, epistemology, and so on set up the rules within which a given frame will appear more or less appropriate. Frames tie content together within culturally constructed "topics" such as environmentalism, the economy, politics, and religion. Ideology cuts across the topics, privileging but not determining certain frames within each topic area.

Although certain frames are better suited to certain ideological structures, frames are not completely determined by ideologies. Frames are more narrowly construed than ideology, and a number of frames would "fit" within a given ideology. On occasion, social groups may exhibit different ideologies and yet apply the same frame to a particular topic. As an example, we found that anarchist protesters who reject the underlying capitalist/democratic ideology of the American system still discussed their actions in terms of a "criminal justice" frame that seems to embrace the rejected ideology (Hertog & McLeod, 1995). One reason is because of the difficulty of communicating to potential converts without adopting a culturally privileged frame. Even beyond communicating with the wider public, the anarchists themselves are members of the wider society and share the dominant frames of the culture. Thus, communication among anarchists was enhanced by the adoption of the frame, even though conveying much of their political critique was made more difficult.

Frames are, however, more comprehensive than issues. Issues are fairly narrowly drawn conflicts over social policy. The positions taken on an issue usually share a number of the underlying presumptions provided by a frame. Opposition usually represents competition over funds or methods of reaching a limited set of goals. Republicans and Democrats debate over the amount of money to be allocated to defense, but not whether there should be a defense department. Under a competing frame, the military could be massively defunded or even eliminated.

Issues reside within frames—that is, frames provide the ground rules necessary for an issue to form. Just as the rules of a sports match must be determined before a game is played, so too must the rules of debate over a social phenomenon be determined before a legitimate issue can arise. In the absence of a common frame, there is no evidence, no weighing the strength of arguments that can be used to determine which "side" should prevail. If the very basis for argument itself is contested, no amount of confrontation, negotiation, and discussion can lead to a solution. In Reese's terms, the issue must be structured by the frame.

FRAMING

Frames are relatively stable cultural structures, but new frames are at times created and existing ones modified or replaced, or they may simply fade from use. The processes by which existing cultural frames change and social phenomena are symbolically connected to existing frames take the active verb form of "frame." As we have noted earlier, frames are produced and shaped by the political economy of the society. In their everyday interaction with powerful organizations and institutions, individuals, groups, and organizations are forced to adopt certain beliefs and behaviors in order to be effective. Beyond personal experience, portrayals of human/organizational/institutional interactions permeate the popular culture, further disseminating and reinforcing frames and at the same time shaping and molding them.

A second source of frames is the deliberate attempt of individuals or groups to structure public discourse in a way that privileges their goals and means of attaining them. In our studies, we have found that radical protest is the attempt of groups to reframe a certain social problem, setting new grounds of debate and privileging a very different set of arguments and proposed solutions than does the dominant frame. Feminists attempt to reframe discussions of the appropriate role of men and women in business organizations. The dominant capitalist/business frame justifies lower wage rates for women by arguing that they are more likely than men to take childbearing time off, to move locations when their spouse gets an offer, and less willing to sacrifice time on weekends. Rather than argue that these claims are false, reframing the argument based on social equity could make them far less effective and increase the weight given other points. One might argue that childbearing is the responsibility of the society as a whole and must be borne by institutions as part of doing business, that social mobility is a right of all Americans and cannot be punished in the hiring/wage process, and that equal pay for equal work is a higher value than organizational profit.

Sometimes the ongoing process of social change will contribute new metaphors, narratives, myths, information, knowledge, even new forms of looking at the world. These cultural features can modify existing frames or even build new ones and tear old ones down. The coming of the computer age has changed lives, redesigned business relationships, provided new means and kinds of communication. All of these changes have the potential to alter the frames within a culture.

Sometimes change in frames may even occur as a result of the ongoing fluctuation of tastes, preferences, and beliefs that results from the constant innovation in popular culture. Changes in fashion, television programming, even widely experienced blockbuster movies, can influence frames. Individual cultural artifacts like national newsmagazines, network television shows, and newswire stories. Armies of patrons experience movies like "Titanic," and those who do not see it in the theater are exposed to its publicity and discussion of it through other media. Professionals with great skill produce popular culture artifacts in the form of mythic narratives that provide a powerful common experience for vast audiences. As an example, the phrase "Wag the Dog" was often mentioned in coverage of renewed U.S. conflict with Iraq. President Clinton was facing impeachment at the time, and one scenario portrayed the decision to send troops as an attempt by the White House to divert attention from the impeachment hearings. Newsweek (12/28/98) coverage asked, "The GOP lawmakers demanded to know: Was this a 'Wag the Dog' scenario? Had the president started a war to stall his own impeachment?"

"Wag the Dog" came from the title of a movie that had been released about a staged war to divert attention from a president's sexual dalliance with a young girl. Although "Wag the Dog" would not by itself qualify as a frame, it fits a more general "elite manipulation" frame of politics in general.

WHAT DO FRAMES DO?

Reese uses the term *organizing* to note how frames "make sense" of sets of ideas and phenomena. When a topic is "framed"—that is, connected to an existing cultural frame—the topic's meaning is heavily determined by the frame. Choosing what frame problematic social phenomena are to be placed in may do more to determine their meaning than lengthy discussions of the facts of or arguments toward them.

Frames provide the widely understood context for understanding new phenomena. When a topic is "framed" its context is determined; its major tenets prescribed; individuals, groups, and organizations are assigned the roles of protagonist, antagonist, or spectator; and the legitimacy of varied strategies for action is defined. Once an unfamiliar idea, topic, action, or event has been framed its interpretation is driven by the frame. The frame also is affected, as its meaning adjusts to the addition of the new concept and the reordering of existing elements.

Social activist groups faced with a commonly held frame that impairs their ability to communicate their case may find it difficult to successfully advance their cause. Like a team playing on a steep slope, regardless of their effort or their abilities, the outcome is preordained, the odds too long, the competition weighted too heavily against them. When the applied frame is too detrimental to the group's efforts, it may be wiser to attempt to reframe the debate so that the odds are more in its favor. This is a difficult task and usually unsuccessful, but it represents a major improvement in the group's chances for ultimate success if it can be accomplished.

STUDYING FRAMES

How, then, can we identify, outline, describe and understand frames? What are the features that can be used to identify and model them? To study frames, we recommend a combination of text analyses, review of informed writings or discussions, depth or focus interviews, and ethnography.

The first step in a frame analysis is to identify the central concepts that make up varied frames. A common feature at the core of most frames is a basic conflict. The Cold War frame revolved around a perceived conflict between the United States and the Soviet Union. All other phenomena reflecting a Cold War frame were interpreted as being the result of the superpower conflict, forcing choices between the "poles" of global influence and/or providing support or comfort to one of the "sides," in a way that affected the "global balance." As radical political change has occurred within the Soviet system and the conflict between Russia and the United States declined, many have declared the Cold War to be over. In the absence of the basic driving force of superpower conflict, the entire frame has been undermined.

One indicator of the central conflict is the choice of actors presenting information, ideas, positions within a text. In news text, the sources chosen will structure the discussion. In primetime programming, the character roles will perform the same function. Who is privileged to speak? What individuals, groups, organizations, and so on, are mere spectators or even have no role to play?

A second feature of frames to seek is a master narrative. Narratives are powerful organizing devices, and most frames will have ideal narratives that organize a large amount of disparate ideas and information. Writings within the capitalist/democratic frame often call upon a "Horatio Alger" story as a means to organize and give meaning to what otherwise might be bewildering events and actions. Myths, closely related to narratives ("mythic narratives" are common within a culture), represent another significant set of concepts that may be central to a frame. Myths may be tied to religions, folklore, organizations, institutions, or other significant societal entities. They are widely shared and understood within the culture, and are especially prone to drawing in a wide array of additional beliefs, feelings, expectations, and values. That is, they are especially efficient in making meaning. The culturally competent researcher will recognize them in context. The main problem is that they may not need to be mentioned often to have a profound effect in the process of framing—their very excess meaning and efficiency may make them hard to identify in text. By calling up a metaphor such as "dog fight" to describe competition among candidates in the week before a Republican primary, for example, the rest of the coverage of the story is interpreted within the terms of the metaphor.

Each frame has its own vocabulary. Though it is less efficient to identify frames by identifying the repetition of certain adjectives, adverbs, verb tenses, and nouns, usage can be employed to induce frames in text. For example, the use of *baby* versus *fetus* signals a very different approach to the topic of abortion. Trouble will come when these terms are employed in multiple frames—as they will do more often than narratives or metaphors. Many of these terms are peripheral to frames, but the quantitative pattern of use of multiple terms can help the researcher identify the frame. Perhaps the greatest value of using adjectives, adverbs, and nouns is in enhancing the researcher's ability to identify frame boundaries and the relationships among frames. How much content is shared by what frames and in what patterns? Certainly this is an important set of questions in the attempt to identify the larger structure of popular culture and ideology.

Preparing for Frame Analysis

To prepare for analysis of media texts, you should read widely among ideologically divergent sources. For a successful frame analysis, you must make yourself aware of an array of potential frames for the topic under study. Most researchers view the world with the dominant cultural assumptions, expectations, and blindspots that they want to study. Their ability to identify frames will be greatly enhanced via exposing themselves to content falling outside the cultural mainstream—texts that make the dominant frames problematic. Scholars who work from within a given frame often fail to recognize the culturally determined nature of their analyses—theory, methods, findings, and conclusions.

Reading widely is more important than reading deeply. That is, beyond your review of scholarly literature, you should expose yourself to popular texts chosen to reflect widely divergent points of view. This wide net should include sources from outside the host culture. Particularly useful in this regard are journals aimed toward politically, socially, and culturally diverse groups. Read, for example, right-wing manifestoes, anarchist tracts, capitalist literature. Bone up on your avant-garde critique, feminist opinion, and deep ecology tracts. Read it in the original. If you cannot understand a piece of writing, you may be confronting a potential frame for your topic.

To reach beyond your own culture and "get outside" its imposed frames, material from culturally dissimilar countries should be viewed. Pore over materials from foreign governments as well as public groups, multinational nonprofits, and news outlets. The goal is to gain a broad understanding of the different ways that the topic is understood, not details on the particular events, data, or proposed solutions.

As an example, an unpublished dissertation at the University of Kentucky addressed coverage of the change of Hong Kong sovereignty from England to China that occurred in 1998 (Zhang, 1998). Associated Press coverage treated the historical event as a threat to individual freedom and the economic welfare of Hong Kong residents. Stories focused on press freedom, voting rights, movement of Chinese troops into the area, and so on. Xinhua, the official Chinese news agency, portrayed the return of a long-lost child to its mother, with attendant celebration and reconciliation. These frames are so different as to defy comparison. Reviewing only American sources, though they be diverse, would not have provided an understanding of framing as it occurred for this topic. The American frame fits an individualist culture with a capitalist/democratic system, the Chinese frame a communalist culture with a centralized bureaucratic government and economy.

Analytical Steps

As a framing analyst, you should use the preliminary investigation outlined earlier to: identify characteristics of your own culture that would otherwise be invisible to you; prepare preliminary models of as many frames and subframes as you can identify; match frames to sponsor groups; sensitize yourself to the ways that frames can be represented symbolically; identify change in frames over time; develop basic hypotheses about the relationships among frames, issues, ideology, and narrative structures; and identify appropriate research methods you can use to approach the study of frames in the context of the chosen topic.

One of the most difficult tasks for the researcher is to critically analyze her own culture and its structure. The very taken-for-grantedness of your own culture blinds you to important assumptions, values, and beliefs that should be a matter of critical analysis. Exposing yourself to very different ways of seeing the world helps to make your own culture more transparent. We learn by comparison and come to recognize the assumptions and unreflective acceptance of our own way of doing things. Once made clear, these features of our own culture should be written into the descriptions of frames identified in the preliminary reading.

As a preparation to approach the text under study, you should model the frames encountered in your background research. Central and peripheral concepts, and relationships among them, should be specified. Without a clear idea of what constitutes the core set of concepts and relations, you may assign texts to inappropriate frames, may be unable to categorize large amounts of text, or may be unable to assign boundaries to frames with overlapping content. Specifying the boundaries among frames before the final analysis of text will be especially helpful in improving the validity of the results.

These frame models should be considered guides rather than hard-and-fast coding categories. Use of the models in the text analysis will help to keep you from straying off-track, blurring frame boundaries or unnecessarily multiplying the number of frames. Knowing which concepts and features of frames are central, and which are peripheral, will aid you in relating material to the correct frame. Identifying concepts and relationships that cut across frames will guide you in designating sections of content according to frame.

One of the most frustrating tendencies in the study of frames and framing is the tendency for scholars to generate a unique set of frames for every study of every social phenomenon. It is one of the reasons we have not developed a set of agreed-upon generalizations or parallel conclusions. In the absence of a disciplined approach to analyzing and interpreting the data, researchers are too easily led to find the evidence they are looking for, to discount negative evidence, and to perceive relationships that support their contentions. Our own experience has led to a fairly expansive list of frames relating to media presentation of social protesters (McLeod & Hertog, 1999). Before adding to this list, we need to review the differences among these subframes to determine whether they represent unique phenomena or variations on a smaller population. To develop the field, frames identified in prior work should always be included and tested in subsequent research. Reducing the total number of proposed frames will enhance the field by moving us closer to developing an inventory of the limited number of frames we believe underlie much of social knowledge.

One of the most valuable research concerns in frame–framing research relates to the impact of framing in political conflict. Groups attempting to influence the social agenda attempt to assign their frames to topics of social concern and to oppose the assignation of other groups' frames. Because there will tend to be a dominant frame that is culturally privileged, the success of groups outside the mainstream in doing so will be rare. However, because reframing of an issue or topic can have significant consequences for the success of varied viewpoints, linking frames to groups will be of great use in analyzing social process. When the connection can be made, study of the means used to frame and reframe conflicts can be carried out and tremendously valuable information for media studies generated.

The researcher should also develop a list of symbols, language, usage, narratives, categories, and concepts note in the content to be evaluated. This list can be used to develop measures for text analysis and to guide the sensitive application of those measures. If you are interested in frame evolution, content from more than one time period should be perused. To develop an idea of the evolution of frames, you must develop frame models from at least two time points and then compare the content and structure at different time points.

To guide analysis, you should develop hypotheses about relations among culture, ideology, frames, issues, and narrative structures. Theory development prior to text analysis is pretty rare in frame studies, contributing to the drift that often occurs during the analysis process. Testing of hypotheses would call for more perusal of more content than we suggest you read or watch at this early stage. Waiting until you are faced with a large body of text to carry out this means of focusing your attention and ordering your measurement will often lead to poorly spent data collection and analysis time. It may even cause you to repeat work or lead you down blind alleys. If you make some calculated guesses based on your preliminary review of the data, you can design your text analysis to see to it that the most

152 HERTOG AND McLEOD

important of the concepts are measured and the critical relationships picked up by the method. Again, adjustment during data collection remains an option where appropriate.

Identify appropriate research methods. There are a number of approaches to the analysis of texts. Exposure to an array of potential frames for your topic will help to sensitize you to what your chosen method will need to provide and what kinds of symbolic content it must be sensitive to. Additionally, the preliminary brush with frame content will influence the goals of your research. Because the goals of the research should always drive the choice of methods, the final decision on the research methods should await the outcome of the preliminary frame review.

Texts ranging from straight news accounts to movies to photos to television melodrama to corporate annual reports to focus group transcripts have been analyzed in framing research. In addition to the diversity of texts for analysis, there are many text analysis methods employed. We recommend the use of both qualitative and quantitative methods. We employed both in our research on anarchist protests (Hertog & McLeod, 1995).

Quantitative analysis applied to framing research is usually a means to identify language use in texts. Counting the number of times certain categories are used, terms relating to a frame employed, column inches devoted to a particular source or source category, or the number of times various categories of sources are quoted can be very helpful in ascertaining the frames employed and the rhetoric applied. Quantitative analyses are most successful when a particular set of concepts is clearly related to a frame and the number of times the concept is used reflects the emphasis of that concept or set of concepts in the text. A promising method for building frame models from text has been introduced by Carley (1997). This computer-driven analysis provides a model of the structure, including nodes and links, among a number of concepts found in text. Although still in its early development, this method could provide a set of interlinked maps that would model frames and their interrelationships derived from any of the texts cited before.

One shortcoming of quantitative text analysis methods, however, is that many very powerful concepts, central to frames, need not be repeated often to have a great impact. One or two references may be enough to set the frame for a large amount of content. As an example, conflict among positions is a normal part of news coverage. One group's success framing the coverage may well provoke repeated attempts by the opposition to reframe the issue. Quantitative analysis would conclude that the coverage was framed in terms of the latter, unsuccessful, but oft-repeated attempt to reframe.

Qualitative study of frames is in some ways inevitable. Researchers must apply their cultural expertise to induce the meaning of texts. Human judg-

ment is necessary to approach the essential question about what could
have been in the content but was not. Computer analyses are poorly suited
to determine what is *not* shown. Additionally, because the interpretation of
the symbolic content is dependent upon the cultural competence of those
involved in the communication itself and can never be completely programmed into a computer, direct researcher interaction with texts should
be part of any framing study. The qualitative analysis of texts should include comparison of the idealized frame models developed in preliminary
work to the text of interest. Qualitative text analysis allows you to discover
new insights as part of the coding process. The frame models are simply
guides, and a deep reading should not be overly constrained by them. You
should be prepared to make note of framing differences among authors, editors, organizations, media, classes, and ideological groups. These observations serve as both hypotheses and data that are useful for your final discussion. Notes in the margins, combinations and recombinations of the
text—perhaps using qualitative computer content analysis programs like
NUD*IST—and ongoing note taking guide a dialogue with yourself that
should provide insights in confronting frames that would be impossible
with quantitative content analysis. The ability to learn as a part of the
method itself is one of the strengths of qualitative analysis and should not
be lost in an attempt at "rigor."

Qualitative analysis of frames does present the possibility of idiosyncratic analysis, however. One of the reasons we recommend a mixture of
quantitative and qualitative analysis is the diffuse nature of frames, and
their openness to varied interpretations. The very point that different
researchers will construct very different frames from the same material
should send up a red flag here. You should use every opportunity to check
your insights against some standard. Interviews with activists, members of
groups portrayed in texts, insights from other researchers, review of additional documents, and analysis of the texts by other coder/scholars are all
valuable checks against interpretations springing more from the researcher's
values and beliefs than from the phenomenon under study. Although careful self-analysis and continuing review of one's own thoughts and developing theories is essential, as in all qualitative study, framing research is inherently open to widely disparate analyses and interpretations of the data.
Multiple analyses using multiple methods is especially wise where no standard content exists, concepts and theories abound and are not widely
agreed to, and many interpretations of the same data are possible.

In addition to the analysis of cultural artifacts, subjects within the culture should be interviewed to determine what frames are employed both in
producing and in consuming texts. In terms of the former, depth interviews
with cultural personnel are of great value. Although you will often need to
engage in primary data collection, interviews with actors, reporters, pro-

ducers, directors, rock stars, evangelists, and others are common fare on
television—especially on cable networks specializing in popular culture. Primary interviews with producers represent one of the most valuable research methods in the study of popular culture. Sensitive questioning can
draw out the basic frames content producers use to organize the world and
how these are translated into texts. Frustrations creative personnel experience in tailoring their work routines and the content they produce to the organizational requisites of production may signal the clash of organizational
and cultural frames. Another topic that is especially valuable in understanding framing as a social process is how the media of communication available to the creative person affect the preferred meaning in texts and artifacts. Creative clashes among artists may help you determine how they
compromise over frame conflict to produce popular cultural artifacts with
hybrid frames.

Interviews with audience members, perhaps best exemplified by focus
groups, deal with the process of framing in consumption. Frames are socially constructed, and their consumption involves social meaning generation as well. The social interaction of focus groups is especially suited for
observation of the construction of frames in consumption as the members
confront texts and construct frames as a group. Dominant social frames are
reflected in the discussion of topics and texts even as those frames are negotiated and changed by the discussion. Purposely congregating groups
comprised of members from different cultures or conflicting groups could
provide an opportunity to observe firsthand the conflict over the framing of
an issue.

Guidance and observation of focus group discussion will be improved by
the preliminary review of literature that highlights the assumptions, presuppositions, topic choices, language use, choice of metaphors, narrative
style and other features of the cultural frame. Those features that are common among the participants present likely features of the dominant frame
for the topic. As a catalyst for such discussion, cultural artifacts—movie
clips, magazine articles, photos, advertisements and so on—can be introduced into the group. The moderator may even challenge the accepted
frame as a means to monitor the reasoning and discussion that such a challenge provokes.

One other set of respondents critical to an analysis of frames, but especially framing, is frame sponsors. Social activists, government officials, or
business spokespersons seek to impose their frames on topics of interest to
them. Interviews with members of these social action groups can help you
determine what critical concepts, relations, metaphors, and so on define
each group's view of the situation, a cornerstone to frame analysis. Questions addressing internal communications among members of the group
and their approaches to external communication are especially useful.

These respondents can provide a great deal of insight into the means by which frame sponsors attempt to frame and reframe topics and issues of importance to them. Only through this method will an understanding of framing strategy be developed. Details on activities and encounters among frame sponsors are not available through mainstream sources, nor do specialized periodicals, newsletters, and so on always fill in the void of knowledge.

Finally, if you are willing to dedicate a great deal of effort to gain a deep understanding of the social framing process in a given case, participant observation might be the method of choice. Observing the process groups go through within their natural environment to make sense of the world provides the researcher with a more detailed and nuanced understanding of the process of framing. You may choose to observe the development of a frame within a group context or the clash generated when groups conflict over the proper frame to apply to social phenomena. The interactions among individuals, groups, organizations, and institutions, when observed naturally, provides information and knowledge unattainable elsewhere. Participant observation presents the danger that the researcher will become socialized to accept the world view of those under study. The acceptance of the rules of behavior within the organization, group or other may lead to uncritical acceptance of the dominant frame. The same concern over inability to step outside the frame and look back in that was voiced in relation to police beat reporters afflicts those who would enter a social group or organization in order to observe frame construction, negotiation and use in natural social settings.

EXAMPLES OF FRAMING ANALYSIS

One focus of our work has been the study of social protest and the media. Framing analysis can contribute mightily to the understanding of social protest, social change, and social control. Major goals in the study of framing and social protest include identifying and outlining the dominant frame for a social controversy—and variations within that frame—as well as alternative frames promoted by challenge groups. A second goal of framing study is identifying the array of strategies and tactics groups employ to influence social framing of a topic. A third is determining the popular "reading" of newspaper stories, televised news coverage, and so forth, in terms of the ultimate framing of the controversy by the wider public. We illustrate our approach to framing research using studies we have carried out on a number of occasions of social protest.

An early study of three demonstrations and a conference held by anarchists in Minneapolis sought to identify influences over a number of content characteristics, including the frames employed. Newspaper coverage, television news accounts, and coverage by anarchist publications were analyzed using both quantitative and qualitative methods to identify bias, sensationalism, and ideology. Framing was considered one form of ideology, as discussed in Hackett (1984). Five frames were identified, including the riot, confrontation, protest, circus, and debate frames. The text features that most distinguished these frames were: the nature of the conflict portrayal; metaphors and narratives used; the emphasis or lack thereof concerning the social critique forwarded by the anarchists; the portrayal of the anarchists themselves; the portrayal of the police; and the role assigned to bystanders. Especially salient features of the stories included headlines, photos, and direct quotes.

The two most common frames were the riot and confrontation frames. The riot frame was organized around a conflict between the anarchists and society. The typical narrative began with a relatively calm protest march, degenerating into illegal or aggressive behavior by the anarchists. Subsequently, riot troops were called in and the violence put down, but the threat of future anarchist action remained. The police symbolized social order and lawful behavior. They were forced to protect bystanders and property when the anarchists became unruly, but did not instigate any violence on their own. The favored phrase describing anarchist behavior was "riot." The video portion of television news coverage emphasized threatening anarchist actions, norm-breaking behavior, and arrests. For example, in one story, the camera was set behind the police as anarchists threw pop cans at them, providing the illusion that the cans were coming at the home viewer. Bystanders were portrayed as being hostile toward the anarchists.

The confrontation frame revolved around the conflict between the anarchists and the police. News coverage even detailed the tactics the two groups employ—from anarchist leaders' advice to marchers on how to deal with mace to the police' review prior to the march on how to use "the sticks" appropriately. Common descriptions of the actions described them as a battle, confrontation, scuffle, clash, etc. The narrative described a pitched battle, often giving a detailed description of the flow of events. The anarchists' social critique was not an important focus of the coverage; in many cases, it was omitted from the story. The anarchists were treated as combatants but not as thoughtful social critics. Bystanders were, for the most part, critical of the anarchists but they may also be critical of the police for overreacting or using mace.

The protest frame made fewer appearances. It centered on the conflict between the anarchists and powerful institutions within society. Accounts focused on the protest activities of the anarchists and de-emphasized clashes with the police. The narrative chronicled protest actions and often gave a fairly detailed account of the progression of the protest from beginning to end (sometimes even including maps of routes taken, etc.). A discussion of protesters' views and symbolic actions accompanied these accounts. The discussion was rarely deep, but the anarchists were able to state their social critique in simple terms. They were treated as a legitimate political group, voicing opinions that merit consideration. Stories did not emphasize bystanders, although anarchist writings occasionally claimed crowd support.

The circus frame did not focus on the conflict as the previous frames had. This frame emphasized the anarchists' deviance from—and general opposition to—all of society. The metaphors "circus" and "carnival" were important features of coverage, along with some related terms like *celebration*. The anarchists' critique of society was downplayed or absent. Instead, the text concentrated on how the group differs from mainstream society—their "oddity." One particularly negative portrayal used terms like *goofballs* and *clowns* to describe the anarchists. Bystanders were portrayed as confused or bewildered by the anarchists.

Debate frame stories presented ideological conflicts between either the anarchists and the powerful institutions of society or conflicts within the anarchist groups themselves. Police and bystanders were peripheral or nonexistent. Debate, discussion, and dialogue were commonly used to describe the important action. In this case, the social critique brought to bear by the anarchists was the main focus of the text. Such stories often presented a more significant and sophisticated discussion of anarchist views as well as points of contention among anarchists. The debate frame was rare in mainstream coverage but common in the anarchist press. As one might expect, anarchists were treated as legitimate and thoughtful social critics, acting in the interests of the public as a whole.

These five frames were expanded upon in our recent discussion of social control and social protest (McLeod & Hertog, 1999). A number of additional frames culled from the literature and our own studies were categorized according to how sympathetic they were to the protesters. Frames were designated as marginalizing (including carnival and riot), mixed (including confrontation), sympathetic, or balanced (including debate).

A study of six protests (stemming from the decision to send national guard troops into action in Honduras) that took place in Minneapolis during 1988 also reviewed framing practices in the mainstream media. In addition to replicating several of the analyses from the anarchist study, this research focused on the framing practices of a number of groups involved in the demonstrations and counter-demonstrations. The protests lasted more than a week, with varying levels of property damage, police confrontation, social support for protesters, and cohesiveness among protesters. As before, we analyzed mainstream media coverage and protest literature. In addition, we interviewed reporters, editors, members of protest groups, and the city chief of police.

Mainstream press coverage of early protests had applied a riot frame to the actions, focusing on property damage and disruption of normal downtown activity. The news coverage, emphasizing protest "violence," contributed to a split in the coalition of protest groups. Groups and individuals less open to militant protest methods broke away from the coalition, not wishing to be part of a violent protest. Five years later, one of the major groups was still suffering organizationally and financially from the loss of members during the fracture of the coalition. One of those members, the wife of the police chief, had been a generous financial supporter.

Interviews demonstrated that journalists were very aware of the attempts of the protesters to reframe the coverage. One local television news producer rejected those attempts by the protesters, "They want to tell me what the story is. *I* decide what the story is."

One especially revealing television program presented a debate between protesters representing three activist groups involved in the protests and three activists opposing the demonstrations. The format of the program was fashioned after the Phil Donahue show of the time, including a host out in the crowd and questions from the audience. The show's format followed and even visually represented the debate frame. The attempt to provide balance was represented by the selection of three speakers from each side, separated on opposite sides of the set, with the host physically separated from the guest speakers (symbolizing neutrality and identification with the audience). The audience was separated (distanced) from the speakers, symbolizing the different roles of actor and audience (activist and bystander) in the dominant frame for social protest.

The show did provide spaces for critique of the dominant frame. When they spoke in their own words, many of the activists questioned the assumptions brought to the show by activists, the host, and the audience. At the outset, the host outlined two topics he wanted to address—why people were protesting and "the manner in which they are doing it." Several participants attempted to frame or reframe the discussion, but were only partially successful due to the forms of control the host was able to bring to bear. For example, when an anarchist in the audience challenged the portrayal of the proceedings as an evenly matched debate, the host provided a curt reply and walked away, taking the microphone and the attention of the camera with him.

Two studies have examined the framing effects of news coverage from these protests demonstrating that the degree to which a particular news frame is adopted and the intensity of that application are also important (McLeod, 1995; McLeod & Detenber, 1999). These experimental studies show that subtle differences in the intensity of news frames can affect audience reactions to the groups involved in the protest. The more accentuated the characteristics of the confrontational frame in television news stories, the more critical that experimental participants were of the protesters and the less critical they were of the police. In addition, participants that saw a more intensely framed news story were less likely to see the protest as being effective, less likely to support the expressive rights of protesters, and less likely to see the protest as a newsworthy story. Finally, these participants perceived public support for the protesters as being significantly lower than participants who saw a less intensely framed news story.

CONCLUSIONS AND RECOMMENDATIONS

Our research and review of the literature indicates that frames are structures of meaning that include a set of core concepts and ideas, especially basic conflicts, metaphors, myths, and narratives. Dominant frames reflect and support the major institutions of society and are widely shared among individual members of society. They shape social understanding and structure the debate over social problems and social policy.

We are still in the early stages in our study of framing and its influence on society. Although we believe frames to be reflective of—and influential in supporting—the powerful institutions in society, the ways in which those institutions and frames intersect and interact are far from clear. The means by which frames influence social policy have not been clearly articulated nor have the ways social structure influences the development and maintenance of dominant frames.

Future study should classify frames according to important dimensions, one of which is their level of abstraction. We have noted the need to identify very abstract frames that encompass a wide range of content within a designated topic area. We have called these cultural frames. At the same time, subframes that stake out more specific approaches to particular social problems must be identified, and the relationships between frames and subframes carefully articulated. Developing a system for classification of frames would advance framing analysis significantly.

The study of frames should generate a relatively stable, widely agreed-upon set of cultural frames and subframes that is valid over time and across varied topics rather than a new set with every study of every topic. To meet most scholars' expectations about the role of frames in society, frames must be widely held and relatively stable. This indicates that researchers can identify and classify a limited number of dominant and alternative frames that are independent of narrowly defined topics. An additional set of subframes, more topical in nature, should also be articulated. Research should begin with a review of these frames and ultimately replicate or challenge them as part of each study.

More work needs to be done to identify the sources of frames and subframes. Our earlier work (Hertog & McLeod, 1995) developed a method for identifying influences according to level of analysis, but little effort to identify the relative influences of multiple contributing factors for popular culture has followed. The role of social institutions, including the media in the development and maintenance of or challenge to frames has not been adequately studied. It is often simply *assumed* that media or some other entity like the executive branch of government has the power to frame issues. Good, solid research is lacking in this critical area of study. One promising area for study is the sociology of media organizations like the work of Tuchman, Gans, or Hess but with an eye toward determining how media organizations frame social topics.

Relating frames to other popular culture phenomena should be an important part of frame studies. For example, our earlier finding that sensationalism and objectivity varied significantly according to the frame applied in news needs further testing and elaboration. We also determined that framing varied by story genre—news, editorial, letter to the editor, and so on. This could certainly be expanded beyond news coverage to include the effect of a wide range of popular genre on framing of social concerns. One fruitful area would be to look at the framing of social concerns in television drama. Research of this type has been carried out in the past, although it has not been labeled framing study.

A great deal more effort in determining how social framing of controversies affects public understanding of those controversies is needed. The findings by McLeod (1995) and McLeod and Detenber (1999) demonstrating a powerful impact of framing in reactions to news depictions of protest calls for research on the impact of framing on public opinion for a much broader range of genre and topics. This research needs to move out of the laboratory and into the realm of popular culture. Depth interviews, focus groups or survey research should relate exposure to media content and public framing of social concerns. Finally, tracing the framing of social concerns within public and private institutions of power and the social impact of such framing must be one of the goals of the program of research. Certainly, one of the assumed reasons for study of the framing of social concerns is that it has an impact on social policy and plays a role in the process of social control. Perhaps analyses of congressional debates and hearings, corporate publications, and stockholder meetings can be combined with popular culture studies on the one hand and policy votes and investment decisions on the other. If, as we believe, framing is one of the most powerful forces in determining public and private social policy, this form of research could stand as some of the most important political and social communication research ever carried out.

REFERENCES

Altheide, D. L. (1979). *Media logic.* Beverly Hills: Sage.

Althusser, L. (1971). *Lenin and philosophy and other essays.* London: New Left.

Carley, K. M. (1997). Network text analysis: The network position of concepts. In C. W. Roberts (Ed.), *Text analysis for the social sciences* (pp. 79–100). Mahwah, NJ: Lawrence Erlbaum Associates.

Hackett, R. A. (1984). Decline of a paradigm? Bias and objectivity in news media studies. *Critical Studies in Mass Communication, 1*(3), 229–259.

Hall, S. (1979). Culture, the media and the 'ideological effect'. In J. Curran, M. Gurevitch, & J. Woollacott (Eds.), *Mass communication and society* (pp. 315–348). Beverly Hills: Sage.

Hall, S. (1984). The rediscovery of 'ideology': Return of the repressed in media studies. In M. Gurevitch, T. Bennett, J. Curran, & J. Woollacott (Eds.), *Culture, society and the media* (pp. 56–90). New York: Methuen.

Hertog, J. K., & McLeod, D. M. (1995). Anarchists wreak havoc in downtown Minneapolis: A multilevel study of media coverage of radical protest. *Journalism & Mass Communication Monographs, 151.*

McLeod, D. M. (1995). Communicating deviance: The effects of television news coverage of social protest. *Journal of Broadcasting and Electronic Media, 39*(1), 4–19.

McLeod, D. M., & Hertog, J. K. (1999). Social control, social change and the mass media's role in the regulation of protest groups. In D. Demers & K. Viswanath (Eds.), *Mass media, social control, and social change* (pp. 305–330). Ames, IA: Iowa State University.

McLeod, D. M., & Detenber, B. H. (1999). Framing effects of television news coverage of social protest. *Journal of Communication, 49,* 3–23.

Zhang, Y. (1998). *Covering the Hong Kong transition: A content analysis of the news stories by China's Xinhua news agency and the Associated Press of the United States between May 1 and August 31, 1998.* Unpublished Doctoral Dissertation, University of Kentucky, Lexington.

8

Framing "Political Correctness": *The New York Times'* Tale of Two Professors

Donna L. Dickerson

Few institutions in our society are less well understood by the general public than America's colleges and universities. With its system of tenure for life, "publish or perish," and rituals of promotion, among many curiosities, higher education has a great capacity to baffle most noninsiders. Nevertheless, most Americans respect universities. Those who educate and are educated are perceived as wise and prescient, credible and responsible, logical and curious, and above all, tolerant and open to new ideas.

At least so it appeared until the "political correctness" debate hit America's campuses several years ago. Political correctness is a complex and multifaceted issue that pits the essential American values of free speech against respect for others. However, the public rarely sees or understands that complexity because of the media's tendency to frame the issue around specific events and personalities on America's campuses rather than as a story about academic freedom, human dignity, freedom of speech, or individual rights (Iyengar, 1994).

These "episodic frames" are exemplars of Entman's (1989) claim that the media use "simplification, personalization and symbolization" in order to appeal to a broad audience (p. 49). Simplification relates to the media's preference for simple stories that strip issues of their context and, consequently, of their complexity. Personalization entices audience interest by telling stories about people—whether they are well known or obscure—to create dramatic force. Symbolization allows journalists to shape a story using an already familiar model. For example, violence in high school is now defined by "Columbine"; American terrorism goes by the moniker "Oklahoma City," stories of abuse of power are simplified by analogy to "Watergate." These symbols not only direct readers' attention away from the complexity of social and political issues but also direct readers how to interpret these events.

This chapter examines two similar stories about political correctness and how, through simplification, personalization, and symbolization, they were framed very differently by the *New York Times*. One story is that of Professor Leonard Jeffries of City College of New York (CCNY), who made what were characterized as "racist and anti-Semitic" comments during a television speech in New York. The other story, which began earlier but eventually paralleled that of Jeffries was that of CCNY Professor Michael Levin, whose various writings and public comments were described as "racist" and demeaning to Blacks.

This chapter follows Entman's (1989) advise that "news slant becomes visible when we compare news stories to each other—not to reality" (p. 40). Entman (1991) studied the contrasting frames that emerged between the stories of the shooting down of the Korean Air Lines flight 007 by the Soviets over the Sea of Japan and the shooting down of Iran Air flight 655 by the United States over the Persian Gulf. He notes that, although the details were different in each case, the principal theme—the killing of more than 300 civilian passengers when an unarmed passenger airliner was shot down by military forces—was the same, and nothing in the reality of events justified the vastly different framing of the stories.

Like the stories Entman studied, the details of the Jeffries and Levin stories were different, but the principal theme—controversial racial remarks by professors protected by academic freedom and the First Amendment—was the same. Why, then, did the *New York Times* treat the stories differently? Whereas most studies select the *New York Times* for study because it is the nation's "newspaper of record," this study selected the *Times* because CCNY is in Manhattan and both stories were local, with all but one story appearing in Sec. B–Regional/Metropolitan.

THE JEFFRIES AND LEVIN STORIES

Professor Leonard Jeffries, then chair of CCNY's Black Studies Department and faculty member since 1969, is a spokesperson for revisionist views of African history and culture. At the time of these events, he served on a governor's advisory board to create and implement a multicultural curriculum in the New York public schools. On July 20, 1991, he spoke about the curriculum at the Empire State Black Arts and Culture Festival in Albany, New York. In that speech he stated, among other things, that Jews and Italians were responsible for the demeaning way Blacks were depicted in American film, that Jews had financed the slave trade, and that American history books do not correctly depict African American history.

As a result of the speech, CCNY removed Jeffries from his administrative position in March 1992. Jeffries sued the trustees for infringement of his academic freedom. In May 1993, a federal jury found that the trustees had abridged Jeffries' freedom of speech and awarded him $360,000 in damages. In August 1993, Federal District Judge Kenneth Conboy ordered Jeffries reinstated as chairman of CCNY's Black Studies Department. After the Court of Appeals upheld the jury's finding (Jeffries v. Harleston, 1994), the case bounced around the court system for another 3 years. The case ended when the Court of Appeals in 1996 reversed its earlier decision after finding that Jeffries' speech had the potential to disrupt the workplace. Later that year, the Black Studies Department was disbanded, and Jeffries was moved into the Political Science Department (Polner, 1996).

Professor Michael Levin had been a philosophy professor at CCNY since 1969 also. He spoke and wrote about ethics, affirmative action, comparable worth, and intelligence scores across racial groups. In lectures, articles, television shows, and letters he stated among other things that Blacks were mentally deficient and less intelligent than Whites, that Whites had good reason to be afraid of Black men, that the police are morally justified in basing searches on skin color, and that homosexuals are abnormal.

In October 1989, students at CCNY called for disciplinary action against Levin after one of his articles was circulated on campus. The article's thesis was that women and Black students had lowered academic standards at American universities and that Blacks were less intelligent than the average White person. The university moved Levin out of his introductory philosophy course, and he sued for infringement of academic freedom.

On May 2, 1990, Levin lectured on the topic of Black crime to a standing-room-only crowd at Long Island University (LIU) in Brooklyn. A group of 50 protestors tried to enter the auditorium, but police used clubs and mace to keep the students from disrupting Levin. In the end, nine students were arrested and four police officers were injured. The speech was followed by student protests at CCNY demanding his removal. Three weeks later, Levin appeared on the "Sally Jessie Raphael" talk show, where he demeaned Blacks, women, homosexuals, and stated that "Nazis may have been on the right track, but went about it wrong" (Lowery, 1990, p. 29).

In September 1992, Judge Conboy ruled that the college had violated Levin's rights by investigating his writings and by establishing separate sections of his course (Levin v. Harleston, 1992). Robert Reno (1991), a *Newsday* columnist, probably characterized these overlapping stories best when he wrote: "[Levin and Jeffries] have become academic symbols of the theory that blacks and Jews have some sort of weird joint obligation to engage in a moral jihad against each other" (p. 48).

FRAME ANALYSIS

To help illuminate the contrasting way the Levin and Jeffries stories were framed, this analysis examined each news article and editorial about Jeffries and Levin published in the *New York Times* between May 7, 1990, and July 1, 1993, the period of greatest overlap between the two stories. Not included were letters to the editor and photographs. In addition, the *New York Post* and *Newsday* were used as a check on how other local newspapers covered these stories. A textual analysis was conducted on each article to define the structural as well as rhetorical elements that related to the principal themes of the stories: the men, their messages, and the controversies. The structural elements included headlines, lead emphasis, backgrounding, length of stories, number of stories, and selection and placement of quotations.

Although there were differences in the details of the Jeffries and Levin stories, the principal theme—controversial racial remarks by professors protected by academic freedom and the First Amendment—was the same. Even the *Times* agreed that the stories were basically the same, noting,

> The cases of Dr. Levin and Dr. Jeffries differ in details, but both involve professors whose unpopular views on race issues have raised questions about the limits of free speech and academic freedom . . . (McFadden, 1992, p. B3)

However, for Jeffries, the *Times* told the story of a discredited Black professor who targets Jews with his peculiar brand of virulent racism—a "delegitimizing" frame. For Levin, the frame de-emphasizes his race and conservative affiliations and instead paints the picture of a stereotypical bespectacled White professor who writes about Black/White issues—a "legitimizing" frame.

Emphasis

Between these two events, the Jeffries story was portrayed by the *Times* as far more important than that of Levin. Not only were there eight times more stories about Jeffries, but the stories were significantly longer. Also, as the amount of information increased, more of it was repeated in subsequent stories as background. A look at the coverage of these stories by the *New York Post* and *Newsday* reveals that a great deal of information about the Levin story was indeed available. For example, *Newsday* ran 33 stories about Levin, 46 about Jeffries, and 14 that included both men.

What factors might account for the difference in sizing? In terms of traditional news values (timeliness, proximity, consequence, and prominence), the Levin story should have been more prominent. The Levin speech was reported immediately; Jeffries' speech was not reported for almost a month. Jeffries gave his speech 375 miles away in Albany; Levin's speech was given next door in Brooklyn. As for consequence, Jeffries' speech was not associated with violence or student protest; Levin's was. A month earlier, students offended by Levin's message broke down CCNY President Bernard Harleston's door as they protested against Levin.

Salience, which is closely related to consequence, would indicate that the closer the story is to the reader, the more important it becomes. At the time the Jeffries story hit the street, the city had just been through several days of riots in the Crown Heights district of Bedford-Stuyvesant, where a Black child was accidentally run over by a Jewish motorist. When Levin made his controversial speech in Brooklyn, the state was trying a Jewish man for the murders of Michael Griffith and Yusef Hawkins, Blacks were boycotting two Korean grocery stores in Brooklyn, and a White jogger had been raped by a Black man in Central Park. These issues would suggest that any related story—whether about Levin or Jeffries—would have salience for New York City readers.

The engine that drove the Jeffries story was the quoted reaction from elite sources. Journalists do express opinion by selecting whom to quote, what to quote, and where to place the quotations in the story (Tuchman, 1972). The placement and repetition of quotations from President Harleston, Governor Mario Cuomo, Senator Alfonse D'Amato, trustees, and other politicians told readers that this was a politically important story. These elite sources invariably appeared at the top of the story, whereas reactions from faculty and supporters appeared at the end of the stories. In addition, Cuomo and D'Amato's original denunciations and those of several local politicians were repeated in the "backgrounding" across more than one half of the stories. This heavy dependence on elite quotes had the effect of overemphasizing the opposition view point that Jeffries was "deviant" or different.

The Levin story, in contrast, was completely void of elite reaction. It was not presented as a story of political consequence. In fact, the coverage of Levin is significant not for what is included in the frame, but for what was excluded. For example, the *Times* did not report that Levin had been repudiated by the Anti-Defamation League and by such prominent leaders as Mayor David Dinkins, Roy Innis of the Congress of Racial Equality, civic leader Al Sharpton, and Governor Cuomo (a year later). The newspaper did not report that the National Association of Scholars had forced Levin off of its board of directors because of "persistent racist remarks" (Innerst, 1990, p. A4), nor did it report his connections with the White supremacist organization, American Renaissance. No one with expertise in the scholarship of intelligence testing was quoted. Those sources were not silent, however. *Newsday* interviewed several academic sources, all of whom repudiated Levin's comments as uninformed and unscholarly.

Text Elements

Repetition of certain words and phrases across the life of a story shapes meaning by telling readers what the important story elements are and how to think about them. In these stories the men, their message, and the nature of the controversies were defined by repetition and helped create the contrasting "legitimizing" and "delegitimizing" frames. Strauss (1992) noted that in normal or natural discourse, there are five methods of legitimation/delegitimation: claiming worth, embodiment of performance standards, setting boundaries, distancing, and theorizing. In these stories, the first three processes appear to be at work in the reporters' coverage.

The most significant means of creating worth for Levin and devaluing Jeffries was in the contrasting way that the reporters used verbs of attribution when describing what the men said. Although the views of both men were delivered through writing and speeches, the dominant verb of attribution for Levin's message was "written": "In *articles* submitted to academic journals, Dr. Levin has . . ." (Gray, 1991, p. A34); "Levin in his academic *writings* asserted that . . ." (Racial Debate 101, 1991, p. A7); "Levin has *written* at least three articles for academic journals that . . ." (Berger, 1990, p. B1).

The citing of Levin's academic articles rather than his several television appearances and local speeches mirrors our culture's respect for the written over the oral, thus legitimizing Levin as a scholar. In contrast, the verbs of attribution used in the Jeffries stories devalue his message by connoting loudness: "His latest diatribe was delivered in July . . ." (Why the Delay, 1991, p. A24). Other terms included "accused," "charged," "blamed," "attacked," "in a diatribe that . . ." Verbs also reflected skepticism: "In his speech, Dr. Jeffries also complained of . . ." (Stanley, 1991, p. B1). Other verbs of attribution included "espouses," "enunciates theories," "propounds that," "has gone public with the notion," and "touts that."

Another pattern that created value for Levin and devalued Jeffries was the manner in which the messages were summarized for the reader. Both Levin's and Jeffries' speeches and writings were available to the media, and *Newsday* ran *verbatim* each of the principal speeches that set off the controversies (In His Own Words, 1991, p. 3; Text of Jeffries' July Speech, 1991, p. 2). The *Times* ran neither. Whereas the nature of a news report does not allow an entire speech to be repeated every time in background, a newspaper can "reconstruct" the speech by selection and repetition of certain elements. Those elements that were repeated throughout the life of the story included Jeffries' statement that Jews and Italians were responsible for the negative portrayal of Blacks in movies; that Jews had financed the American slave trade; that White are "ice people," who are fundamentally materialistic, greedy and intent on domination; and that skin pigment (melanin) may affect intelligence and physical superiority (Text of Jeffries' July Speech, 1991, p. 2).

The speech itself, however, was about the unsuccessful attempts to get a multicultural curriculum for social sciences approved. This context appeared in only 4 of 41 stories. Only two stories mentioned that Jeffries was part of the Governor's advisory committee to review the curriculum. The element of Jews and Hollywood was an aside at the beginning of the speech and given only a few sentences. The element of Jews and slavery, which appeared in 37 stories, did occupy a good deal of the speech as Jeffries recounted his attempt to "re-educate" Mayor Ed Koch about the influence of Jews on American slave trade. Whereas Jeffries cited more than a dozen scholarly works to support his comments, the *Times* never mentioned that the statements were supported by the scholarship of others.

Levin's remarks were not as dramatic, but were certainly as wide-ranging and as inflammatory as those of Jeffries'—criticizing Blacks, women, and homosexuals. The stories about Levin's suit against CCNY paraphrased Levin's writings regarding affirmative action and intelligence of Blacks and women. However, when the stories were about the altercation at LIU, the *Times* never quoted from the content of the speech and instead quoted from an article published 2 years earlier in which Levin stated that Blacks were less intelligent than Whites. Once again, the *Times* neglected aspects of Levin's message that might have undermined his legitimacy.

The symbolization strategy used by the *Times* early in the story was to label Jeffries as a racist, whose speech was racist and anti-Semitic. The phrase "racially charged" was used in more than a dozen stories: "Dr. Leonard Jeffries, Jr., the City College professor who delivered a racially charged speech at a state sponsored conference . . ." (Verhovek, 1991, p. B1). Jeffries' speech also was characterized as "unfortunate and shocking," "grotesque distortions," "mindless denunciations," and "palpably clear expression of bigotry."

Jeffries, the man, was portrayed as "emotional," "defiant," "outspoken," "combative," and "incendiary." One article described Jeffries' career as "distinguished by political activities, little scholarly publication, intense lectures, and a penchant for controversy" (Tierney, 1991, p. B1). Several months into the story, detractors are quoted, calling him "grossly negligent," "preacher of hatred," and "incompetent." By the end of the story, he is labeled as "twisted," "bizarre," "Nazi Dog," "hatemonger," and "odious." Editor Abe Rosenthal wrote that Jeffries was "an unpleasant piece of urban nastiness to step over" (1993, p. A23).

Although the negative characterizations far outweighed the positive, some of Jeffries' supporters did find positive things to say about him. The positive descriptions emphasized his popularity among students. Other characterizations depict him in his present predicament as a "sacrificial lamb" and "courageous."

The *Times* also defined Levin's remarks as racist: "Dr. Michael Levin, a philosophy professor, has made racially charged remarks . . ." (Berger,

1991, p. B2). However, the paper printed only one quote that negatively characterized Levin's remarks—the President of the CCNY Faculty Senate called them "outlandish" (Berger, 1990, p. B1). There were more positive characterizations of Levin than there were negative, such as "brilliant," "riveting," and an "intellectual provocateur."

Neither Jeffries nor Levin spoke from the base of original research. Yet, their "scholarship" is treated very differently. Although Jeffries cited in his speech more than a dozen sources for his statements regarding slavery and Hollywood, he is characterized as a pseudo-scholar: "This has led others to criticize him for teaching pseudoscientific notions about black racial superiority" (Bernstein, 1993, p. B1). Other phrases used to describe his credentials include: "little scholarship published," "no scholarly standards," "scholarship is questionable," "seriously flawed," "incompetent," and "confused." One editorial charged that Jeffries' "unsubstantiated remarks clearly undermine the valid scholarship of his department . . ." (Why the Delay, 1991, p. A24). In addition, the newspaper ran repudiations of his scholarship by several historians.

As noted earlier, the major verb of attribution used by the *Times* to introduce Levin's remarks was "written," providing readers with the sense that his material is more scholarly. The *Times* never attributes Levin's ideas to his speeches or to his television appearance; nor do they seek scholars to repudiate his remarks.

Strauss (1982) noted that setting boundaries is a common delegitimizing strategy. In the few stories that deal with the issue of academic freedom, Jeffries is described as being unprofessional by sharing his opinions with students in the classroom. The argument was that Jeffries would not have been in any trouble if only he had kept his ideas out of the classroom. Almost every story that dealt with both men compared Levin and Jeffries on the classroom issue. For example: "Unlike Dr. Levin, Dr. Jeffries has discussed his own racial theories in the classroom" (Hayes, 1991, p. B2). And in the story announcing Levin's court victory, the lead stated that the court found that CCNY had violated the constitutional rights of Levin "who contended in published letters and articles, *although not in his classes* (italics added), that Blacks on average are less intelligent than whites" (McFadden, 1992, p. B3).

In an article about the limits of academic freedom, there are two mentions of Levin: "Dr. Michael Levin, a philosophy professor, has contended in articles published *outside his academic field* (italics added) that blacks are on average less intelligent than whites" (Weiss, 1991, p. A23). In the same article, Levin's legal battles are summarized: "Professor Levin had sued saying he had never discussed his views in class" (p. A23). Levin becomes legitimized because, unlike Jeffries, he has comported himself within the prescribed limits.

DISCUSSION

Why were these two stories, which were essentially the same, framed so differently by the *New York Times*? According to traditional news values, the Levin story should have been more prominent.

The puzzle was not lost on journalists at the time. A reporter for *Newsday* noted that "the volume level directed against the black professor, Leonard Jeffries, has clearly been louder than that against the white philosophy professor, Michael Levin" (Firestone, 1991, p. 4). The same reporter interviewed both Blacks and Jews to find the reason. A spokesman for the American Jewish Committee posited that it was because Levin's ideas were expressed in journals and at "a small speech in Brooklyn," whereas Jeffries' speech was given at a large state-sponsored festival. The spokesman stated that there is a "quantum leap of difference" when racist comments are made under state sponsorship (p. 4). Long Island University is a state institution, and more than 150 people attended Levin's speech.

Donald Smith, the chair of the Education Department at Baruch College, argued that there was a "double-standard" at work.

> Historically, people like Levin have always made heinous remarks to people of African descent, and I don't recall any widespread effort to remove them from their jobs. But in Dr. Jeffries' case, there are a number of well-organized groups who feel that is in their interest to silence him. (Firestone, 1991, p. 4)

Foucault (1980) argued that individuals are not instrumental in any fundamental way in creating meaning; instead, they are repeating or mirroring a cultural code that controls the character of knowledge. How a story is framed, therefore, is an embedded way of expressing ideas already deeply ingrained in our culture. Our culture determines what kind of discourse is acceptable as true, what techniques are acceptable in acquiring truth, what measures we use to distinguish truth from falsity, and who has authority to say what is true (p. 131). This characterization is just as true for the narrower culture of news production. Consequently, as Schudson (1995) noted, "the press follows more often than leads and reinforces more than challenges conventional wisdom" (p. 76).

Martindale (1992) noted that the failure of the newspapers in America to cover Black issues and concerns stems from a multiplicity of interrelated factors inherent in the American media culture: the need to simplify the complex, reliance on elite sources, and emphasis on events rather than interpretation and process. Added to these institutional routines are the dominance of White ownership of the media, lack of minority representation in the newsroom, and failure to acknowledge that minority groups have economic power. When combined, these elements favor access to the media by elites and promote a focus on White, western, middle-class perspectives of news events (van Dijk, 1986).

Elite sources were very much at work in framing the Jeffries story, where those who "spoke" the loudest represented the racial groups denounced by Jeffries: Italians (Cuomo and D'Amato) and Jews (numerous local politicians and university administrators). The *Times* used these elites to define the situation by allowing their quotations to signify what was legitimate and what was meaningless.

Another source of bias in the distribution of speaker roles is the disinclination of journalists to seek out sources among cultures with which they have no contact. Like everyone else, journalists seek out "their own," and because of the predominance of White journalists in America's newsrooms, members of minority groups are less likely to be interviewed. When combined with the propensity for negative events, this distancing contributes at best to marginalizing minorities, and at worst to a consistent negative framing of minorities (Campbell, 1995; Schudson, 1995). This may explain why *Times'* reporters made no effort to seek out sources within New York City's Black communities who would repudiate Levin's charges. However, it would not explain why other local newspapers such as *Newsday* did seek out minority sources.

Groups with established leaders and formal organizations have greater access to the media (Entman, 1989). In New York City, with a large Jewish population that is organized and well represented in politics as well as in the *Times*, it was very easy for the press to find prominent spokespersons to condemn Jeffries. Not only is reliance on "legitimate political elites" the least expensive way to gather information, but it also has the feel of credibility because elites share the same social class as most readers and journalists. They have "cultural" legitimacy and can provide ready and believable "facts" (Entman, 1989).

Minorities are also considered less credible, and in stories about race minorities are often seen as incapable of being objective. This doubt manifests itself in the tendency to quote, rather than paraphrase, statements that are "questionable" (van Dijk, 1986). This doubt and skepticism are clearly visible in the consistent and explicit use of quotations from Jeffries' speech rather than paraphrases. On the other hand, Levin's statements about Black intelligence are paraphrased in 7 of the 10 instances in which it was referenced. The statement became a "natural" and objective part of the discourse, void of the doubt and distancing that quotations imply.

Levin's statements about Black crime and Black intelligence were deemed credible by the *Times,* not only because they came from a member of a legitimate and organized group, but also because they fall within the traditional stereotypes that have been perpetuated by the media for more than two centuries (Campbell, 1995; Gossett, 1963; Jaret, 1995; Martindale,

1992). Feagin and Feagin (1996) defined traditional racism as containing negative beliefs about Black intelligence, ambition, and honesty. On the other hand, Jeffries' remarks about Jews and Hollywood and Jews and slavery are relatively new within the pantheon of Jewish stereotypes. They are new branches of the old stereotype that the middleman role of Jews as merchants and financiers placed them in positions of exploitation (Feagin & Feagin, 1966). The novelty of the charges increased their consequence and controversy, and they even raised the Hollywood remarks from a mere aside to a major aspect of the speech. In a sense, the *Times*, consciously or unconsciously, recognized a different type of "social knowledge," classified it as "not preferred," and labeled its perpetrator as deviant.

This study shows how the media lead readers toward an understanding of events by placing stories into understandable frames. It also helps us see how journalists, as Foucault (1980) argued, play a predefined cultural role in defining the meaning of events for readers. Journalists, working within the complex news culture, echo and reproduce culturally embedded ways of seeing the world, including stereotyping. They follow cultural codes to distinguish what is of consequence, what is legitimate, and who has the status to say what is true. In these two stories, the failure of the *Times* to recognize and seek voices within the Black community, the inherent skepticism of what is said by Blacks, and the legitimacy of perpetuating old stereotypes all worked together to create the contrasting frames found in this study.

REFERENCES

Berger, J. (1990, April 20). Professor's theories on race stir turmoil at city college. *New York Times*, B1.

Berger, J. (1991, Nov. 16). City College gives a seminar on racial issues, Jeffries case. *New York Times*, B2.

Bernstein, R. (1993, Sept. 12). Jeffries and his racial theories return to class. *New York Times*, B1.

Campbell, C. (1995). *Race, myth and the news*. Thousand Oaks, CA: Sage.

Entman, R. (1989). *Democracy without citizens: Media and the decay of American politics*. New York: Oxford University Press.

Entman, R. (1991). Framing U.S. coverage of international news: Contrasts in narratives of the KAL and Iran air incidents. *Journal of Communication 41*, 6–24.

Feagin, J., & Feagin, C. (1996). *Racial and ethnic relations*. Upper Saddle River, NJ: Prentice-Hall.

Firestone, D. (1991, Aug. 14). Double standard at work. *Newsday*, 4.

Foucault, M. (1980). *Power/knowledge*. New York: Pantheon Books.

Gossett, T. (1963). *Race: The history of an idea in America*. Dallas, TX: Southern Methodist University Press.

Gray, J. (1991, March 24). Educators chided for race remarks. *New York Times*, A34.

Hayes, C. (1991, Sept. 5). CUNY barred from punishing white professor. *New York Times*, B2.

In His Own Words: Text of Levin Speech. (1991, Sept. 5). *Newsday*, 3.

Innerst, C. (1990, June 11). Scholar forced out of NAS over persistent racist remarks. *Washington Times*, A4

Iyengar, S. (1994) . *Is anyone responsible? How television frames issues*. Chicago: University of Chicago Press.

Jaret, C. (1995). *Contemporary racial and ethnic relations*. New York: HarperCollins.

Jeffries v. Harleston (1994). 21 F.3d 1238 (2d Cir.). Rev'd 1995 U.S. App. Lexis 7639 (2d Cir., April 4).

Levin v. Harleston (1992). 966 F.2d 85 (2d Cir.).

Lowery, M. (1990, May 30). CUNY prof. defends racial beliefs. *Newsday*, 29.

Martindale, C. (1992). *The white press and black America*. Westport, CT: Greenwood.

McFadden, R. (1992, June 9). Court finds a violation of a professor's rights. *New York Times,* B3.

Polner, R. (1996, June 1). Academic feud/faculty protest Jeffries move to their department. *Newsday*, 7.

Racial debate 101. (1991, Sept. 8). *New York Times*, A7.

Reno, R. (1991, Sept. 6). Reno at large: To the barricades for their right to be prejudiced. *Newsday*, 48.

Rosenthal, A. (1993, Aug. 13). On my mind. *New York Times*, A23.

Schudson, M. (1995). How news becomes news. *Media Critic*, *2*, 76–85.

Stanley, A. (1991, Aug. 6). City College professor assailed for remarks on Jews. *New York Times*, B1.

Strauss, A. (1982). Social worlds and legitimation processes. *Studies in Symbolic Interaction, 4*, 171–90.

Text of Jeffries' July speech. (1991, Aug. 19). *Newsday*, 2.

Tierney, J. (1991, Sept. 7). For Jeffries, a penchant for disputes. *New York Times*, B1.

Tuchman, G. (1972). Objectivity as strategic ritual: an examination of newsmen's notions of objectivity. *American Journal of Sociology 77*, 660–679.

Van Dijk, T. (1986). Mediating racism: The role of the media in the reproduction of racism. In R. Wodak (Ed.), *Language, power and ideology* (pp. 199–226). Amsterdam: Benjamins.

Verhovek, S. (1991, Aug. 8). Cuomo urges CUNY to act on professor. *New York Times*, B1.

Weiss, S. (1991, Nov. 10). Are there any enforceable limits? *New York Times*, A23.

Why the delay on Jeffries? (1991, Oct. 30). *New York Times*, A24.

9

Covering the Crisis in Somalia: Framing Choices by *The New York Times* and *The Manchester Guardian*

Philemon Bantimaroudis
Hyun Ban

In 1991, pictures of the turmoil in Somalia were broadcast worldwide. A drought and a civil war had brought the country to a dead end. Although news media kept reporting from Somalia, initially the United Nations was indifferent to the troubled African state. However, by the end of the year the U.N., supported by the United States and the outgoing Bush administration, began considering a possible mission in Somalia. It was argued that this Western benevolence was sparked by the graphic media coverage. Others contended that the operation was a great opportunity for public relations for the outgoing Bush administration. No matter the reasons, while the U.S. Navy was approaching the Somali coast, servicemen were startled by bright lights. Soon, they realized that those were camera lights of media personnel waiting for them on the coast. "Operation Restore Hope" had begun.

U.S. AND BRITISH NEWS COVERAGE

Treating American and British media as a monolithic institution does not allow for critical comparisons of Third World coverage within the West. As a matter of fact, European and American journalists often make drastically different decisions in terms of content selection and patterns of coverage. Observing such differences makes audiences aware of more than one perspectives, or points of view, concerning the coverage of the Third World.

According to Hopple (1982), *The New York Times* and *The Manchester Guardian*, both influential newspapers representing the two continents, display interesting differences in terms of their gatekeeping habits and their news selection processes. *The New York Times* tends to be more ethnocentric than *The Guardian*. Hopple (1982) argued that *The Guardian*'s coverage is balanced including developments unfolding in various parts of the world. On the other hand, *The New York Times* covers international issues directly related to U.S. policies.

The current project attempts a similar critical comparison. *The Guardian* and *The New York Times* are major gatekeepers in the United States and Europe, respectively. Their articles are often reprinted by regional media. Thus, investigating their coverage patterns allows scholars to speculate on coverage trends followed by other media in the two continents. The most important implication of the comparison pertains to the notion of the informed citizen. Citizens of the world need to be aware of different perspectives and triangulate their information acquiring habits. Comparing the coverage of two respected daily newspapers cultivates the notion of multiple perspectives and approaches.

MEDIA FRAMING IN SOMALIA

The operation in Somalia was allegedly driven by graphic media coverage of the crisis. According to Minear, Scott, and Weiss (1996), "television news is singled out as the main stimulus in the process, supposedly triggering Washington's military intervention and its abrupt withdrawal" (p. 53). However, such an assessment may not be totally accurate. Livingston and Eachus (1995) argued that the United Nation's decision to plan and carry out a humanitarian mission in Somalia was "the result of diplomatic and bureaucratic operations, with news coverage coming in response to those decisions" (p. 413). Natsios (1997) contended that the Office of Foreign Disaster Assistance, despite its modest staff and resources, is instrumental in setting agendas for humanitarian operations (p. 39). Although the media have the capacity to produce emotional reactions and occasionally affect certain policies, it is usually official actions that lead toward a certain kind of media coverage (Livingston & Eachus, 1995, p. 416). Of course, the media contributed to raising awareness about the issue. And after the decision was made media and military existed in a symbiotic relationship serving each other's agendas and interests.

Although scholars define framing in various ways, they agree that framing constitutes a form of bias, a process of selection and exclusion. Framing involves salience. But, it goes beyond that. Reese (see Prologue, this volume) defines frames as "organizing principles that are socially shared and persistent over time, that work symbolically to meaningfully structure the social world."

Ghanem (1996) identified four distinct categories of frames. Frames can be divided into subtopics, affective elements, cognitive elements, and framing mechanisms. Photographs, quotes, headlines, and subheads are all examples of framing mechanisms. These are means through which frames become salient. Ghanem (1996) pointed out that the frequency with which a topic is mentioned in media content is arguably the most powerful framing mechanism (p. 32). In this context, Tankard and Sumpter (1993) measured the frequency of the term: *spin doctor.* They searched a collection of articles from the LEXIS/NEXIS database and found that in 1987 there were only seven stories that incorporated the specific term. In 1988, there were 131. In 1991, spin doctors appeared in 334 stories and, in 1992, in 1,553 stories. According to Tankard and Sumpter, their "study indicates that journalists may be becoming more and more accepting of spin doctors" (p. 10).

STATEMENT OF THE PROBLEM

The current chapter focuses primarily on framing mechanisms, as found in the key phrases and terms that signify larger frame structures. Ghanem (1996) asserted that the frequency a topic or a stock-phrase is mentioned is a powerful tool that makes frames salient. Previous studies have demonstrated the importance of frame repetition. As suggested earlier, we think choice of language is perhaps the most important framing mechanism. A careful examination of word choices and the extent of their use in news coverage can reveal much about the organizing ideas, the framing choices, of the media. The central question of this chapter is to what extent Western—in this case, American and British newspapers—media resorted to the use of similar framing mechanisms. Thus, the following research questions can be posed:

1. *What are the most commonly observed framing devices used by the two news media?* The project will attempt to identify framing mechanisms widely used by both media.
2. *Which of the two media uses them more extensively?* It is important to know which framing devices were most salient and consequently guided public perceptions in the West.
3. *Was the operation framed as a humanitarian mission or as a military intervention?* The designers of the mission attempted to promote their endeavor as a humanitarian mission—an effort to save lives. It should be observed whether their framing device was utilized by the media. Furthermore, the military intervention aspect of the operation should be

examined since the West often is accused as interfering with other nations' domestic affairs.

4. *Are there any changes in patterns during the 3-year period of the operation?* Changes in framing choices may be indicative of changes in policies and administrative initiatives.

There will be two components in the design of the project: a qualitative and a quantitative analysis. In the qualitative assessment we attempt to identify important framing devices in the news texts. The objective of the section is not quantity but description. In a fairly small number of articles and editorials, we attempt to identify recurring themes, stock-phrases, or keywords that are descriptive of the situation in Somalia but also reveal Western attitudes toward the African state. Then, the identified frames will be more precisely counted during the 3-year period to assess their salience. In doing so, we try to combine both the provocative value of qualitative analysis in identifying frames with the reliability of quantitative measures in assessing their scope. The counting will be achieved through mechanisms provided by the database for maximum reliability.

TEXTUAL ASSESSMENT

To identify important framing devices, the study was not limited to news articles. It was decided that both news articles and editorials contribute to salience and both were examined. In this qualitative, exploratory part of the study, 10 articles were randomly selected and analyzed. Thus, a modest number of articles and editorials were deemed adequate for the analysis, designed to be more exploratory than comprehensive. Thus, five pieces were selected from *The Guardian* and five from *The New York Times*. Out of the 10 pieces, 8 were news articles and 2 were editorials.

Factions and Warlords

Both *The New York Times* and *The Guardian* referred to Somali leaders as "warlords." Warlords and their factions are presented in direct opposition to United Nations forces. Both media implied that the U.N. mission would have succeeded in Somalia if Somali warlords and their factions had not interfered with the United Nations initiative. The two media blamed warlords and their clans for the disaster in Somalia. They stressed the notion that the warlords' ambitions, their violent orientation and their hostility toward the West brought the country in a state of turmoil. Although the United Nations was willing to provide the country with solutions, the media argued, Somali warlords demonstrated their inability to seize the opportunity presented by the U.N. and allow the country to recover. According to *The Guardian* and *The Times*, the warlords often blocked humanitarian aid destined for remote villages and their inhabitants.

Both media used the term *warlords* quite extensively in their coverage. For example, on January 8, 1993, *The New York Times* described the attack of 400 marines against "Mogadishu's treacherous warlord Mohammed Farah Aidid" (Noble, 1993). On February 9, 1993, *The Guardian* described the brutal attack of the "warlord Mohammed Siad Barre" against Somali villagers (Dahlburg, 1993). Furthermore, *The Guardian* on June 21, showed how the "warlord Aidid" prevented peacekeepers from distributing food to civilians (Tomforde, 1993). The newspaper pointed out that "the United Nations abandoned plans to drop food in areas in Mogadishu controlled by Mohamed Farah Aidid yesterday when Pakistani troops supposed to guard it said they feared coming under sniper fire" (Tomforde, 1993). On February 1, 1993, *The New York Times* argued that "clan warfare still rages," and this prevents Somalia from being "a functioning country" (Schemo, 1993). On October 26, 1993, *The Guardian* condemned the deeds of "warlord Aidid" who "took up arms against the UN" (Huband, 1993). This recurrent terminology in the content of both *The New York Times* and *The Guardian* seems to be an important framing device utilized by the two media.

Humanitarian or Military Operation

When President Bush took the initiative to send American forces to Somalia, he claimed it was a humanitarian operation. However, in the news content there were traces of both the humanitarian as well as the military aspect of the mission. American soldiers arrived in Mogadishu, Somalia, on December of 1992, on what *The Guardian* claimed was a short-term, mercy-mission. However, in 1993, U.N. leaders realized that to fulfill their humanitarian objectives, they would have to take care of Somalia's internal instability. Consequently, they found themselves in the middle of a violent conflict without being able to relieve hungry civilians, especially in remote villages.

In 1993, both newspapers focused on children being fed by peacekeepers. Both described the situation in Somalia as horrific. On October 26, 1993, *The Guardian* argued that "children's bellies were distended, their hair has fallen out or turned orange from malnutrition, and they are desperately hungry" (Huband, 1993). *The New York Times* also highlighted the relief aspect of the operation. "In just two months, American forces have nearly completed their assigned mission of providing desperate Somalis with emergency humanitarian relief" (450 Combat Soldiers Return from Somalia, 1993).

However, the mission was not framed exclusively as humanitarian. Both media made extensive references to the military aspect of the operation. They argued that U.N. soldiers—despite good intentions—had to engage in military confrontation. For example, as *The Guardian* pointed out,

the food handout, postponed until today, was supposed to refocus the attention of Mogadishu's million people on the relief role which brought the U.N. to
Somalia in the first place and douse controversy over the killings of civilians
by the peacekeepers." (Tomforde, 1993)

The New York Times also argued that the presence of the military was necessary despite the humanitarian nature of the operation. "Troops were sent to
Somalia in a United Nations effort to insure the safe passage of humanitarian
aid" (450 Soldiers Return Home From Somalia, 1993). Both media explained
the challenges faced by the peacekeepers. Although the "Operation Restore
Hope" was conceptualized as a humanitarian operation, a few months later it
had become an unrealistic vision of Western leaders who were not aware of
the extent of the troubles that plagued the Somali people.

QUANTITATIVE STUDY OF FRAMING MECHANISMS

The terms *warlords* and *factions* emerged in the content of both *The New
York Times* as well as *The Guardian*. Furthermore, the two media framed the
mission both as a humanitarian operation as well as a military confrontation. To precisely measure the occurrence of the foregoing framing mechanisms during the entire operation—from 1992 to 1994—the current project
utilized the database NEXIS/LEXIS which provided an accurate count of the
terms. To search for these terms, the following scheme was utilized: *Somalia* and *warlords* from 1/1/92 to 12/31/92. This method was repeated for every
term throughout the 3-year period. The total population of articles was utilized. *The New York Times* devoted more space to the coverage of Somalia
than did *The Guardian*. The authors reviewed all articles and eliminated re-
dundant pieces and articles that mentioned Somalia in passing. The total
number of articles published by *The New York Times* and *The Guardian* are
reported in Table 9.1.

Because *The New York Times* devoted considerably more space in the
coverage of the mission than *The Guardian*, the authors converted the raw
measures of the keywords to occurrences of the terms per thousand arti-

TABLE 9.1
The total coverage of "Operation Restore Hope"
in Somalia by *The New York Times* and *The Guardian*.

Year	1992	1993	1994
The New York Times (Number of Articles)	427	778	223
The Guardian (Number of Articles)	177	224	75

cles. This was a necessary step to ensure a meaningful comparison of framing mechanisms between the two media. The following framing mechanisms were counted: warlord(s) and faction(s), two common characterizations of Somali leaders; "peacekeeper(s)" and "humanitarian" that dealt with the humanitarian nature of the mission; and "military" and "intervention," which addressed the military aspect of the operation. Tables 9.2 and 9.3 summarize the findings.

Warlords and Factions

The terms *warlord(s)* and *faction(s)* were important framing mechanisms for both media. The data indicate that there were no significant quantitative differences between the two media in terms of this framing mechanism.

TABLE 9.2
A Quantitative Assessment of Framing Mechanisms During
"Operation Restore Hope" in Somalia From 1992 to 1994.

| | The New York Times | | | | | |
| | 1992 | | 1993 | | 1994 | |
Year	Raw Articles	Per 1000	Raw Articles	Per 1000	Raw Articles	Per 1000
Warlord(s)	51	119	153	197	16	72
Faction(s)	108	252	368	473	45	201
Peace-keeper(s)	31	73	243	313	45	201
Humanitarian	119	279	106	136	23	103
Intervention	82	192	147	189	31	139
Military	271	635	320	411	120	538

TABLE 9.3
A Quantitative Assessment of Framing Mechanisms During
"Operation Restore Hope" in Somalia From 1992 to 1994.

| | The Guardian | | | | | |
| | 1992 | | 1993 | | 1994 | |
Year	Raw Articles	Per 1000	Raw Articles	Per 1000	Raw Articles	Per 1000
Warlord(s)	27	152	71	317	12	160
Faction(s)	50	282	59	263	9	120
Peace-keeper(s)	4	23	30	134	10	133
Humanitarian	69	389	54	241	13	173
Intervention	33	186	49	218	8	107
Military	78	440	131	585	28	373

Both used the terms more extensively during the year 1993 than during the other two years. It can be speculated that both frames were significant for Western policies. Perhaps the extensive use of those terms and the portrayal of Somali leaders as warlords and leaders of factions was preparing the ground for the military intervention in Somalia and the elimination of those groups. The use of those frames peaked for both media in 1993 when the military conflict was at its zenith. From a Western perspective, framing those Somali leaders as warlords, did not provide any insight as to how the Somalis themselves perceived their nation's leadership and social structure.

The Humanitarian and the Military Frames

The term *humanitarian* was more salient in 1992 and showed a decline during the years 1993 and 1994. This decline was consistent in the coverage of both media. The term *peacekeeper*, however, reached its peak in 1993 and showed a small decline during 1994, while *The Guardian* emphasized this frame equally during the years 1993 and 1994.

The terms *military* and *intervention* registered strongly during the year 1992 in the case of *The New York Times* and, during 1993, in the case of *The Guardian*. In 1994 they registered stronger in the coverage of *The New York Times*. Although Operation Restore Hope was framed as a humanitarian mission, the term *military* appeared at least twice as much across the board in the coverage of both media. In other words, it can be argued that Operation Restore Hope was framed more as a military operation than as a mercy mission. Although the United Nations itself framed the operation in Somalia as a humanitarian mission—and the media followed the *United Nations* lead, in the process the media ultimately treated the military frame as a more important. The media's framing choices show that the military involvement in Somalia was more salient than the humanitarian initiative. This finding may be indicative of the media being subject to nongovernmental influences. Although policymakers attempt to frame issues and events a certain way, the media often deal with structural and systemic factors that impact their framing choices.

In terms of changing frame patterns, the term *humanitarian* was stronger during the year 1992 and showed signs of decline in 1993 and 1994. This trend held true for both media. Thus, it can be speculated that although the mission was designed and promoted as humanitarian in nature, in the process it became a military operation. In the coverage of *The New York Times*, the military frame remained very strong during the 3-year period. In *The Guardian* it registered very strongly during 1993 and then became significantly weaker in 1994. Overall, the two media showed a consistency in their framing choices. Although *The Guardian* has a reputation as a center/left newspaper which often expresses its opposition to US policies, in this case, it mirrored framing choices pursued by *The New York Times*.

CONCLUSION

Although previous research has shown that Western media are not a monolithic institution, in this case Operation Restore Hope was covered similarly by both European and American journalists. There were no striking differences pertaining to the frames we identified. The identified frames were of major importance for both media. The military aspect of the operation was overemphasized by both media. This is probably indicative of the importance policymakers and the media placed on the presence of military personnel in Somalia. On the other hand, the term *humanitarian* registered strongly in the beginning of the operation and slowly declined. Thus it can be speculated that altruism lost its momentum after a few months in Somalia. Although the framing of Operation Restore Hope as a humanitarian mission was initially successful, the steady decline of the frame may be indicative of a shift in the nature of the operation.

The current project deviates from previous research since it demonstrates that Western media utilized the same framing mechanisms and told virtually the same story. The identified frames were important for both *The New York Times* and *The Guardian*. Is this an isolated phenomenon? Is this a sign of convergence in terms of gatekeeping patterns, source reliance, and styles of coverage? Is this a result of media concentration in the West? The extent to which this trend applies to the coverage of other world events should be subject to further investigation.

As this was only a preliminary study conducted by graduate students in their early stages of familiarization with framing analyses, the reader needs to treat the current results as a case study with a limited degree of generalization to other world events. Future studies should not limit their analyses to framing mechanisms. Other categories of frames should be identified and measured in comparative structures to reveal different attitudes toward the Third World as well as the structural and ideological influences that lead editors and reporters to frame issues a certain way and not another.

REFERENCES

Dahlburg, J. (1993, February 9). "Despair in villages beyond hope." *The Guardian*, p. 11.

Ghanem, S. (1996). *Media coverage of crime and public opinion: An exploration of the second level agenda setting.* Austin: University of Texas Doctoral Dissertation.

Hopple, G. (1982). International news coverage in two elite newspapers. *Journal of Communication, 32,* 61–74.

Huband, M. (1993, October 26). "Somalis die in renewed clan wars." *The Guardian*, p. 10.

Livingston, S., & Eachus, T. (1995). Humanitarian crises and U.S. foreign policy: Somalia and the CNN effect reconsidered. *Political Communication, 12,* 413–29.

Minear, L., Scott, C., & Weiss, T. (1996). *The news media, civil war and humanitarian action.* Boulder, CO: Rienner.

Natsios, A. (1997). *U.S. foreign policy and the four horsemen of the Apocalypse: Humanitarian relief in complex emergencies.* Westport, CT: Praeger.

450 Combat soldiers return home from Somalia. (1993, December 19). *The New York Times*, p. 49.

Noble, K. (1993, January 8). 400 Marines attack compound of Somali gunmen. *The New York Times*, p. 1.

Schemo, D. (1993, February 1). Somali police back on duty. *The New York Times*, p. 7.

Tankard, J., & Sumpter, R. (1993). *Media awareness of media manipulation: The use of the term "spin doctor."* Paper presented to the Association for Education in Journalism and Mass Communication, Kansas City.

Tomforde, A. (1993, June 21). UN Chief offers Bonn his services in court. *The Guardian*, p. 20.

10

Framing the Motorcycle Outlaw

Ross Stuart Fuglsang

Our image of bikers and the framework of perceptions surrounding outlaw motorcycle clubs has changed only slightly in the past 50 years. Badass attitude, black leather jackets, heavy boots, and denim jeans are staples of biker chic. Not even Japan's domination of the motorcycle market in the 1970s and 1980s, the "You meet the nicest people on a Honda" sloganeering of the 1960s, 10 years of *Happy Days* and "the Fonz," or Harley-Davidson's economic renaissance and its wooing of rich urban bikers—rubbies—could dispel the image.

The seed of the outlaw biker image was planted July 4th weekend, 1947, in Hollister, California, but that only began the transformation of a handful of Southern California bikers and nonconformists into a national scourge. How did the news media respond to the perceived threat of bikers and outlaw clubs? How did they construct and use a framework of myth and outlaw imagery to ascribe meaning to the new phenomenon? Mainstream media, as arbiters of right and wrong, relied on a specific array of ritual, myth, and metaphor, first to explain and define motorcycle culture, then to assign bikers a place on the margins of society. Seizing the opportunity, the news media satisfied audience desire for sensation and information, defined the biker "not-a-citizen" and supported America's middle-class norms for civility and propriety.

News media employ specific strategies to cover every exigency of the newsroom and create an illusion of fair and adequate coverage. To explain the similarity of news coverage across media, Cohen and Young (1981) employed the consensual paradigm, which states that journalists share a particular view of the way the world must be. It assumes a preconceived definition of citizenship, social order, and normal human nature. The conventions and practices, which define the newsroom, are socialized into reporters, editors, and photographers from their first day on the job. In the end, the journalist's accepted paradigm of how and why events occur and of what the universe looks like conspire to homogenize the news, no matter how out of the ordinary it may be, into the typically atypical.

Becker (1973) described a process by which some of those events are understood to break the rules and consequently are labeled as deviant. For Becker, there are the acts themselves, and the judgment of those acts. It is in the observance, discussion, and description of alleged deviance, the drama as played out in "moral rhetoric," that definition takes place. Becker focuses on "those sufficiently powerful to make their imputations of deviance stick: police, courts, physicians, school officials, and parents" (p. 196). The mass media are an obvious and necessary addition to this list of "moral entrepreneurs," and to the system of moral judgment overall. Ericson, Baranek, and Chan (1989) suggested that the news media, through recognition of sources and experts, play a unique role as the public's "daily barometer" of how society works: "News is a representation of authority. In the contemporary knowledge society news represents who are the authorized knowers and what are their authoritative versions of reality" (p. 3).

The media interpret and enforce social norms out of self-interest. Their ability to control deviance is a keystone in the construction of administered society and our understanding of what it means to be law-abiding citizens. How and why deviants and deviance are imagined as they are is as important as who is selected for recognition and public approbation. The selection of a narrative framework prods the audience to perceive a story in one way rather than another, to make this mental connection rather than another. Accurate or not, the interpretive frames the media ultimately decide upon create meaning in readers and viewers, place events in a particular context, and serve as persistent reminders of how future stories should be told and understood.

News reports out of Hollister established an early connection between bikers and criminality. Continued reporting made the connection stronger, singling out "one-percenters" as an identifiable threat to safety and stability. The headline beneath *Life* magazine's photo from Hollister read, "Cyclist's holiday. He and friends terrorize a town" (1947, p. 31). Without discriminating among more than 4,000 motorcycle enthusiasts attending the AMA (American Motorcyclist Association) sanctioned rally, the brief story described how bikers "quickly tired of ordinary motorcycle thrills" without first explaining what exactly "ordinary" was (p. 31). Cyclists raced their motorcycles in the streets, disobeyed traffic signs, and damaged a restaurant.

A few were arrested for drunkenness and indecent exposure, but in the end most were guilty simply of a lack of decorum and disorderly conduct.

Defiance of authority, disregard for property, and the necessity of calling other law enforcement agencies for assistance were consistent themes in early reports. An Associated Press story on Hollister noted that 32 officers augmented the town's seven-man police force, and that trouble started when cyclists raced down a "main thoroughfare, paying no heed to orders from police to stop" ("Motorcyclists put town," 1947, p. 19). A year later, during a melee in Riverside, California, the AP reported, "Every police and sheriff's officer this citrus-belt town could muster was called out tonight to defend the town against more than 1,000 cyclists" ("Cyclists rule," 1948, p. 16). Besides racing through the town's business district, they "manhandled" an Air Force officer and trampled the hood of his car. At Angels Camp, California, in 1957 the AP reported that bikers overwhelmed the two-man police force and 48 additional lawmen were brought in to quell the disturbance. Though declaring "main street was not safe for the townsmen," the final paragraph admitted that "except for hundreds of beer bottles and cans littering main street, no damage was done during the disturbance" ("Outlaw cyclists," 1957, p. 7).

A *Los Angeles Times* editorial warned readers of "mobile, mounted hoodlums" in 1948. It compared those early California disturbances to "guerrilla warfare," adding that Hollister motorcyclists "fought, rioted and destroyed, until they were dispersed with the threat of tear gas" ("Swarming," 1948, p. 4). "The rape of Riverside," the article suggested, might have been avoided had local law enforcement been better prepared. It concluded with a dire warning: "This is more than a local problem. Mounted hoodlums who can assemble from all points of the compass and from distances of several hundred miles pose a state problem of policing" (p. 4). It is clear from the *Times'* rhetorical hyperbole that it had identified a threat and that police and "flying squadrons" of the State Highway Patrol ought to react decisively to resolve the problem.

In time, the ubiquity of the Hell's Angels Motorcycle Club would further erode the biker image. Their drunken antics, disheveled and sloppy appearance and general oafishness betrayed bikers as undesirable, even among other motorcyclists. Reporting the Big Bear Run in Victorville, California, in 1961, *Sports Illustrated* advanced the idea of the AMA's separation from the "sideburned delinquents" who made the event a shambles. Opposing respectable motorcyclists were "bearded tough guys in top hats and young swaggerers in black leather jackets with 'Hell's Angels—Berdoo' painted on the back. . . . In short, enough certified kooks to show that the romance had not gone out of California motorcycling altogether" (Murray, 1961, p. 12).

By the end of the decade the nation had seen all it needed of the Hell's Angels. The incidence and severity of violence at rallies and AMA-sponsored events escalated steadily, so much so that a 1963 Labor Day blowout in Porterville and allegations of rape during a 1964 Angels run in Monterey inspired California Attorney General Thomas Lynch to investigate outlaw clubs. Bikers had clearly crossed a line between a level of socially acceptable inconvenience and antisocial depravity, and police and mainstream media reacted in tandem to apprise the citizenry. The outlaw bikers' eccentricities, especially their sexual aggressiveness, were intolerable and their existence was a "mockery of public decency" (Thompson, 1967, p. 116). Lynch's report focused yet more attention on bikers and gave law enforcement greater authority to put the clamps on outlaw clubs. Similarly, the accumulating evidence that the Hell's Angels MC was spreading its influence into middle-class communities further invoked the news media's role as finger-pointing moral barometer.

Time accepted at face value Lynch's indictment of antisocial behavior. Freely citing "facts" and eschewing initiative reporting, *Time* concluded that "no act is too degrading for the pack," then added descriptions of the Angels' deviant sexual practices and thievery, all performed between "drug-induced stupors" ("The wilder ones," 1965, p. 23B). A *New York Times* story also depended on Lynch's accumulated evidence, but reassured readers that all was well by mentioning the report's "intensive" investigation and the new surveillance and intelligence efforts to be implemented in California ("California takes," 1965, p. 15). Lynch got the final word, predicting stronger measures will be taken to investigate and arrest bikers "who threaten the lives, peace and security of honest citizens" ("The wilder ones," p. 23B).

The *Los Angeles Times* put that threat at the top of its story concerning the "long-awaited report," followed by a description of the "voluminous incidents for which club members were responsible" and law enforcement's proposed new tactics ("Hell's Angels called," 1965, p. 1). The import of Lynch's findings was indicated not only by the weight of the Angels' legal infractions, but by the amount of work that went into compiling the facts and statistics, which painted an ugly picture of outlaw clubs. The "mass investigation" entailed "six months of work by the attorney general's office, the California Highway Patrol, 22 district attorneys, 15 sheriffs and 67 police chiefs" (p. 1).

Descriptions of outlaw bikers as less than human and outside the scope of social acceptability were the rule. A focus on appearance and bizarre appetites made them easy to identify in a decade when riots and demonstrations were common. The Angels gained singular notoriety as instigators of violence. They had no agenda other than lawlessness and self-gratification, and their definition of fun was at best unsettling. Their use of random violence and casual intimidation was the nation's worst fear realized. In Laconia, New Hampshire, rioters and Hell's Angels were alleged to have set fire to a car while a family of six was still in it, then faced down National Guardsmen and "unfurled a Nazi flag and set up a chant of 'Sieg Heil'" ("Bikies' fun," 1965, p. 21).

Mok's (1965) Laconia reporting for *Life* was less critical than usual of bikers, observing that "crew-cut college kids whose immaculate chinos could only have been laundered by Mother" joined motorcyclists in the melee (p. 88). Thompson (1967), however, treated the Laconia reports as an example of the mainstream media's focus on outrage stories and their inability to divine the truth amid contradictory accounts. The National Guard, he wrote, expected violence in Laconia and had practiced riot control for 10 weeks previous. Although it was not stated in news reports, Thompson revealed that damage from the riot was minimal, the races went on as scheduled, and townspeople believed the event would be welcomed back the next year. Unfortunately, by the time all of this information was available, no one cared.

After a series of nationally publicized murder trials and the debacle at Altamont Speedway, where The Rolling Stones hired the Angels to act as security for an outdoor concert and they subsequently killed Meredith Hunter, the club involved itself in charity events in an attempt to spruce up its outlaw image. As described in *Newsweek*, an antidrug campaign, blood drives, and toy runs seemed successful, but the bad biker framework proved to be more resilient than the club's public relations moves. Sources quoted in the story "The risen Angels" (1973) are skeptical. One police officer "speculates the new image may in fact be nothing more than a front for expanded narcotics trafficking" (p. 38). *Newsweek's* lead confirmed its own estimation that the gang's image "hit rock-bottom—even by its own less-than-lofty standards," and that they inspire fear even while performing good deeds (p. 38). That they are carrying teddy bears instead of "switchblades and beer bottles" seemed too bizarre to believe.

Ten Hell's Angels, including Ralph "Sonny" Barger, now the club's "godfather," were arrested on conspiracy and drug charges in 1979 ("It may be," 1979, p. 63). Articles in *Time* and *Newsweek* repeated pat biker descriptions created out of Hollister, but described as well a new sophistication which belied the club's reputation. *Time* instilled an ominous tone by noting that officers seized drugs and "a small arsenal of firearms, including some 1,000 rounds of ammunition" ("Hell's Angels: Some," 1979, p. 34). And though they faced up to 20 years in prison, one source made it clear the danger the Angels represented to all of society remained: "'There will be more of them out of prison than in, and you can't change years of a pattern over night'" (p. 34).

The trial foreshadowed a litany of stories concerning drugs, violence, arrests, trials, and mob connections which played throughout the 1980s (See "Busting," 1985; "Gangs that rival," 1986; Penn, 1984; Santos, 1980; Shapiro,

1985; "Speed demons," 1984; Starr, 1981). The Hell's Angels MC continued to establish new chapters across the country, however. Upstart clubs challenged them and the gang wars that followed provided adequate media fodder for anger, outrage, and handwringing. The Angels also continued their low-key, circumspect metamorphosis. Possibly sensing nascent antigovernment opinion, Sonny Barger spoke out against attacks on the club in 1982: "'DEA and ATF on their best days would make the Hell's Angels look like a bunch of Boy Scouts on a Sunday picnic'" (Weissler, 1982, p. 65).

For four decades, Barger was a constant in Hell's Angels reporting. *Newsweek* noted his odor and decadence in 1965 as he "spat out," "'We ain't no homos'" ("The wild ones," p. 25). In 1970, commenting unrepentantly—and again ungrammatically—on Altamont, the malevolence of the "boss Angel" had a stronger undercurrent: " 'Ain't nobody gonna kick my motorcycle' " ("Avenging Angels," 1970, p. 16). Relying on the California Attorney General and former club members, a 1973 *Los Angeles Times* article painted a threatening picture of Barger, if only because it revealed his intelligence and charisma. He created a "Mafia-style monolith, staking out territories and ruling through fear and intimidation," succeeded in harnessing the club's potential, directed its public relations, and "put a lid on the Angels' more raucous entertainment" (Endicott, 1973, p. 3).

In 1994 the archetypal Angel was profiled again in a *Los Angeles Times* piece, this time as an entrepreneur and philanthropist. The biker marketed his own line of salsa and sold T-shirts emblazoned, "Sonny Barger—American hero." Relaxing in his home, Barger was "almost patrician" and the "hard edges have softened." He remained unapologetic, however, and his speaking ability had, amazingly, improved: "'I just believe we have a right to do anything we want to do as long as we're not hurting anyone else, and if anyone tries to stop us, we have a right to step on them'" (Sipchen, 1994, p. E1). He had "melted" into society, but continued to "avoid mainstream society. 'It's not something that appeals to me. . . . I am what I want to be' " (p. E1). Barger, it seemed, was a survivor and a winner, and America loves winners.

Barger's image makeover paralleled the media's handling of the country's changing perceptions of motorcycles and bikers. With continued acceptance of motorcycles and the re-birth of the Harley-Davidson Motor Company in 1982 after years of economic sputtering, mainstream media felt pressure to modify the established biker formula. The portrait Bastoni (1988) sketched in a *Boston Magazine* piece was, at least, ambivalent toward the tried-and-true bad biker image. The Massachusetts Hell's Angels Bastoni interviewed admitted to being convicts and felons, but they argued that fact alone should not reflect on the club. Bouncin' Bob argued that politicians and members of the Knights of Columbus have been convicted of crimes, so "'why aren't they calling the Senate a criminal organization and harassing senators and politicians?'" (p. 101). Another biker claimed that police officers steal cocaine and marijuana from property rooms then resell it, but no one believes they are part of a criminal organization. The club's age-old defense had gained a new resonance in an era of government corruption.

Besides interviewing bikers, Bastoni talked to the club's lawyer, the FBI, and state police officers. With the information he gathered, Bastoni admitted, "Not even the Angels' high-octane blend of paranoia and denial can wipe out the violent record of the Massachusetts club during the last 10 years" (p. 131). Club members were linked to murder and methamphetamine production and hired themselves out to the Mafia. Yet there is no real comparison between the two organizations. Compared to the Mafia "the Hell's Angels pale in significance," the chief of the New England Organized Crime Strike Force said, because their influence is too narrow (p. 135).

In 1997 the Hell's Angels Motorcycle Club was the object of international attention as it established chapters in Sweden and Denmark. The move prompted a "turf war" between the Angels and the Bandidos MC over drug markets. Elements of a page 1 *New York Times* story reporting the incisive actions of a multinational police force used familiar imagery to describe the biker lifestyle. The Angels' clubhouse was a "shack," and they celebrated their newest chapter with "rivers of beer." One particularly surly biker, bearded, tattooed and abrupt, chafed under the "suffocating police surveillance" (Ibrahim, 1997, p. A1).

The article expressed none of the furor and indignation of previous decades' reports, however. Despite the "cycle of attacks and revenge" inflicted on the residents of Copenhagen, Oslo, and Stockholm, the headline merely noted, "Police Spoil Hell's Angels Party." The story described the escalation of violence, the array of weapons employed and the number of "civilians" injured in the war, but the club's activities were related in such a way that they sounded like the actions of a particularly aggressive multinational corporation. A familiar story detail, albeit reserved, was the reported success of law enforcement's crackdown: "The normally liberal Swedish police made sure the 250 to 300 international members of the brotherhood, as the Angels refer to themselves, had a miserable time" (p. A1).

By 1999, the outrage and fear instilled into the outlaw biker framework for decades further dissipated. In an AP story about the club's return to Lynn, Massachusetts, the bikers' neighbors were "pretty upset," but the homeowners' concern was for property values: "As soon as the Hell's Angels signs went up, this property right here dropped 20 grand" ("Hell's Angels are," 1999, p. A7). Residents seemed willing to give the bikers a chance, and City Councilman David Ellis noted their civic involvement and that "they walk both sides of the fence" (p. A7). The established biker framework was recalled in the last half of the article, however, casting a pall over the homecoming. The clubhouse was protected by pit bulls and no trespassing signs threatened death to those who don't pay attention. Before being run out of town in 1997, it was reported, two members admitted murdering a rival gang member and 16 others were arrested for dealing drugs. Federal agents in armored personnel carriers drove them out and destroyed their former clubhouse.

CONCLUSION

The media impart knowledge and create an awareness of the world we experience, as well as those aspects of our existence which remain unexperienced, unexplained, and hidden. Despite the miles between Sweden and Hollister, California, deviant motorcycle clubs and steadfast police will be understood by an international audience. The process of communication begins with imagination, the spontaneous creation of a meaningful image (Adam, 1993). The outlaw biker myth is that image, a multipurpose, meaning-making device. The critical element of the process of communication is not just the act of providing information; for communication to be successful there must exist a shared framework for creating meaning from that information.

Written at first blush, with city officials reeling as bikers incited violence in their sleepy little towns, newspaper and magazine reports inspired public fear and moral outrage. When the facts were discovered, however, and the actual damage was less extensive than originally thought, it was too late to undo the injury, even if the media had wanted to. Why change what effectively called attention to deviance, bad behavior and criminality? From the beginning motorcycle hooligans, one-percenters, and outlaws have stood as effective examples of what is wrong—and only rarely right—with society. They filled the role of "not-a-citlzen," symbols of social and sexual deviance which provided a civics lesson in miniature every time a law was broken and the police brought to justice an unkempt, longhaired biker. It seems only fitting that as a parting shot one-percenters coined "citizen" as a derisive term for those who willingly accepted society's legal and moral strictures.

The outlaw bikers' marginal existence was an invitation for the news media, in their role as moral entrepreneurs and watchdogs of the public good, to exhibit a negative example of citizenship. From the beginning the one-percenters' manner of dress was provocative. So too was their lack of personal hygiene, their insobriety, and the physical menace they cultivated with every swagger. As young people dropped out and civil unrest grew to encompass racial, ethnic, gender, and class dissatisfaction in the 1960s, American self-confidence evaporated. Although other organizations, legal and illegal alike, were more critical of the status quo, the media and law enforcement agencies tagged motorcycle gangs as a dangerous force that needed to be dealt with quickly and effectively. Abhorred by everyone and unprotected by a nation's collective guilt, loosely organized outlaw clubs were easy to single out and offered police departments an opportunity to publicize hard-won victories in the "war against crime."

In the course of their first 40 years, motorcycle clubs' criminal deviance dovetailed with their social nonconformity, making them attractive targets. But by the late 1980s society had come to accept, at least in part, a biker perspective. A newfound cynicism of the mainstream, combined with lack of respect for authority, had more to do with the country's growing acceptance of bikers than did changes in bikers themselves, however. Their success, strength, and longevity offer clues as to why the biker myth has recently enjoyed a popular renaissance. Motorcycle outlaws, who have long cultivated independence and a healthy skepticism of bureaucracy and democracy, have managed to meld with the demands of the age. Even some "true" citizens believe society has too tight a hold on their lives.

Relying on established, readily understood, interpretive frames, mainstream media exploited the image of outlaw bikers, identifying them as a menace to middle-class values. Motorcycle clubs and their activities at once served to define the boundaries of acceptable behavior and reveal the effectiveness of law enforcement procedures against a rising tide of criminal activity. But that line between citizen and not-a-citizen, between wrong and right, and between evil and good, is fluid. Consequently, there will always be a need for the media to define and inform the populace where they believe the line is—and where it ought to be. Cohen (1971) noted that the media give inordinate attention to deviance because it reassures the audience that a line exists between good and evil. More important to the continued analysis of changes in the framing of outlaw motorcycle clubs, however, is Cohen's reminder that "the value of the line must continually be reasserted; we can only know what it is to be saintly by being told just what the shape of the devil is" (p. 10).

REFERENCES

Adam, G. S. (1993). *Notes towards a definition of journalism: Understanding an old craft as an art form.* St. Petersburg, FL: The Poynter Institute for Media Studies.

Avenging angels. (1970, January 5). *Newsweek,* p. 16.

Bastoni, M. (1988, July). Chrome and hot leather. *Boston Magazine,* pp. 98–101, 128–138.

Becker, H. S. (1973). *Outsiders: Studies in the sociology of deviance.* New York: The Free Press.

Bikies' fun. (1965, 5 July). *Newsweek,* p. 21.

Busting Hell's Angels. (1985, May 13). *Time,* p. 28.

California takes steps to curb terrorism of ruffian cyclists. (1965, March 16). *New York Times,* p. 15.

Cohen, S. (Ed.). (1971). *Images of deviance.* Middlesex, England: Penguin Books.

Cohen, S., & Young, J. (1981). Models of presentation. In S. Cohen & J. Young (Eds.), *The manufacture of news: Social problems, deviance and the mass media* (pp. 159–168). Beverly Hills, CA: Sage.

Cyclist's holiday. (1947, July 21). *Life*, p. 31.

Cyclists rule town; 28 held in disorder. (1948, July 5). *New York Times*, p. 16.

Endicott, W. (1973, January 15). Hell's Angels: Some say they're in the big leagues. *Los Angeles Times*, pp. 3, 12.

Ericson, R. V., Baranek, P., & Chan, J. (1989). *Negotiating control: A study of news sources.* Toronto, Canada: University of Toronto Press.

Gangs that rival the mob. (1986, February 3). *U.S. News and World Report*, p. 29.

Hell's Angels are back to tough 'City of Sin.' (1999, March 9). *Sioux City Journal*, p. A7.

Hell's Angels called threat on wheels. (1965, March 16). *Los Angeles Times*, pp. 1, 2.

Hell's Angels: Some wheelers may be dealers. (1979, July 2). *Time*, p. 34.

Ibrahim, Y. M. (1997, March 3). Sweden's courteous police spoil a Hell's Angels party. *New York Times*, p. A1.

It may be the end of a cycle as Hell's Angels 'Godfather' Sonny Barger returns to jail. (1979, July 3). *People Weekly*, pp. 63–64.

Mok, M. 'Come to the riot. See Weirs Beach burn.' (1965, July 2). *Life*, p. 88–89.

Motorcyclists put town in uproar. (1947, July 7). *New York Times*, p. 19.

Murray, J. (1961, January 23). Debacle in the desert. *Sports Illustrated*, pp. 12–15.

Outlaw cyclists alarm a village. (1957, June 3). *New York Times*, p. 7.

Penn, S. (1984, January 11). Rise in crime ventures by motorcycle gangs worries U. S. lawmen. *Wall Street Journal*, pp. 1, 18.

The risen Angels. (1973, December 10). *Newsweek*, p. 38.

Santos, L. (1980, July 24). Gangs of bikers control drugs, DEA report says. *Los Angeles Times*, p. 18.

Shapiro, W. (1985, May 13). Going after Hell's Angels. *Newsweek*, p. 41.

Sipchen, B. (1994, December 14). The rough rider. *Los Angeles Times*, p. E1.

Speed demons. (1984, April 2). *Time*, p. 21.

Starr, M. (1981, November 23). Do the Bandidos fit their name. *Newsweek*, p. 49.

Swarming of the mounted hoodlums. (1948, July 6). *Los Angeles Times*, p. 4II.

Thompson, H. S. (1967). *Hell's Angels: A strange and terrible saga of the outlaw motorcycle gang.* New York: Ballantine.

Weissler, D. A. (1982, September 20). Motorcycle gangs go gray flannel. *U.S. News and World Report*, p. 65.

The wild ones. (1965, March 29). *Newsweek*, p. 25.

The wilder ones. (1965, March 26). *Time*, p. 23B.

11

What's Really Important Here?: Media Self-Coverage in the Susan Smith Murder Trial

Lynn M. Zoch

On May 11, 1995, the *Union* [South Carolina] *Daily Times*, circulation 7,100, published an editorial with the headline, "Be prepared for media show during Smith trial." The editorial read in part:

> Even as these words are being written, media organizations from around the world are gearing up for the beginning of the [Susan Smith] trial. They are doing background stories, exploring every possible angle, and preparing to descend on us like an occupying army. How long they will remain will depend upon the duration of the trial and how many stories they can squeeze out of it ... (W)e set an example for the whole world during the initial rush of publicity and attention that made us the center of the world's attention. . . . Now we have to do it again. (p. A4)

By May 1995 the editorial writer and residents of the small town of Union were already experienced with the problems inherent in being in the media spotlight. The previous October, a life-long resident of the town, 24-year-old Susan Vaughn Smith, had attracted international media attention to Union for the 9 days it took investigators to determine she had drowned her two children—3-year-old Michael and 14-month-old Alexander. Smith originally told police a carjacker stole her car with the two children still strapped in the back seat. Her accusations precipitated a nationwide search for the children and focused media attention on the events taking place in Union.

Some of those events, all covered in meticulous detail by the battalion of print reporters and broadcast camera crews that descended on Union, involved the media itself. The coverage became part of the story, and continued as part of the story during the trial and sentencing of Susan Smith for the murder of her two children. This chapter analyzes how South Carolina newspapers covered the media, particularly the broadcast media, represented in Union during the trial and pretrial period of the case. It then illustrates how the media framed their own importance to, and impact on, the denouement of the unfolding drama that was the Susan Smith case.

FRAMING THE MEDIA EVENT

Most readers and viewers have developed a set of media images, or beliefs and attitudes about the media based on their use of it. "These implicit theories, or schema, represent knowledge structures useful for organizing expectations concerning various phenomena" (Kosicki, Becker, & Fredin, 1994, p. 77). Beliefs such as "the media are accurate" or "the media are biased," "the media tell us what we need to know" or "the media are controlled by special interest groups" are examples of the common-sense theories audiences develop from their personal experience with the media (Kosicki, Becker, & Fredin, 1994). These constructions of common-sense theories about how the media should be understood, especially if the schema is a positive one, may multiply the effect of repetitive media words or images on the audience.

Framing intersects agenda setting when the media go beyond telling us what to think about—the selection of objects, issues, events, or personalities for attention—and the focus becomes how to think about it—the attributes of the object on which to focus attention (McCombs & Shaw, 1993). McCombs and Ghanem (chap. 2, this volume) call this transmission of attribute salience the "second level" of agenda setting. Framing, in this view, selects for the media agenda a restricted number of thematically related attributes related to a topic or news event and thus affects the pictures in our heads relating to that topic or event. In the newspaper coverage of the Susan Smith trial, the focus on the media presence at the trial affected the public's view of what was important and what they should pay attention to. In this sense the media covering the trial became as much a part of the story as was Smith, her lawyers, ex-husband, or the facts of the case.

Whereas Dayan and Katz (1992) view media events—"the high holidays of mass communication" (p. 1)—as unique to television, this chapter posits that television itself, or at least its representatives, can *become* the event. Although agreeing with Dayan and Katz that these events are not routine, and that they must happen live to be considered an event, I extend their definition to include *newspaper coverage* of the "event," as well as the television event itself. Bogart (1992) writes that television increasingly defines significant world events. The problem newspapers face is that readers identify big events with television and see newspapers as the source for local news. Although important to those living in the community, local information does not engage the reader the way major television stories do (Bogart, 1992). In this study, I analyze South Carolina newspapers' attempts to couple a local story with a worldwide story by framing the media, particularly television, as part of that story. The local story is the trial of Susan Smith, a young South Carolina mother who murdered her two children. The more widely publicized international story was the trial of Susan Smith, a woman known for murdering her two adorable toddlers, and for repeatedly lying to the American public by appearing on national television news shows begging the "kidnapper" to return her children to her unharmed.

Media events studies tend to "view the public realm as capable of alteration and replenishment through rhetoric and symbols" (Peters, 1995, p. 26). This is a view that also fits well with framing research, which may look for verbal and visual cues that direct the audience's attention in one direction while serving to obscure another. "Media content takes elements of culture, magnifies them, frames them, and feeds them back to an audience" (Shoemaker & Reese, 1991, p. 49). Schudson (1995) writes that "when the media offer the public an item of news, they confer upon it public legitimacy . . . they not only distribute the report of an event or announcement to a large group, they amplify it" (p. 19). The magnification or amplification these researchers refer to is the power inherent in the media's ability to frame a particular event or issue.

The metaphor of a media event, which can also be considered as an item of news or an element of our culture, as *theater* or *drama*, is also a recurring one. Peters (1995) refers to actors taking part in a media event, and compares these events to theatrical performances, while Weaver (1994) writes that "news isn't simply a report of what happened yesterday. It's a story, with characters, action, plot, point of view, dramatic closure" (p. 1). Gripsrud (1992) critiques the European press and its use of melodrama to tell the story.

If the media itself is considered part of the event it is covering, then well-known media personalities and "celebrities" become actors in the drama and worthy of coverage themselves. And television personalities are the actors the audience knows. After all, we invite them into our houses on an almost daily basis. Networks bid increasingly astronomical sums to lure "stars" to build ratings, while local television stations put together their own news "teams" to build audience share (Cook, Gomery, & Lichty, 1992). Television talk show hosts, some on a first-name basis with the audience, become celebrity actors in the unfolding drama. In the media event that was the Susan Smith trial, Oprah [Winfrey], Sally Jesse [Raphael], Phil

[Donahue], and Susan [Rook of CNN's "TalkBack"] all became stars to be covered as part of the drama.

METHOD AND SOURCES

I conducted a qualitative frame analysis on articles that referred to media involvement in the Susan Smith case and trial in any way. The frame analysis empirically tracked key words, phrases and themes that served to focus attention on journalists, media celebrities, the technology of news coverage, and the media itself as an integral part of the Susan Smith trial and overall story that was presented to the reading public.

The body of coverage for this study is composed of 107 newspaper articles published from May, the period leading up to the trial, through August, 1995, when the final wrap-up articles were published. Newspapers within South Carolina and the region, rather than a nationwide sample, were used because they contained the heaviest overall coverage of the trial. I purposively chose the four largest newspapers in the state—*The* [Columbia] *State*, *The* [Charleston] *Post & Courier*, *The Greenville News*, *The* [Spartanburg] *Herald-Journal*—as well as *The Charlotte* [North Carolina] *Observer* and the *Union Daily Times* for analysis. Only the state's largest papers were chosen because the smaller papers tend to use wire reports, often those submitted by reporters from the larger papers, and did not have their own reporters on the scene. The Union and Charlotte papers were included because Union was the site of the murder and the trial, and Charlotte, while in North Carolina, is close to Union with a major metropolitan paper.

Whereas television news broadcasts and talk shows offered intense coverage of the trial that was similar in content and scope to the print coverage, newspapers focused most heavily on the media presence and involvement at the trial. The newspaper body of coverage that was analyzed included hard news, feature articles, editorials, and commentary. The unit of analysis for this study was a statement referring in any way to the media's presence or impact as reported in the analyzed newspapers. In many cases whole articles were devoted to the media "take-over" of Union, while in other cases the media coverage and impact on the town and people was a peripheral issue and only comprised a few lines in the story.

IDENTIFYING THE FRAME

The frame analysis supported the idea that the media had become part of the story in the Susan Smith case. Of the six newspapers analyzed, all focused on the broadcast media to the exclusion of the print media in their coverage of media presence at the trial. *Newsweek* reporter Ginny Carroll, who covered the story, tried to put this attention on the broadcast media into perspective:

> Television's impact is so enormous that it almost inevitably becomes part of any story. And newspapers have almost built it in to their list of "what we have to do." Print has almost built that element into its coverage. Print does not have that impact and never will. The role of print remains the explainer (personal interview, September 19, 1997).

Carroll continued by pointing out that the television "cult of celebrity" also had an effect on why television's presence was considered newsworthy.

> (A)s this "cult of celebrity" continues to grow you get more and more people ... sort of using the national television personalities as a barometer of the importance of a story.
> And that's something else that happens in smaller newspapers. They use that to frame an event, to put it into perspective for their readers. [The event] is important enough that this person and that person is here. But the bottom line is television's impact is so enormous you just can't ignore it (personal interview, September 19, 1997).

Within the frame of "media are part of the story," and beyond the focus on television, I identified six additional themes that recurred repeatedly in the newspaper coverage: events that occurred only because of the media presence in Union; reportage of reporters working; local interaction with the media; local people as media (mostly broadcast) celebrities; comparisons to the "media circus" that the O.J. Simpson trial became; and outside forces—individuals and other media—that focused the media coverage in a particular direction.

To make sense of how these themes were used within the frame, I used the five devices identified by Gamson and Modigliani (1989) to group them. Of the five devices—visual images, metaphors, catchphrases, depictions, and exemplars—all but catchphrases were used by the newspapers to develop the frame of media as part of the story.

Use of Visual Images

The visual element of the frame was one area all newspapers had in common, and that served to unify the frame. The images of cameras and satellite trucks became ubiquitous throughout the period analyzed, both in actual photographs and in descriptions of the scene. A favorite visual for the newspapers was a view of the Union County Courthouse, all but obscured by scaffolding for television news crews, satellite trucks, and miles of wiring for telephones and cable feeds.

"Outside the courthouse, all the major networks had set up their satellite dishes" (*The Charlotte Observer*, July 11, 1995, p. A4). "Before the days of Court TV, CNN and satellite trucks, big trials just weren't quite as BIG," reported *The State* on June 24, p. A1. Even though Judge Howard had banned cameras from the courtroom during the trial, "(s)till, the major networks— CNN, NBC, ABC, CBS, all plan extensive coverage. On Main Street, TV stations have turned storefronts into temporary newsrooms. Huge trucks with satellite dishes are stationed like warships outside the Courthouse" (*The Charlotte Observer*, July 10, 1995, p. A1).

Descriptions such as "satellite dishes stationed like warships" are plentiful in the stories and commentary about the trial. "Dozens of television cameras, photographers and reporters buzzed outside the courthouse . . ." (*Greenville News*, July 11, 1995, p. D1) and "the endless foam-wrapped microphones swarming toward anyone ready to impart opinion" (*Charlotte Observer*, July 11, 1995, p. A4) are only a prelude to the ultimate visual metaphor: "In front of the courthouse, a dozen or so TV satellite trucks are parked, their dish antennas aimed toward a satellite somewhere in the heavens" (*The State*, July 13, 1995, p. A10). The reader can immediately visualize that satellite beaming the Susan Smith trial to one of the 65 national and international media outlets covering the trial.

In each of these cases the newspaper reader can easily visualize the television reporters and technology being described. Why? Because each image is something we've seen dozens of time in the background of a television live shot, as the reporter shouts to be heard over the noise of bystanders and other reporters doing their own live shots. Because the visual image of some unlucky local reporter being hit in the face with a boom mike has played coast to coast on syndicated "Bloopers" shows. Because in the spring and summer of 1995 we were in the middle of the O.J. Simpson trial, and we *knew* what reporters did at high profile trials.

Metaphors

Of equal importance to the visual images, and sometimes overlapping them, were the metaphors used to describe the scene in Union. While I identified three metaphors—the parallels to the "media circus" of the O.J. Simpson trial, the town as a "war zone" and the event itself as theater or drama, with the setting reminiscent of a movie set—the primary metaphor was the event-as-theater. This involved looking at the event itself as a story, with "stars" taking the roles of characters in the drama, action, plot, point of view, and dramatic closure. This drama metaphor is actually embedded in all of the reporting about the case. Each description of the media takeover of the town of Union describes the scene, the "set" if you will. The courthouse and scaffolding surrounding it are where the action takes place, the filled-to-capacity parking lots of satellite trucks and the Main Street buildings taken over by the networks—"storefronts, transformed shoe shops and doctors' offices" (*The State*, July 30, 1995, p. A13)—can be considered the backlot and trailers assigned to the stars. The cameras and microphones are the props used by the actors—in this case the media representatives. There are even cameos by television personalities like Susan Rook and Phil Donahue, who pop in and out of town.

The people of Union can be considered either spectators or extras, or perhaps both. A photo of a group of young boys in front of the courthouse with a television camera and reporter in the foreground makes this point. The photo is captioned "Derrick Keisler, 12, of Union S.C. is interviewed by Jerry Carnes of Atlanta's NBC affiliate channel Tuesday in front of the Union County Courthouse. Derrick and his YMCA day camp were there to see the *murder trial scene* in their hometown" (italics added; *Charlotte Observer*, July 12, 1995, p. A6). They are there not to attend the trial itself, but to see the scene surrounding the trial, as though the trial might be of lesser importance than what is going on around it, and they are drawn into the drama as bit players.

The principals in the trial are seen as actors too, with *The Charlotte Observer* printing "profiles" of both attorneys, prosecutor Tommy Pope, and lead defense attorney David Bruck. Pope, who rejected a plea bargain and went for the death penalty in the case, was accorded "star" treatment. "Oprah Winfrey sent a limo to pick him up for a live broadcast in Union" (*Charlotte Observer*, July 9, 1995, p. A1). Pope, unlike some of the actors, was credited with understanding the role he played in the drama. A July 9th editorial in *The State* was titled "If prosecutor makes a deal, he can't play The Game" (p. D2). The editorial writer comments that if Pope deals (accepts the plea bargain), there's no show. "The press, the TV, the lights, all pack up and go" (p. D2).

Exemplars

The impact of the media presence on the town of Union and the trial itself was also framed through the use of exemplars that highlighted how the media were becoming part of the story. These exemplars are identified as "events occurring because of the media presence" and came in two forms— those which were representative of how the media affected the trial, and those which represented the media's effect on the town.

The Trial. The greatest impact the media presence had on the trial itself was when Judge Howard "ordered cameras out the courtroom, giving TV crews five minutes to pack their gear" (*Post & Courier*, July 8, 1995, p. A1). The argument set forth by David Bruck, Smith's attorney, was that "coast-to-coast televised coverage would hurt his client's right to a fair trial. He said the presence of cameras might alter the way witnesses testify. 'The paramount obligation of both sides to this case is not to present a televised spectacle but to reach a just result at the lowest possible cost in resources and additional human suffering,' his motion says" (*Post & Courier*, June 30, 1995, p. A23).

The televised spectacle of the O.J. Simpson trial, where the media and the tendency of the principals in the case to play to the media are both thought to have affected the ultimate outcome of the criminal trial, also influenced the Smith trial and its judge.

> Some had predicted that the trial would take more than two months and compared it with the murder trial of O.J. Simpson in California. But Howard served notice immediately that the trials would be different. He banned cameras from the courtroom, enforced a gag order by ordering a reporter to jail and charged a juror with criminal contempt when he learned that she had lied about her criminal record. (*Greenville News*, July 29, 1995, p. A1)

The media coverage of the case also affected spectators at the trial. "Smith's story and her trial attracted so much national attention, people from all over felt a connection to the dead boys. During the trial's last days, spectators began lining up at 5 a.m. to get a seat in the courtroom" (*Charlotte Observer*, July 30, 1995, p. A1). Tourists with expectations for attending the trial, particularly during the sentencing phase, arrived from as far away as Ohio and Michigan, and newspaper photos showed people waiting in line for a chance to enter the courtroom.

The Town. In analyzing the effect of the media on Union, I found that the media became part of the story when newspaper reports repeatedly reminded readers of media representatives' impact on the town's economy and the residents' psyche. Initially the town of Union expected an economic bonanza from the presence of hundreds of media representatives. For real estate agents "the media influx is boosting spirits with a small economic boom at the cost of spreading the town's worst scandal all over the world. The upside for Union is that half a dozen vacant buildings on the two-lane Main Street are rented to media organizations, some of whom are making repairs at their own expense" (*The State*, July 3, 1995, p. A1).

The downside to the media influx into Union was traffic snarls and no parking downtown: "The city is encouraging employees who work in the general area (of the courthouse) to carpool" (*Post & Courier*, June 25, 1995, p. A1); no time off for Union police and safety officers; relentless questions

from reporters who stopped anyone who would talk with them and omni-
present cameras.

> By the end of the sentencing phase the "people who live and work in Union
> seemed grateful that the end was drawing near . . . Union has been turned up-
> side-down since then, and not much good has come of it. The hoped-for retail
> bonanza downtown hasn't materialized, except for some motel owners and a
> few Main Street vendors. Reporters are not spending much. And it is not the
> kind of event where you buy souvenirs" (*The State*, July 23, 1995, p. A8).

The remaining themes identified—coverage of reporters working; local
interaction with the media, local people as media (mostly broadcast) celebrities, and outside forces (individuals and other media) that focused the
media coverage in a particular direction—fit into the final framing device of
depictions. Each of these themes, which overlap and intertwine in the newspaper stories, describes an aspect of how the media, their representatives
and technology, became part of the story of the Susan Smith trial.

CONCLUSIONS

Even though South Carolina has recently made the "Top 10" list for states
with the highest rates of violent death, a case like that of Susan Smith, with
its accompanying high-profile trial and media frenzy, is not a usual occurrence. To have the case investigated and tried in the small, rural county
seat of Union added additional stresses to the town's citizens and to the
media representatives sent to cover the trial. Not only did Union lack the infrastructure to support the influx of technology-dependent media, it also
lacked the size to insulate its residents from the needs and wants of dead-
line-driven reporters.

In addition to putting Union under the microscope, media representatives put themselves on the slide to be viewed. Not only did they cover the
story, the "American Tragedy" that was the Susan Smith case, they covered
themselves as part of the story. In particular, as presented in this study, the
six newspapers analyzed covered television covering the story, and they
covered the effect on a small town when the media take it over for their
own uses. It must be noted at this point that had I chosen to conduct a nationwide sample, or to use only the major national newspapers, the findings
might have differed. As presented here, the frame identified is of regional
importance, because I cannot say definitively that all newspapers covered
the media as part of the story. Anecdotal evidence indicates, however, that
the media "takeover" of Union was reported internationally, as well as nationally.

The broadcast media became the "star" of this coverage for many reasons, not the least of which is the recognition audience members give to it. We "know" the people on TV. Also important to why television was covered to the exclusion of print media is the sheer *size* of its presence. Television is big in more ways than one. As Ginny Carroll explained:

> A reporter with a notepad is not a very visible or obstructive thing. A still cameraman, one lone still cameraman is not terribly noticeable unless he really wants to be. Take four or five networks who typically bring 20 or 30 people to a media event, with somewhat smaller equipment than used to be, but still pretty visible equipment, and you just create a huge intrusion on space, on people's space, on a town's space. It's the bulk of it and the volume of it. And it doesn't bear exclusively on television. But as more and more news organizations have gotten the technological capabilities, local TV stations send a truck and a crew and somebody to go on live. (personal interview, September 19, 1997).

During the trial and pretrial period of the Susan Smith case the media did more than cover the event. As this study shows it not only *became* part of the event, it *covered itself* as part of the event. And that coverage was framed so that the reader accepted the media presence as an integral part of what should be, and needed to be, covered in the trial and its setting. The media were part of the story.

The importance of the media as part of the story can be seen in the framing of "events that occurred only because of the media presence in Union." The newspapers analyzed carefully covered the media impact on both the trial and the town of Union. The visuals used in the coverage also supported the omnipresence of the media. Aside from pictures of Susan Smith entering or exiting the courthouse, almost all pictures were either media-directed or had cameras and microphones in the background or foreground.

Reporters also covered themselves working, although to a fairly small degree compared to other self-coverage. Local interaction with the media, particularly how generic "reporters" (obviously never the reporter writing the story) hounded local people for interviews was also a regular topic for coverage.

Comparisons to the media circus that the O.J. Simpson trial became represented only one of the metaphors used in the reporting of the trial. Perhaps of more importance is the drama or theater metaphor. Reporters saw this trial as a denouement to the American Tragedy of the entire Susan Smith case. As ABC producer Claudia Pryor said, "(the case) was almost like a bruise felt nationally" (*The State*, July 9, 1995, p. A1). Thus they reported events surrounding the trial as a drama and viewed themselves as part of the cast.

Ultimately the question becomes "what's really important here?" If the media is covering itself as part of the story because there are no other news developments, it brings into question the economics of assigning teams of reporters and producers to cover a trial in a small town where the judge had banned cameras from the courtroom. If the media is covering itself as part of the story because the reporters at the event saw themselves and their colleagues as a newsworthy component of the event, then the power of the media to change events it covers is a force that must be considered. Whichever is the case for other events, the media representatives in Union in the summer of 1995 considered their own importance to the event to be such that they framed themselves as part of the last chapter of the Susan Smith story.

REFERENCES

Bogart, L. (1992). The state of the industry. In P. Cook, D. Gomery, & L. Lichty (Eds.), *The future of news: Television-newspapers-wire services-newsmagazines* (pp. 85–103). Washington, DC: The Woodrow Wilson Center Press.

Cook, P., Gomery, D., & Lichty, L. (1992). *The future of news: Television-newspapers-wire services-newsmagazines.* Washington, DC: The Woodrow Wilson Center Press.

Dayan, D., & Katz, E. (1992). *Media events: The live broadcasting of history.* Cambridge, MA: Harvard University Press.

Gamson, W. A., & Modigliani, A. (1989). Media discourse and public opinion on nuclear power: A constructionist approach. *American Journal of Sociology, 95,* 1–37.

Gripsrud, J. (1992). The aesthetics and politics of melodrama. In P. Dahlgreen & C. Sparks (Eds.), *Journalism and popular culture* (pp. 84–95), London: Sage.

Kosicki, G. M., Becker, L. B., & Fredin, E. S. (1994). Buses and ballots: The role of media images in a local election. *Journalism & Mass Communication Quarterly, 71,* 76–89.

McCombs, M. E., & Shaw, D. L. (1993). The evolution of agenda- setting research: Twenty-five years in the marketplace of ideas. *Journal of Communication, 43,* 58–67.

Peters, J. D. (1995). Historical tensions in the concept of public opinion. In T. L. Glasser & C. T. Salmon (Eds.), *Public opinion and the communication of consent* (pp. 3–32). New York: Guilford.

Schudson, M. (1995). *The power of news.* Cambridge, MA: Harvard University Press.

Shoemaker, P. J., & Reese, S. D. (1991/1996). *Mediating the message: Theories of influences on mass media content.* New York: Longman.

Weaver, P. H. (1994). *News and the culture of lying.* New York: The Free Press.

12

Frames of Conviction: The Intersection of Social Frameworks and Standards of Appraisal in Letters to the Editor Regarding a Lesbian Commitment Ceremony

Ernest L. Wiggins

Like few other events in recent memory, the reporting of the commitment ceremony of Jennifer Colella and Dewey Scott-Wiley on January 18, 1996, revealed the ability of a newspaper to excite and unnerve its community of readers. Published in Columbia, South Carolina, a state that explicitly prohibits same-sex marriages, *The State* newspaper ran the story about the courtship and "wedding" of two local, openly homosexual women (Hogan-Alback & Butler, 1996). Appearing on the front page of the Thursday "Living" features section, the story included full-color photographs of the ceremony, performed in a Unitarian Universalist Fellowship hall, and black and white photographs of the women during private moments in their home. In the same issue and same section of was an article about the 50th anniversary of several heterosexual couples. The article preceded by 6 months the passage by the U.S. House of Representatives of the Defense of Marriage Act, which restricts marriage to one man and one woman. Although the newspaper addressed the legal and political implications of same-sex unions, the tone and structure of the story characterized the women's relationship as a romantic and spiritual union, aspects that are associated with routine wedding coverage.

In the 2 weeks immediately following publication of the story, *The State* received more than 100 letters to the editor, which offered a unique opportunity to examine how readers make sense of their relationships with one another and with the local newspaper. Would readers employ language

used in the national debate on same-sex marriages to judge the women's actions and the newspaper's framing of the commitment ceremony? Although
formal analysis of letters to the editor suffers the same limitations of any
pool created through self-selection, such letters reveal not only how readers make sense of what they read, but also how discourse employed by political and cultural organizations can direct readers in their interpretation
and evaluation of the newspaper's text and its role in the community (Nord,
1995).

Employing Social Frameworks

In his early explication of frame analysis, Goffman (1974) delineated the difference between natural and social frameworks, schema used to render
meaning to the world. Natural frameworks are used by individuals to understand events that are "due totally, from start to finish, to natural determinants." No human agent guides the actions. When social frameworks are
employed, however, the individual sees the event

> incorporate(s) the will, aim, and controlling effort of an intelligence, a live
> agency, the chief one being the human being. . . . These doings subject the
> doer *to "standards," to social appraisal of his action based on its honesty, effi-
> ciency, economy, safety, elegance, tactfulness, good taste, and so forth.* (p. 22; ital-
> ics added).

Goffman's proposition can be applied to the present case in a number of
meaningful ways. First, social frameworks were utilized by both the media
and the public in evaluating the actions of the two women. The newspaper's
reporters and editors employed a standard in determining that the wom-
en's private lives and commitment ceremony were generally newsworthy
and would be of interest to readers. Similarly, those who responded publicly to the article used standards to evaluate the women's actions, variously describing them as immoral and courageous. Second, readers who responded publicly used social frameworks to evaluate the newspaper's
actions in publishing the story, many charging the newspaper with failure
to appreciate or respect the beliefs of its readers. It is my contention that
these social frameworks, and the standards used to appraise the women at
the center of the story and the newspaper, informed the letter writers'
choice of language as they engaged in public discourse.

FRAMES AND LANGUAGE

It is commonly held by frame analysis researchers that individuals employ
frames to process information (Entman, 1993; Goffman, 1974). When that information comes from newspaper articles, Nord (1995) asserted, the proc-

ess involves a transaction between text and reader. Baylor (1996) stated that this transaction is dependent on there being culturally available frames that are shared by the media and the public. Using a common stock of key words, phrases, and images, members of the public construct the terms on which public discourse takes place (Gamson, 1992; Graber, 1988). Additionally, as Kosicki and Pan (1996) stated, media "provide raw materials, conceptual frames and vocabulary" that are used to construct a platform on which members of society think and talk about public issue, even those issues, I would add, involving the doings of the media, themselves.

Nord (1995) suggested that political and religious organizations have strongly influenced public discourse. This is no less true concerning public issues regarding gays and lesbians, particularly the issue of same-sex marriage. Published objections to gay and lesbian marriages, including those articulated by the leadership of prominent and powerful political organizations, such as the Christian Coalition, often employ framing elements related to religious convictions, which construct same-sex marriage as abnormal, sinful, and illegal in the eyes of God (Lawsky, 1996). Public expressions in defense of same-sex marriage, most often articulated by representatives of the gay and lesbian activist community, invoke references to normality and civil and social tolerance (Nava & Dawidoff, 1994, p. 147). Both camps have applied social frameworks, although different standards, in appraising the issue. The former used religious standards, whereas the latter used civil or secular standards. And this appears to have been reflected in the public discourse at the local level.

FRAMING CONVICTIONS

Evidence of this divergence in language and standards between opponents and proponents of same-sex marriage was initially observed in a cursory reading of letters to the editor following the publication of the lesbian wedding story. Referring to the lesbian commitment ceremony article as "fawning" and "florid," some readers who were opposed to the publication of the article accused the paper of promoting a sinful, abnormal lifestyle that constituted a threat to the spiritual and civic health of the community. As one reader wrote:

> I read (and saw) with disgust and repugnance your garrulous and prolific feature article "Do you, Jennifer, take Dewey" on the homosexual "union" of two women in Columbia. I was appalled at the acceptance and prominent status *The State* gave this amoral, aberrant and anti-family lifestyle issue. (Bob Wechtel, January 24, 1996)

Other opponents viewed the newspaper as indifferent to or abusive of the public's trust.

> Your major story of the lesbian marriage was highly irresponsible. . . . Your newspaper is a major media influence in our community. I urge you to exercise more wisdom and courage with these kinds of issues in the future. (Robert Cline, January 25, 1996)

In contrast, supporters commended the newspaper and the wedding's participants for their courage and praised the paper for its positive acknowledgment of a diverse community.

> A news organization has an obligation to feature stories that reflect all facets of life, not just the areas of our society that are mainstream and less subject to discussion (Clay Owens, February 1, 1996).

In addition, many of the article's supporters took opponents to task for their lack of religious and social tolerance.

> As a heterosexual, I am disgusted with the letters from my segment of the population. This is not to say that your newspaper shouldn't have published the "hate letters." On the contrary, I feel that everyone's opinion should be heard. But reading them served as a reality check. There are too many people still filled with mean-spirited prejudice against anyone who doesn't conform to their values (Elaine Gillespie, January 29, 1996).

Although the letters largely mirrored the national debate about the legality and morality of same-sex marriages, readers also charged that the newspaper was promoting a social or political agenda in reporting the ceremony. Those opposed to the publication of the story argued that *The State* betrayed its moral responsibility to the community while rejecting the values of its largely conservative readership.

> I call to task *The State* for "selling" this kind of behavior as just one more flavor in the big ice cream shop of life, and isn't-it-wonderful-these-two-have-found-each-other, etc. . . . There is a narrow line between tolerance and acceptance, a line that the media and the gay community consistently blur. (Marcia Kalayjian, January 24, 1996)

Those supporting the publication of the article commended the newspaper for widening its scope to include those in the community who had long been ignored by the local media.

> Thank you for providing reportage that is inclusive of all *The State's* readers. (Glenn Farr, February 1, 1996)

These responses showed the strikingly different ways in which readers describe, interpret, and evaluate the newspaper text and the newspaper's role in the community.

ANALYZING THE FRAMES

In this study, I sought to measure the intersection of social frameworks and standards of appraisal in letters to the editor sent to *The State* after the publication of the lesbian commitment ceremony article. I hypothesized that those who opposed the publication of the article were more likely than supporters to employ religious terms in framing their arguments, because such terms were emblems of the standard used by prominent opponents to appraise such events. Likewise, I posited that supporters were more likely to couch their arguments in civil or secular terms.

A formal analysis of the 106 letters received by *The State* during the 2 weeks immediately following the publication of the story uncovered recurring patterns of words and phrases used to frame arguments opposing or supporting the publication of the article. Assuming that vocabulary serves as markers of the religious and political discourses that structure the national debate about same-sex marriage, I identified 12 terms or their variants employed in the national debate: *Bible, God, Christianity* (including Christ and Jesus), *other religions, family* (or children), *sin, normalcy* (normality or abnormality), *conservatism, morality, tolerance, offensiveness*, and *newspaper bias*. These terms were categorized as indicators of either discourse rooted in religious conviction, as that employed by prominent opponents to same-sex marriage, or discourse rooted in social justice or civil rights convictions, as that used by those supporting the issue. Religious terms were *Bible, God, Christianity, other religions, and sin*. The other terms were classified as elements of civil discourse.

Each letter was placed in one of two categories—those opposed to the publication of the article and those supporting publication of the article. Crosstabs were generated to assess whether the type of vocabulary used was related to the letter writer's position.

The audit revealed 298 terms of interest: 138 religious terms and 160 civil or secular terms. Of the 199 terms of interest present in the 65 letters opposing publication, 85 were religious, and 114 were civil. Letters written in support of publication contained a total of 99 terms of interest, 53 religious terms, and 46 civil terms. A test of independence revealed no significant relationship between the letter writer's position and the use of religious versus civil terminology, which suggests that both opponents and supporters drew from the same pool of vocabulary, and that neither "owned" a specific type of discursive vocabulary when framing their arguments.

Aftermath: *The State* Responds

The 2 weeks following the publication of the lesbian wedding story were capped by an extraordinary comment written by the publisher of *The State*, Frederick B. Mott, Jr., for the editorial page. Mott acknowledged problematic framing elements:

> In the eyes of many of our readers . . . the story's length and the four accompanying color photographs went beyond acceptable coverage. To many, it seemed that we were "promoting" a homosexual lifestyle. (February 4, 1996, p. D3)

Mott, himself, went on to employ a framing device not unlike that used by writers who opposed the article, that is, applying a religious standard to evaluate the women's doings.

> I discussed my feelings with a friend, a pastor in our community. . . . The presentation of our story with its length, color, photographs, church setting and reference to Jesus could only be interpreted, he explained, as an attack upon the biblical family and the sanctity of marriage. I respect that belief. (p. D3)

Mott concluded the column by conceding that the newspaper had not properly framed the story for its readers and apologized.

> While we never want to dilute the facts or back away from a tough issue, there are times when it is wise to seek the input of as many different points of view as possible. Had we discussed this sensitive issue more fully, our presentation (frame?) might have been different. We meant no harm. (p. D3)

The implication is clear. Had newsroom editors consulted those who were likely to oppose the story, the frame of the story as a romantic and spiritual union might have been changed to one about community opposition to such unions on social and religious grounds. In short, the frame, having been influenced by more conservative elements of the community, would have shifted from one of commitment to one of conviction.

In the wake of the lesbian wedding story, *The State* initiated a year-long project to mend the rift between the paper and religious conservatives. This initiative included (1) lunch hour discussions with religious scholars and pastors in the community to help staff members understand conservative religious perspective, (2) reader focus groups to discuss the paper's performance in covering religious issues and secular issues with religious undertones, and (3) the assigning of two staff writers to the coverage of religious news and features.

CONCLUSION

This study sought to measure the intersection of social frameworks and standards of appraisal, as defined by Goffman, using letters to the editor reacting to a news article on a lesbian commitment ceremony. Using the seminal work of frame analysis researchers as a foundation, I hoped to find associations among frameworks, standards, and language used to appraise both the actions of the women at the heart of the story and the newspaper's decision to publish the article. I expected the language to resemble that used by prominent opponents and supporters of same-sex weddings, language that had been employed in public discourse on the national level for several years. I hypothesized that letter writers opposed to the article were more likely to use religious terminology than proponents, while proponents would be more likely to use civil or secular language. Though the results of the analysis did not support the hypothesis, this case study points to a number of areas for further inquiry and discussion.

The results suggest that neither side of the issue of same-sex marriage has proprietary rights to religious or secular terminology. These results might also suggest a disconnection between a researcher's understanding of the religious *vis à vis* civil terms and that of the letter writers. That is, because religion and religiosity is so thoroughly inculcated in the social frameworks of the South, readers may not as readily use the religious and secular delineations applied in this study. If this is the case, what does this suggest for media professionals who are seeking stronger community connections and for those responsible for public policy? If the religious and secular are interwoven in the Bible Belt, what does this mean for newspapers that have traditionally kept God on the religion page? Would it be appropriate to ask public officials questions related to their own religious beliefs or those of their constituents?

Perhaps this study suggests that Goffman's social frameworks and standards of appraisals, at least as evidenced in the South, are not so easily circumscribed. I would suggest, however, that attempts to explore and explain the intersections could have profound and lasting benefits for both newspapers and those who read them.

REFERENCES

Baylor, T. (1996). Media framing of movement protest: The case of American Indian protest. *The Social Science Journal, 33*(3), 241–255.

Entman, R. M. (1993). Framing: Toward clarification of a fractured paradigm. *Journal of Communication, 43*(4), 51–58.

Gamson, W. A. (1992). *Talking politics.* New York: Cambridge University Press.

Goffman, E. (1974). *Frame analysis: An essay on the organization of experience.* Cambridge, MA: Harvard University Press.

Graber, D. A. (1988). *Processing the news: How people tame the information tide* (2nd ed.). New York: Longman.

Holgan-Albach, S., & Butler, P. (1996, January 18). "'Do you, Jennifer, take Dewey . . .' Lesbian Union Mirrors National Debate on Same-Sex Marriages." *The State,* p. D1.

Kosicki, G., & Pan, Z. (1996). *Framing analysis: An approach to media effects.* Paper delivered at International Communication Association Conference, Chicago, Illinois.

Lawsky, D. (1996, July 13). *House passes anti-gay marriage bill.* Washington, DC: Reuters News Service.

Nava, M., & Dawidoff, R. (1994). *Created equal: Why gay rights matter to America.* New York: St. Martin's Press.

Nord, D. P. (1995). Reading the newspaper: Strategies and politics of reader response, Chicago, 1912-1917. *Journal of Communication, 45*(3), 66–93.

13

The Role of Images in Framing News Stories

Paul Messaris
Linus Abraham

How does visual communication function as an agent of framing? In what ways is the framing process affected by the use of visual images? In answering these questions, we begin by examining what makes pictures different from verbal language as a medium of communication. Our discussion focuses on three distinctive properties of visual images—their analogical quality, their indexicality, and their lack of an explicit propositional syntax—each of which may make visual framing less obtrusive than verbal framing. On the basis of this examination of the general characteristics of images, we then offer a more detailed look at a specific illustration of the potential implications of visual framing—namely, the presentation of African Americans in the news. This examination leads us to the conclusion that visual framing may convey meanings that would be more controversial or might meet with greater audience resistance if they were conveyed through words.

CHARACTERISTICS OF VISUAL IMAGES

What are the distinctive properties of images (including movies and television as well as individual pictures) as media of communication? With regard to the issue of framing, the most relevant properties are those that have the capacity either to enhance or to mitigate its consequences. If the impact of framing is crucially dependent on its being taken for granted, on audience members not being too aware of it, then anything that can affect the audience's awareness may also make a considerable difference on the ultimate outcome of the framing process. The three visual characteristics listed earlier all have significant implications regarding the likelihood that a viewer will take what she or he sees for granted. These three characteristics—which, taken together, account for much of the core quality of pictures as means of communication—are closely related to each other, and it is often difficult, if not impossible, to impute a viewer's response to any one of them by itself. Nevertheless, for the purposes of this introductory discussion, it may be helpful to treat them separately. In the course of examining each of them, we review some earlier visual research that illustrates how they might affect viewers' responses to framing.

The Analogical Quality of Images

The central characteristic of images, which most clearly distinguishes them from words, is the fact that images constitute a largely analogical system of communication, whereas words are almost wholly arbitrary. This familiar distinction refers to the fact that the relationship between most words and their meanings is purely a matter of social convention, whereas the relationships between images and their meanings are based on similarity or analogy. Although this point may seem intuitively self-evident, it is in fact . one of the most controversial topics in visual scholarship, and several well-known writers (Eco, 1975; Gombrich, 1960; Goodman, 1976) have disputed—or seemed to dispute—the idea that pictures look like the things they represent. This is not the place for a detailed discussion of that controversy, which has been addressed at length in a previous publication by one of the authors of this chapter (Messaris, 1994).

For present purposes, the following points should be borne in mind. First, systematic research with a variety of viewers (people looking at culturally unfamiliar pictures, blind people examining raised outline drawings, and even animals) has consistently found that the recognition of objects in pictures does not appear to require prior familiarity with the particular representational conventions of those pictures (for reviews of this research, see Danto, 1990; Kennedy, 1993; Messaris, 1994, pp. 60–64). In other words, this finding is in accord with the notion that picture perception is based on similarity or analogy. Second, both this research and a growing body of scholarship in cognitive studies (Anderson, 1997; Marr, 1982; Reeves & Nass, 1996) suggest that the brain's ability to make sense of pictures does not require that pictures be exact replicas of the appearance of reality. Rather, the brain is perfectly capable of working with partial analogies, such as those found in black-and-white outline drawings (which represent shape but not color) or even stick figures (which represent overall structure but no details).

As far as viewers' responses to framing are concerned, the analogical quality of images has the following consequence. Precisely because it can make images appear more natural, more closely linked to reality than words are, it can also inveigle viewers into overlooking the fact that all images are human-made, artificial constructions. This is one sense, then, in which visual framing may be less obtrusive, more easily taken-for-granted than verbal framing. Evidence of the potential unobtrusiveness of visual framing has existed for some time in studies on viewers' reactions to the formal conventions of visual communication (close-ups vs. long shots, editing, and so forth).

One such study, a classic experiment, looked at the effect of camera angle on viewers' perceptions of a political figure mentioned and shown in a news broadcast. Using a fake news item read by a real television newsman and inserted into a tape of a real broadcast, Mandell and Shaw (1973) found that viewers' evaluations of the power of a person mentioned in that fake news item were affected significantly by the camera angle from which that person was photographed (lower angles produced higher power ratings). However, even though the viewers in this study were all college students majoring in broadcast media, most of them showed no awareness of the use of camera angle in the fake news segment. Out of a total of some 70 students who saw either a low or a high angle, only 13 indicated that they had noticed the presence of this device.

The Indexicality of Images

The term *indexicality* comes from the writings of the philosopher C. S. Peirce (1991), who used it to single out photographs from other types of images. Because a photograph is in a sense an automatic product of the effects of light on lenses and film (or video and other electronic media), the connection between photograph and reality has a certain authenticity that human-made pictures can never have. This true-to-life quality of photographs, their ability to bypass human agency in certain respects, is the basis on which Peirce called them "indices" (i.e., direct pointers, as opposed to constructed representations of reality). Because of their indexicality, photographs come with an implicit guarantee of being closer to the truth than other forms of communication are. Consequently, the use of photographic media (including television and video) in the framing process could diminish the likelihood that viewers would question what they see.

A substantial body of literature explores how viewers' perceptions can be shaped as a consequence of unwitting faith in the connection between photographs and reality. Although this literature does not refer specifically to framing as such, much of it has a direct bearing on this process. A dominant theme in this literature is the exploration of various photographic practices that can potentially mislead a viewer who is insufficiently attentive to them. These practices include the unacknowledged staging of images appearing in the news or other nonfictional contexts, and the unacknowledged alteration of images by computer manipulation or other means. See Messaris (1997) for a review of literature in this area. However, despite the sensational nature of these forms of photographic deception, there is another, much simpler photographic practice whose implications for the framing process are probably much more far-reaching. The practice in question is the simple act of selection—choosing one view instead of another when making the photograph, cropping or editing the resulting image one way instead of another, or simply just choosing to show viewers one image out of the many others that may have been produced at the same place and time. Unlike staging or alteration, selection is an inevitable part of every act of making a photographic image and displaying it to the public. Hence its special relevance for the process of visual framing.

The potential consequences of the photographic selection process have been studied systematically in one of the seminal pieces of visual communication research, Lang and Lang's (1952) investigation of how television editing can shape viewers' perceptions of a real event. The Langs' study was conducted during the Korean War, following President Truman's recall of General Douglas MacArthur from his command of U.S. military operations in that war. As a show of support for MacArthur, a number of cities around the country staged parades and other festivities in his honor. Focusing on MacArthur Day in Chicago, they employed teams of coders to rate the behavior of the crowds participating in the event. One set of ratings was conducted on-site at the event itself; a second, parallel set of ratings assessed the televised presentation of the crowd behavior.

Observing that the crowds seemed much more enthusiastic on television than in person, the Langs ascribed this difference to editing. By selectively transmitting images of people applauding and waving, and failing to transmit images of more subdued behavior, the television broadcasts of this event may have created an exaggerated impression of the strength of public support for MacArthur—and, by implication, public disapproval of Harry Truman. Because the television broadcasts' effectiveness in conveying their own version, or frame, of the MacArthur Day events depended on the viewers' implicit trust in the veracity of the television image, the Langs' findings can be seen as a paradigmatic illustration of the relationship between visual indexicality and framing.

Images' Lack of an Explicit Propositional Syntax

Up to this point, our discussion has dealt with properties of individual images. The third item on our list has to do with the relationship between images, that is with visual syntax. One of the distinctive properties of verbal language is its elaborate and explicit set of syntactic devices for making propositions. In the course of making claims, we use these devices routinely as means of setting forth propositions about causality ("x happened *because of* y," "x is *due to* y," etc.), comparisons ("x is *similar to* y," "x is *the same as* y"), generalizations ("x is *typical of* y," "x is *an exception to* y"), or whatever other types of connections we wish to make among the various entities that are encompassed in our topic.

In contrast to verbal language, visual communication does not have an explicit set of syntactic conventions for making such propositions. Although causality and similarity, for example, are often implied in the visual structure of commercials, political ads, or other visual formats, the conventions for making such connections are loose, imprecise, and unsystematic. Thus, the very same syntactic device—for example, a dissolve—can be used for diametrically different reasons—in one case, to imply simultaneity; in another, to imply a time lapse (see Messaris, 1998, for a detailed discussion of these issues).

In comparison with verbal language, then, visual propositions are more reliant on the viewer's ability to make intuitive sense of implicit meanings on the basis of contextual or other cues. Consequently, viewers may be less conscious of having been presented with a fully articulated set of claims than they would be if those claims were made verbally. Evidence in favor of this notion comes from a recent study of the legal aspects of commercial advertising claims. Khoury (1997) examined the use of visual juxtaposition as a means of making implied product claims in magazine ads, such as a picture of a nutritional supplement juxtaposed with an image of a couple engaged in passionate sexual activity.

In a systematic comparison of such visuals with the ads' verbal text, Khoury found that the images often appeared to be making implicit product claims that went beyond what was spelled out explicitly in the text and that, indeed, could have led to legal or regulatory problems if made verbally. This finding suggests that, at least as far as the legal and regulatory context is concerned, the implicitness of visual syntax does seem to result in a less vigilant response. Supportive evidence regarding viewers' comparative lack of awareness of visual syntax also comes from a study of people's interpretations of a political video (Messaris, 1997). Faced with the kind of ambiguous visual syntax mentioned earlier, the viewers in this study were readily able to provide interpretations but were frequently unaware of the visual structures from which these interpretations were derived. In short, as with the other two characteristics of visual communications that we discussed earlier, this one too appears to lead to a reduced awareness of the process by which a particular visual impression is generated. Here too, then, we find what is arguably a precondition of effective framing. With this theoretical perspective in mind, we now turn to an examination of two specific examples of visual framing, one drawn from the news, the other from fiction film.

VISUAL FRAMING OF AFRICAN AMERICANS
IN TELEVISION NEWS

Although television news analysis often ignores the visual aspects of the news text, much of the meaning of news narratives may be generated by the relationship between particular images and their verbal components (Hartley, 1982). And it is important to point out that newscast video images do not always just support the verbal text; they may sometimes convey implicit information that is "factual and evaluative beyond that asserted orally and in sending competing and perhaps discrepant stimuli" (Adams, 1978, p. 169). Thus implicit information from visuals may contribute significantly to the semantic interpretation of news stories.

Visual Images and Ideology

The special qualities of visuals—their iconicity, their indexicality, and especially their syntactic implicitness—makes them very effective tools for framing and articulating ideological messages. It has been noted that ideology works subtly—by camouflaging its constructed nature, hiding its historical and social roots, and appearing to be natural and commonsensical (Hall, 1982). The iconic ability to seemingly reproduce nature means that visual images are capable of producing documentary evidence to support the commonsensical claims of ideology, and in turn to use the very appearance of nature (seeming factual representations) to subtly camouflage the constructed, historical, and social roots of ideology. Thus, Woollacott (1982) noted that, "Film and photography . . . operate upon us in a manner which suppresses and conceals their ideological function because they appear to record rather than to transform or signify" (p. 99).

For these reasons visuals come in handy in framing subtle messages—especially messages that may be socially risky if stated explicitly (Burgoon, Buller, & Woodall, 1996). For such messages relying on visual imagery, because of their lack of explicitness, may provide a broadcaster or journalist with a shield of deniability, of a kind that cannot be claimed with verbal persuasion. Thus, visual imagery may be effective for ideological exposition and manipulation.

Subtle Racism and Implicit Visual News Imagery
of Blacks

One such area of social risk (perhaps due to the media's fear of being branded racist) where implicit visual information may be used to frame messages is in the depiction of African Americans in negative story contexts that are perceived to be stereotypical and prejudicial. Contemporary studies on the production of prejudice in the media now emphasize the subtlety of racial appeals (Campbell, 1995; Entman, 1994b). This reflects notions of more subtle forms of prejudice or racism, which are said to work in veiled and indirect ways (Meertens & Pettigrew, 1997). Van Dijk (1988) argued that, "Whereas the racial slur, the graffiti, or the old movie may be blatantly racist, many other present-day types of talk may communicate racism in a more veiled way" (p. 18).

Racial appeals now often take place through visual imagery, without any explicit or overt reference to race (Mendleberg, 1996). Van Dijk (1988) commented that, "Even more than physical racism (or sexism for that matter), symbolic racism allows for subtlety, indirectness, and implication. It may, paradoxically, be expressed by the unsaid" (p. 18). The visual modality in television news, because of its iconic and descriptive nature, provides a rich source of imagery about ethnic groups. The visuals present physical and behavioral features that affect our perception, often evoking stereotypes (Cowen, 1991). In the presence of a member (or symbolic equivalent—as in media images) of an ethnic group, the stereotypes may be activated automatically, even if unintentionally (Devine, 1989). Visuals can therefore provide implicit and subtle stereotyping that calls little attention to the artifice of construction. And because it seldom proclaims itself openly, visual stereotyping can be insidious and, perhaps, more potent than explicit verbal stereotyping (Browne, Firestone, & Mickiewicz, 1994).

Implicit visual imagery is increasingly being used to frame messages that involve the representation of African Americans in news. For example, Bird (1996), studying a sensational AIDS story that circulated in the Dallas media, commented on how television news coverage of the story did not make an issue of race verbally, but visually tended to reinforce stereotypes of African-American sexuality: "Stories repeatedly used the same footage of Black people dancing in dimly-lit nightclubs, apparently disregarding the beautiful threat lurking among them" (p. 53). Entman (1994a) and Martindale (1995) have also noted how news stories make implicit links between Blacks and negative thematic concepts—such as violent crime, drugs, poverty, prisons, drug-addicted babies, AIDS victims, and welfare—by predominantly juxtaposing or illustrating stories with images of African Americans. The selective use of African-American images for juxtaposition with negative verbal text is of direct relevance to the framing of meanings in news stories. How a story is framed has the potential of determining what most people will notice, understand, and remember about an event, as well as how they evaluate and choose to act upon it (Entman, 1993).

For example, implicit visual information helped to create racial subtexts of meaning, not explicitly stated in the verbal text, in an opinion piece that appeared in *The Daily Pennsylvanian*—the student newspaper of the University of Pennsylvania (February 28, 1995). The story titled, "The Buck Stops

Now, Men Must Be Responsible," exhorts all men to take responsibility in helping stop rapes. The written text of the story—which makes no mention of the race of the men who are guilty of rape and those who should help stop the rapes—is illustrated with a drawing of a White man restraining a muscular and menacing Black man, with the word "rapist" written across the front of the Black man's briefs.

The racist propensity of this visual image may or may not have been intended by the writer; but whether it was intended or not, one cannot overlook the subtle and indirect racist implications. The racial subtext created by the juxtaposition of the visual with the written text creates very powerful racist connotations and activates myths of Black sexuality, although these are not stated explicitly in words. They are rather expressed through the "unsaid"—the visuals. Blackness, as race, in American culture has historically been perceived as synonymous with deviance. In many cases "blackness" has become a conventional notation symbolizing abnormality. Its racist symbolic use is so ingrained that, after years of supposed egalitarian trends in the culture, this symbolic notation still appears, albeit subtly, in arenas where racist language would otherwise be eschewed.

A second example illustrates how visual imagery can be used to frame (intentionally or unintentionally) racial subtexts of meaning in the news. An NBC evening news story that broadcast on September 10, 1993, told the story of a program in Cleveland that effectively moved people from welfare to work. Although it uses two individuals (one White and one Black) as case studies to personalize and illustrate the point of the story, the lengthy introductory run-up to the story gives a thematic profile of those on welfare—a profile that explicitly refers to the subjects as "people who have been on welfare all their lives." The series of images juxtaposed with this introduction, and whose summary is captured by the just stated quotation, are visual shots of African Americans. The first 14 shots in the story are all images of Blacks, none of whom is individualized by name. As a result, the total structure of the story, with its preponderance of Black images, creates an overall sense that most people on welfare are Black—the subjects the story is discussing are predominantly Black. The text does not state this explicitly; this is a meaning that comes through implicitly, by the preponderance of images of Blacks juxtaposed with the text.

Visual Associations of Blacks With Urban Pathology

The media have developed an elaborate language of pathology in reporting about the urban environment (Ettema & Peer, 1997). As opposed to the suburb, which is often represented in more positive terms, the media's reporting of the urban space is laden with stereotypic expectancies that depict the urban community as unsafe, violent, unaesthetic, and unpleasant (Boskin 1980). It has also been noted that, increasingly, the news media associate Blacks with urban pathology (Boskin, 1980; Gray, 1989). However, this association is often achieved through implicit visual imagery rather than being stated explicitly in words.

A story that illustrates how, through visual framing, Blacks are associated with urban pathology was broadcast by ABC on its national news, on October 14, 1996. Anchoring from a studio in Detroit, Peter Jennings, in his introduction, comments that the state of the country's cities is not an issue in the 1996 presidential election. Field reporter Steve Reynolds then proceeds to develop the reason for this. Over a sequence of images showing a high-rise building being torn down, groups of Blacks watching, and new town-houses being constructed, his voice-over intones that "in Detroit, this morning, it was down with the old, down with the high-rise symbols of urban rot, to be replaced by new neighborhoods." He calls attention to 25 housing projects started in Detroit since the Clinton administration took office. A "sound-bite" of Detroit mayor, Dennis Archer, follows, in which he comments on the positive relationship between the city of Detroit and Washington. Then, over images of neighborhoods populated by Blacks, revealing run-down buildings, men and boys walking down dusty and dirty alleys, children and adults idling outside a liquor store, the reporter comments that, "one reason why there is so little debate about the state of the city in this presidential campaign" is because Clinton has the support of so many mayors.

The reporter goes on to develop the thesis that cooperation with the administration (the establishment of specially designated empowerment zones) has lured private investors to the troubled cities. In a "stand-upper" concluding the story, shot in a run-down part of the city, the reporter goes on to state that the empowerment zones "are located in six troubled urban areas across the country." He then adds that, "there are those who believe that a more Republican self-help solution, not federal aid, is best for what ails the city." There are some important racial, spatial–aesthetic, and attitudinal–behavioral cues—communicated implicitly through the visuals—that have to be deconstructed to reach deeply imbedded cultural meanings in this story.

Racial Cues. No part of the verbal rendition of the story refers explicitly to the race or color of those who occupy the space characterized as "cities," at some points referred to as "troubled," and described as spotting the symbols of "urban rot." However, throughout the story, through visual juxtapositions and associations, we are implicitly provided a picture of those who occupy this space. By logical deduction, we conclude that Blacks occupy these areas of urban pathology. The choice of diction, "symbol of urban rot," is telling and revealing of the perception of the city and the urban environment. The visual manifestation of this phrase is a high-rise building, which juxtaposed with the Black spectators watching, connotes the public housing projects that are increasingly populated by Blacks. In the middle of the story, where the reporter explicates what the "empowerment zones" are about, he comments that, "they are located in six troubled urban areas across the country." Once again, the images juxtaposed with this phrase are images of dilapidated neighborhoods occupied by Blacks.

Spatial-Aesthetic Cues. The story provides us with an example of the visual realization of the aesthetic dimension of the urban pathology. In its aesthetic form it explicates itself as urban = unaesthetic, dirty, and ugly. In the story, urban pathology is made visually manifest in its aesthetic ugliness—the dilapidated buildings, the shanty structures, and the dirty and run-down neighborhoods. The perception of Blacks as dirty people has been a common traditional stereotype in American culture. And though it may not be expressed openly now, the images of dirty and run-down neighborhoods populated by Blacks in the news implicitly activate and connote this stereotype.

Attitudinal-Behavioral Cues. Imagery of Blacks shown not engaging in purposeful activity is a recurring pattern in news stories (Entman, 1994). These images function as attitudinal–behavioral cues that mythically connote laziness and a lack of individual drive. This myth is implicitly manifest in the visual rendition of the story. With the exception of the few Black construction workers shown working on the housing projects, most Blacks shown are idling. This implicit visual manifestation is confirmed and made explicit when the reporter articulates the preferred conservative ideology— "there are those who believe that a more Republican self-help solution, not federal aid, is best for what ails the city." These verbal pronouncements, and their visual renditions, activate connotations of Blacks as lazy and dependent people, and Black areas as receptors into which government aid is poured—for example, the empowerment zones have been established with the aid of the federal government.

Thus the news media use visuals to subtly frame racial subtexts to their narratives on urban pathology. Whereas in the news stories overtly bigoted myths of Blacks are not stated explicitly, through implicit visual imagery old stereotypes of Blacks as dirty, lazy, and dependent, and myths of Black inferiority are subtly suggested. In doing this television news continues to perpetuate traditional negative stereotypes of Blacks in American culture.

CONCLUSION

We began this chapter with a discussion of three central characteristics of visual communication: the analogical nature of visual representation, the indexicality of photographic images, and lack of explicit propositional devices in visual syntax. On this basis, we argue that viewers may be less aware of the process of framing when it occurs visually than when it takes place through words. Consequently, visual images may have the capacity of conveying messages that would meet with greater resistance if put in words, but which are received more readily in visual form. This point is exemplified in our illustration of the process of visual framing in journalistic references to African Americans.

In our analysis of news stories, we discussed the ways in which visual imagery is used to associate African Americans with a variety of negative concepts and social problems. It is worth repeating that the verbal text of the news stories we looked at does not specifically refer to African Africans. The framing of social problems in terms of African Americans is a product of the images, not the words. We take this disparity to be a demonstration of our general point about images' ability to convey controversial messages with greater impunity. We assume that a verbal reference to African Americans would have come under tighter scrutiny by the news organization itself, whereas the images may have more readily been taken for granted.

Both in principle and in practice, then, the distinctive qualities of pictures make the study of visual communication especially relevant to the concerns of framing theory. Pictorial framing is worthy of investigation not only because images are capable of conveying unverbalized meanings, but also because awareness of those meanings may be particularly elusive. If one of the main goals of culturally oriented research on framing is to uncover the tacit assumptions through which social communication affects public perceptions and values, the investigation of visual images surely deserves to play a central role in that research.

REFERENCES

Adams, W. (1978). Visual analysis of newscasts: Issues in social science research. In W. Adams & F. Schreibman (Eds.), *Television network news: Issues in content research* (pp. 155–173). Washington, DC: George Washington University Press.

Anderson, J. (1997). *An ecological theory of cinematic perception.* Minneapolis: University of Minnesota Press.

Bird, S. E. (1996). CJ's revenge: Media, folklore, and the cultural construction of AIDS. *Critical studies in mass communication, 13,* 44–58.

Boskin, J. (1980). Denials: The media view of dark skins and the city. In B. Rubin (Ed.), *Small voices and great trumpets: Minorities and the media* (pp. 141–147). New York: Praeger.

Browne, D. R., Firestone, C. M., & Mickiewicz, E. (1994). *Television/radio news and minorities.* Queenstown, Aspen Institute.

Burgoon, J. K., Buller, D. B., & Woodall, W. G. (1996). *Nonverbal communication: The unspoken dialogue.* New York: McGraw-Hill.

Campbell, C. P. (1995). *Race, myth and the news.* Thousand Oaks, CA: Sage.

Cowen, P. S. (1991). A socio-cognitive approach to ethnicity in films. In L. D. Friedman (Ed.), *Unspeakable images: Ethnicity and the American cinema* (pp. 353–378). Urbana & Chicago: University of Illinois Press.

Danto, A. (1990). *Beyond the Brillo box*. New York: Columbia University Press.

Devine, P. G. (1989). Stereotypes and prejudice: Their automatic and controlled components. *Journal of Personality and Social Psychology, 56*, 5–18.

Eco, U. (1975). *A theory of semiotics*. Bloomington: Indiana University Press.

Entman, R. M. (1993). Framing: Toward clarification of a fractured paradigm. *Journal of Communication, 43*, 51–58.

Entman, R. M. (1994a). African-Americans according to television news. *Media Studies Journal*, Summer, 29–38.

Entman, R. M. (1994b). Representation and reality in the portrayal of Blacks on network television news. *Journalism & Mass Communication Quarterly, 71*, 509–520.

Ettema, J. S., & Peer, L. (1996). Good news from a bad neighborhood: Toward an alternative to the discourse of urban pathology. *Journalism & Mass Communication Quarterly, 73*, 835–856.

Gombrich, E. H. (1960). *Art and illusion: A study in the psychology of pictorial representation*. Princeton, NJ: Princeton University Press.

Goodman, N. (1976). *Languages of art: An approach to a theory of symbols*. Indianapolis, IN: Bobbs-Merrill.

Gray, H. (1989). Television, Black Americans, and the American dream. *Critical Studies in Mass Communication, 6*, 376–386.

Hall, S. (1982). The rediscovery of 'ideology': Return of the repressed in media studies. In M. Gurevitch, T. Bennett, J. Curran, & J. Woollacott (Eds.), *Culture, society and media* (pp. 56–90). London and New York: Routledge.

Hartley, J. (1982). *Understanding news*. London & New York: Methuen.

Kennedy, J. M. (1993). *Drawing and the blind: Pictures to touch*. New Haven, CT: Yale University Press.

Khoury, J. (1997). *Implicit propositions in advertising messages: Legal and regulatory aspects*. M.A. thesis, Annenberg School for Communication, University of Pennsylvania.

Lang, K., & Lang, G. E. (1952). The unique perspective of television and its effect: A pilot study. In W. Schramm & D. F. Roberts (Eds.), *The process and effects of mass communication* (rev. ed., pp. 169–188). Urbana: University of Illinois Press, pp. 169–188.

Mandell, L. M., & Shaw, D. L. (1973). Judging people in the news—unconsciously: Effect of camera angle and bodily activity. *Journal of Broadcasting, 17*, 353–362.

Marr, D. (1982). *Vision: A computational investigation into the human representation and processing of visual information*. New York: Freeman.

Martindale, C. (1996). Newspaper stereotypes of African-Americans. In P. Lester (Ed.), *Images that injure: Pictorial stereotypes in the media* (pp. 21–26). Westport, CT: Greenwood.

Meertens, R. W., & Pettigrew, T. F. (1997). Is subtle prejudice really prejudice? *Public Opinion Quarterly, 61*, 54–71.

Mendleberg, T. (1996, September). *Implicitly racial appeals and the impact of campaigns*. Paper delivered at a seminar for Annenberg Research Fellows, Annenberg School for Communication, University of Pennsylvania.

Messaris, P. (1994). *Visual "literacy": Image, mind, and reality*. Boulder, CO: Westview Press.

Messaris, P. (1997). *Visual persuasion: The role of images in advertising*. Thousand Oaks, CA: Sage.

Messaris, P. (1998). Visual aspects of media literacy. *Journal of Communication, 48*, 70–80.

Peirce, C. S. (1991). *Peirce on signs: Writings on semiotics by Charles Sanders Peirce*. Chapel Hill: University of North Carolina Press.

Reeves, B., & Nass, C. (1996). *The media equation: How people treat computers, television, and new media like real people and places*. New York: Cambridge University Press.

Van Dijk, T. A. (1988). Introduction. In G. Smitherman-Donaldson & T. A. van Dijk (Eds.), *Discourse and discrimination* (pp. 11–22). Detroit: Wayne State University Press.

Woollacott, J. (1982). Messages and meanings. In M. Gurevitch, T. Bennett, J. Curran, & J. Woollacott (Eds.), *Culture, society and the media* (pp. 91–111). New York: Routledge.

14

The Effects of Value-Framing
on Political Judgment
and Reasoning

Dhavan V. Shah
David Domke
Daniel B. Wackman

Certain enduring norms of newsworthiness, in combination with routines of media production, encourage journalists to organize—to frame—their reports in predictable ways (Dennis & Ismach, 1981; Shoemaker & Reese, 1996). To personalize news and make it appear timely, media professionals tend to construct stories in episodic terms, focusing on specific instances and individuals, rather than presenting issues in their larger thematic context (Iyengar, 1991). Likewise, when covering campaigns and government, reporters and editors increasingly downplay in-depth coverage of public policy positions and initiatives, instead choosing to attend to the more dramatic and oppositional elements of politics such as the "horse-race" between candidates, and the strategic motives and efforts of politicians (Cappella & Jamieson, 1997). Such *episodic* and *strategic* framing of news has been shown to influence citizens' information processing and political judgments, altering the criteria used to evaluate politicians and shaping assessments of governmental effectiveness and responsiveness.

These approaches to the study of news framing, however, suffer from two important limitations. First, they confound differences in news frames with variance in the substantive content of news. Second, they fail to acknowledge the degree to which extramedia factors, particularly the rhetorical strategies of political elites, influence news framing. The approach to framing advanced in this chapter attempts to avoid these limitations. In our research, we conceive of framing in terms of the different sets of *values* that provide the underlying rationale for particular policy discussions (Shah, Domke, & Wackman, 1996). From this perspective, framing concerns the presentation of an equivalent set of considerations in the context of different themes, or organizing principles (see Kahneman & Tversky, 1984; Lau, Smith, & Fiske, 1991; Tversky & Kahneman, 1981).

In general, we believe, there are two overarching sets of values used by political elites to justify their policy stands: *ethical values*, which often become most explicitly apparent in discourse about rights, morals, and basic principles; and *material values*, which are often manifest in discussions of economics, pragmatics, and practicality (Abramson & Inglehart, 1995; Ball-Rokeach & Loges, 1996; Shah, 1999). Our theory of *value-framing* asserts that politicians and social activists struggle over the values used to define issues to build public support for the perspectives they endorse. In turn, journalists construct policy debates in (a) the language of rights and morals, (b) the language of economics and pragmatics, or (c) both, to simplify news production and ease the dissemination of information to the broader public. Finally, the public processes news discourse about policy positions and makes a range of political judgments based on the cues provided in journalists' reports.

Notably, many issues discussed by political elites and news media in terms of what Haider-Markel and Meier (1996) termed *deeply held values*, such as abortion and gay rights, have been found to influence voting behavior in both national and state elections (Abramowitz, 1995). Scholars assert that citizens, particularly those with strong religious convictions, are often concerned with the symbolic importance of such issues and use them to assert their values in political contexts (Klein, 1984; Olson & Carroll, 1992; Sears & Funk, 1991). Relatively unexamined, however, are the ways in which political behavior may be influenced by the particular values emphasized in the framing of campaign issues.

In this chapter, we expand upon our program of research exploring how shifts in discourse interact with individuals' cognitions and motivations to shape political evaluations. To date, this line of experimental inquiry has examined how the value-framing of campaign information can not only shape individuals' interpretations of issues, but also can encourage voters to make attributions about candidate character, apply social cognitions to policy evaluations, and modify their decision-making processes (Domke, McCoy, & Torres, 1999; Domke, Shah, & Wackman, 1998a; Shah, Domke, & Wackman, 1996). Extending our research, this chapter examines the direct and mediated effects of value-framing on the vote-choice process across two very different research populations, evangelical Christians and undergraduate students.

Value-Framing

Although too often unacknowledged in content analyses, it must be recognized that individuals "do not slavishly follow the framing of issues presented in the mass media"; rather, people "actively filter, sort, and reorganize information in personally meaningful ways in constructing an understanding of public issues" (Neuman, Just, & Crigler, 1992, pp. 76–77). When confronted with information, individuals are thought to first locate relevant schemas to guide processing. Research suggests that frequency and recency of use influence which schema is activated. For familiar objects, relevant schemas are highly—even chronically—accessible due to frequent activation (Fazio, 1989; Higgins & King, 1981; Krosnick, 1988); with less familiar objects, however, recently activated schemas brought into active thought by contextual cues may guide information processing (Chaiken, 1980; Tourangeau & Rasinski, 1988).

Similarly, Zaller and Feldman (1992) asserted that most people are internally conflicted with multiple, often opposing "considerations" on most political issues and do not exhaustively search available considerations. Rather, individuals sample from their available cognitions, oversampling those that are easily brought into conscious thought. According to this perspective, the ordering, or framing, of textual materials activates certain considerations, which interact with a person's political predispositions to guide political judgments (Krosnick, 1991; Zaller, 1992). This is consistent with the findings of Iyengar and Kinder (1987), who argued that media emphasis on particular issues *primes* certain ideas for individuals, which are then more accessible for evaluations of politicians.

Subtle shifts in message frames also have been found to influence the process and outcome of a wide range of social and political evaluations, from the price elasticity of goods to political tolerance judgments (Green & Blair, 1995; Nelson, Clawson, & Oxley, 1997; Nelson, Oxley, & Clawson, 1997; Tversky & Kahneman, 1986). In our research, we have discovered that the *ethical framing* of political issues activates considerations about rights and morals in the minds of some citizens, who then use these standards in their interpretation of campaign issues and carry them over to other campaign evaluations. Specifically, individuals who encounter an issue framed in ethical terms become more likely to view not only that issue but also other issues, perhaps even issues typically understood in economic and pragmatic terms, as connected with basic moral principles (Shah et al., 1996). They also apply these ethical criteria to candidate character evaluations, such that attributions to the morality, honesty, and compassion of candidates (or lack thereof) tend to increase when an ethically framed issue is part of the political discourse (Domke et al., 1998a).

Similarly, research on "value-choice" frames asserts that political candidates and politicians struggle over the construction of issues "to legitimate to themselves and to communicate to others why their choice is more moral or competent than their opponent's" (Ball-Rokeach & Loges, 1996, p. 279; Ball-Rokeach, Power, Guthrie, & Waring, 1990). As this work suggests, media emphasis on particular values may influence individuals' judgmental processes when selecting between options, as is the case in voting behavior. Because values can function as heuristics, individuals may adjust the complexity of their judgment processes in relation to the values—the value-choices—they encounter (Tetlock, 1986; Shah, in press). This perspective, then, implies that individual values and basic motivations should receive greater consideration when examining the impact of value-frames on the vote-choice process.

Motivation and Decision Making

Motivational approaches to personality and attitudes suggest that mental systems serve both a "schematic" function, providing individuals with a frame of reference for understanding and ordering attitude objects, and an "expressive" function, affirming core values and defending self-image (Herek, 1986; Snyder & DeBono, 1987, 1989). Particular attention has focused on phenomena that demonstrate and maintain an individual's sense of self, with some scholars positing that the expression of core values allows individuals to support their self-concepts (Greenwald & Breckler, 1985; Rokeach, 1973). Especially relevant for this research, Tetlock (1989) argued that individuals' reasoning about political issues is "powerfully shaped by the fundamental values they are trying to advance in particular policy domains" (p. 130).

These insights, then, suggest that voting may be a means for individuals to validate core aspects of their self-conception, or more specifically, the sense of values that they believe are at stake in a given political context (Abelson, 1988; Steele, 1988). Primarily, individuals' value priorities may interact with news frames to shape interpretations of political issues. Evidence from our program of research confirms this relationship. The framing of a campaign issue often is accepted or rejected, in part, on the basis of the strength individuals assign to the values emphasized in news coverage (Shah, forthcoming). It appears, then, that individuals' value priorities and media's value-framing of political issues work together in shaping issue interpretations.

Further, our research consistently has found that issue interpretations grounded in concerns about rights and morals play an overriding role in the candidate selection process, leading voters to truncate their decision making (Domke, Shah, & Wackman, 1998b; Shah et al., 1996; Shah, forthcoming). It seems likely, then, that the effect of value-frames on the vote-choice process is mediated by individuals' issue interpretations, for as Tetlock

(1986) asserted, "it is dissonant and threatening to [individuals'] self-esteem to acknowledge that they are capable of cold-blooded trade-off decisions that require compromising basic values" (p. 819). Thus, media frames may have both direct and mediated effects on electoral decision-making processes, altering the underlying strategy that voters employ in making a candidate choice.

Behavioral research that examines how individuals decide between two or more alternatives, using their cognitive capacities to process information and reduce conflict, has identified decision-making strategies that fall under the rubrics of *compensatory* and *noncompensatory* processing (Billings & Marcus, 1983; Hogarth, 1987; Wright, 1975). In a *compensatory* model, positive and negative evaluations on several criteria can offset one another—that is, individuals can make tradeoffs among valued attributes to determine which alternative has the greatest overall worth (Beattie & Baron, 1991; Payne, Bettman, & Johnson, 1990). This multiple-criteria model—with its weighting and summing of attributes—shares theoretical commonality with rational choice models of voting behavior (Herstein, 1981; Hinich & Pollard, 1981).

However, both compensatory and rational choice models have been criticized because of their assumptions of highly calculative decision makers (Green & Shapiro, 1994; Onken, Hastie, & Revelle, 1985; Rabinowitz & Macdonald, 1989). Hence, *noncompensatory* strategies, in which positive evaluations cannot offset negative evaluations, have also been theorized. In these models, which recognize that decision makers often use an overriding or contingent criterion, "trade-offs may not be made explicitly in many cases" (Payne, Bettman, & Johnson, 1992, p. 93; Wright & Barbour, 1975). Instead, the noncompensatory decision maker adopts an inflexible position concerning the choice that focuses on one or two key attributes. As such, noncompensatory decision strategies are qualitatively distinct from their compensatory counterparts.

HYPOTHESES

This research explores three major hypotheses: the first concerns whether media frames influence individuals' issue interpretations; the second concerns whether media frames affect voters' choice processes; the third concerns the mediating role of subjects' issue interpretations for framing effects on the vote-choice process.

We posit that value-frames in news content, by selecting and emphasizing certain aspects of an issue, influence citizens' application of particular values in interpreting issues. Specifically, we expect that voters form distinct *interpretations* of issues based on the activation of different sets of values. Individuals who assign an *ethical interpretation* to an issue understand the issue in terms of their sense of right and wrong grounded in beliefs about human rights, civil rights, religious morals, or personal principles. Individuals who assign a *material interpretation* to an issue understand the issue in terms of tangible concerns grounded in economics, expedience, practicality, and personal self-interest (see Domke et al., 1998a; Shah et al., 1996). Schemas related to moral or ethical values are likely to be closely related to one's self-conception and thus be both highly accessible and particularly powerful. These factors increase the likelihood that an ethical media frame will foster an ethical interpretation of issues. Thus, the first hypothesis may be stated:

> H1: *Individuals receiving an issue with an ethical value-frame will be more likely to form an ethical interpretation of the issues they encounter than individuals receiving the same issue with a material value-frame.*

We further contend that individuals' processing of campaign issue information activates certain schemas that then become likely to serve as a basis for judgment. For example, if an issue's frame emphasizes moral or ethical values, schemas activated in the processing of this information will motivate the use of such criterion in judgment. Therefore, by activating particular schemas an ethically framed issue may not only encourage an ethical interpretation but may also, in turn, influence the use of ethical comparisons as a primary method of judgment and decision making. In this way, the comparison of alternatives using an ethical criterion will encourage the use of a noncompensatory decision-making strategy: that is, tradeoffs between options become less likely because positive evaluations on other issues cannot compensate for a negative evaluation on the ethical issue. Thus, the second hypothesis may be stated:

> H2: *Individuals receiving an issue with an ethical value-frame will be more likely to use a noncompensatory decision-making strategy than individuals receiving the same issue with a material value-frame.*

Further, our program of research suggests that individual interpretations of issues may serve as a critical mediating factor between value-frames in news texts and decision making (Domke et al., 1998b; Shah et al., 1996). Individuals with an ethical interpretation of an issue seem likely to focus on that issue as they assess electoral information because their sense of "right and wrong" is critical to maintaining their self-conception. In evaluating a set of candidates, then, individuals with an ethical interpretation of an issue will first consider each candidate's position on that issue, shaping the manner in which information is processed to arrive at a candidate decision. That is, voters with an ethical interpretation of at least one issue seem likely to use a noncompensatory decision-making process: that is, candidates who do not share their ethical position may be eliminated or, in a more simplified approach, the vote may be made solely on that issue.

In contrast, individuals with a material interpretation probably do not link the issue to their sense of self with the same intensity, even though there may be potential personal consequences. As a result, when politicians are evaluated on issues assigned material interpretations, individuals seem likely to allow candidates' stands on various issues to offset or balance one another, resulting in more integrative, or compensatory, processing. Thus, the third hypothesis may be stated:

> H3: *Individuals' issue interpretations will mediate the effects of value frames on the decision-making strategy.*

METHODS

We test the theoretical relationships proposed here by exploring how two subpopulations, evangelical Christians and undergraduate students, process the same media messages about particular issues. Concurrent study of these two groups provides a strong test of the hypotheses linking media frames, issue interpretations, and voter decision making. Although not mutually exclusive in all ways, these two populations differ considerably in their ideological orientations and political attitudes. Parallel results across these two very different subject groups would provide strong support for the generalizability of our theory.

In the overall study, 172 members of five evangelical Christian churches and 201 undergraduate students in a large Midwestern city were presented copies of newspaper articles and a questionnaire. The research discussed in this chapter focuses on 83 of the Christian subjects and 101 of the undergraduate subjects, who received an experimental manipulation regarding the framing of one issue within otherwise controlled political information environments. Of the evangelical Christians, 51% were men; ages ranged relatively evenly between 20 and 76; and 94% had attended at least some college. Of the undergraduate students, 53% were men and 83% were between the ages of 18 and 25. Most respondents took 35–45 minutes to read the newspaper articles and complete the questionnaire.

Research Design

The core of this research strategy is the controlled presentation of political information environments. Each environment included newspaper articles about a Congressional primary in a neighboring state that presented the contending views of *three candidates on four issues*. In this study, all subjects received the same articles on three issues: economy, education, and government cuts. Two experimental conditions were created by differently framing a fourth issue, health care, which was value-framed in ethical terms in one condition and in material terms in the second. In the first case, the issue was presented in terms of rights and morals by pitting equality and compassion in access to medical treatment against personal responsibility to provide for one's self. In the second, the issue was presented in terms of economics, expedience, and practicality by pitting the merits of the free market against the need for government intervention to control costs. Candidate quotations echoed the general framing of the issue. The other issues—economy, education, and government cuts—were framed to emphasize material values.

In carrying out the manipulation, candidate positions and policy implications were the same in both conditions; only the rationale underlying candidate positions was varied. In the articles, a number of possible confounding variables (e.g., political party affiliation, gender, and subject familiarity with candidates, as well as order of issue and candidate information) were controlled to guard against potential confounds. For the stimulus materials and other methodological details, see Shah et al. (1996).

Questionnaire

After reading the articles, subjects completed a questionnaire about their voting process that began by asking them which one of the three candidates they would vote for in the primary election. To measure the decision-making strategy, a series of open-ended questions asked subjects to describe their candidate choice process. Research suggests that questions about information processing can effectively elicit a "memory dump" if asked immediately after a task has been carried out (Ericsson & Simon, 1984; Zaller & Feldman, 1992). Guided by research on compensatory and noncompensatory strategies, we coded responses into these two categories.

In brief, if subjects (a) indicated that they eliminated a candidate early in their evaluative process because of his stand on a particular issue, or (b) based their decision on a single overriding criterion, they were coded as noncompensatory. Conversely, if subjects indicated that they weighted candidates' stands on a variety of issues, allowing them to compensate for one another, in arriving at a vote choice, they were coded as compensatory. Among the evangelical Christian subjects, of the 167 usable responses, two coders agreed on 140 as compensatory or noncompensatory (alpha = .84). Among student subjects, of the 193 usable responses, coders agreed on 166 as compensatory or noncompensatory (alpha = .86). For examples of the types of responses coded into these content categories, see Shah, Domke, and Wackman (1997).

Individual interpretations of issues were measured next with three open-ended questions that asked subjects to engage in a thought-listing procedure exploring how the issues related to their personal sense of values, their more broadly construed concerns about society, as well as their personal life-situations. Each issue was coded as having received primarily an ethical interpretation, material interpretation, or as not mentioned/stated as ignored. An issue was coded as receiving an ethical interpretation if the individual primarily discussed it within the framework of personal principles, basic rights, or religious morals. An issue was coded as receiving a material interpretation if the individual primarily discussed it in terms of economics, pragmatics, or self-interest. Among the evangelical Christian subjects, of the 165 usable responses, two coders agreed on 590 of 660 individual-issue codings (alpha = .89). Among student subjects, for the 200 usable responses, two coders agreed on 719 of 800 individual-issue codings (alpha = .90). For examples of the types of responses coded into these content categories, see Shah et al. (1997).

Individual-issue codings were combined to create a variable assessing a subject's interpretation of the overall issue environment. Individuals who assigned an ethical interpretation to at least one issue were coded as having an ethical interpretation of the issue environment. Individuals who did not assign an ethical interpretation to at least one issue, but who did have at least one material interpretation were coded as having a material interpretation of the issue environment. This classification system accounted for all subjects.

The questionnaire also contained four statements concerning the amount of information subjects reported processing while making the voting decision. Subjects rated their agreement with the statements using a five-point Likert scale. Among the evangelical Christian subjects, the additive index had mean interitem correlations of .48 and a Cronbach's alpha of .79. Among student subjects, the index had mean interitem correlations of .39 and an alpha of .72.

RESULTS

Hypothesis 1 predicted that individuals receiving an issue with an ethical value-frame would be more likely to form an ethical interpretation of the issue environment than individuals receiving the same issue with a material value-frame. To test this hypothesis, crosstabulations were run between the experimental conditions and subjects' interpretations of the issue environment (see Table 14.1). As predicted, subjects receiving health care with an ethical frame were significantly more likely to interpret the issue environment in an ethical manner than subjects receiving health care with a

TABLE 14.1
Value-Frame of Health Care by Environment Interpretation

Evangelical Christians

	EXPERIMENTAL GROUP	
Interpretation	*Ethical Value-Frame*	*Material Value-Frame*
Ethical	61.5%	21.6%
Material	*38.5*	78.4
Totals	100%	100%
	(*n* = 39)	(*n* = 37)
	$X^{2(1)} = 12.4, p < .001$	

Undergraduate Students

	EXPERIMENTAL GROUP	
Interpretation	*Ethical Value-Frame*	*Material Value-Frame*
Ethical	48.1%	16.3%
Material	*51.9*	83.7
Totals	100%	100%
	(*n* = 52)	(*n* = 49)
	$X^{2(1)} = 11.6, p < .001$	

material frame. These results were found in both research populations. Among evangelical Christians, nearly two thirds of subjects (62%) receiving the ethical value-frame of health care ascribed an ethical interpretation to the issue environment, compared to only 22% of subjects receiving the material value-frame of health care. Parallel results were found among undergraduate students: nearly half of subjects (48%) receiving the ethical frame of health care ascribed an ethical interpretation to the issue environment, compared to only 16% of subjects receiving the material frame of health care.

Hypothesis 2 predicted that individuals receiving an issue with an ethical value-frame will be more likely to use a noncompensatory decision-making strategy than those receiving the material value-frame. To test this hypothesis, crosstabs were run between the experimental conditions and the decision-making measure, which coded subjects' descriptions of their candidate selection process as either compensatory or noncompensatory. As predicted, subjects receiving health care with an ethical frame were more likely to use a noncompensatory strategy than subjects receiving the same issue with a material frame (see Table 14.2). These results were found in both research populations. Among evangelical Christians, a solid majority of subjects (58%) receiving the ethical frame of health care used a noncompensatory strategy, compared to less than one fourth of subjects (24%)

TABLE 14.2
Value-Frame of Health Care by Decision-Making Strategy

	Evangelical Christians	
	EXPERIMENTAL GROUP	
Strategy Used	Ethical Value-Frame	Material Value-Frame
Compensatory	42.5%	76.3%
Noncompensatory	57.5	23.7
Totals	100%	100%
	($n = 40$)	($n = 38$)
	$X^{2(1)} = 9.2, p < .01$	

	Undergraduate Students	
	EXPERIMENTAL GROUP	
Strategy Used	Ethical Value-Frame	Material Value-Frame
Compensatory	59.2%	84.1%
Noncompensatory	40.8	15.9
Totals	100%	100%
	($n = 49$)	($n = 44$)
	$X^{2(1)} = 7.0, p < .01$	

receiving the material frame of health care. Among undergraduate students, although less than half of subjects in both groups used a noncompensatory strategy, a great deal more did so in the group receiving the ethically framed version (41%) than in the group receiving the materially framed version (16%).

Hypothesis 3 predicted that individuals' issue interpretations will mediate the effects of value-frames on the decision-making strategy. To test this hypothesis, causal modeling analysis was performed using OLS regressions to estimate path coefficients. Information processing is included as a second mediating variable in the model, as it might provide an alternative explanation for some of the observed relationships. It seems plausible that the linkage between value-framing and the decision-making process might be a function of the amount of information subjects bothered to read and put to use. Indeed, some psychologists argue that noncompensatory strategies are used because individuals are "cognitive misers," unwilling to process much of the information they encounter (see Fiske & Taylor, 1991). Accordingly, truncated voting decisions may result from a limited processing of the available information, which in turn may be caused by exposure to the ethical framing of issue information.

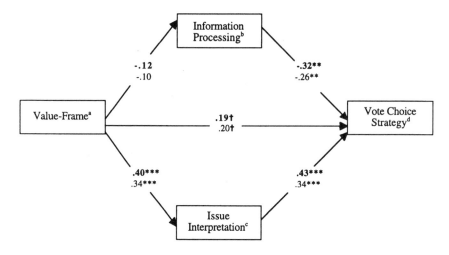

FIG. 14.1. Path analysis of mediational role of issue interpretation for framing effects. *Notes.* Coefficients are equivalent to standardized partial regression (β) weights. Coefficients in bold typeface are evangelical Christian, coefficients in regular typeface are undergraduate students.
[a]Coded as 0 = material value-frame, 1 = ethical value-frame.
[b]Less information processed = low, more information processed = high; Explained variance = .01 for evangelical Christians and .01 for undergraduate students.
[c]Coded as 0 = material interpretation, 1 = ethical interpretation; Explained variance = .16 for evangelical Christians and .11 for undergraduate students.
[d]Coded as 0 = compensatory, 1 = noncompensatory; Explained variance = .47 for evangelical Christians and .24 for undergraduate students.
† < .10; *p < .05; **p < .01; ***p < .001

The path model presented in Fig. 14.1 lends stronger support to the theory advanced in this chapter than the alternative explanation for noncompensatory voting decisions. The effect of value-framing on decision making appears to be largely mediated by individuals' issue interpretations. However, although this indirect effect of value-framing on the decision-making strategy substantially attenuates the relationship observed in tests of Hypothesis 2, the direct path remains marginally significant (p = .051 for evangelical Christian subjects; p = .056 for undergraduate student subjects). Further, information processing is not significantly influenced by the framing of the health care issue, but nonetheless is negatively related to noncompensatory decision making. That is, individuals who reported that they considered all the campaign information they encountered tended to make decisions that reflected a weighing and summing of candidate attributes. The results, once again, are parallel for both sets of subjects, albeit generally stronger among the evangelical Christians.

DISCUSSION

The findings presented here support the perspective that news frames influence the issue interpretations and electoral decision-making strategies of citizens. Thus, it appears that individuals possess a variety of cognitions from which they form their conceptions of political issues and rely on contextual cues in constituting their political judgments. If political elites and advocacy groups discuss political issues in terms of contrasting sets of values to build public support *and* journalists adopt this discourse in their coverage to simplify news production and public consumption, as research suggests and we believe, then our investigation indicates that the value-framing of issues that results from this dynamic can activate especially powerful mental constructs that shape a wide range of judgmental processes. Primarily, these considerations mold individuals' interpretations of the issues they encounter and, to a lesser degree, provide criteria for electoral reasoning.

Indeed, causal modeling analysis across both research populations indicates that the effect of value-framing on the candidate selection strategy, although largely mediated by individuals' issue interpretations, is not completely attenuated by this indirect relationship. Nonetheless, it appears that voters with an ethical interpretation of an issue, due to the strong linkage of concerns about rights and morals to the self-concept, place that issue at the center of their evaluation of the issue environment. In this context, their own stands on the issue function as a filter through which candidate information will first be processed, encouraging a noncompensatory decision-making process. These findings also indicate that, for individuals who do not ascribe an ethical interpretation to an issue, there is less of a filtering process; instead, materially interpreted issues are likely to compete in a relatively equal manner as these issues are not linked to an individual's identity as centrally as are issues tied to ethics or morals.

Therefore, results provide support for the perspective that media frames *directly* and *indirectly* influence voters' political judgments and reasoning processes. Media framing of issues in ethical terms may lead to more noncompensatory decision making by (a) *activating* ethical schemas or attitudes, which *motivate* voters to make judgments in ethical terms; and (b) *providing* specific information on ethically based candidate positions, which *encourage* ethical interpretations of issues and *enable* voters to apply these ethical considerations in judgment. An individual encountering a campaign issue framed in ethical terms, then, becomes quite likely to use an overriding criterion as the means of deciding between candidates. This simple conclusion may go a long way towards explaining the role of news media—as well as political elites—in the rise of "hot-button" issues in American electoral politics (Abramowitz, 1995; Cook, Jelen, & Wilcox, 1994; Haider-Markel

& Meier, 1996). It may be that ethical framing of issues, such as abortion and gay rights, has helped to polarize the electorate and foster simplified voting decisions, geared toward expressing values and not advancing interests.

As noted earlier in this chapter, our research program also indicates that the highlighting of ethical concerns in news discourse has a considerable impact on citizens' judgments about the integrity of political candidates. Although these data are not presented here, the implications of a relationship between value-framing of issues and evaluations of candidate character are considerable. In particular, this linkage suggests that image-based voting represents the outcome, in part, of perceptions encouraged by individuals' exposure to subtle shifts in the framing of campaign issue information. That is, the value-framing of issues also may trigger priming effects that begin with voters' thoughts about issues and issue positions and then "carry over" to shape evaluations of the integrity of political candidates. Given that issue-based evaluations of candidates appear to contribute to image-based voting, our research findings question the long-standing dichotomy between the roles of political issues and candidate images in electoral behavior.

In sum, the theory outlined in this chapter suggests that political communication research needs to adopt a more nuanced understanding of (a) what qualifies as media framing and (b) what direct and indirect consequences media framing has for individuals' psychological and behavioral functioning. Our approach to framing, which defines frames narrowly and draws a sharp distinction between ethical news frames and material news frames, has been shown to have a range of implication for electoral judgment and reasoning processes. To date, we have devoted most of our effort to exploring the implications of value-framing for candidate evaluations and voting behavior. Future research needs to look beyond this context to examine the effects of value-framing on individuals' political knowledge, opinion expression, civic engagement, and political participation. It seems likely that the phenomena that foster attributions to candidate integrity and truncated decision making might also encourage greater levels of learning about certain issues, make the expression of minority opinions more permissible, and sponsor greater levels of involvement in public life. This is because individuals who come to understand an issue as linked to core values are driven to defend their self-conception by *acting upon* this set of concerns.

REFERENCES

Abelson, R. (1988). Conviction. *American Psychologist, 43,* 267–275.

Abramowitz, A. I. (1995). It's abortion, stupid: Policy voting in the 1992 presidential election. *Journal of Politics, 57,* 176–186.

Abramson, P., & Inglehart, R. (1995). *Value change in global perspective.* Ann Arbor: University of Michigan Press.

Ball-Rokeach, S. J., & Loges, W. E. (1996). Making choices: Media roles in the construction of value-choices. In C. Seligman, J. Olson, & M. Zanna (Eds.), *Values: The Ontario Symposium, Vol. 8* (pp. 277–298). Hillsdale, NJ: Lawrence Erlbaum Associates.

Ball-Rokeach, S. J., Power, G. J., Guthrie, K. K., & Waring, H. R. (1990). Value-framing abortion in the United States: An application of media system dependency theory. *International Journal of Public Opinion Research, 2,* 249–273.

Beattie, J., & Baron, J. (1991). Investigating the effect of stimulus range on attribute weight. *Journal of Experimental Psychology: Human Perception and Performance, 17,* 571–585.

Billings, R. S., & Marcus, S. A. (1983). Measures of compensatory and noncompensatory models of decision behavior: Process tracing versus policy capturing. *Organizational Behavior and Human Performance, 31,* 331–352.

Cappella, J. N., & Jamieson, K. H. (1997). *Spiral of cynicism: The press and the public good.* New York: Oxford University Press.

Chaiken, S. (1980). Heuristic versus systematic information processing and the use of source versus message cues in persuasion. *Journal of Personality and Social Psychology, 39,* 752–766.

Cook, E. A., Jelen, T. G., & Wilcox, C. (1994). Issue voting in gubernatorial elections: Abortion and post-*Webster* politics. *Journal of Politics, 56,* 187–199.

Dennis, E. E., & Ismach, A. H. (1981). *Reporting processes and practices.* Belmont, CA: Wadsworth.

Domke, D., McCoy, K., & Torres, M. (1999). News media, racial perceptions, and political cognition. *Communication Research, 26,* 570–607.

Domke, D., Shah, D. V., & Wackman, D. (1998a). Media priming effects: Accessibility, association, and activation. *International Journal of Public Opinion Research, 1,* 51–74.

Domke, D., Shah, D. V., & Wackman, D. (1998b). "Moral referendums": Values, news media, and the process of candidate choice. *Political Communication, 15,* 301–321.

Ericsson, K. A, & Simon, H. (1984). *Protocol analysis.* Cambridge, MA: MIT Press.

Fazio, R. H. (1989). On the power and functionality of attitudes: The role of attitude accessibility. In A. R. Pratkanis, S. J. Breckler, A. G. Greenwald (Eds.), *Attitude structure and function* (pp. 153–179). Hillsdale, NJ: Lawrence Erlbaum Associates.

Fiske, S., & Taylor, S. (1991). *Social cognition.* New York: McGraw-Hill.

Green, D. P., & Blair, I. V. (1995). Framing and the price elasticity of private and public goods. *Journal of Consumer Psychology, 4,* 1–32.

Green, D. P., & Shapiro, I. (1994). *Pathologies of rational choice theory: A critique of applications in political science.* New Haven, CT: Yale University Press.

Greenwald, A. G., & Breckler, S. J. (1985). To whom is the self presented? In B. R. Schlenker (Ed.), *The self and social life* (pp. 126–145). New York: McGraw-Hill.

Haider-Markel, D. P., & Meier, K. J. (1996). The politics of gay and lesbian rights: Expanding the scope of the conflict. *Journal of Politics, 58,* 332–349.

Herek, G. M. (1986). The instrumentality of attitudes: Towards a neo-functional theory. *Journal of Social Issues, 42,* 99–114.

Herstein, J. A. (1981). Keeping the voter's limit in mind: A cognitive processing analysis of decisionmaking in voting. *Journal of Personality and Social Psychology, 40,* 843–861.

Higgins, E. T., & King, G. (1981). Accessibility of social constructs: Information-processing consequences of individual and contextual variability. In N. Cantor & J. Kihlstrom (Eds.), *Personality, cognition, and social interaction* (pp. 69–121). Hillsdale, NJ: Lawrence Erlbaum Associates.

Hinich, M. J., & Pollard, W. (1981). A new approach to the spatial theory of electoral competition. *American Journal of Political Science, 25,* 323–333.

Hogarth, R. M. (1987). *Judgment and choice.* New York: Wiley.

Iyengar, S. (1991). *Is anyone responsible?: How television frames political issues.* Chicago: University of Chicago Press.

Iyengar, S., & Kinder, D. (1987). *News that matters.* Chicago: University of Chicago Press.

Kahneman, D., & Tversky, A. (1984). Choice, values, and frames. *American Psychologist, 39*, 341–350.

Klein, E. (1984). *Gender politics.* Cambridge, MA: Harvard University Press.

Krosnick, J. A. (1988). The role of attitude importance in social evaluation: A study of policy preferences, presidential candidate evaluations, and voting behavior. *Journal of Personality and Social Psychology, 55*, 196–210.

Krosnick, J. A. (1991). Response strategies for coping with the cognitive demands of attitude measures in surveys. *Applied Cognitive Psychology, 5*, 231–236.

Lau, R., Smith, R. A., & Fiske, S. T. (1991). Political beliefs, policy interpretations, and political persuasion. *Journal of Politics, 53*, 644–675.

Nelson, T. E., Clawson, R. A., & Oxley, Z. M. (1997). Media framing of a civil liberties conflict and its effect on tolerance. *American Political Science Review, 91*, 567–583

Nelson, T. E., Oxley, Z. M., & Clawson, R. A. (1997). Toward a psychology of framing effects. *Political Behavior, 19*, 221–245.

Neuman, W. R., Just, M. R., & Crigler, A. N. (1992). *Common knowledge: News and the construction of political meaning.* Chicago: University of Chicago Press.

Olson, D. V. A., & Carroll, J. W. (1992). Religiously based politics: Religious elites and the public. *Social Forces, 70*, 765–86.

Onken, J., Hastie, R., & Revelle, W. (1985). Individual differences in the use of simplification strategies in a complex decision-making task. *Journal of Experimental Psychology: Human Perception and Performance, 11*, 14–27.

Payne, J. W., Bettman, J. R., & Johnson, E. J. (1990). The adaptive decision maker: Effort and accuracy in choice. In R. M. Hogarth (Ed.), *Insights in decision making: A tribute to Hillel J. Einhorn* (pp. 129–153). Chicago: University of Chicago Press.

Payne, J. W., Bettman, J. R., & Johnson, E. J. (1992). Behavioral decision research. *Annual Review of Psychology, 43*, 87–131.

Rabinowitz, G., & Macdonald, S. E. (1989). A directional theory of issue voting. *American Political Science Review, 83*, 93–121.

Rokeach, M. (1973). *The nature of human values.* New York: The Free Press.

Sears, D. O., & Funk, C. L. (1991). The role of self-interest in social and political attitudes. *Advances in Experimental Social Psychology, 24*, 1–91.

Shah, D. V. (1999). *Value judgments: News framing and individual processing of political issues.* Unpublished doctoral dissertation, University of Minnesota.

Shah, D. V. (in press). The collision of convictions: Value-framing and electoral judgment processes. In R. P. Hart & D. Shaw (Eds.), *Communication and U.S. elections: New agendas* (pp. 55–74). Lanham, MD: Rowman and Littlefield.

Shah, D. V., Domke, D., & Wackman, D. B. (1996). "To thine own self be true": Values, framing, and voter decision-making strategies. *Communication Research, 23*, 509–561.

Shah, D. V., Domke, D., & Wackman, D. B. (1997). Values and the vote: Linking issue interpretations to the process of candidate choice. *Journalism & Mass Communication Quarterly, 74*(2), 357–387.

Shoemaker, P., & Reese, S. (1996) *Mediating the message: Theories of influence on mass media content.* White Plains, NY: Longman.

Snyder, M., & DeBono, K. G. (1987). A functional approach to attitudes and persuasion. In M. P. Zanna, J. M. Olson, & C. P. Herman (Eds.), *Social influence: The Ontario symposium* (Vol. 5, pp. 107–125). Hillsdale, NJ: Lawrence Erlbaum Associates.

Snyder, M., & DeBono, K. G. (1989). Understanding the function of attitudes: Lessons for personality and social behavior. In A. R. Pratkanis, S. J. Breckler, & A. G. Greenwald (Eds.), *Attitude structure and function* (pp. 339–359). Hillsdale, NJ: Lawrence Erlbaum Associates.

Steele, C. M. (1988). The psychology of self-affirmation: Sustaining the integrity of the self. In L. Berkowitz (Ed.), *Advances in experimental psychology* (Vol. 21, pp. 261–302). New York: Academic Press

Tetlock, P. E. (1986). A value pluralism model of ideological reasoning. *Journal of Personality and Social Psychology, 50,* 819–827.

Tetlock, P. E. (1989). Structure and function in political belief systems. In A. R. Pratkanis, S. J. Breckler, & A. G. Greenwald (Eds.), *Attitude structure and function* (pp. 129–151). Hillsdale, NJ: Lawrence Erlbaum Associates.

Tourangeau, R., & Rasinski, K. (1988). Cognitive processes underlying context effects in attitude measurement. *Psychological Bulletin, 103,* 299–314.

Tversky, A., & Kahneman, D. (1981). The framing of decisions and the psychology of choice. *Science, 211,* 453–458.

Tversky, A., & Kahneman, D. (1986). Rational choice and the framing of decisions. *Journal of Business, 59,* 251–78.

Wright, P. (1975). Consumer choice strategies: Simplifying vs. optimizing. *Journal of Marketing Research, 12,* 60–66.

Wright, P., & Barbour, F. (1975). The relevance of decision process models in structuring persuasive messages. *Communication Research, 2,* 246–259.

Zaller, J. (1992). *The nature and origins of mass opinion.* Cambridge, England: Cambridge University Press.

Zaller, J., & Feldman, S. (1992). A simple theory of the survey response: Answering questions versus revealing preferences. *American Journal of Political Science, 36*(3), 579–616.

15

Issue Frames That Strike a Value Balance: A Political Psychology Perspective

Thomas E. Nelson
Elaine A. Willey

Like its sister disciplines, political science has pounced on framing as a conceptual tool of impressive power for describing and analyzing important political phenomena. It wasn't always this way; hard-nosed, quantitatively minded political scientists used to shy away from slippery and hard-to-measure concepts like "frame." Perhaps the epitome of this attitude is Iyengar and Kinder's (1987) program of research on agenda-setting and priming summarized in the modern classic, *News That Matters*. Not much content analysis can be found in that book; the main story is about how the *frequency* of news coverage of an issue affects political judgments relating to that issue (How serious a problem is it? Does the president's handling of the issue matter to my judgment of his overall performance?). Yet both members of that team have recently turned to questions of content in their separate and quite distinct research on framing (Iyengar, 1991; Nelson & Kinder 1996; Kinder & Sanders 1996). Many others have come along for the ride, and as a certain anonymous manuscript reviewer can attest, there is a lot of interest in framing in political science now.

Framing takes many forms and suits many purposes, and the accumulated scholarly record reflects this diversity. Nearly all the research, however, views framing as a constituent of political communication. Communicators frame messages, with implications (not always intended) for how receivers think about the message's subject. Scholars have bestowed the lion's share of their attention on a frame's origins, generating numerous bold theories and illuminating analyses of the social, political, economic, and institutional forces that affect the generation and dissemination of frames. Some of the most imaginative framing work examines both the sender *and* the receiver (e.g., Iyengar, 1991; Snow, Rochford, Worden, & Benford, 1986), but generally speaking, less has been said about the frame's destination, the ordinary citizen. Frame responses have been subjected to fairly conventional social–psychological analyses, with a strong emphasis on citizens as limited-capacity information processors. As useful as these treatments have been, we believe that this broad and complex phenomenon requires a creative and nuanced battery of theories on *both* sides to best illuminate it.

Our team has expounded a broad theory of framing that tries to be faithful to both sides of the transaction without pretending to be comprehensive (Nelson, Clawson, & Oxley, 1997; Nelson & Oxley, 1999; Nelson, Oxley, & Clawson, 1997). In this chapter, we describe this theory and relate it to other work on the subject, especially in political science. We single out for extended treatment one aspect of the theory that speaks loudly to contemporary public opinion scholarship: a view of framing as a compass for navigating value conflicts. We finish with a brief description of one set of experiments that exemplifies our empirical approach.

SPECIES OF FRAMES

There is more than one kind of frame swimming in the political information stream. The most politically relevant species are *collective action frames* (Gamson, 1992; Snow et al., 1986); *decision frames* (Kahneman & Tversky, 1984); *news frames* (Iyengar, 1991; Price & Tewksbury, 1997); and our favorite, *issue frames* (Nelson & Oxley, 1999). To propose a single, comprehensive theory covering the generation of and response to all types of frames would be laughably naïve. We will get to the last one eventually, but let us start with a brief treatment of the first three to set properly the context.

Credit for collective action frames properly belongs to the sociologists, not the political scientists, starting with Goffman's (1974) description of frames as interpretive structures laid atop an otherwise ambiguous stream of events. The most passionate promoters of this kind of framing analysis see it as a way of re-injecting ideational considerations into the study of social movements, a field otherwise dominated by materialistic approaches. Snow and colleagues talk of how movements must "align" their frames with those of their supporters and constituents in order to thrive (Snow et al., 1986; see also Gamson, 1992). Events and circumstances must be effectively framed as injustices that challenge important interests and values to inspire the kind of collective demands that get government attention. Gamson proposes the most detailed collective action frame anatomy and physiology, and explicitly ties frame production to dissemination via mass media outlets (e.g., Gamson & Meyer, 1996).

Psychological research presents a very different species—decision frames—that nevertheless echoes the broader point that it is not so much the facts of the matter as their interpretation that governs human behavior. In this case, the behavior is the choice between two alternatives with the same expected value, one that involves risk and the other a sure thing. It turns out that when the alternatives are framed as "gains," experimental participants favor the sure thing, but when the same alternatives are frames as "losses," participants favor the gamble. Kahneman and Tversky, who uncovered this framing effect and proposed Prospect Theory as its explanation, argue that losses "loom larger" than equivalent gains. Losses are felt more acutely and so carry greater weight in our decisions.

Political scientists, especially those who study leader decision making, have been intrigued by prospect theory, although many have pointed out that the principles don't always translate readily to actual decision scenarios. Those who look toward mass politics take greater interest in how individuals and institutions, particularly the mass media, frame messages for popular consumption. There is a peck of research linking news frames to institutional imperatives of the media industry, often with a strong critical eye toward frame-imposed distortions that may bias public opinion. General news frames include the "strategic" or "game" frame for campaign coverage (Patterson, 1993), the "episodic" versus "thematic" frames for social issues coverage (Iyengar, 1991), and the pervasive "conflict" and "personalization" frames (Price & Tewksbury, 1997).

Somewhat overshadowed by the concern with news frames is the work on issue frames. The distinction is admittedly a little murky, not the least because the news media are the most likely conveyors of issue frames. Still, it is important to draw a line between issue frames that the media simply *report* versus those that they *impose* out of organizational habit and marketplace demand. News frames like *conflict* arise from the perceived need to seek market share by highlighting or exaggerating dramatic confrontation. Like the others, this frame can (and usually does) structure nearly every kind of story. Issue frames are content-specific (though not exclusive), and usually originate from professional politicians, advertisers, spokespeople, editorialists, think-tankers, and others who care about molding public opinion. The mass media tote these frames to their targets either directly via paid advertising, letters to the editor, and op-ed pieces; or indirectly via quotations and other borrowing from the source that is reported as part of a news story.

Issue frames are descriptions of social policies and problems that shape the public's understanding of how the problem came to be and the important criteria by which policy solutions should be evaluated. Gamson (1992) has done the most to detail the components of an issue frame. Most issue frames can be summarized by a simple tagline, such as "reverse discrimination" or "right to life," but the best contain a medley of elements that fit together, gestalt-like, to form a total interpretive package that makes sense of the issue and suggests a course of action. "Right to life" might contain stereotypic caricatures like greedy doctors and charmless, masculine working women; catchy slogans like "abortion stops a beating heart"; and vivid iconic images such as a pair of tiny fetal feet.

Although Gamson and colleagues have traced the "public careers" of frames for such issues as nuclear power and welfare spending, Kinder and colleagues have examined the consequences of framing for individual opinions (Kinder & Sanders, 1996; Nelson & Kinder, 1996). Using survey-based question-wording experiments, Kinder and colleagues have shown how framing alters the "mix of ingredients" that individuals bring to their issue ruminations. Framing affirmative action as "reverse discrimination" brings Whites' self-interest concerns to the fore, whereas framing it as an "undeserved advantage" privileges Whites' potentially hostile attitudes toward Blacks. One of us (Nelson), in collaboration with Kinder, found that "group centered frames"—that is, frames that play on stereotypes and hostile attitudes toward groups such as Blacks and gays—guided respondents to think of social issues in light of their beliefs and feelings about the groups involved, rather than some other way of conceptualizing the issue (Nelson & Kinder, 1996). Likewise, Shah, Domke, and Wackman (chap. 14, this volume) have presented experimental evidence that "value frames" for issues encourage audiences to think about issues in light of their fundamental political principles rather than, for instance, their material costs and benefits.

THE VALUES CONNECTION

We too are interested in framing's relevance to values-based political attitudes, but our cut is different. We are interested in how frames help citizens manage *value conflict*. Value conflict pervades pluralistic democratic cultures such as the United States and infiltrates the opinions of many citizens. As communicators vie for a larger slice of public support for their policies, they frame issues so as to tip the balance between conflicting values in their favor, hoping that opinions follow suit.

Belief Systems and Value Systems

Before we spell out our approach, however, let's review a little background on values and public opinion. Our story begins with the pioneering studies of citizen political thought undertaken at the University of Michigan in the late 1950s and summarized in Philip Converse's (1964) landmark chapter, "The Nature of Belief Systems in Mass Publics." Converse argued that citizens' attitudes about major social and political issues—the kind that preoccupy politicians, journalists, and the politically aware laity—are, to put it charitably, curious. When citizens actually *hold* real opinions (and, depending on the issue, that opinionated segment could be the minority), these opinions are isolated from opinions on other issues and other kinds of abstract political ideas. Converse singled out for specific debunking the suggestion that the average citizen deduces issue opinions from an abstract, articulated, and stable political *ideology*.

More than 35 years later Converse's conclusions are still debated (e.g., Kinder 1998), but scholars generally agree that, while this research got some things wrong, what it probably got right is that abstract ideology of the liberal–conservative type doesn't guide the political thoughts and opinions of most citizens to any serious extent. Does that mean that these opinions are devoid of *any* general political ideas? Not at all. For many citizens, social and political *values* fill the ideological gap. A value is not an ideology, in the sense of a prescriptive political outlook derived from a few core assumptions about human nature, justice, and the proper role of government in human affairs. Values are general claims about desirable social and personal conditions, or "end states," such as *equality*, *freedom*, and *a world of beauty* (Rokeach 1973).[1]

In effect, a value is a positive attitude toward some general state of affairs, even if that state of affairs is an unattainable ideal. Unlike ideologies, values are not overtly political in content, rather they help shape political outlooks. Values are not "core beliefs," as they make no existential claims (e.g., that people are inherently selfish, or that capitalism yields the greatest good for the greatest number). The two distinguishing attributes of a value are its *evaluative flavor* (a claim about goodness or desirability) and its *target* (an abstract quality or condition).

What is the evidence that values enjoy privileged status in the average citizen's political thinking? Social psychologists and political scientists alike have shown how core values such as *freedom*, *equality*, and *individualism* contribute to attitudes on social policy matters like welfare spending and affirmative action (Bobo & Kluegel, 1993, Rokeach 1973). Rokeach (1973) argued that major political ideologies such as socialism and liberal capitalism are extensions and elaborations of the core values *freedom* and *equality*

---

[1]The grandfather of this research, Milton Rokeach, famously distinguished between *terminal values* (end states) and *instrumental values* (ways of behaving). *Equality* is a terminal value, whereas *industriousness* is an instrumental value, for example. Schwarz (1994) has effectively argued that this distinction is more semantic than real, and that all values are really esteemed social or individual conditions. So, according to Schwarz, *responsibility* is not so much a way of doing things as a personal condition or characteristic.

(see also Inglehart, 1990). Feldman (1988) linked core values, especially *equal opportunity* and *work ethic*, to opinions on various domestic policy issues, presidential performance evaluation, and attitudes toward candidates. Feldman and Zaller (1992) showed that the relative balance of *individualism* and *equal opportunity* strongly influenced respondents' welfare attitudes.

We have described values as lacking the strict organization and internal consistency we usually attribute to ideologies. Nevertheless, scholars speak of value *structures* or *systems*. Rokeach depicted values as organized hierarchically, with most people reporting a stable sense of the priorities among values. Thus, some would place equality near the top of their list, and consequently favor policies that promote this value, while others might rank morality at the top, and therefore lean toward morality-friendly policies. American political culture allegedly strongly endorses individualism and the work ethic, and the bulk of public opinion favors policies that agree with these values (McClosky & Zaller, 1984).

Schwartz (1994) proposed the major alternative to Rokeach's system. Situating his model within a general theory of motivation, Schwartz described a circular arrangement of values governed by two universal dimensions of human needs: *openness to change versus conservation* and *self-transcendence versus self-enhancement*. The circular blueprint makes clear the affinities and antagonisms between value pairs. Values that promote the same motive are compatible, whereas those that promote opposite motives conflict. So, for example, *universalism* and *benevolence* both promote self-transcendence and so are compatible, but each conflict with *achievement* and *power*, two self-enhancement values. Schwartz (1994) presented cross-cultural data showing broad adherence to his general scheme. Individuals do not depart significantly from the structure, but differ in the *emphasis* they place on different values.

A common point among the various theories is the presumed stability in value orientations. Although gradual change over the life span occurs, most scholars believe that value systems are established in early adult socialization and persist long enough to shape the contours of the individual's major social and political beliefs and behavioral tendencies. Rokeach himself pioneered one method for inducing value change, the "self-confrontation" technique, but emphasized the limitations of this method for effecting truly fundamental alterations in value structures (Rokeach & Grube, 1979).

Values, Attitudes, and Behavior

Viewed as stable, long-term needs or goals, values can serve the same orienting and motivating function for political attitudes and behaviors as material interests. Although many political scientists see rational-actor models of citizen political action as incompatible with psychological approaches

(Green & Shapiro, 1994), in the study of values and behavior, the psychologists speak the economists' language. Norman Feather (1995) provided a succinct statement of his theory:

> Like needs, values function to induce valences on objects and events . . . These value-induced valences would be expected to influence the choices that a person makes between alternatives in a given situation. Consistent with the general framework of expectancy-value theory, I assume that a person's choice between alternatives would be influenced by his or her valences or subjective values and by the expectations that the person holds. (p. 1136)

Political action, like any human behavior, becomes a way not just to further one's own comfort and well-being, but also to advance one's treasured values and thwart those despised ones. Variation in political behavior arises not only because people have different material interests (e.g., some people want parks while others want malls) but also because people have different social and political values (e.g., some want greater economic equality while others want more a more moral and reverent society). Likewise, Katz's (1960) venerable "functional" approach emphasized the value-expressive purpose of attitudes. We hold political attitudes in part because we see them as relevant to our treasured values, and as opportunities to voice those values.

Value Conflict and Ambivalence

Even as scholars accumulated evidence about the importance of values to political attitudes, they began to show how the translation of abstract values into concrete opinions is often difficult and uncertain, not the least because politics exposes troubling value *conflicts*. Politics can be a boxing ring where well-matched opponent values go toe-to-toe for several rounds until one is declared the winner—only to have the loser demand a rematch. In Rokeach's model, potential conflict could be found between values of similar high rank, depending on the specific application. So, although it would be terrific to create social policies that strengthen both equality and freedom, many issues support one *at the expense of the other*, fostering value conflict among those who treasure both (Tetlock, 1986).

For Schwartz, value conflict is inevitable because one cannot simultaneously pursue values that satisfy opposing needs, such as self-transcendence and self-enhancement. Value conflict has caught the attention of many public opinion and political attitudes scholars (Alvarez & Brehm, 1995; Gibson, 1998; Smelser, 1998; Zaller, 1992). Many view value conflict as part of the explanation for the instabilities and lack of cohesion in political attitudes that Converse and company described long ago. Rejecting Converse's explanation—that disorganized and unstable attitudes were really vacuous "nonattitudes"–this view portrays public opinion as rife with *ambivalence*: a mix of positive and negative inclinations born of value conflict. Pulled in opposite directions by their conflicting values, many citizens vacillate on specific issues, and their totality of political views lacks the organization that a single dominant value would provide.

Nearly every contentious issue on the contemporary American political scene exposes an entrenched value conflict that torments many who respect both values. Take school vouchers: They mix better educational opportunity (a noble egalitarian motive) with taxpayer funding of religious institutions (a threat to civil libertarian values). For this and other issues, a kind of hydraulic system governs the values involved, wherein strengthening one weakens the other. Dogmatists and utopian idealists aside, it seems that most citizens are aware that, in politics at least, you can't have it all. The value conflict–ambivalence thesis appeals to us because it both makes sense of research observations and captures our intuitions and experiences about political conundrums. It also forces us to reconsider some assumptions about the hierarchical arrangement and long-term stability of individual value structures. The value conflict–ambivalence approach suggests that value hierarchies are flexible and socially negotiated, subject to influence from forces like issue framing. Value hierarchies that prevail for an issue might be overturned, depending on shifts in frame.

This is all very nice in theory, but how do communicators use frames to effect such a change? Based on our informal analyses of political rhetoric on a number of contemporary issues, we can suggest a small list—by no means exhaustive—of the communication forms that persuaders brandish to affect value priorities through framing.

Policy Categorization and Labeling. If there is one refrain that has sounded most consistently in contemporary scholarship of social and political cognition, it is the chronic need for humans to simplify the unmanageable informational demands of their universe (Fiske & Taylor, 1991). We have at our disposal an impressive range of cognitive tools for culling, storing, and using social and political information; one of the choicest is *categorization*: the assignment of novel objects to familiar classes. Issues, too, may fall into several different categories; the one we ultimately choose could determine the goals and values we honor when evaluating the issue.

> People will see a problem quite differently if it is put into one category rather than another. Thus, much of the struggle over problem definition centers on the categories that will be used and the ways they will be used. You may not be able to judge a problem by its category, but its category structures people's perceptions of the problem in many important respects. (Kingdon, 1995, p. 111)

As a rhetorical tactic, categorization carries broad powers, one of which could be the setting of goal and value priorities. The Food and Drug Administration, for example, with President Clinton's encouragement, has considered classifying nicotine as "a drug" and cigarettes as "drug delivery devices."[2] The controversy over smoking regulation exposes a fundamental conflict between the values of protecting the public from harm and preserving individuals' basic freedom to put themselves in an early grave. The FDA's new classifications will probably change few beliefs about the lethality of smoking, yet they will radically change the institutional impetus to regulate tobacco products. They might also change the public's views about the urgency of new smoking restrictions by elevating the value of public protection relative to personal freedom.

Successful issue categorization may sometimes require directly refuting the applicability of an alternative category, thereby denying the relevance of a rival goal or value. Thus, abortion opponents try to remind us that "It's a child, not a choice." Commenting on a controversy over a child's choice of a religious book for "read aloud day" at school, the Morgantown (West Virginia) *Dominion Post* opined:

> This isn't about free speech. This isn't about separation of church and state. This isn't even about some serious educational issue that would have significant impact on a great number of children. This is about adults who make questionable judgments, then hide behind serious constitutional issues, hire lawyers, tie up court time and eventually add to the suffocating weight of laws to protect us from stuff that demands no protection.[3]

Goal Ranking. This is accomplished when the communicator makes a straight declaration about the superior status of a value or goal, either absolutely or relative to others. Explicit goal comparisons and direct goal-ranking might be a rhetorical tool to which a communicator resorts when the facts of a case are especially clear and ignoring the other side would be a strategic mistake. The communicator might seek to minimize that damaging information by trivializing its perceived importance or relevance to the issue. In a pro-gun-control essay, writer Daniel Lazare (1999) readily conceded opponents' claim that the Second Amendment protects individual gun ownership but then asserted the will of the people as supreme to the Founding Fathers:

> So why must we subordinate ourselves to a 208-year-old law that, if the latest scholarship is correct, is contrary to what the democratic majority believes is

---

[2]Linda Greenhouse, "Justices Skeptical of U.S. Effort for Jurisdiction Over Cigarettes." *New York Times*, Dec. 2, 1999.

[3]Quoted in "Other viewpoints." *Columbus Dispatch*, November 10, 1999, p. A10.

in its best interest? Why can't *we* create the kind of society we want as opposed to living with laws meant to create the kind of society *they* wanted? They are dead and buried and will not be around to suffer the consequences. We the living will. (pp. 57–65)

Partisans might choose not to mention competing goals and values, but rather simply assert the preeminence or rising prominence of their favorite. When the Clinton Administration suspended road-building in old-growth forests, a spokesman explained the decision by stating, "The Vice President is the one who has been pushing for this. He feels strongly that after a century of Federal forest management, it is time to give stronger weight to forest values like clean water, recreation and wildlife" (Cushman, 1998). Sometimes assertions reach beyond any specific controversy to become general manifestoes for one goal. Some civil libertarians, for example, are well-known for asserting the dominance of free expression values over all competitors in all circumstances, proudly labeling themselves "free speech fundamentalists" (Gross & Kinder, 1998).

Institutional Role Assignment. Communicators often contend that certain kinds of social and political goals are the special dominion of key institutions and organizations. This allows endorsement of a goal within a narrow domain without necessarily upsetting one's global value hierarchy. A free speech controversy within a school setting might be modified by the claim that a school's sacred duty is to protect the well-being of children, even if doing so requires restricting freedom of expression by, for example, establishing a dress code. In a syndicated column, Sowell (1993) spoke out against allowing gays to serve in the military by suggesting their presence would thwart the military's special duty: "The military exists to carry on a life-and-death business, and how well they do their job affects not only the lives and deaths of the troops themselves, but of the whole society whose security and national interests they are defending" (p. A11).

Sometimes the "institution" might be as big as "the government" or perhaps "the nation." Communicators might declare "what this nation should stand for" or "what this government is all about." Following the 1998 midterm elections, which many interpreted as a mandate from the nation to drop the whole impeachment process against President Clinton, House Judiciary Chairman Henry Hyde lamented that "we should have a Government of laws and not of men, but I'm afraid we're going in the opposite direction" (Greenhouse, 1998, p. A1). Contradicting the perceived will of the electorate is always daunting; Chairman Hyde's dilemma was to assert the Constitutional imperative of the impeachment hearings without disrespecting the public. Ultimately, differing notions about the proper role of government lie at the heart of modern liberalism and conservatism. As Converse and company pointed out, however, ordinary citizens adhere to such abstract claims inconsistently (or, if you prefer, flexibly). They might well be persuaded to accord more respect to a goal or value if it is framed as the "government's business." More generally, American political history can be described as an evolving idea about the kinds of social and political conditions that the government ought to be concerned with (Mutz, 1998).

THE PSYCHOLOGICAL RESPONSE

Psychologically speaking, we have located most of the framing action within the individual's dynamic, issue-specific values structure (see also Chong, 1993; Jones, 1994). This is surely not the only way framing can influence attitudes, however. Indeed, the same frame could have multiple effects at various levels of message processing, with different consequences for different audiences. Most scholars in the framing business think the heart of these effects lies in the varying levels of cognitive accessibility possessed by political beliefs (Zaller, 1992). Coming straight out of the cognitive miser and bounded rationality perspectives in psychology, the accessibility argument stresses that most citizens have a limited ability and motivation to attend carefully to all the relevant information about an issue in their memories, so they economize by considering only the first few items that come to mind (Fiske & Taylor, 1991). In other words, they will not take into consideration all of the *available* information (information stored in memory but not necessarily readily retrieved), only the most *accessible*.[4] Frames affect opinions by priming specific beliefs; that is, by selectively boosting their accessibility in memory. So, for example, framing affirmative action as "reverse discrimination" will prime whatever beliefs the individual has about the chances that affirmative action programs will disadvantage majority group members. Once primed, these beliefs have their best chance to influence opinion. Had a different frame appeared, these beliefs have remained buried in long-term memory, beyond the reach of today's opinion.

The accessibility approach could readily apply to issues characterized by value conflict. If genuinely torn about affirmative action because one values creating new opportunities for minorities—but not at the expense of op-

---

[4]Most models of this sort declare, or at least strongly imply, that attitudes are reconstituted from individual bits of information every time they are expressed, whether in response to a survey question or in a casual conversation. Surely this cannot be true, at least not for all attitudes. The major competitor to this "memory-based" model, the "online model" (Lodge, McGraw, & Stroh, 1989), argued that attitudes exist as general evaluative orientations that are updated only when relevant information is encountered; the information itself is then forgotten. While the description of our model probably resembles the memory-based model more closely than the online model, in fact it is comfortable with either.

portunities for majority group members, the reverse discrimination frame might resolve the conflict (temporarily) by priming that competitor alone. But framing might also affect the *content* of those beliefs. The reverse discrimination frame might not just prime beliefs about majority group vulnerability, it might actually *create* those beliefs among those who had never considered affirmative action's possible effects on majority group members. Indeed, frames that act in this way stretch the boundaries of what we should consider true "framing effects." If frames actually supply new information that alters our beliefs and expectations about policy change, then how are they any different from conventional persuasive messages (Nelson & Oxley, 1999)? Framing as we understand the term is best reserved for messages that don't supply new information, but rather restructure or reinterpret existing information.

Belief content and accessibility are both necessary for attitude change. One must convince the receiver that a social policy will have salutary or disastrous consequences, and these beliefs must be accessible at the time the attitude is being (re)considered. But how do we judge if a particular consequence is salutary, disastrous, or merely irrelevant? Sometimes the material costs and benefits of policy change are obvious, but what of more "symbolic" issues that fire our passions without necessarily affecting our pocketbooks? Mathematically the process is no different: We figure the costs and benefits and judge accordingly; but the costs and benefits are in the denomination of values, not dollars and cents. So we must judge which of several competing values really counts the most. This is where the sorts of frames described earlier have their biggest impact.

To illustrate the important differences among these processes, we take you back to the chaotic month of January 1999, the peak of the impeachment frenzy. By then President Clinton had finally admitted to the "improper relationship" with "that woman," and the release of the Starr report had made the details of that relationship all too graphically clear for most of the American public. The report, House impeachment hearings, and Senate trial did not put to rest *all* questions of fact, especially those pertaining to the effort to conceal the affair. Still, by January, nearly everyone who cared about the Clinton–Lewinsky affair agreed about what actually happened between the two principals in the White House. So what impact did the revelations have on public opinion toward the president, and how did framing intervene?

First, there were clear differences in citizens' evaluations of the president's conduct. Although few went on record as approving of what he did, the public's *disapproval* varied from abhorrence to annoyance to indifference. Still, the stability in the president's general approval rating ran contrary to the disapproval of his personal conduct. So, was it the case that thoughts and feelings about the affair were *inaccessible* to citizens as they responded to the nearly incessant stream of public opinion polls during this period? Hard to believe, with the broadcasts of the Senate trial and saturation coverage of the story by national and international media organizations. What about the pundits' favorite explanation—that disapproval of the affair was overwhelmed by giddy approval of Clinton's stewardship of the vigorous American economy? No doubt the economy contributed to Clinton's good marks, but even the healthy economy could not have saved Clinton from such a high-profile, sordid scandal, complete with the president's admission to lying on national television, *if the public believed the scandal were truly important and relevant to their feelings about Clinton's performance as president.*

With the help of the President's defenders, most of the American public framed the scandal as a *private* matter, with little bearing on the President's public duties. Some went even further—again, with the help of Democratic Party elites and like-minded opinion molders—by framing the impeachment itself as a mean-spirited and cynical overthrow of the democratic process by sanctimonious, hypocritical Republican sore losers. Thus, the president's enemies, who thought his infidelities and deceit should overshadow everything, watched in disbelief as those matters took a back seat to other concerns for most of the American public (Bennett, 1999).

PIZZA "REDLINING" EXPERIMENT

We want to give some flavor for our research paradigm by describing our study of one vivid example of issue framing: the case of pizza delivery redlining. Our experiments on this issue sought to combine several virtues. We wanted to draw from a real-world framing struggle—one that, while perhaps not as momentous as the impeachment battle, still had real consequences. We combined a rough-and-ready analysis of the framing tactics employed by the interested parties in this dispute with a laboratory experiment's specification and systematic manipulation of communication elements. We also wanted to test our hypotheses about the psychological mediators that are (and are not) responsible for carrying a frame's energy through to its intended target: the audience's opinions.

In many large cities, some pizza delivery companies will not provide service in high-crime areas, a practice known as *redlining.* Redlining came to national attention during the summer of 1996 when Willie Kennedy, a San Francisco city supervisor, accused Domino's Pizza and other companies of racial discrimination because the redlined areas are mostly Black. Domino's called the racism allegation unfair and claimed that their actions were taken merely to protect their employees, some of whom had been robbed, assaulted, and even murdered on the job.[5]

The pizza delivery controversy presented an appealing venue for testing our model of framing effects. It was a relatively novel entry onto the issue scene when we began our investigations, thus allowing us to examine opinions in-the-making. Although the issue was novel, it was hardly bizarre, as it touched on the perennial burdens of crime and racial prejudice. Finally, the issue presented a particularly vivid study of issue categorization in that it fundamentally entailed a dispute over proper labeling and interpretation. Although the "facts" of the case were mostly not in dispute, the categorization of those facts was hotly contested. To the extent that the pizza delivery companies succeeded in confining the discussion to crime, they could count on a great deal of sympathy and support for their actions. On the other hand, if they could make the racism label stick, Kennedy and other members of the San Francisco city council were prepared to require pizza companies to serve all addresses within their delivery area.

We created an experiment to examine how the framing rhetoric surrounding the San Francisco pizza redlining controversy influenced opinion on the issue. We constructed two bogus news stories about the San Francisco case—one representing the "crime" frame, and the other representing the "racism" frame—by borrowing from the public statements of political leaders, activists, and editorialists. Our two guiding research questions were: (a) Would the alternative frames significantly influence participants' attitudes toward redlining?; and (b) How would belief content, belief accessibility, and weighting of competing values mediate any communication effects we might observe?

Method

Three-hundred thirty undergraduate students enrolled in political science courses in the fall of 1997 through the winter of 1999 participated in the experiment.[6] Participants received extra credit for attending the session. The sample was 52% female and ranged in age from 17 to 44 years old. Thirty-eight percent of participants reported identifying with the Republican party, 40% identified with the Democratic party, and 22% were independents. The experiment was described as a study "to see how well computer-based news services provide information to the public." Participants used a

---

[5]Redlining is certainly not confined to the pizza delivery business. In recent years banks, insurance companies, and home mortgage lenders have all been accused of practices that discriminate against low-income minority customers.

[6]Although the experiment took place over several years, we do not believe that time effects affect our findings. First, our results replicate for each group of participants. Second, the redlining issue did not become particularly salient at any point during our experiments.

personal computer to read news stories and enter their responses to our questions. They viewed a story about the San Francisco controversy that was purportedly posted on the campus newspaper's web site. The computer program automatically assigned participants at random to the crime or race framing condition.

Issue Frames

The two stories were closely modeled on actual news coverage of the San Francisco pizza delivery dispute. Factual content was held constant across the two versions. All participants read that several delivery drivers had been attacked on the job, and also that residents of the affected, mostly Black neighborhoods had complained about racial discrimination. The stories varied in headline, lead paragraph, quote, and accompanying photo, which collectively represented the frame. The crime frame featured a photo of a pizza delivery driver, and included a quote from a "Domino's spokeswoman" claiming that safety was their top priority and that race had nothing to do with their decision. The race frame featured a photo of an attractive Black family and included a quote from a "neighborhood resident," claiming that the new delivery policy was unfair to Blacks.

Opinion and Mediator Measures

After participants answered a few filler questions relating to the readability and informativeness of the news story (to maintain the credibility of our cover story), they expressed their opinions on the issue. Respondents were asked the degree to which they approve or disapprove of the pizza companies' practice of refusing to deliver to certain neighborhoods.

To measure the effects of framing on the cognitive accessibility of concepts relating to crime and race, we then led participants through a reaction-time procedure (Fazio, 1990). Participants were told that we were examining the effects of distractions on reading through a word recognition test. Participants viewed a prompt on the screen, either "pizza" or "ice cream," followed by a target word. There were four types of target words: crime words (e.g., *crime*); race words (e.g., *racism*); neutral words (e.g., *comment*); and nonsense words (e.g., *bolau*).[7] Participants indicated whether the target word represented a real word or a nonword by pressing one of two keys on the computer keyboard. The appearance of the prompt and target words were randomized, but each target word (and nonword) ap-

---

[7]The exact words that were used for the reaction time procedure were: crime, danger, robbery, and driver as "crime" words; racism, prejudice, unfair and customer as "race" words; sight, comment, monthly, and external as "neutral" words; and gooyen, bolau, curagsua, viyed, ivotcurs, dape, fekruk, and udahrob as "nonsense" words.

peared twice: once preceded by *ice cream* and once preceded by *pizza*. So that participants would remain focused on the task, they were also asked to count the number of appearances of the words *pizza* and *ice cream* preceding the target words. Before beginning the reaction time test, participants were given several practice words to become familiar with the procedure. Relatively fast reaction times would indicate a highly accessible association between the prime and the target concepts. For example, responding quickly to crime-related words following the *pizza* prime (relative to the *ice cream* prime) would suggest a strong cognitive association between pizza and crime.

We also sought to measure the relative emphasis participants placed on competing values in the controversy. The *crime* frame championed protection and security values, while the *race* frame upheld fairness and equality values. We therefore included two questions concerning these values. The first asked, "When you think about whether or not pizza companies should be required to deliver to all homes in their delivery area, how important to you is protecting driver safety?" The second asked, "When you think about whether or not pizza companies should be required to deliver to all homes in their delivery area, how important to you is treating both Black and White citizens equally and fairly?" Participants responded by manipulating a 100-point sliding scale with the top of the scale (100) labeled *extremely important* and the bottom of the scale (1) labeled *not important*.

Last, six items measured the beliefs of participants about the safety of pizza delivery and the fairness of delivery company policies. These items asked respondents to rate the safety of pizza delivery as an occupation, and also to judge whether pizza delivery would be safer or more dangerous if companies were required to deliver to all addresses within their area. Respondents also judged whether or not redlining policies were unfair to Black citizens, and indicated whether they thought delivery would become more or less fair if companies were required to deliver to all addresses. Finally, respondents indicated how much they "generally approved" of protecting driver safety and fair and equal treatment for Black and White citizens.

We expected that framing would influence redlining attitudes such that participants in the crime frame would express greater approval of redlining than those in the race frame. We also expected that framing would influence the relative importance attributed to protecting driver safety and treating black and white citizens fairly and equally, with the "crime" frame enhancing the importance of the former and the race frame enhancing the importance of the latter. Based on prior research, we expected fairly minimal effects of framing on belief content and belief accessibility. Finally, not only should framing affect redlining opinion and the importance attributed to driver safety, but we further expected that the importance judgments should at least partially mediate the effect of framing on opinion.

Findings

Table 15.1 shows the mean redlining opinion, relative importance rating, and beliefs about redlining by framing condition. The pattern of means corresponds quite well with our predictions. Framing had a statistically significant effect on opinion toward redlining, with respondents in the race condition expressing greater opposition than those in the crime condition. The relative importance of safety and fairness was also affected by the framing condition. To create an index of relative importance, we subtracted the importance attributed to treating Black and White citizens fairly from the importance attributed to protecting driver safety. Although the average importance attributed to driver safety exceeds that attributed to fair and equal treatment even in the race condition, the difference is significantly greater in the crime condition. As expected, subjects in the crime condition

TABLE 15.1
Opinion, Belief, and Importance Items, by Framing Condition

	Crime Frame	Race Frame	p
Redlining opinion[a]	2.55	3.01	.01*
	(1.54)	(1.63)	
Relative importance[b]	9.45	4.44	.10*
	(31.37)	(29.9)	
Belief about the safety of drivers[c]	4.67	4.83	.16#
	(1.17)	(1.06)	
Belief about safety without redlining[d]	5.45	5.52	.56#
	(1.17)	(1.21)	
Belief about the fairness of redlining[e]	3.84	4.06	.26#
	(1.78)	(1.64)	
Belief about the fairness without redlining[f]	3.72	3.78	.68#
	(1.34)	(1.39)	
Belief about making drivers safe[g]	1.64	1.66	.92#
	(.887)	(1.08)	
Belief about making delivery fair[h]	1.64	1.08	.53#
	(1.75)	(1.28)	

*One-tailed test
#Two-tailed test
[a]Higher numbers indicate greater opposition to redlining policies
[b]Higher number indicate greater importance attributed to protecting driver safety, relative to providing fair and equal treatment to Blacks and Whites.
[c]Higher numbers indicate belief that pizza delivery is dangerous.
[d]Higher numbers indicate belief that pizza delivery would be more dangerous if drivers were forced to visit all addresses.
[e]Higher numbers indicate belief that redlining is unfair to Blacks.
[f]Lower numbers indicate belief that delivery would be more fair if redlining were eliminated.
[g]Lower numbers indicate greater approval of protecting driver safety.
[h]Lower numbers indicate greater approval of fair and equal treatment.

rated protecting driver safety more important than did subjects in the race condition.

Framing's effect on belief content was weaker and somewhat inconsistent. None of the effects reached statistical significance. Participants in the race condition rated redlining as slightly more unfair to Blacks than did participants in the crime condition, but they paradoxically also rated pizza delivery as slightly more dangerous. Again, somewhat surprisingly, participants in the race condition were slightly more inclined to believe that pizza delivery would become *more* dangerous if drivers were required to visit every address. Finally, these respondents were less likely to agree that such a requirement would lead to more equal treatment for Blacks and Whites. One shouldn't make much of these effects because of their small magnitude, but clearly the overall pattern does not correspond to a belief-based explanation for framing effects.

Before analyzing the reaction time data, we used a linear reciprocal transformation to correct for skewness in the raw scores (Fazio, 1990).[8] Outliers (reaction times greater than three standard deviations beyond the mean) were also eliminated. Two patterns of results from the reaction-time portion of the experiment would be consistent with a priming or belief accessibility hypothesis. If the frames simply made crime- or race-related concepts more accessible in general, participants should be able to recognize target words corresponding to the frame they saw more quickly, regardless of the prime. Alternatively, framing might strengthen the association between pizza delivery and crime or race. Response time should then be facilitated when the prime *pizza* is followed by a crime-related word (for the crime framing condition) or a race-related word (for the race framing condition). A repeated-measures analysis of variance indicated that neither of these predicted interactions reached statistical significance.[9] Framing did not affect the speed of recognition of crime or race words in general, nor did framing affect the relative accessibility of these concepts following the *pizza* versus *ice cream* primes. The means appear in Table 15.2.

CONCLUSION

Our approach to framing encompasses both sides of political communication. On the communicator side, we have paid close attention to the content

---

[8]Because many of the reaction times were less than 1 second, we used the transformation $1/[x+1]$ to transform the data.

[9]The interaction between race words and the race frame has a p value of .049, but the means indicate that the relationship is in the wrong direction. Participants in the race frame were slower to respond to race words than participants in the crime frame, opposite of the relationship predicted if the frame facilitates the accessibility of associated constructs.

TABLE 15.2
Reaction Time Results

Target Words	Prime	Crime Frame	Race Frame	p
Crime words	pizza	645.7	654.5	.59
		(141.0)	(181.0)	
	ice cream	657.5	690.0	.15
		(188.4)	(202.0)	
Race words	pizza	659.9	674.2	.41
		(153.3)	(145.3)	
	ice cream	689.3	711.6	.30
		(176.8)	(201.8)	
Neutral words	pizza	681.1	691.9	.63
		(185.1)	(202.8)	
	ice cream	671.2	690.9	.32
		(165.8)	(176.6)	
Nonsense words	pizza	714.3	727.8	.49
		(170.2)	(173.4)	
	ice cream	710.7	730.1	.33
		(169.6)	(179.4)	

Note. Scores are raw (untransformed) reaction times. Standard errors appear in parentheses. Outliers have been eliminated. All tests two-tailed.

of persuasive framing rhetoric and have tried to understand its generation within the modern political milieu, particularly the mass media environment. On the receiver side, we have elaborated the psychological processes that regulate framing's impact on political attitudes. The model challenges cognitive miser-like assertions in the political science literature that framing relies exclusively on limited attention and cognitive accessibility. Priming and accessibility processes certainly explain some framing effects, but we believe that frames do more than simply prime certain ideas—they establish hierarchies among competing values. We further challenge the assumption that individual value structures are strictly ordered and free from domain-specific considerations. An individual's choice among values in a particular area is not an inviolable, isomorphic translation from his or her general-purpose hierarchy. It is susceptible to contextual forces, including framing. Thus, our model of political attitudes relates long-term individual elements (beliefs, values, and expectations) to short-term social forces (priming, framing, and information).

Every year it seems that politics gets louder and louder, but the public hears less and less. The excitement over an apparently competitive party primary season gave way to the inevitable tedium of a Bush–Gore presidential battle. It's not just the healthy economy that has the public generally bored with the 2000 election, it is the lukewarm feeling many citizens have toward two candidates that seem overproduced. The underdogs' appeal came not from their maverick policy positions but from their apparent genuineness, in contrast to the *image* of genuineness that, like everything else about the victorious nominees, seemed carefully cultivated since their youth. We live in a framing age, alas, where citizens watch with increasing disgust as officially appointed spin-doctors battle with congenitally skeptical journalists to shape public comprehension of the political world (Kurtz, 1998). Although a political campaign may be the most obvious framing arena, nonelectoral issue battles stage their own epic framing contests. As Schattschneider (1960) observed, this war of words can be momentous:

> Political conflict is not like an intercollegiate debate in which the opponents agree in advance on a definition of the issues. As a matter of fact, the definition of the alternatives is the supreme instrument of power; the antagonists can rarely agree on what the issues are because power is involved in the definition. He who determines what politics is about runs the country, because the definition of the alternatives is the choice of conflicts, and the choice of conflicts allocates power. (p. 66)

We have labeled this definitional activity *issue categorization.* Alongside value ranking and institutional role assignment, it is a species of framing that acts upon a citizen's value priorities and their application to matters of public concern. We usually think of our values as private, beyond the reach of the framers and manipulators of the world. As general, long-term guides for our attitudes and actions, values do exist apart from everyday political jockeying and the vicissitudes of our mediated social life. The inherently social or public nature of politics, however, forces a gap between the citizen's personal needs and values and their political opinions (Mutz, 1998; Stoker, 1992). Deciding which values truly matter in a specific domain does not simplify to a mechanical application of an all-purpose formula. It depends importantly on judgments and interpretations that reach beyond the individual's world to the surrounding social and political setting.

REFERENCES

Alvarez, R. M., & Brehm, J. (1995). American ambivalence towards abortion policy: Development of a heteroskedastic probit model of competing values. *American Journal of Political Science, 39,* 1055–1082.

Bennett, W. J. (1999). *The death of outrage: Bill Clinton and the assault on American ideals.* New York: Free Press.

Bobo, L., & Kluegel, J. R. (1993). Opposition to race-targeting: Self-interest, stratification ideology, or racial attitudes? *American Sociological Review, 58,* 443–464.

Chong, D. (1993). How people think, reason, and feel about rights and liberties. *American Journal of Political Science, 37,* 867–899.

Converse, P. E. (1964). The nature of belief systems in mass publics. In D. Apter (Ed.), *Ideology and discontent* (pp. 206–261). New York: Free Press.

Cushman, J. H., Jr. (1998, January 10). U.S. to suspend road building in many national forest areas. *New York Times,* p. A1.

Fazio, R. (1990). A practical guide to the use of response latency in social psychological research. In C. Hendrick & M. S. Clark (Eds.), *Review of personality and social psychology, Vol. 11: Research methods in personality and social psychology* (pp. 74–94). Newbury Park, CA: Sage.

Feather, N. T. (1995). Values, valences, and choice: The influence of values on the perceived attractiveness and choice of alternatives. *Journal of Personality & Social Psychology, 68,* 1135–1151.

Feldman, S. (1988). Structure and consistency in public opinion: The role of core beliefs and values. *American Journal of Political Science, 32*(2), 416–440.

Feldman, S., & Zaller, J. (1992). The political culture of ambivalence: Ideological responses to the welfare state. *American Journal of Political Science, 36*(1), 268–307.

Fiske, S. T., & Taylor, S. E. (1991). *Social cognition* (2nd ed.). New York: McGraw-Hill.

Gamson, W. A. (1992). *Talking politics.* Cambridge, England: Cambridge University Press.

Gamson, W. A., & Lasch, K. E. (1983). The political culture of social welfare policy. In S. E. Spiro & E. Yuchtman-Yaar (Eds.), *Evaluating the welfare state* (pp. 395–415). New York: Academic Press.

Gamson, W. A., & Meyer, D. S. (1996). Framing political opportunity. In D. McAdam, J. D. McCarthy, & M. N. Zald (Eds.), *Comparative perspectives on social movements* (pp. 275–290). New York: Cambridge University Press.

Gibson, J. (1998). A sober second thought: An experiment in persuading Russians to tolerate. *American Journal of Political Science, 42*(3), 819–850.

Goffman, E. (1974). *Frame analysis: An essay on the organization of experience.* Cambridge, MA: Harvard University Press.

Green, D. P., & Shapiro, I. (1994). *Pathologies of rational choice theory: A critique of applications in political science.* New Haven, CT: Yale University Press.

Greenhouse, L. (1998, November 10). It's impeachment or nothing, scholars warn lawmakers at hearing. *New York Times,* p. A1.

Gross, K., & Kinder, D. R. (1998). A collision of principles? Free expression, racial equality, and the prohibition of racist speech. *British Journal of Political Science, 28*(3), 445–471.

Huckfeldt, R., Levine, J., Morgan, W., & Sprague, J. (1999). Accessibility and the political utility of partisan and ideological orientations. *American Journal of Political Science, 43*(3), 888–911.

Inglehart, R. (1990). *Culture shift in advanced industrial societies.* Princeton, NJ: Princeton University Press.

Iyengar, S. (1991). *Is anyone responsible?: How television frames political issues.* Chicago: University of Chicago Press.

Iyengar, S., & Kinder, D. (1987). *News that matters.* Chicago: University of Chicago Press.

Jones, B. D. (1994). *Reconceiving decision-making in democratic politics.* Chicago: University of Chicago Press.

Kahneman, D., & Tversky, A. (1984). Choices, values, and frames. *American Psychologist, 39,* 341–350.

Katz, D. (1960). The functional approach to the study of attitudes. *Public Opinion Quarterly, 24*(2), 163–204.

Kinder, D. R. (1998). Opinion and action in the realm of politics. *Handbook of social psychology, 4th edition* (pp. 778–867). New York: McGraw Hill.

Kinder, D. R., & Sanders, L. M. (1996). *Divided by color: Racial politics and democratic ideals.* Chicago: University of Chicago Press.

Kingdon, J. W. (1995). *Agendas, alternatives and public policies, 2nd edition.* New York: HarperCollins.

Kurtz, H. (1998). *Spin cycle.* New York: Touchstone.

Lazare, D. (1999, October). Your constitution is killing you. *Harper's Magazine*, 57–65.

Lodge, M., McGraw, K. M., & Stroh, P. (1989). An impression-driven model of candidate evaluation. *American Political Science Review, 83*, 399–419.

McClosky, H., & Zaller, J. (1984). *The American ethos. Public attitudes toward capitalism and democracy*. Cambridge, MA: Harvard University Press.

Mutz, D. C. (1998). *Impersonal influence*. New York: Cambridge University Press.

Nelson, T. E., & Kinder, D. R. (1996). Issue frames and group-centrism in American public opinion. *Journal of Politics, 58*, 1055–1078.

Nelson, T. E., Clawson, R. A., & Oxley, Z. M. (1997). Media framing of a civil liberties conflict and its effect on tolerance. *American Political Science Review, 91*, 567–583.

Nelson, T. E., & Oxley, Z. M. (1999). Issue framing effects on belief importance and opinion. *Journal of Politics, 61*, 1040–1067.

Nelson, T. E., Oxley, Z. M., & Clawson, R. A. (1997). Toward a psychology of framing effects. *Political Behavior, 19*, 221–246.

Patterson, T. (1993). *Out of order*. New York: Knopf.

Price, V., & Tewksbury, D. (1997). News values and public opinion: A theoretical account of media priming and framing. In G. Barnett & F. J. Boster (Eds.), *Progress in the communication sciences* (Vol. XIII, pp. 173–211). Greenwich, CT: Ablex.

Rokeach, M. (1973). *The nature of human values*. New York: Free Press.

Rokeach, M., & Grube, J. W. (1979). Can values be manipulated arbitrarily? In M. Rokeach (Ed.), *Understanding human values* (pp. 241–256). New York: Free Press.

Schattschneider, E. E. (1960). *The semi-sovereign people*. Hinsdale, IL: Dryden.

Schwartz, S. H. (1994). Are there universal aspects in the structure and contents of human values? *Journal of Social Issues, 50*, 19–45.

Smelser, N. J. (1998). The rational and the ambivalent in the social sciences. *American Sociological Review, 63*, 1–16.

Snow, D. A., Rochford, E. B. Jr., Worden, S. K., & Benford, R. D. (1986). Frame alignment processes, micromobilization, and movement participation. *American Sociological Review, 51*, 464–481.

Sowell, T. (1993, July 27). Sexual orientation isn't issue, but effect on performance, morale is. *Arizona Republic*, p. A11.

Stoker, L. (1992). Interests and ethics in politics. *American Political Science Review, 86*, 369–380.

Tetlock, P. E. (1986). A value pluralism model of ideological reasoning. *Journal of Personality and Social Psychology, 50*, 819–827.

Zaller, J. (1992). *The nature and origins of mass opinion*. New York: Cambridge University Press.

Zaller, J., & Feldman, S. (1992). A simple theory of the survey response: Answering questions versus revealing preferences. *American Journal of Political Science, 36*(3), 579–616.

THE NEW MEDIA
LANDSCAPE

16

Frame Breaking and Creativity: A Frame Database for Hypermedia News

Eric S. Fredin

The scale of computer networks and the relatively low cost of posting material mean that an enormous range of viewpoints on political social issues will be potentially available. Such variety is generally seen as fundamental to good journalism. However, for most people, the sheer volume of material will undercut the possibility that they will be able to encounter, let alone think about, a wide variety of news and commentary. Individuals cannot sort through the volume of available material themselves; hence, as a practical matter, organizational and institutional powers will largely control the scope and nature of the variety that is readily available to them, and, as a consequence, certain viewpoints and understandings will not appear while others will be stressed (Gandy, 1997).

This situation implies that frames will continue to be a basic characteristic of news. A frame, to paraphrase Entman (1993), is a device for organizing material that emphasizes some aspects of an issue, event, or situation and downplays or ignores others. Frames can provide definitions, causal interpretations, moral evaluations, or recommendations for action. Frames clearly can have an enormous impact on how people think about issues, but that is not the end of the matter. People do have some capacity to decide what to think. John Dewey (1927/1954) argued that this volition is an essential part of real political communication, which he did not consider as accomplished by transmitting knowledge that is complete and contained within itself. Rather the political communication itself makes political knowledge complete because individuals transform the knowledge by de-

veloping and adding their own understandings to it. Hence, the kind of political communication that is essential for a participatory democracy involves creativity.

The thesis of this essay is that computer networks such as the Internet
can increase creativity in political thinking among the public, and I propose
that journalists develop a sophisticated frame database that individuals
could manipulate using the interactive tools that are the core of hypermedia as a communication medium. Hypermedia news thus would consist
of news stories, as is the case now, plus frame databases (FDBs). I lay the
groundwork for this argument by first discussing basic cognitive characteristics of people, and then by discussing some of the characteristics hypermedia news could have and how people might interact with it. Next I discuss some basic properties of creativity, sketching an example of a person
using an FDB to think creatively about a political issue.

Characteristics of human information processing are part of the reason
that people cannot effectively cope with the enormous and diverse volume
of material on the Internet. Basically, people have a very limited capacity
for information processing, even when they are concentrating, and hypermedia news must encourage creativity within these constraints. There are
three important processing bottlenecks. First, short-term or working memory, roughly what appears in consciousness, is extremely small, hence people cannot work with much material at once. Second moving material from
short- to long-term memory takes time and effort. Third, there is a great
deal of information in long-term memory, but retrieving relevant material is
highly dependent upon the available cues.

Against this general backdrop, I discuss a few aspects of how information is organized in memory and retrieved from it. People have frames that
are in many ways quite similar to the frames found in news. The frame as a
mental construct is generally referred to as a schema in the psychological
literature. As is the case with news frames, schemas are organizations of
knowledge, ideas, values, and affect, though they are sometimes treated as
being composed of knowledge only. Schemas function as efficient ways to
quickly interpret events in daily life. In this regard, they are structures of
expectation (Chafe, 1990), guiding people toward what to look for in various
people and situations. Schemas also fill in gaps in available information. Evidence indicates that people are often better able to recall material that fits
their schemas , unless the material is shocking or cannot be readily ignored
(e.g., Hamil & Lodge, 1986).

Schemas are important in coping with news; they are a central part of
what Graber (1984) labeled "taming the information tide." Schemas are triggered by labels, phrases, or images in a news story. Repeated use of the
same frames in news stories would encourage frame-to-schema matching
because a frame would include information and material that the audience

member would come to expect. Schemas thus tend to direct people toward confirming rather than disconfirming evidence. Because information about an event is always incomplete, schemas are used to fill in the gaps with information from previous events that fit the schemas. A quick processing of a news story, therefore, often can result in people mostly learning what they already know.

Frames incessantly repeated in news can thus have considerable control over how people think about various issues and events. If elites largely control the frames, and people basically learn and use these frames to interpret the world, then it can be asked, in what sense is there an independent public opinion (Entman, 1993)? People do have volition, however, and there is evidence that when people think about issues, they sometimes ignore or reject news frames, and that they draw upon general cultural themes as well as their own experiences and those of people they talk to (Gamson, 1992; Neuman, Just, & Crigler, 1992). The power of frames, however, is considerable.

A process related to schema is priming. People are highly susceptible to priming, that is, to being prepared to look at an event with a particular schema or point of view. In other words, the frame or perspective used on an earlier event is used again for a later event that appears to be similar. Looked at this way, priming seems quite sensible. If two events are similar, then why not approach them similarly? The problem is that if a different frame had been evoked by the earlier event, then that frame probably would have been used for the later event. The individual involved did not really select the frame to be used. Neither frame may be completely inappropriate, but they may be inadequate. For example, when evaluating a public official, priming partly sets the standards by which the official is judged (Iyengar & Kinder, 1987). The problem is that if the news stories in the previous week emphasized the environment, then environmental problems tend to be heavily weighted in the evaluation of the official. If news stories stressed defense, then defense issues tend to be heavily weighted (Iyengar & Kinder, 1987).

The term *priming* is being used metaphorically here, and like any metaphor, the term does *not* fit in some ways. The word itself means to prepare something or someone for a particular activity, as in priming a pump, a wall, or a witness. However, psychological priming is not necessarily done deliberately by anyone. Rather it just happens during the often confusing, haphazard, and arbitrary course of daily events. The particular schema evoked may arise because it is the one of many relevant schema used most recently, or because the schema fits a mood triggered by an unrelated event, or because the schema involves strongly held beliefs that, on second thought, may not be very relevant.

Schemas and priming are limiting, but often they are quite effective. They get people to act quickly, smoothly, and appropriately in many situations. Without the incessant use of schema and priming, people would constantly have to think things through, which is ludicrous and impossible. On the other hand, schema and priming can also leave people in the grip of frames that people would otherwise disagree with. A serious concern, then, is the conditions under which people are likely to break out of frames. It takes effort. The phrase "second thoughts" is apt because in most situations people will have quick responses based on schema and stereotypes. Hence, it is often the more deliberate reaction to this first response that makes a difference in people's thoughts, feelings, and actions (Gilbert & Malone, 1995; Reeder, 1997). People can be forced by external events to have second thoughts, as when the misreading of a situation creates serious consequences.

Often, however, second thoughts are a matter of volition, and volition is central to thinking about hypermedia news stories. To make hypermedia work, people must frequently make coherent choices. Furthermore, because choices are a basic property of hypermedia, there must be many choices within news stories, not just between them, if journalism is to take full advantage of the medium. Thus, although a hypermedia news story cannot force a person to act with volition, it can be encouraged and made worth while. Organizing structures of choices is therefore an important part of designing a hypermedia news story.

THE SIMPLE DIGRESSION-FORMAT

One such structure of choice, a rather conservative one, is the simple "digression-format." In this format, a standard hard-news story is broken into segments about the length of three to six newspaper-style paragraphs. Each segment becomes a separate computer file. Numerous files of relevant information are linked to each segment. Individuals can read down the main story and digress to other files, then return to the story. Headlines, often summaries of the digression files, are placed on the screen around the window showing the main story. Calling up a digression file places that file in a second window alongside the main-story window to facilitate comparisons. Digression files would contain a wide variety of material including editorials, opinion pieces, copies of relevant documents, maps, statistical data, and other news stories. The material would be organized and labeled by type, and links to the main story would indicate the relationship between the main story and the digression. Link labels could be derived from story syntax categories already in use such as "previous events," "background," and "detail." "Conflict" or "conflicting view" could also be labels. Each digression file can be linked to many segments in a story, not just one, and users can move up and down in the main story or a digression story. (This and other formats are discussed in Fredin, 1997.) It is important to note that the simple digression-format would also include a sophisticated glossary. For example, once the entry for a technical term is called up by clicking on it, then that entry would appear again automatically whenever the term reappears. This glossary can serve as a reminding mechanism, and not just a list to be called upon.

In designing and constructing simple digression-format stories, journalists need to consider two psychological constructs: namely, metacognition and self-efficacy. Metacognition, which is thinking about thinking, can be divided into two parts. The first involves monitoring how well the reading, listening, or viewing is going, and the second part consists of strategies and rules for how to go make things go better if something seems not quite right. Many of the rules will be simple but need to occur automatically, that is, without conscious thought. Thus, one metacognitive rule for using a hypermedia news story may be clicking on a term that is not well understood in order to look at a definition in the glossary. Reading will be smoother if such a rule is followed automatically.

Self-efficacy is closely related to actually following such a rule. Self-efficacy is the sense that one can accomplish a given task even if it isn't entirely clear what the task will entail. People have different levels of self-efficacy for different tasks and different situations (Bandura, 1989a, 1989b), and the level is set partly by experience. Hence an individual may automatically start to click upon an unknown term, but might stop because of low self-efficacy—the glossary doesn't really help, or is too much work.

THE HYPERSTORY INTERACTION CYCLE

Theoretically, self-efficacy plays an important role in all the decisions an individual makes in using a hyperstory. Self-efficacy is part of a cycle called the Hypermedia Interaction Cycle (HIC; Fredin & David, 1998). The cycle is intended to answer, in part, two questions: What are the dynamics of user interactions with a hypermedia story? What drives a person to continue with the next interaction? The cycle is a microlevel model of hypermedia use. For example, as an individual reads the main story, he or she may decide at any point to scan the list of headlines of related material, perhaps read a file or two, then return to the story. This digression can be treated as one cycle. An entire session with a hyperstory can be treated as a series of cycles, each cycle involving goals and motivation, of which self-efficacy is a key part. Each cycle has three phases: preparation, exploration, and consolidation.

In the preparation phase, goals are foreshadowed. The goals often will be vague in that there may be many of them or they can be reached in many ways. Next is the exploration phase, which would include scanning, searching, and following links from file to file, as well as looking at summaries and longer files. In the consolidation phase the user evaluates what he or she found, then moves to another cycle, perhaps related to what was just found, perhaps not. The level of self-efficacy at the start of each cycle affects the number and breadth of goals. Evaluation at the consolidation stage in turn affects the level of self-efficacy. The motivation itself may arise from the anticipated feelings one will have upon reaching or not reaching a goal. The feelings can affect self-efficacy, which in turn can affect goals for the next cycle. The self-efficacy in this situation is largely local in that it is only partly dependent on prior experience with other news hyperstories. In general, higher self-efficacy leads to greater and more persistent effort, which is definitely needed to explore a hyperstory and to use it creatively.

The goals involved in the HIC are contingent, emergent, flexible, and partly intrinsic. They are contingent because goals set in a later cycle depend partly on the outcome of previous cycles. They sometimes are emergent as well, because software in the story may select files presented to the user based on what the user has selected earlier. The goals are intrinsic in that they have to do with the content of the story. Fredin and David (1998) found evidence for the cycle in a pilot study of students looking for ideas for news stories in a specified section of the World Wide Web. In this instance, broader goals increased self-efficacy, whereas narrower goals reduced it.

From the journalists' perspective, encouraging exploration and creativity means creating a story environment that fosters serendipity and surprise. Surprise is important because it can prompt a rethinking. Surprise implies that something encountered has violated expectations. Evidence indicates that surprise information can get people to break out of schemas (Kunda, Miller, & Claire, 1990). Surprise may also encourage people to think more imaginatively about the hyperstory and what it means. Some material encountered may not agree with people's ideas about the story topic, but disagreement can foster new insights as well.

BROWSING, IMAGINATION, AND CREATIVITY

The HIC of preparation, exploration, and consolidation can be seen as a process of browsing, which is central to using hyperstories and is an important process in creativity. Browsing is an iterative process, a kind of partially structured searching in which "the initial search criteria or goals are only partly defined or known in advance" (Chang & Rice, 1993, p. 233). In browsing, one remains open to unexpected possibilities. Browsing can involve finding interesting material, continuing to browse, and returning on occasion to material already seen (Bates, 1989). In the context of a hypermedia story browsing would include scanning the headlines of linked files. Such scanning would be an instance of intrinsic goals dovetailing with extrinsic goals, which are goals not related to the content itself. An extrinsic goal may be to scan all the headlines on the screen. The intrinsic goal may be to evaluate each headline with reference to what has already been encountered in the hyperstory and recalled from memory. The layout of screens should be designed to encourage such dovetailing.

A second process that may be very important to creative use of hyperstories is imagination, the act of forming ideas or mental images of something not present in the senses or never entirely seen in reality. However, being imaginative goes further in that it requires that various real-world inhibitors are ignored or suspended. The suspension of inhibition grants some freedom to think about an idea before one automatically dismisses it as being ridiculous or unrealistic. Use of the imagination may be a way to weaken the hold of priming, because elaborating various ideas or spinning various scenarios may involve using several frames or combinations of them. Being imaginative involves spontaneity but is not necessarily effortless. Being imaginative can shade into what Salomon and Globerson (1987) called mindfulness, which is volitional and often involves conscious effort. Mindfulness also involves reflecting upon a range of possibilities and having second thoughts. Mindfulness can sound grim but need not be, partly because people using a hyperstory have an interest in the story topic in the first place. Surprise, disagreement, or serendipity during browsing may open up a space for considering what implications arise from what was just encountered. But using the space and keeping it open involves imagination and mindfulness, which in turn may produce goals and subgoals to be acted upon in the HIC.

In broad terms, creativity refers to "mental processes that lead to solutions, ideas, conceptualizations, artistic forms, theories or products that are unique and novel" (Reber, 1985, quoted in Johnson-Laird, 1988, p. 203). With regard to audience members using hypermedia news stories, being creative is in large part the process of building a new understanding of a situation or event or issue. Simply learning more facts or the latest events is not creative; neither is applying the first available explanation from memory. But restructuring how one thinks about something is. Certainly such restructuring can happen away from the computer. Thinking about the hyperstory topic at other times can be creative, but the process of using a hyperstory can be a central part of the entire creative process.

A range of studies supports the idea that creativity is strongly linked to intrinsic motivation—interest in doing an activity for its own sake. "People will be most creative when they feel motivated primarily by the interest, enjoyment, satisfaction, and challenge of the work itself—not by external pressures" (Hennessey & Amabile, 1988, p. 11). A study of highly visible, creative people in areas from business to science to the arts supports the importance of intrinsic motivation in creativity (Csikszentmihalyi, 1996). It would seem that intrinsic motivation could be encouraged or invited by a good hyperstory.

Creativity is often considered as a kind of talent or personality trait, and some people are undoubtedly more creative than others. However, research also indicates that creativity involves various skills and processes that can be learned and practiced (Sternberg, 1988). Creative activity in almost any area seems to involve several situations in common, which should be considered from the perspective of a hypermedia story.

Sorting Through Choices

Creativity usually involves sorting through vast numbers of alternatives to look for those with potential (Getzels & Csikszentmihalyi, 1976; Perkins, 1988). The number of alternatives can quickly become overwhelming. As composer Roger Sessions put it, "it is not sufficient to have the whole world at one's disposal—the very infinitude of possibilities cancels out possibilities, as it were, until limitations are discovered" (Sessions, quoted in Goodman, 1976, p. 127). One of the main forms that limitations take are the rules and heuristics found in any style of art. The need for limiting rules is apparent in musical improvisation. No matter what the style, improvising requires considerable knowledge of the rules for melodic contours, harmonic progressions, rhythmic patterns, and overall musical structure. Improvisation occurs within this set of rules. The rules cut down the number of possibilities for each beat, each note, and each chord as the piece unfolds, which allows the improviser to achieve coherence in real time, and the listener to detect it (Johnson-Laird, 1988).

Skilled use of a good digression-format hyperstory is a kind of improvising, because at each step an individual user has a large number of choices, which take the form of the links to related files and the continuation of the main-story. A sequence of files selected by the user might be the equivalent of a theme or melody. Looking at some additional material might be a simple embellishment of a melody. Variations on a theme might be accomplished by going through the same sequence of files but looking at different digression files, thus creating a new context for the sequence (Fredin, 1997).

Thus, the journalist in constructing a digression-format hyperstory is laying out structures of choices that encourage improvising on the part of the user. The rules that journalists might use to create an environment for improvising have not for the most part been invented. But a place to start can be suggested. As already alluded to, links from a main-story to a related file can be classified using terms such as such as *conflict, background,* or *counter-*

argument. Categorization of links is a way of organizing alternatives so that it is easier for users to narrow the alternatives they consider as they move through a hyperstory. Later rules might involve form or phrasing. Perhaps it will usually be best to go from the second file of the main story to a background file, then to two files outlining conflicting views, then another background file, and then a third viewpoint, and back to the next file of the main story. The quality of improvisation will depend partly on the richness of the environment created by the journalist, but quality will depend also upon the approach that the user takes. A largely schema-driven selection would generally result in improvisations that are hackneyed and trite. As in any art, imagination and mindfulness can enlarge the interesting alternatives considered by helping break out of current schemas.

Metaphor

A second process often found in creative action is the sudden insight that comes from recognizing a good metaphor, if metaphor is taken broadly to include models, images, and similes. Langley and Jones (1988) made the interesting point that often the metaphor is found when someone is *not* thinking about the problem to which the metaphor applies, but rather is doing something unrelated and suddenly makes the connection back to the problem. Looking for a metaphor is looking for an unusual comparison. It may be that this aspect of hypermedia news and creativity will occur when the user is away from the hyperstory, though finding a metaphor could impel people to return to a hyperstory, or an updated version of it.

Boundary Fiddling

A third aspect of creativity, which can be encouraged in a hyperstory, is what Perkins (1988) called "boundary fiddling" (p. 373). Creativity often occurs at the intersection of two fields of research or two styles of art. Creativity also occurs at boundaries formed by rules; a person may alter a few rules of a standard form and style, then follow some of the consequences of the change.

In hyperstories one boundary may be between fact and opinion. Facts linked to values, ideas, and assumptions create arguments, and working at the boundary between fact and opinion could generate better or new arguments about issues, actors, and events. Arguments can also increase interest in a story—and the pertinent facts—because, unlike so many news stories, arguments explicitly involve values and beliefs, some of which users feel strongly about. In Dewey's (1927/1954) terms, "what is kept apart from values depresses thought and renders values sparse and precarious ..." (p. 173). Merritt (1995) argued that newspapers have lost readers because of the way values are hidden in the objective style of news stories. For these reasons, many files in a hyperstory should be arguments. Of course they must be clearly marked, and, to be fair, related arguments should be linked so the user can move readily among them. As this last remark implies, boundary fiddling could also occur at the juncture of two frames that cover the same issue. Different aspects of two frames could be mixed or changed to see how the two then mesh or better account for difficult facts. I return to this idea shortly, but one more aspect of hypermedia must be introduced.

First a Little, Then a Lot

Creativity would end and self-efficacy would sag without the addition of a rule that is quite straightforward. The rule in presenting any material is "first a little, then a lot." Almost any material would have at least three versions: short, medium, and long. The three or more levels give the user far more control over the hyperstory. Thus, a short explanation for a glossary term may be no more than a line shown directly above the term. But if a person pushes the mouse farther to right, a longer definition will appear. And if a person pushes the mouse farther, a separate file discussing the term in some detail may appear. This file may in turn be linked to other news stories in which the term plays a central role. Thus, what is a quick-to-use glossary on the surface can lead to entire hypermedia stories. News can be accessed by a term or phrase treated as a glossary entry.

The "ramp-up" rule of "first a little, then a lot" would apply to almost any file linked to the main-story files in the digression-format. The rule gives far greater control over the hyperstory in all its variety. Without it, improvising probably stops. Consider what would happen with a complex glossary term if the rule is not followed: A person clicks on a term and receives a long file. The person can ignore the file, thus not learning about the term. The person can read the whole file, which is distracting and irritating. Much of the material is irrelevant, and at the end, the person probably has lost the sense of the original story. Or instead of reading the entire file, the person could jump around arbitrarily in the file trying to find a quick definition, a bothersome task that may not work either. The rule implies that many news stories must be summarized in different ways and to different degrees to link effectively with other news stories.

Metaphorically, the application of the first-a-little-then-a-lot rule means people can slide up and down slopes of glossary terms or linked files that are next to the path of the main story, rather than suddenly being confronted with a cliff to scale—that is, a long and complex file. Sliding in and out of files gives the user far more control over where the story is going, and this in turn should make the story much more interesting.

A FRAME DATABASE

A summary level would be one of the most important aspects of a frame database (FDB). The summary level, which would be linked to daily news stories, would lay out a broad context that could be reviewed quickly. An FDB would have to be used for more than a digression in a news story if it is to be a powerful aid to creativity. The goal of creativity is to start inventing new frames by devising speculations, ideas, and hypotheses. New frames, however, will arise largely from fragments of old frames, partly because frames are not simply right or wrong, true or false. Even a frame one disagrees strongly with may have some facts and values that one considers relevant and valid. The summary level of a frame database will be important because it will allow the user to mix and compare different segments of frames quickly.

An excellent example of the summary level of such a database was constructed for other reasons by Gamson and Lasch (1983). Part of their summaries of frames concerning welfare are reproduced here to illustrate how an FDB might work (see Table 16.1). After discussion of their summaries, I consider a number of extensions. Their frame matrix can encourage creativity chiefly because it segments the frames. Each row represents a frame, and each column represents property held by all frames. The frame categories in Table 16.1 can themselves be divided into two supercategories (Gamson & Lasch, 1983). The first supercategory contains categories concerning "reasoning devices that justify what should be done" about the issue (Gamson & Modigliani, 1989, p. 3): Core Frame, Core Position, Roots, Appeals to Principle, and Consequences.

These five "reasoning device" categories lay out a value-driven model of the issue, from causes to consequences. The Core Frame defines the essential questions. The Core Position states general goals that are closely related to general principles. Appeals to Principle might be labeled Cultural Themes to stress the origin of the themes, and also to indicate that the themes generally have a dialectic (Gamson & Modigliani, 1989). For every theme there is a countertheme. Thus, for the Welfare Freeloaders frame, Appeals to Principle could include the theme of self-sufficiency, while the countertheme would be "help those truly in need."

The Consequences category is labeled Consequences of FAP, a label that needs some clarification. This category is tied to a particular event, namely President Nixon's proposal of a Family Assistance Plan in the early 1970s. In the consequences category are the interpretations each frame has of the FAP. A major function of frames is to interpret ongoing events (Gamson, 1992; Gamson & Modigliani, 1989), hence each major event involving an issue could have its own Consequences category in the FDB. The Consequences of FAP also can be seen as summarizing a standard news story on

TABLE 16.1
Frame Matrix for Welfare Issue

Title	Core Frame	Roots	Core Position	Appeals to Principle	Consequences of FAP	Metaphor	Exemplars	Catchphrases	Depictions
Welfare freeloaders	The issue is how to keep the country from going broke supporting a huge welfare bureaucracy and a lot of blacks and other minorities who are too lazy to work.	Welfare rolls are inflated because of individual laziness and personal failure to acquire adequate work skills on the part of the recipient.	Able-bodied people should not be given any money without requiring that they work for it.	Rewards should be commensurate with effort. People should not be rewarded unless they have earned it through honest, hard work.	FAP would set a bad precedent since the support floor will inevitably be raised and the work incentive portion attacked as some sort of slavery or forced labor.	Cartoon showing a gluttonous bureaucrat sharing a generous meal with a well-fed welfare bum at the public expense.	Stories of welfare fraud; welfare recipients driving Cadillacs. Lesson: Undeserving people are taking advantage of welfare.	Workfare, not welfare.	Welfare recipients as "freeloaders," "bums," "chiselers." Welfare payments as "handouts."
Working poor	The issue is how to provide welfare recipients with an incentive to work while providing adequate coverage for their basic needs.	Welfare roles are inflated because the poor lack adequate job skills, have poor motivation, and have been socialized into a self-perpetuating culture of poverty, and because the welfare system provides disincentives to work.	A minimum support level should be provided so that no one starves while at the same time, manpower training and extra rewards should be offered to encourage the able and willing to work.	No one should receive more for being idle than for working. It is morally wrong for a family that is working to try to make ends meet to receive less than the nonworking family across the street.	AntiFAP1: The floor for minimum support is not high enough. AntiFAP2: The work incentive is too weak and ineffective.	Cartoon showing a poor person disdaining a handout while eagerly accepting an offer of honest work.	Stories of deserving poor who choose work over the dole but find that they lose money by doing so. Lesson: Many on welfare would prefer to work given adequate incentives and skills.	A way to independence through the dignity of work. The government's willingness to help the needy is linked to the willingness of the needy to help themselves. When you pay people to be poor, there are going to be plenty of poor people.	Present welfare system as offering disincentives to work and degrading recipient by encouraging dependency.

Poverty trap	The issue is how to help the victims of poverty out of a trap that is not of their own making.	Economic policies that fail to provide full employment.	Welfare measures such as a universal family allowance, income maintenance, and unemployment insurance for the long-term unemployed should be provided along with programs aimed at creating more jobs.	Every citizen has the right to a life of dignity, free of the despair wrought by poverty.	FAP is inadequate because most welfare recipients are unable to work and it fails to address the economic roots of poverty.	Requiring a dehumanizing means test is like knocking someone down and then demanding that he produce a doctor's certificate before he can be treated.	Family allowance programs in European welfare states. Lesson: A universal payment system protects the dignity of the poor and makes sure that all can live adequately.	Blaming the Victim. Guaranteed income. The disillusioned poor trapped in a prison of poverty and despair. It does not serve the nation or its people to train the unemployed for jobs that don't exist.	Poverty as a trap; the welfare system as a treadmill; means tests as an affront to dignity or humiliating; the idea of welfare recipients as being able bodied is false and a myth.

Abridged from Gamson and Lasch (1983).

reactions to Nixon's proposal. The Consequences category could serve as an important link between later news stories and the context provided by the rest of the FDB.

The second supercategory of Gamson and Lasch (1983) contains a set of categories that describe how to think about the frames. There are six categories: Metaphors, Catchphrases, Exemplars, Depictions, Package (frame) Title, and Visual Images. (This last category, suggested by Gamson and Modigliani [1989] is not shown in Table 16.1.) This descriptors supercategory represents an operationalization of a basic property of schemas, namely that recall of a schema as a whole is triggered by symbols—whether images, sounds, or words. These symbols in the description categories clearly could be linked to mentions in daily news stories. Each frame in an FDB thus would potentially have many entry points. People's recall of a frame may often be incomplete, because a thorough description of a frame is rarely found in public discourse. Often there are only the references and allusions to the description categories (Gamson & Modigliani, 1989).

Fact Categories

The frames as laid out thus far are mostly missing an important class of material, namely data, or facts. Conceptually, frames include facts, as do schema. In general, facts have no fixed, simple relationship to the reasoning or descriptor categories, because facts do not explain themselves. Hence, facts need their own set of categories and their own row for each frame in the FDB. As with the other categories, segmenting of facts into categories can encourage people to move sections around as an aid to raising new questions and hypotheses. Rows and columns could be reordered, and one row or column could be slid along another as a literal way of running through possible comparisons in order to find potentially interesting ones. Also, the user could copy cells from the FDB into her own Issue Space, which would be a separate window on the computer screen.

Pertinent data or facts are central to arguing for or against all or part of a frame. The key term here is *pertinent*. Lasch (1990) argued that the news inundates people with facts, but that people ignore most of these facts because they seem irrelevant to their own concerns (see also Merritt, 1995). Research in cognitive and political psychology indicates that people are more likely to attend to information that fits with their existing schema (e.g., Graber, 1984; Hamil & Lodge, 1986). Thus, relevance often may be narrowed to fit what a person already knows or believes. These general considerations lead to two important points. First, many facts may be pertinent to only one frame, and second, many of the pertinent facts may come from the criticisms of an opposing frame.

For instance, the idea that women on welfare purposely have more children in order to get a larger welfare check could be placed in the Exemplar category of the Welfare Freeloaders frame (see Table 16.1). Those holding to other frames may dismiss this exemplar as an offensive and irrational attack on welfare mothers, but still there is pertinent data: The average family size for Temporary Assistance for Needy Families (TANF) families is 2.8; 40% of the families had one child, and 10% more than three (Temporary Assistance for Needy Families Program, 1999). This fact is pertinent to the Welfare Freeloaders frame. However, it is not particularly central to the Working Poor frame or the Poverty Trap frame. This example indicates that two categories are needed for the face row of each frame: Supporting Facts and Contrary or Difficult Facts. The latter is probably the more important for encouraging creativity.

Facts that are pertinent to all or most frames would go in a General Facts category. These would be facts that describe something of the scale, scope, and nature of the issue; hence, many of these facts will be statistical in form. Because numbers take on meaning by being compared to other numbers, each statistical fact should carry an additional snippet of context as well. Thus the general facts would provide context and bring with them hints of larger contexts. These nested contexts are one point where it is particularly clear that much of an FDB can be general, factual, perhaps valid, but not objective.

For example, one general fact for the Welfare FDB could be the amount of federal money allotted to welfare, estimated at $110 billion for fiscal 2001 (Executive Office of the President, 2000). To establish a larger context for this figure, the amount could be expressed as a proportion of the federal budget outlays, about 6%. By comparison, Social Security is about 22%. Of course, comparison with Social Security could be seen as biased, although it can be justified too. Likewise the percent of the budget can be seen as minimizing the expense. However, if the monetary amount is stated alone—as is often done in the news—the amount probably seems huge to most people. Hence it would be easy to conclude that the amount is too much. An FDB should help put general context around the smaller context of a particular issue.

Using the FDB Creatively: A Scenario

With the addition of fact rows, a fairly complex scenario of using the FDB creatively can be sketched. An FDB could be useful for boundary fiddling (Perkins, 1988). The boundaries in this instance are boundaries between frames and boundaries between facts, the reasoning categories, and the descriptor categories. The fiddling consists of juxtaposing material from both frames—both on the screen and in the user's Issue Space—to see what the mix suggests.

In this scenario, a user who hasn't paid much attention to welfare comes into the database from a story link. She thinks that the Working Poor frame has a good point under Catchphrases—that government will help those who help themselves. But there's the very different point made by the Poverty Trap frame under Roots—that economic policies fail to provide needed jobs. The user isn't so sure of this idea, but juxtaposes the two—literally on the screen by placing the boxes side by side in her Issue Space window. She can organize boxes in the Issue Space however she wants, and she can also hide parts of boxes. This way, she can place more boxes in the space, and can also hide detail in order to get a sense of the larger picture (see Table 16.2).

The juxtaposition leads to some general questions. The first might be phrased, irreverently, "so show me . . . does the government have programs that help those who help themselves?" Because the user hasn't followed the welfare issue, she looks first under the category General Facts and finds that there is summary information about the major welfare programs. One is Temporary Assistance for Needy Families (TANF), which in 1996 replaced Aid to Families with Dependent Children (AFDC). The TANF program has rather strict rules about getting an education or finding a job. People violating various rules are denied some or all benefits for some time. TANF also limits lifetime benefits to 5 years. Another program is also outlined—Earned Income Tax Credit (EITC)—under which workers with low salaries get a break on federal income taxes or, if poor enough, are given money by the federal government. The user is curious about the program and does a "burst" on the EITC facts. A burst command brings up a ring of headlines around a statement, each headline being a link to more material. She looks at the "exemplar" link, which leads to a thumbnail sketch: A woman has two children in college and earned $19,000 in 1999, and $660 was taken from her pay for federal income taxes. Under the EITC, she would get the $660 back plus $1,779 (Earned Income Tax Credit Campaign, 2000). The contextual information is that the TANF plan gives a great deal of latitude to the state governments on how to implement the program. From this information the user concludes that, yes, it seems that the government is helping people who help themselves. She moves the General Fact information to her Issue Space (see Table 16.2).

The user then thinks about the economic boom. At this point, she could simply conclude that the welfare problem is going away, what with TANF, EITC and the booming economy. And her schemas might well suggest this, since filling in gaps is one of the basic functions of schemas. Instead, recall of the economic boom leads to another "so show me" question—how is the unemployment rate? For the Poverty Trap frame in the Supportive Facts cell, is a report that unemployment in February, 2000, is 4.1% (5.8 million), and the rate has been under 5% since July, 1997, and under 4.5% since April, 1998 (Bureau of Labor Statistics, 2000). The context information for this is that median wages in 1999 have reached 1989 levels but not 1973 levels

TABLE 16.2
Completed Issue Space for Creative Scenario

TANF CONSEQUENCES: Pertinent Facts *for the Working Poor frame*	*TANF CONSEQUENCES: Pertinent Facts* *for the Poverty Trap frame*
Women getting off of welfare often return: One study:	Reasons for drop in welfare cases 1996-1999:
return within one year 25% return within five years 41%	Economy 10% Minimum wage increase 10% TANF 33%
Reasons for no longer working: *job-related,* including being fired, laid off, not liking the job, and low wages; 57% *personal reasons* including health, child-care, and family problems 43%	Percent who have left welfare who are working: 50–70% Percent who were sanctioned who are work- ing: 20–50%
But real resilience in finding jobs:	Context fact: There are fewer poor children, but those who are poor have gotten poorer
Context fact: for both is that those working often cannot raise themselves out of pov- erty or advance:	A substantial percent of welfare cases have various mental and physical health prob- lems that hinder working.

General Facts:
  Earned Income Tax Credit (EITC):
    Workers with low salaries get a break on
      federal income taxes
  If poor enough, are given money by the
    federal government

Working Poor: Catchphrases	*Poverty Trap: Roots:*
The government's willingness to help the *needy is linked to the willingness of the* *needy to help themselves.*	*Economic policies that fail to provide full em-* *ployment.*

| General Facts:
 Temporary Assistance to Needy Families
 (TANF):
 In 1996 replaced Aid to Families with
 Dependent Children
 Has rather strict rules about getting an <br> education or finding a job. People violat-
 ing rules are denied some or all benefits <br> for some time. Limits lifetime benefits to <br> five years. | Poverty Trap: Supportive Facts
 Unemployment:
 Under 5.0% since July '97
 Under 4.5% since April, '98
 In mid 1999 median wages returned to
 '89 level, still below '73 |

(Continued)

TABLE 16.2
(Continued)

TANF CONSEQUENCES: Pertinent Facts for the Working Poor frame	TANF CONSEQUENCES: Pertinent Facts for the Poverty Trap frame
Consequence of TANF: GENERAL welfare caseload: 12.6 million recipients in 1996 7.3 million in March, 1999, a drop of about 40 percent.	Interpretation, Consequence of TANF: Poverty Trap frame Fed Reserve hike done to keep wages down, particularly at lower end of the scale?
Pct under poverty line in 1998: 18.9 percent of children under 18 10.5 percent of adults 18 and over	Seems to be no real evidence for inflation push from wages.
Questions How are state agencies and community-building groups supposed to work together successfully if the Federal Reserve is keeping down wages just when they have started to rise? How can the poor get higher wages? Will the state governments pay attention to children and those with various disabilities? Can they be helped in many ways by participating in the community building projects? Perhaps because it seems many are in need of some confidence and some sense of initiative and responsibility.	Collaborative Filtering Suggestion Community building as a way of building up neighborhoods, social and human capital — initiative, confidence, responsibility. There have to be jobs that pay above the poverty level for community building to work.

Note. The user would copy the cells from the FDB, and would hide some facts. (These are mentioned in the text as are references.) A summary from a user's space identified by collaborative filtering is also in the table, and the user's final questions are in the lower left cell.

(Paycheck Economics, 2000). The user drags a copy of this cell next to the other material she has gathered in her Issue Space. Now there are the two values side by side along with some facts (and context) about TANF, EITC, and unemployment. And looking at the collection the user has gathered, she raises another general question: What happened to them—are people getting jobs and getting off welfare?

The table constructed by Gamson and Lasch (1983) must now be updated by adding Consequences categories for the TANF and the EITC programs. There are three Consequences categories for each program, one for General Facts, one for Pertinent Facts, which go in the fact rows, and one for Interpretation. Gamson and Lasch (1983) had only one Consequences category for the FAP, but this was only a proposal. Once an event occurs, such as a law going into effect, there needs to be categories for each frame for pertinent factual consequences and interpretations of these consequences. Because the TANF is a major change, there is also a General Facts category for it.

The General Facts cell for the Consequences of TANF category states that the welfare caseload has dropped from 12.6 million recipients in 1996 to 7.3 million in March, 1999, a drop of about 40%. About 2.7% of the population is in the TANF program (Temporary Assistance for Needy Families (TANF) Program, 1999, August). The contextual snippet for this fact states that in 1998, about 18.9% of children under 18 lived below the poverty line, compared to 10.5% of adults over 18 (Census Bureau, 2000). The user drags a copy of this information into her Issue Space (see Table 16.2).

By juxtaposing the data on the change in number on welfare and what the TANF law requires, the user can arrive at another iteration of the general question What happened to them? Specifically, do those now off welfare have jobs? How about those still on welfare? The user moves to the Pertinent Facts category for the Poverty Trap frame, and finds the following information:

- First, 8%–10% in the decline in welfare cases from 1996 to 1999 is due to the economy, about one-third to the new TANF law, and about 10% to the increase in the minimum wage (Council of Economic Advisors, 1999).
- Second, state studies indicate that 50%–70% of those leaving welfare are employed or have work earnings, but of those sanctioned for not complying with TANF rules, 20%–50% have jobs (Tweedie, Reichert, & O'Connor, 1999).

The context fact for both is that the poorest are getting poorer: from 1995 to 1998 there has been a $245 increase in the average amount by which incomes of poor families fall *below* the poverty line (Greenstein, Jaffe, & Kayatin, 1999).

- Third, a substantial percent of welfare cases have various mental and physical health problems that hinder working: Studies in Michigan and Utah found that, among TANF recipients, 25%–40% suffered from serious depression, about 7% had general anxiety, about 20% suffered from substance abuse, and about 14% had posttraumatic stress disorder (Sweeney, 2000). Other studies show 33%–40% have learning disabilities (Sweeney, 2000).

The user copies this cell into her own issue space, hides some of the statistical information, and then looks at the Pertinent Facts cell under the Working Poor frame. She finds:

- First, again the data about the effects of the economy, minimum wage, and the TANF program on the welfare rolls.
- Second, studies show that women who get jobs and off welfare often return: One study found that 25% of women who leave welfare for work return within a year, and that 41% return within 5 years (Pavetti, 1997, cited in Brown et al., 1998).
- Third, one study looking at recipients' reasons for no longer working: 57% said one reason was job-related, including being fired, laid off, not liking the job, and receiving wages that were too low; 43% gave personal reasons including health, child-care, and family problems (Hershey & Pavetti, 1997, cited in Brown, Ganzglass, Golonka, Hyland, & Simon, 1998).
- Fourth, there is resilience in finding jobs—an Oregon study during the late 1980s and early 1990s, found that 61% of women who left welfare for work, lost their job within a year; however, 78% of these women found another job within a month. And 57% of these women lost their second job, but 69% found a third (Herr, Halpern, & Wagner, 1995, cited in Brown et al., 1998).

The context fact is that those working often cannot raise themselves out of poverty or advance: One study estimates that wages over 11 years starting in 1979 increase less than 1% per year (Burtless, 1997, cited in Brown et al., 1998). The user copies this cell into her Issue Space, and again hides some of the statistical material.

Thus far the user has been through a maze of policies and statistics. Most statistics have an exemplar link, however. These link the statistics to stories of individuals. The user does a "burst" on the context fact that indicates poor children are getting poorer. Among the headlines is a story about children in one school and the effects of TANF on them.

A key power to the FDB is the exemplar–statistics links and the rule that the links go both ways. Each provides meaning to the other. Often an exemplar may be true but relatively unusual. The feature story about a unmarried teen mother on TANF is thus linked to data that in fiscal year 1998 about 4% of TANF adult recipients were teen parents whose child also received TANF money (Temporary Assistance for Needy Families Program, 1999, August). On the other hand, the stories of individuals give the issue frames a power they may otherwise lack. Participation in social action is often helped by stories of individuals suffering injustices (Gamson, 1992).

After viewing some exemplars, the user returns to the disability data she found in the Pertinent Facts cell of the Poverty Trap frame. She slides these facts past the Exemplars and Depictions for the three frames, and notes that all three frames are basically silent about children and the disabled. The Poverty Trap has a phrase that might refer to the disabled in the Consequences of FAP cell. She then returns to her Issue Space and after looking over the various cells of information does a "burst" on the information on the context information that wages are finally rising. (This is in the Supportive Facts category of the Poverty Trap frame, Table 16.2.) The headlines there lead her to the summary of an article that argues that Alan Greenspan, head of the Federal Reserve bank, seems to be raising its key interest rate—not to stop the possibility of inflation but to keep low-end wages from rising; there is no evidence of inflation as yet, and the stock market excesses do not have to be handled through changing key interest rates (Faux, 2000). She goes back to the working poor, does a burst on the chronic return to welfare rolls and finds an article stating that the major challenge for states in the next few years is to devise programs to keep people at work and in jobs that eventually lead them out of poverty (Brown et al., 1998).

At this point she stops her improvising, but takes one more step. The website with the FDB does collaborative filtering, and she sends data on her issue-space cells to the filtering process. Collaborative filtering is a key social aspect of using the FDB and a process that gives immense leverage to the results of improvising an understanding of an issue. Collaborative filtering, in general, takes a pattern of responses, then searches through databases to find a double, a person with nearly the same response pattern. That double may have also looked at something the first person did not. Collaborative filtering suggests that the first person try this additional material (e.g., Gladwell, 1999; Wittenburg, Das, Hill, & Stead, 1998).

From the user's double comes the suggestion to look at material about community-building approaches to poverty: "It works by building community in individual neighborhoods: neighbors learning to rely on each other, working together on concrete tasks that take advantage of new self-awareness of their collective and individual assets and, in the process, creating human, family and social capital" (Kingsley, McNeely, & Gibson, 1999, p. 1). From the double's Issue Space also comes two points from the conclusions of the community-building paper (Kingsley, McNeely, & Gibson, 1999): First, neighborhood groups engaged in community building projects should seek to work with all levels of government, and government agencies should work to support the groups. Second, community building cannot help much if, among other things, the economy does not produce jobs or if the only jobs pay lower-than-poverty wages and there is no backup support, because the poor themselves and society at large see employment as the way out of poverty.

Glancing back over the cells she collected and also some of the cells of the three frames, she notes that none mention community-level factors.

CONCLUSION

Results of this improvising session are laid out in Table 16.2. In the center are the phrases taken from the Catchphrase category for the Working Poor frame and the Roots category of the Poverty Trap frame. Around these cells are arranged the various cells she dragged into her issue space, along with the collaborative filtering suggestion. She hides some facts in the boxes. And last she adds some questions of her own: How are state agencies and community-building groups supposed to work together successfully if the Federal Reserve is keeping down wages just when they have started to rise? How can the poor get higher wages? Will the state governments pay attention to children and those with various disabilities? Can they be helped in many ways by participating in the community building projects? Perhaps because it seems many are in need of some confidence and some sense of initiative.

The output of her creative work is the Issue Space and the questions she has posed. She has not constructed wholly new schema, but with the questions she has combined segments of two frames and brought in other elements, some found through collaborative filtering. And arguably she is quite some distance from where she was when she first started manipulating the FDB. Her questions do point toward rather different problems and solutions than the three frames in the FDB. Her questions are visible results of creative activity. The questions arose from boundary fiddling and sorting through choices—data and interpretations—mostly with the summary information for the Poverty Trap and the Working Poor frames.

Two final points. First, an FDB would need updating, obviously, but at the summary level at least, many aspects may not change very much for years. After all, the FDB sketched out by Gamson and Lasch was printed in 1983 and was to cover Nixon's welfare proposal made in the early 1970s. Yet the frames are recognizable if not entirely up to date. And finally, constructing and maintaining an FDB would be an art form, or a new genera. And using it will require new kinds actions. Using the FDB is not the same as reading or surfing the Internet, and it is not the same as a discussion. Of course, if FDBs are ever developed at all, they may look nothing like this sketch. But things will change. Books printed during the first 50 years after the printing press are sometimes referred to as *incunabula*, a term to indicate that book printing was in its infancy. Among what needed to be developed were proofs, paragraphing, page numbering, prefaces, and chapter divisions (Murray, 1997). We are in another incunabula stage.

ACKNOWLEDGMENTS

This chapter benefited from discussions with Prabu David, Barbara Fredin, and Joy Heselton.

REFERENCES

Bandura, A. (1989a). Human agency in social cognitive theory. *American Psychologist, 44,* 1175–1184.

Bandura, A. (1989b). Regulation of cognitive processes through perceived self-efficacy. *Developmental Psychology, 25,* 729–735.

Bates, M. J. (1989). The design of browsing and berrypicking techniques for the online search interface. *Online Review, 13,* 407–424.

Brown, R., Ganzglass, E., Golonka, S., Hyland, J., & Simon, M. (1998, July). *Working out of poverty: Employment retention and career advancement for welfare recipients.* Washington DC: NGA Center for Best Practices, Employment and Social Services Policy studies Division, National Governors' Association. (http://www.nga.org/Welfare/EmploymentRentention.htm)

Bureau of Labor Statistics (2000). *Labor force statistics from the Current Population Survey,* Series ID: LFU21000000. (http://stats.bls.gov/webapps/legacy/cpsatab1.htm)

Burtless, G. T. (1997). Welfare recipients' job skills and employment prospects. *The Future of Children, 7,* 45.

Census Bureau (2000). *Poverty by selected characteristics 1989, 1997, and 1998.* (http://www.census.gov/hhes/poverty/poverty98/pv98est1.html)

Chafe, W. (1990). Some things that narrative tells us about the mind. In B. K. Britton & A. D. Pellegrini (Eds.), *Narrative thought and narrative language* (pp. 79–98). Hillsdale, NJ: Lawrence Erlbaum Associates.

Chang, S. J., & Rice, R. E. (1993). Browsing: A multidimensional framework. *Annual Review of Information Science and Technology, 28,* 231–236.

Council of Economic Advisers (1999, August 3). *The Effects of Welfare Policy and the Economic Expansion on Welfare Caseloads: An Update.* Washington D. C.: Executive Office of the President. (http://www.whitehouse.gov/WH/EOP/CEA)

Csikszentmihalyi, M. (1996). *Creativity: Flow and the psychology of discovery and invention.* New York: HarperCollins.

Dewey, J. (1927/1954). *The public and its problems.* Athens, OH: Swallow.

Earned Income Tax Credit Campaign (2000). *The EIC: Extra money for people who work.* Washington D. C. Center on Budget and Policy Priorities. (http://www.cbpp.org/eic2000/extra.pdf)

Entman, R. M. (1993). Toward clarification of a fractured paradigm. *Journal of Communication, 43,* 51–58.

Executive Office of the President (2000). A citizen's guide to the federal budget: Budget of the United States Government, fiscal year 2001. Washington DC: Government Printing Office. (http://www.access.gpo.gov/usbudget/fy2001/guide302.html)

Faux, J. (2000, March, 3). *The Fed's unnecessary assault on wages.* Issue Brief, 136. Washington DC: Economic Policy Institute. (http://epinet.org/Issuebriefs/Ib136.html)

Fredin, E. S. (1997). Rethinking the news story for the Internet: Hyperstory prototypes and a model of the user. *Journalism Monographs, 163,* September.

Fredin, E. S., & David, P. (1998). Browsing and the hypermedia interaction cycle: A model of self-efficacy and goal dynamics. *Journalism and Mass Communication Quarterly, 75,* 35–54.

Gamson, W. A. (1992). *Talking politics.* Cambridge, England: Cambridge University Press.

Gamson, W. A., & Lasch, K. E. (1983). The political culture of social welfare policy. In S. E. Sprio & E. Yuchtman-Yaar (Eds.), *Evaluating the welfare state* (pp. 397–415). New York: Academic Press.

Gamson, W. A., & Modigliani, A. (1989). Media discourse and public opinion on nuclear power: A constructionist approach. *American Journal of Sociology, 95,* 1–37.

Gandy, O. H., Jr. (1997, October). comments prepared for the conference: *Framing in the new media landscape,* University of South Carolina, Columbia, SC.

Getzels, J. W., & Csikszentmihalyi, M. (1976). *The creative vision: A longitudinal study of problem finding in art.* New York: Wiley.

Gilbert, D. T., & Malone, P. S. (1995). The correspondence bias. *Psychological Bulletin, 117,* 21–38.

Gladwell, M. (1999, October 4) The science of the sleeper: How the Information Age could blow away the blockbuster. *The New Yorker,* 48–50, 52, 54–55.

Goodman, N. (1976). *Languages of art: An approach to a theory of symbols.* Indianapolis, IN: Hackett.

Graber, D. A. (1984). *Processing the news: How people tame the information tide.* New York: Longman.

Greenstein, R., Jaffe, J., & Kayatin, T. (1999, October 1). *Low unemployment, rising wages fuel poverty decline: Concerns remain amidst the good news.* Press release. Washington DC: Center on Budget and Policy Priorities. (http://www.cbpp.org/9-30-99pov.htm)

Hamil, R., & Lodge, M. (1986). A partisan schema for political information processing. *American Political Science Review, 80,* 505–519.

Hennessey, B. A., & Amabile, T. M. (1988). The conditions of creativity. In R. J. Sternberg (Ed.), *The nature of creativity: Contemporary psychological perspectives* (pp. 11–38). Cambridge, England: Cambridge University Press.

Herr, T., Halpern, R., & Wagner, S. L. (1995). *Something old, something new: A case study of the postemployment services demonstration in Oregon.* Chicago: Project Match.

Hershey, A. M., & Pavetti, L. (1997). Turning job finders into job keepers, *The Future of Children, 7,* 78.

Iyengar, S., & Kinder, D. R. (1987). *News that matters: Television and American opinion.* Chicago: University of Chicago Press.

Johnson-Laird, P. N. (1988). Freedom and constraint in creativity. In R. J. Sternberg (Ed.), *The nature of creativity: Contemporary psychological perspectives* (pp. 202–219). Cambridge, England: Cambridge University Press.

Kingsley, G. T., McNeely, J. B., & Gibson, J. O. (1999). *Community building: Coming of age.* Oakland, CA: National Community Building Network. (www.ncbn.org/docs/Resources/ R_ncbnpubs/cbage/index.htm)

Kunda, Z., Miller, D. T., & Claire, T. (1990). Combining social concepts: The role of causal reasoning. *Cognitive Science, 14,* 551–557.

Langley, P., & Jones, R. (1988). Problem solving and creativity. In R. J. Sternberg (Ed.), *The nature of creativity: Contemporary psychological perspectives* (pp. 177–201). Cambridge, England: Cambridge University Press.

Lasch, C. (1990). Journalism, publicity, and the lost art of political argument. *Gannett Center Journal, 4,* 1–11.

Merritt, D. (1995). *Public journalism and public life: Why telling the news is not enough.* Hillsdale, NJ: Lawrence Erlbaum Associates.

Murray, J. H. (1997). *Hamlet on the Holodeck: The future of narrative in cyberspace.* Cambridge, MA: MIT Press.

Neuman, R. W., Just, M. R., & Crigler, A. N. (1992). *Common knowledge: New and the construction of political meaning.* Chicago: University of Chicago Press.

Pavetti, L. (1997, July). *How much more can they work? Setting realistic expectations for welfare mothers.* Washington DC: The Urban Institute.

Paycheck Economics (2000). Wage and income trends—Up the down escalator: Executive summary. Washington DC: Economic Policy Institute. (http://epinet.org/Paycheck/Wages/summary%20wages.html)

Perkins, D. N. (1988). The possibility of invention. In R. J. Sternberg (Ed.), *The nature of creativity: Contemporary psychological perspectives* (pp. 362–385). Cambridge, England: Cambridge University Press.

Reber, A. S. (1985). *The Penguin dictionary of psychology.* Harmondsworth, Middlesex: Penguin.

Reeder, G. D. (1997). Dispositional inferences of ability: Content and process. *Journal of Experimental Social Psychology, 33,* 171–189.

Salomon, G., & Globerson, T. (1987). Skill may not be enough: The role of mindfulness in learning and transfer. *International Journal of Educational Research, 11,* 623–637.

Sternberg, R. J. (Ed.). (1988). *The nature of creativity: Contemporary psychological perspectives.* Cambridge, England: Cambridge University Press.

Sweeney, E. P. (2000, February 29). *Recent studies make clear that many parents who are current or former welfare recipients have disabilities and other medical conditions.* Washington DC: Center on Budget and Policy Priorities. (http://www.cbpp.org/2-29-00wel.htm)

Temporary Assistance for Needy Families Program (1999, August). *Characteristics and financial circumstances of TANF recipients, fiscal year 1998: Second Annual Report to Congress.* Washington, DC: Office of Planning, Research and Evaluation, Administration for Children and Families, Department of Health and Human Services. (http://www.acf.dhhs.gov/programs/opre/characteristics/fy98/sum.htm)

Tweedie, J., Reichert D., & O'Connor, M. (1999). *Tracking recipients after they leave welfare.* Washington DC: National Conference of State Legislatures. (http://www.ncsl.org/statefed/welfare/leavers.htm)

Wittenburg, K. Das, D., Hill, W., & Stead, L. (1998). *Group asynchronous browsing on the World Wide Web.* Fourth International World Wide Web Conference, Boston, December, 1995. (http://www.w3.org/Conferences/WWW4/Papers/98)

17

Connectivity and Continuity: Influences of the Digital Realm on the Visual Information Structures of Print

Eric Paul Engel

Every generation inherits a unique legacy of technology. The dominant emerging media technology at the close of the 20th century has been the computer. One application of this technology in particular has until recently remained relatively obscure, generally considered a mysterious realm of "techies" conversing in what the layman would consider "computer gibberish." With the invention of hyperlinks in 1989 and graphical browsers in 1993, however, previous notions of communication were forever altered.

Despite the colossal potential of the Internet, it remained an enigma for over two decades in large part due to its cryptic, text-driven nature. Few in the general public proved brave enough or stubborn enough to learn its codes and unlock its secrets. As late as 1989, the Net was described as "the world's largest library with all the books thrown on the floor and the card catalog burned" (Bock & Senne, 1996, p. 19). With the invention of hyperlinks and GUI (graphical user interface) technology, however, the text-driven limitations of the Internet were overcome, revealing a new realm of information to millions of "newbies" the world over. With this new expansion of users, the Internet concurrently experienced a marked increase in its utilization as a medium for business communication. The Internet and the World Wide Web emerged as an untapped market with boundaries limited primarily by economics and imagination.

As computer technologies (both hardware and software) have emerged as dominant communication media, a new "rhetoric of the page" has emerged as well. The virtual page, however, expands upon all previous notions of what constitutes a "page." With web pages, graphic composers are no longer limited to the physical confines of two dimensional, static space. Software developers are continually improving on real-time interactive audio and video as well as graphic capabilities (including fluid 3-D animation). Web pages are limited solely by the imagination of their creators, the latest software, time, and money. An entire industry has emerged to unite the four resources, every day the software is becoming more capable and dreams are becoming realities.

In response to this new visual rhetoric, many traditional print publications have experienced a transformation in their own formats. Through careful examination, this chapter intends to explicate the tales surrounding digital and print pages. By analyzing design and indexing trends within the digital realm, as well as concurrent trends in the visual rhetoric of traditional print media, communication scholars can begin to knowledgeably examine the implications of computer mediated information dissemination and a newly emerging "rhetoric of the page."

The influence of computers (and hyperlinks and GUI technology, in particular) is profound. At every turn the human enterprise is bounded by bytes and bits. In the 1996 Presidential election, presidential and vice-presidential candidates from the Democratic, Independent, Libertarian, Natural Law, Reform, Republican, and Socialist parties embraced the new medium by posting home pages for all the world's netizens to see (no matter how naively designed or poorly implemented). Numerous magazines have appeared to help usher in this new revolution in communication, both in supporting roles for the hardware and software, as well as by providing social and cultural commentary on the implications of and possibilities for the new medium.

By examining the unique visual attributes of both web pages and traditional print media, this chapter highlights the ways computers have redefined the notion of "the page." Due to the nature of the medium, computer web pages offer a very different rhetoric than traditional print pages. I review defining features of the visual information structures employed by traditional print media as well as those on the Internet, offering parallels as well as detailing some of the unique ways in which digital pages are influencing and transmutating the look and feel of their relations (dead tree documents)—emphasizing notions of connectivity and continuity across communication media. Although this chapter specifically examines the intertextual relationship between print publications and digital pages in cyberspace, the phenomenon is also notably prevalent amidst television programming.

THE NETWORK AND ITS FEATURES

A good analogy for the kind of change society is currently experiencing is the introduction of television (Bock & Senne, 1996). Although the first commercial broadcasts appeared in the 1930s, it was not until 1953 that television sales experienced significant growth. This situation is similar to what we are experiencing daily with the Internet. The Internet's exponential growth would have never been possible if it weren't for two key inventions, which revolutionized the Internet as a communication medium: hyperlinks and the graphical browser. The graphical browser overcame the text-driven nature of the Internet by providing point and click simplicity, thus allowing millions upon millions of computer users access to a world of resources. With the introduction of hyperlinks and GUI technology, the Internet became an inviting multimedia tapestry woven of nothing less than pure imagination.

Especially important is the quantity and quality of information which can be collected "anonymously" when visitors view and download a web site. Web servers can be configured to log the number of online visitors, noting which information files are opened and which files are downloaded, in what order the files are opened, where the visitor's path "dead ends," the time and date the visit took place, as well as the visitor's Internet domain.[1] Such information helps to establish whether the server is reaching the intended audience, what files generate the most interest, and what files generate the least interest (based on the number of "dead ends"). Print oriented media can only dream of such conditions. By providing for instantaneous and continuous feedback, web publishers are able to tailor the content of their creations much more fluidly than their traditional print counterparts.

The Page and Information Structure

Information Management: Indexing. When examining the information structure of a page, careful attention must be paid to the indexing features as well as the visual design of the page. Indexing has referred to some form of classification list complemented by the appropriate pagination with which to locate the desired information quickly and easily (*The Chicago Manual of Style*, 1993; Grodsky, 1985; Oster, 1994; SARA, 1991). Considering the nature of Web documents, however, the concept of chronological pagination becomes something of a moot point. Other various kinds of indexes include subject, author, title, product, and content. Some authors, however, referred to the notion of indexing separate from that of direct pagination and list formatting, instead highlighting the filing or cataloging nature of indexing. Wilson (1994), in particular, expressed this perspective by emphasizing the orderly location of records as being "indexed."

---

[1]Yahoo's Internet Life "Surf Lingo" glossary defines a *domain* as follows: "Domain (.edu, .com, .mil, .net, .uk, et al.): Just as a PCs file extensions (such as .doc for MS Word files) give some indication of what kind of file it is, the last part of an Internet site's domain name tells what kind of site it is. The most rapidly expanding of these is '.com' as in www.yil.com. . . . Other common domains include .edu for educational institutions, .gov for government, and .mil for military sites. For sites based outside the U.S., there are plenty of others. You can guess the origin of .uk, for instance. It gets more confusing once you start dealing with other countries' subdomains, such as the UK's '.ac' for academic."

This last conception more accurately reflects the original notion of indexing, which began with manuscript culture. "Index" is a shortened form of the original *index locorum* or *index locorum communium* ("index of places" or "index of commonplaces") which traces back to rhetorical foundations in orally based formulas. In *Orality and Literacy*, Walter Ong (1982) pointed out that

> the indexer of 400 years ago simply noted on what pages in the text one or another *locus* was exploited, listing there the locus and the corresponding pages in the *index locorum*. The *loci* had originally been thought of as, vaguely, "places" in the mind where ideas were stored. (p. 125)

As many netizens would agree, such is the case when dealing with hyperlinks.

Several generalities emerged within the literature regarding the conceptual notion of indexing. Its purpose was uniformly accepted as an aid for readers in their search for information. By identifying categories of information, indexes offer readers efficient direction as well as providing at-a-glance overviews of the subject matter. The importance of an explicit logic in the creation of indexes and the resulting efficiency was also noted (Grodsky, 1985; Muya, 1993; Oster, 1994; SARA, 1991; Vogel, 1996; Wilson, 1994), with Gardner (1995) capturing the running sentiment succinctly, "With an illogical system you waste time" (p. 145).

Information Management: Design. *Design* describes the actual structuring of information on the page visually. Of primary importance in both indexing and design is the issue of consistency (Cooper, 1995; Dern, 1993; Grodsky, 1985; Hart-Davidson, 1996; Hassett, 1996; Keyes, 1993; Oster, 1994; "Businesses Seek Solutions," 1996; Wilson, 1994). The use of consistent document design (be it a single publication, a series of publications, or a series of web pages) not only informs one's reading through familiarity with consistent visual cueing, but also allows quick assessment of the contents.

Consistency can be created through the use of key terms. Grodsky (1985) mentioned indexing as the "important points" covered on each page. According to *The Chicago Manual of Style* (1993), indexing is distinguished by "pertinent statements" as opposed to "peripheral statements." Oster (1994) commented on "the important information in the document." Although all of these discussions are drawn from research concerning traditional print documentation, their lessons apply to indexing and issues of consistency in the design of web documents.

Hassett's (1996) categorical overview of document design noted that information designers generally worked with the notion of readability as primary, whereas graphic designers assume aesthetics are primary. Rarely, however, has document design been approached in light of readability and aesthetics *as well as* rhetorical value. Whereas Bosley (1993) commented on current conventions of visual design, emphasizing format and style over rhetorical considerations of audience, context, and purpose, Hassett (1996) detailed four basic rhetorical functions that should be addressed when considering document design: alignment, invitation, credibility, and persuasion.

According to Hassett (1996), alignment means making a document look like other documents that are already familiar to the reader, again emphasizing the importance of consistency in design. Hassett, however, does not limit the issue of consistency in design to key terms, instead stressing a much broader definition that addresses documents holistically. When Hassett speaks of invitation, he refers to the idea that design either encourages or discourages readers from attempting to read a document. This point is particularly poignant when it comes to pages on the web, where catching and keeping the reader's eyes is paramount to "making the sale." If the page isn't visually stimulating enough to hold the viewer's attention, it is ultimately of little value. Although Hassett's terminology is unique within the literature, the notion that the amalgam of images, fonts, white space, and other design features contribute to a document tone, which can be either inviting or discouraging is generally accepted (Dyrud, 1996; Hart-Davidson, 1996; Keyes, 1993; King, 1994).

Both Hart-Davidson (1996) and King (1994) addressed the page as a visual unit which must be holistically embraced when considering effective document design. By seeing the page as a composition of visual elements promoting a unified message (or collection of messages), both writers and readers can more effectively and efficiently communicate. The most significant visual elements to be considered when designing documents are generally held to be typography, layout (white space), and illustrations (Coffee, 1993; Cooper, 1995; Hart-Davidson, 1996; Keyes, 1993; King, 1994). Utilizing symbols as the raw material of visual communication, designers incorporate such tools as area, line, shape, color, and texture in the creation and manipulation of fonts, layout, and illustrations. To be maximally effective, these elements must be addressed in the context of certain commonly accepted design principles: simplicity, balance, emphasis, movement, and harmony.

The synergy between typography and layout facilitates audience understanding and use of information in a variety of ways. The most profound principle of design in this regard is the notion of visual information structure. Headers, type changes, color, the manipulation of white space, and the employment of lines and texture all serve as structural and organizational cues regarding content, essentially facilitating the preprocessing of content by revealing an underlying organization (Keyes, 1993).

If done well, the visual organization is actually "perceived unconsciously (preattentively) by the reader while scanning—*before* the effort of conscious focus and reading" (Keyes, p. 1993, p. 639). This will become a particularly important issue for web page designers as modem speeds approach "fluid surfing" status.

In this chapter, the magazine advertisements of a variety of businesses with web presence were examined in order to identify the ways print ads incorporate visual navigation and framing techniques common to the digital environment. The principles detailed earlier regarding information management (both indexing and design) are explicated in reference to the specific advertisements under investigation.

METHODS

The following study involved reviewing two issues of three separate magazines: *Fast Company* (February–March 1997 and April–May 1997), *Macworld* (April–May 1997), and *Wired* (August 1996 and March 1997). The three magazines were chosen for their emphasis on, acceptance of, and active integration with technology. As they describe themselves on their web sites,

> *Fast Company*'s mission is to define the new World of business and to capture the spirit of the men and women who are making it happen. It serves as a handbook for the business revolution: a manifesto for change and a manual for achieving it. It's both a resource and a mentor, dedicated to improving and innovating work.

> *Wired* covers the most important phenomenon of our times, the Digital Revolution, for the people who are making it happen. *Wired* focuses on the individuals, companies, and ideas transforming our world. To a community overwhelmed by raw data, *Wired* supplies meaning and context. People are currently getting *Wired* throughout the United States and in 88 countries worldwide.

Although *Macworld* has an online counterpart, their web site failed to provide a clear, concise statement of purpose.

The symbols and symbolism of the magazines were explored in detail: the amalgam of design features such as images, illustrations, typography, area, line, shape, color, texture, alignment, invitation, credibility, and persuasion. Upon careful review of the pages, a series of similarities emerged in the stories being told. In the end, 27 advertisements (36 pages) were selected to provide a visual context for the analysis.

Critical Examination

What follows is an examination of the unique structures of discourse for both traditional print media as well as digital (the Internet, in particular). By detailing some of the defining features of the visual information structures found in recent magazines, this chapter highlights some of the ways in which the computerized digital realm has influenced the visual discourse of the print media.

Observations have been grouped under six headings. Their ambiguity is emphasized as an acknowledgment that, as with all interpretive endeavors, subjectivity plays a critical role. The initial investigation was prompted by previous explorations into the graphic composition of web pages. Upon examination, *Fast Company, Macworld,* and *Wired* revealed a recurring discourse of connectivity and continuity manifested through visual "sampling" from the digital realm. The analysis and descriptions to follow begin by focusing on connectivity as a feature of traditional print media and information structures, gradually shifting and ultimately focusing on a synergy between traditional print and emerging digital pages and their information structures.

Connectivity as a Feature of Traditional Print Information Structures

The use of lines to connect ideas visually on the page is nothing new to traditional print media such as newspapers and magazines, and the *Fast Company* section highlights two common methods in which lines were employed to frame and guide reading. The first three pages were advertisements from Hyatt Hotels & Resorts (*Fast Company*, 1997a, p. 31; *Fast Company*, 1997b, pp. 32–33). A thin, wrap around border unites the questions "Have you ever noticed how much you don't notice?" and "Has the world become less interesting? Or have you?" with the Hyatt logo in the bottom right corner of the page (as if to suggest you need only visit a Hyatt Hotel or Resort to find the answers). Using line as a dominant design tool, the page designers provided navigational landmarks for our reading in an attempt to visually unify portions of the page. With the line doubling as a border, the narratives of the ads were also "framed" for easier consumption. Interestingly, Hyatt was one of only two pages in my entire study which failed to provide a URL somewhere on the page as a further resource. (Hyatt does in fact have a homepage.)

The final page in this section is an advertisement for the Multipath Back-UPS Office, a surge protector from American Power Conversions (*Macworld*, 1997a, p. 73). This page employs line as a descriptive device, uniting a small portion of text visually with the product or feature itself. (Anyone familiar with the "balloon help" feature in many computer programs will be familiar with this use phenomenon.)

Connectivity and Continuity: Moving Toward a Visual Rhetoric of Hypermedia

The first three advertisements (four pages) in this section visually simulate the notion of hypermedia through the use of dotted lines or rules—literally guidelines to frame your reading. Epson promotes "the world's best color ink jet printer" with an underlying theme of connectivity (*Wired*, 1996, pp. 2–3). Text boxes are united in a networked configuration. Epson also employs rules in their more traditional use as descriptors. Again using rules to unify ideas on the page, a portion of text is highlighted under a magnifying glass (an icon frequently employed in graphic user interfaces, emphasizing familiarity and continuity in design across media). Suggesting that the entire magazine spread is actually a computer screen, the graphic designer even went so far as to place an "Epson" button in the lower right corner (complete with a commonly employed cursor pointer).

The next advertisement is from NEC Multimedia (*Fast Company*, 1997a, pp. 62–63). Three images are united through the use of a large dotted rule, with arrow endcaps emphasizing notions of global interconnectivity and intersubjectivity. The content of the pictures themselves is noteworthy—a close-up of a White male, a picture of a large satellite dish, and a group of "foreigners" united around a computer monitor in an outdoor setting (visually suggesting an interactive feed between a White male educator and an African class half a world away). The largest text box summarizes the argument and highlights the notion of connectivity, "Finally, a vision of multimedia that links more than just words, pictures and sound."

Selling their search engine, HotBot also employs a large dotted line to simulate a hyperlinked button (the HotBot logo in the bottom right corner of the page) (*Wired*, 1996, p. 199). As if to suggest that whatever you seek can be found at the end of the next link, the rule leads to nowhere (somewhere?) just off the page. The ad also employs a smaller dotted line to unite the picture of a parked car at sunset with the text, "Oh, HotBot, you . . . you . . . you found it."

The final page in this section is an advertisement by the PointCast Internet news network (*Wired*, 1997, p. 209). A large text box with a black background divides the page, with the text in the box ("Your live [**news**] feed from the world") simulating a hyperlink through the use of color. From this text a thin line unites with the service's URL, ultimately pointing to the PointCast logo in the bottom corner of the page—a transmission tower (implying an extended connection with the world).

Connectivity and the Human Touch

Using close-up enlargements of human hands and computer mice as the most pronounced images on the page, advertisements for UPS Shipping and Microsoft's IntelliMouse suggest connectivity as a dominant theme as well (emphasizing "a human touch" in and "hands on" approach to users interface with technology and business). This reading is further supported by the advertisements' use of line. UPS suggests a notion of global connectivity just at your finger tips (waiting to be accessed and shipped to) through its use of image (a hand on a computer mouse), line, and a virtual button (*Wired*, 1996, p. 49). As with the Epson button mentioned earlier, the "UPS OnLine" button comes complete with a cursor pointer hovering near.

Microsoft's IntelliMouse follows suit, with a line uniting a human pointer finger and a "raised rubber wheel" (used to navigate and manipulate the computer page) (*Wired*, 1997, p. 48). With a text line at the base of the hand reading "Where do you want to go today?", the reader is visually guided up the page to the tip of the finger, over and down to the mouse via a solid rule, and ultimately (as implied by the mouse bleeding out of view on the bottom right of the page) to the world. Global connectivity at your fingertips complete with point and click simplicity.

Windows, Buttons, and Drop-Down Menus

This portion of my examination combines a variety of magazine pages united by their use of design features native to the graphic user interfaces of the digital realm: windows, buttons, and drop-down menus. Many of the pages also highlight notions of connectivity and continuity through their manipulation of common design tools like line, color, texture, and space.

In Hassett's (1996) terms, the magazine pages frequently strive for alignment with computer pages through the manipulation of dominant, familiar symbols of the digital realm (such as windows, buttons, and drop-down lists or menus). The pages visually present a symbolic rhetoric of transmedia or intertextual continuity. Pages from a magazine become virtual desktops suggesting point and click access to the amassed knowledge of the world. Hassett also commented on the use of headings as a persuasive rhetorical device, "Headings can (and should) be used to encourage the reader to remember material in a particular, persuasive fashion" (pp. 66–67). By employing "virtual" hyperlinks (signified visually through colored text or implied through the use of rules), print publications visually incorporate a persuasive rhetorical device (visually indexical headings). In this context, lines serve as two-dimensional indexing tools.

The following is a list of pages examined within this section of the analysis, with brief insights for each entry.

Wacom Graphics Tablet. A Wacom advertisement explores the notions of connectivity and continuity through the use of dotted rules, framed boxes, and "cut-outs" complete with tool icons in their top left corners. This is an excellent example of the traditional descriptive feature of line being reconstructed in terms of a new rhetoric of connectivity and hypermedia (*Macworld*, 1997a, p. 44).

WAV. Combined with a miniature window to emphasize continuity across media, the solid rules in this advertisement suggest the hyperlinking of text (while actually functioning more traditionally as descriptors or balloons) (*Macworld*, 1997b, p. 18).

Pantone. In this advertisement, rules relate connectivity between the computer and the printer via the data in the window (the Pantone color choices). The page designers not only included the window detailing the color selections, but they even went so far as to include a floating tool bar. Continuity is seen through both the screen color and the "virtual" windows environment (*Macworld*, 1997a, p. 37).

Power Computing. A simulated graphic interface dominates this page. Here is an excellent example of the entire page engaged as a virtual desktop, complete with drop-down menus, scattered windows, and numerous buttons. (Noticeably, it's a Mac desktop environment!) (*Macworld*, 1997b, inside back cover)

GoLive CyberStudio. Here, again, the page designer has simulated a digital environment by depicting the entire magazine page as a single window. Unifying the information by framing its contents in a virtual window, the page emphasizes continuity across media. The coordinated use of space, the placement of text and graphics, and the coloring of both bullets and headings visually imply virtual hyperlinks (*Macworld*, 1997b, p. 95).

Telecom Interactive 97 Forum and Exhibition. Here is a human hand commanding a remote control visually hyperlinked by a thick dotted line which leads to a Windows 95 environment (sporting twin rotating globes and drop-down menus) backgrounded by 20 small maps of the world. A thin rule frames this testament to the religion of connectivity and the notion of "keeping in touch." Notably, the caption at the top of the page posits the question, "Are you ready for this?" (*Wired*, 1997, p. 169)

Xerox. A two-page spread incorporates a virtual desktop complete with textured background, windows environments (even really small ones), and a simulated hyperlink button ("Color The Document") (*Fast Company*, 1997b, pp. 40–41).

IBM. An IBM advertisement parodies a message window with option buttons (a visual that's very familiar to many computer users, "Server unavailable. Try again later.") (*Wired*, 1996, p. 101).

Symantec. Symantec provides an excellent example of the notion of drop-down menus employed as a graphic device to guide the reader's reading of the page. By coloring the text containing the web addresses orange, the page implies hyperlinked qualities as well (*Wired,* 1996, p. 44).

Umax Computer Corporation. This two-page spread implies hyperlinks and hypermedia by uniting a picture of a computer with a series of monitor images via a thick dotted rule. The virtual link itself (the rule) offers three drop-down menus as well. The first menu actually offers descriptors, while the second menu implies a list of bundled software options (tempting the computer literate reader with promises of powerful resources). Connectivity and continuity are creatively constructed—an alluring array of options on a virtual desktop (*Macworld,* 1997b, pp. 29–30).

Mita. A single drop-down menu in the center of the page offers virtual connectivity to a multitude of resources. Thick, red dashed rules with arrowhead endpoints imply hyperlinking to places randomly "out there" (cyberspace) and "in there" (internal to the document or program itself). In the bottom right corner of the drop-down menu, the pointer is found highlighting "can help" (complete with a cursor pointer) (*Fast Company,* 1997b, p. 113).

MultiMedia, HyperMedia, and the Notion of Networking

This collection of pages emphasizes grandiose visions of connectivity and continuity, with particular attention paid to the uniting of individuals over vast geographical distances. Notably, five of the eight pages in this section are advertisements from Microsoft, a superpower in the world of the digerati.

Pioneer Multimedia. Graphically as well as textually, this spread explicitly states a case for extreme connectivity. A multimedia array of images (satellite, broadcast, digital cable TV, DVD, and computer networking) is backgrounded by a picture of the Earth on the left page of the layout and a graphic reminiscent of the fragile soap bubbles of childhood (yet infused with overtones of the digital realm) on the right page of the layout (*Wired,* 1997, pp. 124–125).

Sprint Drums. Computer monitors (labeled "Wallace, Idaho" and "Los Angeles, CA") bleed off into the margins at the top left and bottom right corners of the page in this Sprint advertisement, visually united by similar tool bars (and similar iconography), a background picture of an exploding volcano, and a rule simulating a hypermedia videoconference (*Wired*, 1997, p. 60).

Microsoft Team Manager 97. The inclusion of multi-layered windows (a la Windows 95) emphasizes notions of continuity, while the use of green, underlined copy (within a larger mass of black text) suggests the notion of hyperlinkage. Microsoft advertisements are by design skillfully crafted to have the look and feel of hypertext (*Fast Company*, 1997b, p. 140).

Microsoft Internet Explorer 3.0 for Mac. This two-page spread is an outstanding example of the digital realm being translated visually in a print medium. A thin rule links a portion of a window (a la Internet Explorer) to a large Internet Explorer icon, with the line ultimately exiting the page at the far right. Similar lines unite portions of text (visually hyperlinked through the use of coloring and underlining), further suggesting universal connectivity as they vanish from the page to the left and to the top (into cyberspace?). The company's advertising campaign slogan ("Where do you want to go today?") borders a visual of deep space, suggesting that the reader need only download Microsoft's Internet Explorer software to visit the furthest reaches of the universe (*Macworld*, 1997a, pp. 2–3).

Microsoft FrontPage. A Windows 95 "Start" button and thin dotted rules with bulleted ends imply hyperlinks to information randomly scattered across a two-page spread, visually carrying this theme further by incorporating a background image of a spider's web hung heavy with pearls of dew (*Wired*, 1996, pp. 8–9).

A Vision of Things to Come

To complete this analysis, three pages from the March 1997 issue of *Wired* were examined. At the base of the first page a series of images are united by a single thin line (p. 175). Starting with a text box containing a URL for Geocities, the reader is guided to a web page from which a drop-down menu links with yet another Geocities menu, from which a clipping of the Mona Lisa has been sampled, from which a pink collage of the Mona Lisa with long blond hair and a human torso in a bikini has been composed. By visually explicating a single path in a virtual world, the graphic composers of this page highlight the random, yet systematic nature of hyperlinking in cyberspace.

The final item is a two-page spread—*Wired* 5.03: Table of Contents. Here we see an example of the digital realm and the print realm combining in one of the most comprehensively integrated visual formats encountered. *Wired* exists as both a print publication and a virtual, online ezine. As a result, both publications have employed unique transmedia indexing cues to provide continuity and to aid the reader's navigation, whether reading the print or the online version of the magazine. From the inclusion of a text box (pill) containing the URL for *Wired* 5.03 to the staggered pattern in which the articles are located on the page visually (nontraditionally from left to right across the spread staggering material both up and down, as well as in a traditional top to bottom, column format on the far right of the spread), the graphic representation of the page mimics the "feel" of reading and indexing in cyberspace. Further, the page numbers corresponding to the article titles are colored orange, suggesting virtual hyperlinked extensions—realities just out of reach.

CONNECTIVITY, CONTINUITY, CREATIVITY, COGNITION, AND COORDINATES

The page is at once simple and complex. It is a collection of meanings which together pose an argument, which together tell a story. As I studied the pages of *Fast Company, Macworld,* and *Wired,* I found myself admiring, criticizing, and questioning the page makers' design decisions. I marveled at the ways in which graphic composers visually construct meaning and facilitate the framing of readings.

Print graphic designers are increasingly sampling from the rhetoric of the digital realm to simulate hyperlinking (a fundamental element of navigation and orientation in cyberspace). Some of the most common features employed are rules (dotted or solid), the underlining of text, and the use of windows, buttons, and drop-down menus. Through the frequent repetition of such design elements, print graphic designers are effectively simulating on static two-dimensional pages the digital, interactive environment of the Internet. Graphic designers are well aware of the value of visual continuity. With thousands of new consumers daily joining the ranks of the online masses, the transmedia marketing of products places new emphasis on both continuity and connectivity as defining features of life in a wired world.

In previous research, I have explored theories of design structure in relation to traditional print publications in an attempt to better understand the composition of web pages in cyberspace. My research here leads me to believe that just as the synergy between typography and layout facilitates audience understanding and use of information, so too does the synergism of print and electronic publications contribute to a collective emphasis on temporal and spatial connectivity. We are a culture obsessed with the here (and everywhere else) and now (and "everywhen" else). This chapter has attempted to relate some of the ways in which visual information structures (both in print and in cyberspace) have contributed to and reconstructed a sociocultural discourse of connectivity and continuity.

REFERENCES

Bock, W., & Senne, J. (1996). *Cyberpower for business.* Franklin Lakes, NJ: Career Press.

Bosley, D. (1993). A study of gender and its influence on visual design. *Technical Communication, 40*(3), 543–547.

Businesses seek solutions to filing frustrations. (1996, May). *Supervision, 57*(5), 8–9.

The Chicago Manual of Style (14th ed.). (1993). Chicago: University of Chicago Press.

Coffee, P. (1993). Page description is a breakthrough tool. *PC Week, 10*(2), 36.

Cooper, A. (1995). Designers on design. *Mediaweek, 5*(42), 56–59.

Dern, D. (1993). The well-organized marketer: To become more productive, try these tech tips and tricks. *Home Office Computing, 11*(3), 26–28.

Dyrud, M. (1996). Teaching by example: Suggestions for assignment design. *Business Communication Quarterly, 59*(3), 67–70.

Fast Company (1997a, February–March). [Advertisements, pp. 31, 62–63]. Published raw data.

Fast Company (1997b, April–May). [Advertisements, pp. 32–33, 40–41, 113, 140]. Published raw data.

Gardner, G. (1995). Taming the paperwork monster. *Medical Economics, 72*(22), 145.

Grodsky, S. (1985). Indexing technical communication: What, when, and how. *Technical Communication, Second Quarter,* 26–30.

Hart-Davidson, B. (1996). Teaching the page as a visual unit. *Business Communication Quarterly, 59*(3), 71–73.

Hassett, M. (1996). Teaching the rhetoric of document design. *Business Communication Quarterly, 59*(3), 64–67.

Keyes, E. (1993). Typography, color, and information structure. *Technical Communication, 40*(4), 638–654.

King, W. (1994). Training by design. *Training & Development, 48*(1), 52–54.

Macworld (1997a, April). [Advertisements, pp. 2–3, 37, 44, 73]. Published raw data.

Macworld (1997b, May). [Advertisements, pp. 18, 29–30, 95, Inside back cover]. Published raw data.

Muya, E. (1993). Information management–Indexing. *Information Resource Sharing and Networking. 2nd Revised and Amended Edition.* (Report on Three Training Courses. Arusha, Tanzania, Oct. 22–Nov. 2, 1990; Mombasa, Kenya, April 15–26, 1991; Arusha, Tanzania, March 23–April 3, 1992). Tanzania: Eastern and Southern African Management Institute. (ERIC Document Reproduction Services No. ED 360 975)

Ong, W. J. (1982). *Orality and literacy.* New York: Methuen.

Oster, S. (1994). Indexes in computer documentation. *Technical Communication, 41*(1), 41–50.

Postman, N. (1985). *Amusing ourselves to death: Public discourse in the age of show business.* New York: Penguin.

SARA (State Archives & Records Administration). (1991). *Records legislation for local governments.* Albany, NY: New York State Education Department. (ERIC Document Reproduction Services No. ED 342 370)

Vogel, P. (1996). Know your business: Build a knowledgebase! *Datamation, 42*(13), 84–87.

Wilson, P. (1994). Alphabetic filing rules: Fundamentals for records managers. *Records Management Quarterly, 28*(1), 18–21.

Wired (1996, August). [Advertisements, pp. 2–3, 8–9, 44, 49, 101, 199]. Published raw data.

Wired (1997a, March). [Advertisements, pp. Table of contents, 48, 60, 124–125, 169, 175, 209]. Published raw data.

Yahoo! Internet Life (1997, April 12). *Internet glossary.* [WWW document]. URL *http://www.zdnet.com/yil/content/surfschool/lingo/lingotoc.html*

Zakon, R. H. (1998, April 12). *Hobbes' Internet Timeline v2.5* [WWW document]. URL *http://info.isoc.org/guest/zakon/Internet/History/HIT.html*

18

News Framing and New Media: Digital Tools to Re-engage an Alienated Citizenry

John V. Pavlik

New media storytelling tools are altering, or will likely alter, the framing of news in the digital age. To help understand these changes this chapter examines a number of such tools, including hypermedia, omnidirectional imaging, and object-oriented multimedia. Hypermedia are the online tools that allow journalists and other storytellers to create electronic links between their stories and other online content. Omnidirectional imaging refers to 360-degree view imaging systems, including still or full-motion video, which permit viewers to pan, tilt, or zoom about a visual space not possible through conventional imaging technologies. This viewer navigational capability puts in the hands of the audience new levels of control over what is seen in a video story.

Object-oriented multimedia refers to the creation of digital objects in full motion video and audio. Using MPEG-4 or even next-generation Web technology, storytellers can create content that incorporates both linear and multilinear narrative forms by making every image within a video stream a digital object. Each object, such as a person, place, or building, can be encoded with layers of additional content, such as textual description, interactive graphics, and animation, or additional motion video or audio, all retrievable with a mouse click, remote control, or voice command. Thus, a reporter might create a standard two-minute report for the evening news, but also encode another hour or more content accessible to viewers who are interested in more depth, but not forced upon those who prefer more passive viewing of the news.

Together, these new tools present the opportunity for storytellers, such as journalists, to create much more engaging, navigable, contextualized reports that tell the day's events more accurately, fully and dynamically. In the end, these tools create the possibility to create news reports that are less bound by the typical one-dimensional, episodic-frame storytelling used in most contemporary U.S. news reporting. Instead, there is the possibility to place stories into a more complex frame that more closely approximates the multidimensional nature of most social and political realities.

At least, that is the potential. Included as well is a review of selected news prototypes developed at Columbia University using each of these new tools. This chapter both describes the implications of these emerging tools and speculates on their likely adoption, evolution, and impact on news framing.

FRAMING NEWS STORIES

Despite the editor's well-worn admonition to "Let the facts speak for themselves," most journalists are accustomed to framing their news stories. In newsroom parlance it's called "the angle." "What's the angle?" on this story is perhaps the second-most frequently asked question in editorial meetings, second only to, "Who are your sources?" The simple fact is that in most traditional newsrooms the culture of journalism is to determine the basic nature of a story before assembling all, or even most of, the facts. Just as many theorists develop a working hypothesis before collecting the data, many journalists are used to formulating the angle, or frame, of a story before they interview anyone, read a document, or collect any other facts. Sometimes they are more apt to follow the adage, "Never let the facts get in the way of a good story."

Why is this? The reasons are many.

On a theoretical level, a frame is used as a central organizing idea for making sense of pertinent events and processes. News and information in isolation can have little intrinsic meaning. Thus, when reporting the news it helps to place the facts into a meaningful context to provide coherence. Context is the connecting tissue that ties isolated facts into a whole. News stories are told most commonly as narratives, based on facts, but woven together into a coherent package via framing techniques. Britton (1993) explained,

> Experience is kaleidoscopic: the experience of every moment is unique and unrepeatable. Until we can group items in it on the basis of their similarity we can set up no expectations, make no predictions: lacking these we can make nothing of the present moment. (p. 26)

A variety of scholars have conducted research potentially relevant to this issue, including Cappella and Jamieson (1996), whose work helps delineate between strategy versus policy analysis in a framing context. Perhaps the most relevant, however, is the work of Iyengar (1991), who has conducted extensive research on the framing effects of news coverage on public opinion and political choice. He describes two forms of media frames, what he calls the *episodic* and *thematic*.

Iyengar presents evidence that television news routinely report events in the context of specific events, or "episodic" news framing. Episodic framing presents concrete events to illustrate broader issues, whereas thematic framing offers aggregate or general evidence. Research shows that broadcast media are particularly likely to use an episodic frame for public affairs reporting in which political issues are portrayed in terms of concrete instances. For example, in terms of crime reporting, the focus of the typical local news story is often on an act of violence by a specific (usually non-White) perpetrator.

All this matters because framing affects the audience's perception of reality. As Iyengar argues, through episodic news framing the media help maintain the status quo by rarely placing news events and issues into a broader context. News events are framed within the prevailing paradigm of social and political reality, reinforcing stereotypes, existing political agendas, and prevailing conventional wisdom.

More than this, however, the media of the analog world rely on generally preset episodic frames. There is a limited set of episodic frames that reporters draw upon for each story, report, or beat (the term for a general coverage area). Although there is little research to date to delineate these preset episodic frames, most journalists know them, at least intuitively, for their assigned beat. When covering the education beat in New York, a common frame is the tension between Mayor Rudolph Giuliani and School's Chancellor Rudy Crew. Anything that happens is always placed in that context, or frame. When 21,000 of the students who were required to attend summer school in 1999 failed (14,000 didn't even attend the classes) and were ordered to repeat their previous grade, the story was reported against the backdrop of the Crew–Giuliani strained relationship (the two have not seen eye-to-eye on how to administer the city's troubled public school system).

On a practical, newsroom level, the reasons for episodic framing, particularly that which uses a familiar frame, reduce largely to economics. In most newsrooms, journalists are under enormous pressure to produce news on a daily basis. They are expected to generate news copy, video, or audio as a baker produces bread. As Frank (1991) observed and echoed in Auletta's (1992) broadcast news critique, the changing economic structure of the television networks has eroded the newsroom values in the three traditional commercial networks, ABC, CBS, and NBC. Where once a culture committed to great journalism flourished, a culture dominated by MBAs and financial accountability has taken its place. Accountability to shareholders has replaced accountability to democracy and the citizens it serves.

A similar transformation has occurred in many newspaper and magazine newsrooms, as once-independent, family-owned print media have been swallowed up by increasingly large chains whose focus is on the bottom financial line, and double-digit profits are demanded by large institutional investors. As a result, fewer and fewer journalists are given the support to conduct extensive, often time-consuming investigations, or risky enterprise reporting that may not lead to a publishable story.

This is not the ideal way to develop a story. It is preferable to follow this 15-step iterative procedure:

1. Identify a possible story based on a hunch, suspicion or lead from a source.
2. Collect some preliminary data, or facts.
3. Formulate a working hypothesis.
4. Collect additional data.
5. Refine or reformulate the hypothesis, or thematic frame.
6. Collect more facts.
7. Draft the story based on the facts as currently framed.
8. Collect more facts and begin checking the facts already assembled both from original sources and news sources who can corroborate those facts.
9. Reconsider the story frame in the context of the assembled facts.
10. Prepare a second draft of the story.
11. Collect more facts and do more fact checking, and then when confident of the facts and the thematic frame or angle developed for the story.
12. Publish the story.
13. Re-assess story based on audience feedback.
14. Conduct relevant additional reporting.
15. Revise story if and as necessary.

This rigorous procedure emphasizes many of the most important rules and standards of journalistic excellence, including using multiple sources, extensive fact checking, and most importantly, letting the facts determine the story. Perhaps most importantly, this procedure allows the reporter to place the story into a more thematic frame that has not been preset, and that enables the audience to see how a story based on even a single event fits into a broader social or political reality.

Unfortunately, these procedures require a commitment of time, resources and hard work. In an age of real-time publishing deadlines, escalating competition and powerful economic pressure, most journalists operate in a pack mentality driven by leaks from anonymous sources, public relations (including press releases, press conferences, and staged events) and the Associated Press daybook. Today's typical journalist is expected to produce daily stories, whether in print or broadcast media. Frequently, the story is framed by someone other than a journalist, someone with a vested interest in how the story is spun, or it is set by journalists working for a wire service and only a local "angle" may be added by a journalist working for a local newspaper or broadcast outlet.

Consider how the media report on Alan Greenspan, the chairman of the Federal Reserve Board. On April 2, 1998, Greenspan delivered a speech at the annual convention of the American Society of Newspaper Editors (ASNE) in Washington, D.C. Greenspan delivered a fresh, original, and provocative speech about how information technology (IT) has eliminated compassionate capitalism. He argued that IT has destroyed inefficiency in the world's markets and thus has made it impossible for even the most compassionate of capitalists to show any flexibility in his or her accounting and investment practices in the world's emerging economies.

Unfortunately, Greenspan's speech didn't fit into the standard episodic frame used by traditional media in reporting on the Fed Chairman's pronouncements. The standard frame involves interpreting any remarks by Greenspan in terms of how the world's markets, especially those of the United States, respond. Do they tremble, rise, or fall? A typical report framed Greenspan's speech as a financial story, and concluded that the chairman's views on information technology had little effect on the world's financial markets. The report mentioned virtually nothing about the focus of the speech—the relationship between IT and capitalism. A report from *USA Today* (Belton & Miller, 1998) illustrates:

Federal Reserve Chairman Alan Greenspan voiced uneasiness about sky-high stock prices Thursday as the Dow Jones industrial average neared 9000.

He stopped well short of predicting any sudden reversal in the stock market. But Greenspan asked whether forecasts of sharply higher corporate earnings that are driving up stock prices are realistic.

In remarks to the American Society of Newspaper Editors, Greenspan said those forecasts seem based on the belief that the U.S. economy has entered a new era of continuous steep gains in productivity . . . Greenspan gave no hint Thursday about the future direction of interest rates. (p. 12)

Similar stories ran in *The Washington Post, Milwaukee Journal Sentinel, The Financial Times Limited*, and elsewhere. One exception was the *Investor's Business Daily*, which described his speech as a "Manifesto," a "landmark speech" (1998).

Against this tide, what impact can developments in new media have? In reality, probably very little. They may even make the situation worse by applying pressure to report not just daily but hourly in some cases, such as the financial news Internet sites which demand continual updating. Moreover, the pressure for speed, to the get the story first, leaves little time for the more thoughtful contemplation necessary in thematic framing. The economic forces are severe and the culture of pack journalism is still strong.

However, with effective leadership in both journalism education and the journalism industry, new media can significantly influence the framing of news events. This influence is likely to come in at least three forms. First, new media storytelling tools, especially those involving the Internet, provide an opportunity to report news events and processes in much greater context than in traditional media. Second, through the Internet, citizens are gaining unprecedented access to information. Third, the confluence of these two trends will likely lead to an evolution in the role of the journalist from the primary, and often times sole provider of news, to one of sensemaker and interpreter.

The remainder of this chapter examines these three trends and describes how new media storytelling tools may present particularly significant implications for the framing of news.

NEW MEDIA STORYTELLING TOOLS

Although the convergence of computing, telecommunications, and traditional media has spawned a diverse range of new media tools for storytelling, three in particular have important implications for the framing of news. These three are hypermedia, omnidirectional imaging, and object-oriented video. Hypertext, a term coined by futurist Ted Nelson in 1961 in his vision of a world-wide linked publishing environment he called Xanadu, refers simply to nonlinear text or other content, and has given rise on the World Wide Web to hypermedia, or the use of electronic pointers that connect one term or digital object (such as a graphic, animation or image) to another digital object, perhaps an associated web page. Hypermedia is critically important to the framing of news stories because it enables the journalist to provide links between stories and related online content that can provide additional background, detail and, most importantly, context. It permits the journalist to connect stories to broader themes, issues, or events outside a single episodic frame.

Hypermedia

Although many analysts point to the multimedia nature of the Web as perhaps its most salient storytelling feature, recent evidence suggests that
hypermedia may be at least as important in placing news in a more complete context. Fredin and David (1998) provided an example to illustrate
why hypermedia is so important in providing greater context for the news.

> On a Web site such as CNN Interactive, a typical news story about the 1996
> presidential elections had links to stories on the same topic that were done
> earlier in the campaign. The earlier stories in turn were linked to candidates'
> home pages and platform positions. Some news stories were linked to the
> home pages of relevant federal agencies, to home pages of interest groups, or
> to enormous on-line news archives such as Lexis/Nexis. The result is a mas-
> sive and interconnected information network. The fact that massive reposito-
> ries of information are only a few mouse clicks away offers a richness to
> hypermedia that set it apart from traditional media. (pp. 35–36)

A study conducted in the spring of 1998 demonstrates that those news
consumers who make particularly heavy use of the Internet as a news medium, younger Americans, place great value on the richer context provided
online through hypermedia (Kohut, 1998). Among 18- to 29-year-olds, 77%
say they like having so many information sources to chose from, while the
percentage tails off for older age groups. Just 70% of 30 to 49 year olds say
they like this diversity, 64% of 50 to 64 year olds, and 52% of those 65 or
older.

Although this evidence is by no means conclusive, it suggests that more
contextualized news, news with a wider frame, is especially appealing to
the next generation of news consumers. An increasing amount of evidence
also suggests that this more contextualized news framing makes Internet-
delivered news more credible. A Gallup poll reported in the *American Journalism Review* shows that in a national survey of 1,009 Americans news
delivered via the Internet is perceived as fair and impartial by more Americans (53%) than via any other medium (Newport & Saad, 1998). Just 51%
view local TV news as fair and impartial, followed by national cable TV
news (47%), radio news (46%), national network news (43%), weekly news
magazines (42%), local newspapers (40%) and national newspapers (39%).
Roper poll data collected in 1997 present similar patterns. In a survey of politically interested Web users, the study found that online media tended to
be judged more credible than their traditional versions, and that because of
this greater credibility, news consumers increasingly prefer to obtain their
news from the Internet (Johnson & Kaye, 1998). Again, these findings suggest that better hypermedia, because of their contextualization, provide an
increasingly compelling form of news.

Hypermedia can enable the journalists to increasingly present stories that reach beyond the traditionally narrow frame used in most print and broadcast media. By enabling the news consumer to see a story from multiple perspectives or points of view, thus expanding the news frame, news consumers are able to understand news events in a more complete context. Importantly, evidence is increasingly suggesting that news consumption habits are changing and that younger news consumers prefer their news in a more contextualized frame.

Omnidirectional Image and Object-Oriented Video

Omnidirectional imaging and object-oriented video are two important emerging new media tools that can greatly increase this capability to place news stories in an expanded frame. Omnidirectional imaging refers to 360-degree view cameras, including still or full-motion video, which permit viewers to pan, tilt, or zoom about a visual space not possible through conventional imaging technologies. This viewer navigational capability puts in the hands of the audience new levels of control over what is seen in a video story. Consider news reports about the "Million Youth March" in Harlem, New York City, September 5, 1998. News reports about the controversial event framed the story as largely one of confrontation between march organizer Khallid Abdul Muhammad and New York City police and emphasized an apparent discrepancy in the expected and Mayor Giuliani-estimated crowd size. The Associated Press (1998), for example, gave this account of the event.

> Filled with fiery rhetoric against whites, Jews and police, the Million Youth March ended with a clash between police and ralliers after an organizer riled up the crowd Saturday.
>
>   At the end of the event billed as a black empowerment rally, organizer Khallid Abdul Muhammad called the police names and told participants to "beat the hell out of them with the railing if they so much as touch you."
>
>   "We have a right, a God given right, a constitutional right to defend ourselves against anyone who attacks us," said Muhammad, dismissed as an aide to Nation of Islam minister Louis Farrakhan after a 1994 speech in which he referred to Jews as "bloodsuckers" and insulted Pope John Paul II, homosexuals and whites.
>
>   Muhammad, who went minutes over a court-ordered time limit of four hours, told the thousands of participants to leave peacefully. As the crowd dispersed, a police helicopter flew in low, angering some members who threw bottles and other debris. Police said 16 officers and five civilians were injured.
>
>   Police in riot gear quickly took the stage while officers on horseback and motorcycles occupied the rally area in the city's Harlem neighborhood. A Dal-

las man was arrested on charges that include disorderly conduct. More arrests were expected.

More than 3,000 police officers were at the rally, which Mayor Rudolph Giuliani estimated about 6,000 people attended. Organizers had expected 50,000.

Use of an omnidirectional video camera (see www.cyclovision.com for an online demonstration of an omnidirectional imaging system) could have added significant context to this news report and expanded the "crowd size" frame used in the story. For example, an omnidirectional video report from the event would allow news consumers to pan, tilt or zoom about the scene, observing for themselves the size of the crowd, the police presence, and the nature of the violence that ultimately erupted. Such an omnidirectional video report was used by students at Columbia University's Center for New Media in the spring of 1997 to report on the Irish Lesbian Gay Organization (ILGO) Protest of the annual St. Patrick's Day Parade in New York City. The report is available on the Web (http://comet/ctr.columbia.edu/~laitee/NewsLab/Omnicam/).

Through this navigable report, viewers can make up their own minds as to the nature of the ILGO protest and the arrests that resulted. Although the journalist still plays a central role in creating the news report, it is a role that emphasizes inclusiveness of perspectives much more than in traditional journalism. The report allows the viewer to look around the scene and draw her or his own conclusions to a much greater extent than in traditional media.

Object-oriented multimedia refers to the creation of digital objects in full motion video and audio. It offers an opportunity to journalists to provide even greater context in news reporting. Additional information on the background of Khallid Abdul Muhammad, the reasons motivating the march and the Giuliani Administration's reasons for providing a strong police presence could all have been layered in. Notably, object-oriented storytelling allows reporters to move beyond the standard fare of event-based, episodic news framing, and into what Dennis (1990) described as "process-oriented" news. This process-oriented, thematic framing of news is of critical importance in making connections between apparently isolated events and longer term trends in society and their links to international developments.

This is all the more important, since as Iyengar demonstrates, episodic framing is at its most intense level of practice in television news, especially local news. Television's importance as a leading provider of news in the U.S. makes episodic news framing especially problematic. As we move into a digital television environment, we have a unique opportunity to re-invent the news production process and place greater emphasis on using these new tools to produce stories embracing more thematic frames.

CONCLUSIONS

By many accounts, journalism is in crisis. The credibility of traditional news providers is at an all-time low, as measured by a variety of pollsters such as Gallup, Times Mirror, and Roper. Newspaper readership has fallen steadily since World War II. Network television news viewership has fallen steadily since the 1970s, and overall television viewership for the first time ever dropped in 1997, largely as a result of the rise of new media alternatives, especially the Internet. Moreover, as Stein (1998) and Hickey (1998) pointed out in the *Columbia Journalism Review*, journalism has faced "one screaming mess after another."

Perhaps most importantly, the framing of news has become increasingly problematic in traditional news outlets. As Joan Konner, former publisher of the *Columbia Journalism Review* and Dean Emerita of the Graduate School of Journalism at Columbia University, observed (1998), news is frequently dominated by a frame of "beware": "Beware of the stock market, beware of hurricanes, beware of Black youth in Harlem" (p. 2), are some all-too-common frames in today's news.

Can new media provide an alternative? By providing the tools to create more contextualized stories, new media at least present the possibility of an expanded news frame that emphasizes broader social and political themes. News consumers increasingly value the diverse perspective provided by online news sources. Expanded framing may prove central to re-engaging an increasingly distrusting and alienated citizenry in a 21st Century democracy.

REFERENCES

Associated Press (Sept. 5, 1998). *Million youth march.*
Auletta, K. (1992). *Three blind mice: How the television networks lost their way.* New York: Random House.
Belton, B., & Miller, R. (April 3, 1998, Final ed.). Greenspan leery of sky-high stocks, *USA TODAY,* 12.
Britton, J. (1993). *Learning and language,* 2nd ed. Montclair, NJ: Boynton/Cook.
Cappella, J. N., Jamieson, K. H. (1996). News frames, political cynicism, and media cynicism, *Annals of the American academy of political & social Science, 546,* 71–84.
Dennis, E. E. (1990). *Reshaping the media.* Newbury Park, CA: Sage.
Frank, R. (1991). *Out of thin air: The brief wonderful life of network news.* New York: Simon & Schuster.
Fredin, E. S., & David, P. (1998). Browsing and the hypermedia interaction cycle: A model of self-efficacy and goal dynamics. *Journalism & Mass Communication Quarterly, 75,* 35–36.
Hickey, N. (1998). Ten mistakes that led to the great CNN Fiasco. *Columbia Journalism Review, 38,* 26.
Investor's Business Daily (April 14, 1998). Greenspan's manifesto, non-bylined article, A6.
Iyengar, S. (1991). *Is anyone responsible?* Chicago, IL: University of Chicago Press.

Johnson, T. J., & Kaye, B. K. (1998). Cruising is believing? Comparing Internet and traditional sources on media credibility measures., *Journalism & Mass Communication Quarterly, 75*, 325.

Kohut, A. (1998). Internet news takes off. *Research report*, The Pew Research Center, *8*, 1.

Konner, J. (September/October 1998). Beware, *Columbia Journalism Review*, 2.

Newport, F., & Saad, L. (1998). A Matter of Trust. *American Journalism Review, 20*, 33.

Stein, N. (1998). Banana Peel. *Columbia Journalism Review, 38*, 46.

19

Textual Framing as a Communication Climate Factor in Online Groups

Edward A. Mabry

Framing is a complex concept that functions as a root metaphor about the symbolic representation of social reality (Reese, prologue, this volume). Frames are linguistically and semantically rendered inflections in the construction of shared meaning. Berger and Luckmann (1966) used the term *commutation* in a similar way. Commutation refers to a social constructive mechanism for differentiating between the intersubjective experience of everyday, or routine, social reality and other meaningfully interpretable embedded senses of reality contexts in which individuals also interact. Commutation is seldom a mindful activity but it can be consciously engaged. A journalism student, for example, driving to a part-time job might begin to reinterpret that experience through the lens of a journalist covering a story about transportation problems and, then, introspectively compare those perspectives. Likewise, parents anecdotally report construing the ways they relate to their children as parallels to business relationships (and vice versa). It was in this sense that Bateson (1972) discussed the concept of *perceptual framing* as integral to understanding how individuals construe social situations. He saw it as the constant juxtaposing of foreground (meaning of the moment) and background (meanings of a given class of social experiences) dimensions of social perception.

A construct so fundamental to explicating the essence of social meaning can seem praxiologically distant. Rhee (1997), for example, suggested that frames operate similarly to a preprocessing (or mentative) stage in the social–cognitive process of message interpretation. I assume the use of framing is sufficiently rooted in our intersubjective social practices that it functions on the level of taken-for-granted social knowledge. However, this need not render frames inaccessible to systematic analyses.

I make a second assumption about framing that constitutes a key issue with respect to its empirical goals. As interpretive devices, frames must defer to the spatiotemporal structure of a social situation (Berger & Luckmann, 1966). This is consistent with Bateson's (1972) thinking because it reflects a topological perspective about social situations. How we perceive (and symbolically interpret) the immediate (or foreground) experience is influenced by the contours of the background on which it's projected.. Thus, frames are multidimensional. They are the interpretive nexus of *situated* meaning. As Bateson (1972) suggested, perceptual framing is conditioned by the *where* and the *how* of social interpretation.

Rhee's (1997) study of political campaign coverage is helpful in illustrating this point. Rhee (1997) found that journalists cover political campaigns guided by either or both of two interpretive frames of reference: strategy and issue coverage. Strategy coverage emphasizes campaign process management and control. Issue coverage focuses on the rhetorical engagement of social issues candidates employ in self-definition. Yet, a crucial point with respect to frame dimensionality can be found in the question: Would these same frames be intuitively appealing for reporters' coverage of a different social space? Thus, for instance, would reporters symbolically frame the story of a five-alarm fire in a downtown warehouse in a similar way?

I assume the answer to these questions is "No." Interpretive framing and framing devices are more or less situation-bound and intersubjectively layered. A situated frame functions first to form a sense of meaning-in-context about one's proximate social ecology and, second, to stimulate an identification of symbolic resources that are appropriate and available for implementing the actor's egocentric goals through the construction of shared meaning. This perspective on framing is especially probative to a study of framing practices in social groups like the ones observed in this study.

The social context of groups that use computer-mediated communication [CMC] technology is substantially defined by the form, content, emotional tone, and sequencing of electronic messages (e.g., email) exchanged by group members (Mabry, in press; Scott, 1999). The overall purpose of this study is to investigate how participants in groups that use CMC technology (e.g., Internet newsgroups or listserver groups) overtly employ technologically implemented framing devices through message construction and editing features in the software supporting group communication. These message forms are termed *textual frames* because they shape electronic discourse in ways that are interpretively reflexive.

Communicators can ground their actions using prior messages, comprising a group's cumulative message environment, while simultaneously attending to specific points at issue through textually manipulated punctuated commentary. More specifically, this study focuses on potential relationships between textual framing, group identity (the shaping of a distinctive communication environment), group moderation (or nominal leadership), and the stylistic qualities of message expression.

PARTICIPATING IN COMPUTER-MEDIATED GROUPS

The growing use of CMC is fostered by expanding access to technology and user awareness of the global computer communications network known as the Internet. The Internet's popularity is due to the inexpensive and efficient means of relaying electronic files (containing correspondence, documents, catalogues, and databases) and multimedia images (video and audio signals) it affords for users of desktop computing equipment with network access.

Internet use has increased as network members have created and maintained a wide variety of specialized *discussion* groups for exchanging messages using electronic mail. These electronic groups vary in their formality and conversation-like continuity of message exchanges (Rafaeli & Sudweeks, 1998). Group membership and participation is dynamic. Some function as electronic mailing lists—or bulletin boards—for distributing and seeking information (often used by professional and technical organizations).

Many online groups are formally structured. They use volunteer *moderators* that screen contributions for topical appropriateness, politeness, and blatant commercialism. Yet, the majority of online groups are *unmoderated* and function as vehicles for exchanging information and opinion on various thematic issues. They form relatively open communication environments that only loosely conform to the topical identity originally projected by their organizers—whose computer facilities often support a group's message distribution system (Rheingold, 1993). Permissive environments tacitly, if not actively, encourage the airing of controversies and usually evidence substantial tolerance in supporting ongoing arguments and disputes.

Argumentative exchanges among members of online groups are quite prevalent. The intensity and deviance potential for such disembodied communication contexts can lead to quite heated and destructive exchanges (Hiltz, Turoff, & Johnson, 1989; Kiesler, Zubrow, Moses, & Geller, 1985). The norms of network usage (referred to as "netiquette"), inculcated and reinforced among net users, specifically stress obligations for group and self-monitoring to insure that members maintain civility and communicative relevance. One frequently sanctioned breach of netiquette involves "flame" messages; messages that are precipitous, often personally derogatory, *ad hominem* attacks directed toward someone due to a position taken in a message distributed—*posted*—to the group (Lea, O'Shea, Fung, & Spears, 1992; Mabry, 1998; Siegal, Dubrovsky, Kiesler, & McGuire, 1986).

The management of conflict discourse like flaming in online groups underscores the importance of group identification for helping to provide an intersubjective grounding members must have in order to construct social frames of reference on which social control mechanisms and group cohesiveness rest. This social identification that emerges in online groups is often referred to as "community" (Baym, 1993, 1995; Jones, 1995). Baym (1993, 1995), in her investigations of online groups, found that, group members evolve unique styles of expression that anchor their online presence and foster an overall sense of group identification. Relationships and group expectations are framed by members' constitutive meanings of sociability and appropriateness.

TEXTUAL FRAMING AND THE HUMAN–TECHNOLOGY INTERFACE IN COMPUTER-MEDIATED COMMUNICATION

Some aspects of expressive style appropriations used by online group members are artifacts of computer-mediated communication systems. Virtually all computer software supporting asynchronous electronic mail [email] includes so-called "cut-and-paste" message editing features. The combination of electronic filing (or archiving), making it possible to save exchanged messages, and efficient keyboard editing utilities represent very powerful message construction tools. It is these types of software-driven instrumentalities that provide the communication resources for enacting textual message framing.

One place where textual framing is especially useful is in online argument. An online arguer can easily create a *new* message, say a counterargument to a position advanced by an adversary in a previously distributed message, by inserting segments of the disputed message along with counterclaims the arguer wishes to advance. In this way, edited insertions function as a tactical highlighting of the point in dispute in a way that *frames* the arguer's new discursive moves by selectively focusing attention on the arguer's interpretation of the dispute (Antaki & Leudar, 1992; Govier, 1985; Holtgraves, 1996; Snoeck Hankemans, 1989, 1991). A brief, modestly confrontational, exchange of electronic mail messages employing cut-and-paste editing is presented in Table 19.1.

Earlier, I have studied the use of cut-and-paste editing as a form of textual framing in online groups, observing that framing tactics were used in ways similar to the rationalized placement of refutational arguments in ar-

TABLE 19.1
Example of Cut-and-Paste Arguing

_____#: 123456789/Xemailr
10-Oct-98 10:52:21
Sb: Impeach Him Now!
Fm: <Pseudonym A>
To: <Pseudonym B>
>If you lie, you get busted. Period! When you lie under oath
>you're a criminal. Anybody can see that.
There's an old saying in Washington: if everyone that lied
about having an affair was fired or sent to jail, nobody would
be left to run the country. :-)
>The Constitution says the President can't be a criminal.
>He lied. He's toast!
But, he hasn't been convicted of anything—including lying
in court. So, where's the crime?

Note. Text segments with > (bullets) are cut and paste inserts from a message received from Pseudonym B by the message sender Pseudonym A. Message text is fictitious.

gumentative discourse (Mabry, 1998). I hypothesized that the amount of emotionality used in online messages would be curvilinearly related to the amount of textual framing employed in message construction. Message editing (e.g., use of inserted quoted material, cut-and-paste editing) and narrative references to prior messages were expected to increase with a message's emotional tone until messages reached levels of significant negative affect (antagonism and hostility typical of so-called "flame" messages) at which point messages would become less structured and textual editing would decline. I found partial support for the expected relationship between emotionality and technologically implemented framing (Mabry, 1998). Narrative references to prior messages followed the expect trend. However, message editing followed a simple linear trend; emotional tone of messages increased as the use of editing increased.

RESEARCH OBJECTIVES AND HYPOTHESES

The present study extends this work in three ways. First, it expands the investigation of causal factors that might influence the use of textual framing tactics to variables other than those that are part of the message. Thus, the study of textual framing can move beyond being a message bound phenomenon. Second, the study incorporates information about online group goals and process structure against which the use of textual framing tactics can be compared. Third, this study expands my original classification of online messages to account for expressive attributes of message content which could be more sensitive gauges of social context framing.

Online groups are formed to satisfy various objectives. In this study, these objectives were assessed by researchers involved in message coding. Groups were classified as academic, technical, social, or mixed purpose. Academic groups focused on scholarly-like themes (e.g., literature, pedagogy). Technical groups included members with vocational or avocational interests in specific technologies (e.g., computer programming languages). Social groups were dedicated to particular interests or topics (e.g., StarTrek; hockey). Mixed groups included online support groups or groups that were so broadly engaged that no specific theme could adequately describe their activities.

A second contextualizing factor of online groups is the amount of control over message flow they impose. This involves the role of group moderation. Some online groups are structured around a moderator that functions as a gatekeeper, but most online groups are not moderated because of the large amount of time involved in successfully moderating an active group.

This study defines group purpose and group moderation as independent variables that can separately or in combination function as contextualizing frames. The expressive content of online messages, dependent variables in this study, is defined according to McKelton, Mabry, and Katzman's (1997) investigation of sincerity affectations in online groups. In that study they delineated three types of expressive styles in online messages: relational involvement, topical involvement, and formality. Relationally involved messages can include self-disclosure, metacommunication, agreement, challenges, and similar social bonding themes. Topical involvement includes statements of opinion, nonpersonal information, questions, and other nuances directed towards thematic analysis of a topic. Formality involves the style of linguistic and compositional formatting instantiated into a message (e.g., presence or absence of colloquialisms, proper sentence and paragraph construction, or icons).

Goals an online group expects to satisfy, the presence (or absence) of a group moderator, and group members' use of textual framing tactics contribute to the communicative environment that supports its social cohesion (or community). Therefore, these variables should have an effect on the expressive styles of messages enacted in online groups. This reasoning leads to the following hypotheses:

Hypothesis 1: Group objective, group moderation, and message framing should significantly interact with the extent of relational involvement enacted in the message.

Hypothesis 2: Group objective, group moderation, and message framing should significantly interact with the extent of topical involvement enacted in the message.

Hypothesis 3: Group objective, group moderation, and message framing should significantly interact with the extent of formality enacted in the message.

METHODS

Overview

Data used in this study was obtained as part of an international project in computer-mediated collaborative research. This project was the outgrowth of mediated group discussion over the Comserve system's Internet "hot-line" on organizational communication (sponsored by the Communication Institute for Online Scholarship). The principal goal of the project was to investigate CMC by collecting and analyzing messages from online discussion groups active on the Internet. Over a span of approximately 2 years, an international group of researchers planned and implemented a research design for developing a database of time-sampled messages from a randomly selected set of online discussion groups. A full explanation of the project is available in Rafaeli, Sudweeks, Konston, and Mabry (1998), and only information pertinent to the present study is summarized here.

Message Sampling

Online discussion groups conducted in English that met certain message activity thresholds comprised the sample of groups. Various computer bulletin boards, lists, and newsgroups were canvassed for a period of approximately 1 month. Messages were randomly sampled across days and times. Message sampling terminated when a target of 100 messages was reached. Messages were sampled beginning with a randomly chosen Monday and took, in some cases, a period of months before the target number of messages was reached. Approximately 3,000 messages, from 30 different online discussion groups, were collected and coded for inclusion in the project's database.

Message Coding

A standardized message content analysis coding protocol was collaboratively developed by participating project members. The content analysis instrument measured 46 message variables: 40 variables were manually coded by the researchers and 6 were coded using automated techniques (see, Rafaeli et al., 1998, for an extended explanation of message analysis). The coding protocol required trained coders to read the literal text of a message and apply all defined variables to each message (wherever possible). A message was evaluated on whether it contained content descriptive of the following: facts, opinions, humor, challenges, metacommunications, presence of graphic art, formality of composition, quoted material, emotional tone (e.g., neutrality, agreement, disagreement, hostility—flames), and sender characteristics (e.g., gender, status).

More than 40 people participated as coders. Coders were furnished with materials (e.g., codebook) electronically and given online training activities and guidance. Training involved coding a set of sample messages chosen to cover the range of defined variables. Coders rated the messages and returned results via electronic mail. High agreement with predetermined responses to training messages qualified the person as a coder for the purpose of receiving messages to be analyzed in the main study. A low rating on the training messages sample led to coaching by a senior researcher and another set of training messages testing the trainee. Coders were sent sets of 100 messages. Coders were also given a posttask questionnaire requesting impressions of the list coded and information about their coding and reporting practices. Completed sets of formatted codes were returned via electronic file transfer to a host computer system. Work was automatically screened using custom software to debug technical errors (e.g., off line formats, typographical errors) and any rejected codes were sent back to the coder for correction.

Reliability

Given the project's methodological approach, coding reliability was rather difficult to assess. Online discussions among researchers indicated that initial efforts at establishing reliability proved inconsistent. Difficulties included both listwise (sampled group) and variable-specific results that yielded outcomes with high variances and, for some variables, modest to low reliability.

Two conventional methods for assessing reliability were used in preparing data for this study: Brennan and Prediger's (1981) modification to Cohen's *kappa*, $k_{(n)}$, coefficient and Cronbach's (1951) *Alpha* coefficient. The $k_{(n)}$ coefficient permits an assessment of interrater reliability under conditions where marginal values of an $n \times n$ coding matrix are free to vary. *Kappa* was computed for all variables used in this study. Alpha was computed for items that were treated as scalable.

A sample of 1,000 messages, 100 cross-coded messages from 10 computer-mediated discussion groups/lists, constituted the data for reliability analyses. Because coders were not fixed across lists, reliability calculations were performed on a listwise basis (for each 100 cross-coded message sample) and averaged. Listwise Alpha coefficients could not be computed for some items (e.g., conciliation and challenges variables) due to attentuated variances caused by high percentages of agreement among coders (in excess of 90%). Reliability and descriptive statistical information for variables used for testing study hypotheses can be found in Mabry (1998). Two variables, Opinionation and Fact, did not attain acceptable $k_{(n)}$ coefficients but were deemed critical to an adequate test of the hypotheses and were retained.

Measures of expressive style were derived from message codes analyzed as composite variables. Message codes were converted to scalable items and summed to form relational involvement, topical involvement, and formality measures. Acceptable alpha coefficients were obtained for the three composite measures (see McKelton et al., 1997).

RESULTS

Validity Analyses

The independent variables of group objective and moderation were obtained through independent ratings of message coders and required an analysis of their validity. The independent variable of message framing was empirically derived from the coded messages and assumed to possess face validity.

Coders rated each online group from which their set of messages were drawn on six 5-point scales: member homogeneity, emotional range, verbosity, seriousness, supportiveness, and message utility. These items were defined as a vector variable in multivariate discriminant function and classification analyses computed on the group objective and moderation variables (Tatsuoka, 1971).

Neither discriminant function analysis produced a significant discriminant function. However, the data indicated that uneven distributions of cases (i.e., online groups) across levels of both independent variables led to weak outcomes. Multiple classification analyses should be less sensitive to this problem and were used to assess validity.

The initial results for group objectives were weak as classification efficiency was only 57.60%. However, the social and mixed purpose groups' profiles were very similar. Therefore, these two groups were combined and the classification analysis recomputed. The classification efficiency for group purpose improved to 72.70%. Given this result, the number of levels for this independent variable was decreased to three: academic, technical, and social/mixed purpose groups.

Results for group moderation also failed to reach significance. However, classification efficiency results were a strong 87.90%. This suggested that,

even with somewhat unequal distribution of cases, moderated and unmoderated groups could be differentiated on the basis of coders' perceptions of the groups. Yet, this independent variable had to be dropped from
subsequent analyses due to insufficient data bearing on the interaction hypotheses when it was combined with the other independent variables. Hypotheses are adjusted accordingly.

Tests of Hypotheses

Hypothesis 1. Restated, group objective and message framing should significantly interact with the extent of relational involvement enacted in the
message. Both ANOVA main effects were significant, but the two-way interaction between group objective and message framing was not significant ($F(2,
2391) = .21, p > .80$), therefore the hypothesis was not supported. The main ef-
fect for group purpose was $F(2, 2391) = 8.62, p < .001$. A conservative Scheffe
post hoc test (Winer, 1971) showed the mean amount of relational involvement sentiment expressed in messages from academic groups ($M = 1.84$) was
significantly lower than the ratings of relational involvement found in messages from technical ($M = 1.88$) or social/mixed groups ($M = 1.88$). The main effect for message framing was $F(1, 2391) = 7.65, p < .006$. There was more relational involvement in online messages containing edited text. The mean
amount of relational involvement for messages containing textual framing
was $M = 1.89$, whereas the relational involvement mean for messages not containing technically framed text was $M = 1.87$.

Hypothesis 2. Restated, group objective and message framing should
significantly interact with the extent of topical involvement enacted in the
message. The ANOVA main effect for message framing was significant ($F(1,
2391) = 31.28, p < .0001$), but the main effect for group objective was not ($F(2,
2391) = p > .30$). However, main effects were not interpretable because the
two-way ANOVA interaction was significant and supported the hypothesis
$F(2, 2391) = p < .001$.

Table 19.2 contains means for the two-way effect. A Scheffe post hoc
analysis of means showed a complex ordering. Topical involvement was (a)
highest in academic and social/mixed purpose groups that used message
framing, (b) significantly lower in academic and technical groups that did
not use message framing, and (c) also significantly lower in technical
groups that did use message framing and social/mixed purpose groups not
using message framing.

One anomaly in these results is the lower mean for technical groups engaged in message framing tactics. The only plausible explanation is that
technical groups are highly information oriented, and message segmentation leads to relatively short, very particularized and narrow informational

TABLE 19.2
Two-Way Interaction Means for Topical Involvement

	Framed Messages	
Group Purpose	Yes	No
Academic	1.63	1.53
	(*n* = 99)	(*n* = 201)
Technical	1.46	1.53
	(*n* = 129)	(*n* = 471)
Social/Mixed	1.64	1.49
	(*n* = 402)	(*n* = 1095)

Note. Higher scores indicate greater topical involvement.

statements. Brevity attenuates the compound score as only one or two message analysis codes contribute item scores over one.

Hypothesis 3. Restated, group objective and message framing should significantly interact with the extent of formality enacted in the message. The ANOVA main effect for group objective was significant ($F(2, 2391)$ = 54.85, $p < .0001$) but the main effect for message framing was not ($F(1, 2391)$ = 3.60, $p > .05$). Main effects were not interpretable however because the two-way ANOVA interaction was significant and supported the hypothesis ($F(2, 2391)$ = 10.04, $p < .001$).

Table 19.3 contains means for the significant two-way interaction term. Higher means indicate less formality of expression. The Scheffe post hoc test indicated that social/mixed purpose, technical, and, academic groups, respectively, were significantly ordered from most to least informal in style of expression for messages that did not contain edited text. Overall, there was more informality in online group messages containing edited text. However, variance produced from the increase in informality that accompanied

TABLE 19.3
Two-Way Interaction Means for Formality

	Framed Messages	
Group Purpose	Yes	No
Academic	1.38	1.27
	(*n* = 99)	(*n* = 201)
Technical	1.36	1.35
	(*n* = 129)	(*n* = 471)
Social/Mixed	1.41	1.42
	(*n* = 402)	(*n* = 1095)

Note. Higher scores indicate less formality.

the use of textual message framing in academic online groups was almost totally responsible for the significant interaction effect.

DISCUSSION

Two of the three amended hypotheses were supported. There were statistically significant interactions between group objectives and the presence (absence) of textual framing tactics related to scores for topical involvement and formality in the expressive style of online group messages. This interaction effect was not observed for scores for relational involvement messages. Only once did message framing fail to be a significant contributor to hypothesized interaction effects or to produce significant main effects in the statistical designs.

The implications of these findings are intriguing. First, they clearly indicate that computer-mediated discourse containing message structuring devices influences the emotional tone and issue involvement of messages in online groups. Technologies supporting mediated groups offer text processing resources that facilitate the use of complex, adaptive message strategies necessary for developing cohesiveness that makes these groups a uniquely interpretable social context. Moreover, face-to-face communicators often appear to have only weak command over similar strategic tactics, or experience less powerful outcomes, when the applications are solely reliant on orality (Mabry, in press).

Second, the results indicate that online groups are situated. Members construct communication environments through their appropriating technologies reflecting their groups unique goals. As Jones (1995) argued, online groups are social spaces that evolve much like face-to-face environments. This also supports the inference that mediated communication provides communication resource opportunities similar to those expected from face-to-face interaction (Baym, 1995). And, it adds support for the notion that mediated environments are another in a wide range of social contexts for which communication processes need to be accounted (Kiesler & Sproull, 1992).

Turning to more technical considerations, as was apparent in both the discussion of producing satisfactory reliability analyses for this very unique database and the modifications to the original conceptualization of independent variables in the research design, there is a need to revisit methodological practices employed in creating such databases. The nature of the collaborative effort used in obtaining these data also created unique problems for ensuring empirical consistency, without an inordinate loss of efficiency, and needs to be addressed in subsequent research (Galegher, Kraut, & Egido, 1990). In recognition of the underlying power of the study, it should be pointed out that the results, although significant, were relatively weak. Fractional differences in means were enhanced by the study's large sample of messages. This is offset by the fact that hypotheses were directional and most results displayed trends in the expected directions.

Understanding how symbolic representations of social contexts are enacted through the appropriation of CMC system resources is important. How we co-produce meanings-in-context with other actors is a central issue in understanding our socially competent performances. Compared to online groups, conventional face-to-face group settings differ markedly in the continuity with which their patterns of entertainment and performance consequences can be revealed and included as manifest constituents of a social context (Mabry, 1999, McGrath & Hollingshead, 1994). By contrast, CMC provides denser, but far more immediately accessible, symbolic resources (Messaris, 1998). Thus, it seems essential for communication scholars to continue developing insights about communication practices like textual framing in mediated contexts.

REFERENCES

Antaki, C., & Leudar, I. (1992). Explaining in conversation: Towards an argument model. *European Journal of Social Psychology, 22,* 181–194.

Bateson, G. (1972). *Steps to an ecology of mind.* New York: Ballentine.

Baym, N. (1993). Interpreting soap operas and creating community: Inside a computer-mediated fan culture. *Journal of Folklore Research, 30,* 143–176.

Baym, N. (1995). The emergence of community in computer-mediated communication. In S. G. Jones (Ed.), *Cybersociety: Computer-mediated communication and community* (pp. 138–163). Thousand Oaks, CA: Sage.

Berger, P., & Luckmann, T. (1966). *The social construction of reality: A treatise in the sociology of knowledge.* Garden City, NJ: Doubleday.

Brennan, R. L., & Prediger, D. J. (1981). Coefficient kappa: Some uses, misuses, and alternatives. *Educational and Psychological Measurement, 41,* 687–699.

Cronbach, L. J. (1951). Coefficient alpha and the internal structure of tests. *Psychometrika, 16,* 297–334.

Galegher, J., Kraut, R. E., & Egido, C. (1990). *Intellectual teamwork: Social and technical foundations of cooperative work.* Hillsdale, NJ: Lawrence Erlbaum Associates.

Govier, T. (1985). *A practical study of argument.* Belmont, CA: Wadsworth.

Hiltz, S. R., Turoff, M., & Johnson, K. (1989). Experiments in group decision making, 3: Disinhibition, de-individuation, and group process in pen name and real name computer conferences. *Decision Support Systems, 5,* 217–232.

Holtgraves, T. (1986). Language structure in social interaction: Perceptions of direct and indirect speech acts and interactants who use them. *Journal of Personality and Social Psychology, 51,* 305–314.

Kiesler, S., Zubrow, D., Moses, A. M., & Geller, V. (1985). Affect in computer-mediated communication: An experiment in synchronous terminal-to-terminal discussion. *Human Computer Interaction, 1,* 77–104.

Jones, S. G. (1995). Understanding community in the information age. In S. G. Jones (Ed.), *Cybersociety: Computer-mediated communication and community* (pp. 10–35). Thousand Oaks, CA: Sage.

Kiesler, S., & Sproull, L. (1992). Group decision making and communication technology. *Organizational Behavior and Human Decision Processes, 52,* 96–123.

Lea, M., O'Shea, T., Fung, P., & Spears, R. (1992). 'Flaming' in computer-mediated communication: Observations, explanations, implications. In M. Lea (Ed.) *Contexts of computer-mediated communication* (pp. 89–112). London: Harvester Wheatsheaf.

Mabry, E. A. (1998). Frames and flames: The structure of argumentative messages on the net. In F. Sudweeks, M. McLaughlin, & S. Rafaeli (Eds.), *Network and netplay: Virtual groups on the internet* (pp. 13–26). Menlo Park, CA: AAAI Press/The MIT Press.

Mabry, E. A. (1999). The systems metaphor in group communication. In L. R. Frey, D. S. Gouran, & M. S. Pool (Eds.), *The handbook of group communication theory and research* (pp. 71–91). Thousand Oaks, CA: Sage.

Mabry, E. A. (in press). Technology as task: Rethinking the role of communication modality in the definition of group work and performance. In L. R. Frey (Ed.), *New directions in group communication.* Thousand Oaks, CA: Sage.

McGrath, J. E., & Hollingshead, A. B. (1994). *Groups interacting with technology.* Thousand Oaks, CA: Sage.

McKelton, D. -M., Mabry, E. A., & Katzman, S. (1997, November). *Sincerity in mediated communication.* Paper presented at the annual meeting of the National Communication Association, Chicago.

Messaris, P. (1998). Visual aspects of media literacy. *Journal of Communication, 48,* 70–80.

Rafaeli, S., & Sudweeks, F. E. (1998). Interactivity on the nets. In F. Sudweeks, M. McLaughlin, & S. Rafaeli (Eds.), *Network and netplay: Virtual groups on the internet* (pp. 173–190). Menlo Park, CA: AAAI Press/The MIT Press.

Rafaeli, S., Sudweeks, F., Konstan, J., & Mabry, E. (1998). ProjectH: A collaborative quantitative study of computer-mediated communication. In F. Sudweeks, M. McLaughlin, & S. Rafaeli (Eds.), *Network and netplay: Virtual groups on the internet* (pp. 265–281). Menlo Park, CA: AAAI Press/The MIT Press.

Rhee, J. W. (1997). Strategy and issue frames in election campaign coverage: A social cognitive account of framing effects. *Journal of Communication, 47,* 26–48.

Rheingold, H. (1993). *Virtual communities.* Reading, MA: Addison-Wesley.

Scott, C. R. (1999). Communication technology and group communication. In L. R. Frey, D. S. Gouran, & M. S. Pool (Eds.), *The handbook of group communication theory and research* (pp. 432–472). Thousand Oaks, CA: Sage

Siegel, J. Dubrovsky, V., Kiesler, S., & McGuire, T. (1986). Group processes in computer-mediated communication. *Organizational Behavior and Human Decision Processes, 37,* 157–187.

Snoeck Henkemans, A. F. (1989). Analyzing argumentative texts; The normative reconstruction of multiple and coordinatively compound argumentation. In B. E. Gronbeck (Ed.), *Spheres of argument: Proceedings of the Sixth SCA/AFA conference on argumentation* (pp. 331–334). Annendale, VA: SCA.

Snoeck Henkemans, A. F. (1991). The analysis of dialogical elements in argumentative texts. In F. van Eemeren, R. Grootendorst, J. A. Blair, & C. A. Willard (Eds.), *Proceeding of the Second International Conference on Argumentation* (pp. 365–370). Amsterdam: SICSAT.

Tatsuoka, M. M. (1971). *Multivariate analysis: Techniques for educational and psychological research.* New York: Wiley.

Winer, B. J. (1971). *Statistical principles in experimental design* (2nd. ed.). New York: McGraw-Hill.

20

The Transference of Frames in Global Television

Chris A. Paterson

People who do not live in or routinely travel to other countries have little opportunity to challenge their conception of the mass media provided "reality" of those countries. Mass media are almost wholly responsible for shaping that reality, and among mass media, television news is especially influential, for it alone provides our contemporary visual representations of most of the world (Behr & Iyengar, 1985; Larson, 1984; Ogundimu, 1992). Television news providers, in turn, receive most of their images and information relating to most of the nonlocal world from just a few global news organizations: television news agencies.

Many studies of television news are based on the concept of a shared reality manufactured by the social practices of journalists. I adopt this perspective to compare the framing of our political world by television broadcasters with that of their key sources—news agencies. This comparison of the actual texts of television newscasts from around the world with the stories distributed by their sources is intended to contribute to understanding the role of these few key sources for broadcasters in determining the framing of international news.

International newsgathering is a far too costly affair for all but the largest broadcasters, and even they (BBC, CNN, and the like) typically devote their own resources to just a few international stories at any one time. The wholesale level of global television news produces and disseminates the source material (video, sound, and information) for broadcasters worldwide which the broadcasters themselves cannot obtain with their own resources. This level of the television news sector consists of two commercial news agencies and a variety of cooperative news exchanges (the largest being Eurovision, based in Geneva). The television news agencies are the audio-visual counterparts to the wire services and are one and the same—Reuters and Associated Press.

These companies exercise considerable control over the world's television news agenda, for most broadcasters have few or no other nonlocal sources. There has been little study of these companies, their processes of news selection and production, or the effect of this concentration of sources. (The few recent analyses include Cohen, Levy, Roeh, Gurevitch, 1996; Hjarvard, 1995a, 1995b; Paterson, 1997, 1996; and Putnis, 1996).

Reuters Television is the former VisNews. AP's television division, APTN, is the newly formed combination of Worldwide Television News (WTN), itself once UPITN, and Associated Press Television (APTV). VisNews and WTN evolved from newsreel companies in the 1950s; APTV began in 1994, and bought WTN from its parent, Disney, in 1998. With the demise of WTN, the Associated Press and Reuters are now likely to remain the major providers of international television news for the foreseeable future. Each has made know its intention of dominating multimedia information provision.

These London based companies gather videotaped pictures and sound and story information continuously from about a dozen major bureaus and scores of minor ones, a far larger number of stringers, and from client television stations worldwide. The largest, Reuters Television, claims about 70 worldwide bureaus and over 220 client broadcasters in about 85 countries. They also pull stories from the European Broadcasting Union's (EBU) news exchange mechanism and other exchanges. They subsequently edit together their own story "packages" consisting of video and "natural" sound (that is, no added narration on most), and transmit them via satellite to clients in any of several daily "feeds," and via the EBU's Permanent News Network. Some audio commentary and electronic text (or "scripts") are also provided to clients, providing information to accompany the visuals.

News agencies do more than merely set news agendas, for they make the first decisions on how and if international stories—particularly those from the nonindustrialized world—will be covered. The traditional cost and difficulty of coverage make this especially true for television. News agendas are set and the framing of stories is determined through the choice of where to allocate agency resources, the selection of stories they distribute to clients, the amount of visuals provided, and the nature and amount of accompanying audio and textual information. Satellite capacity is costly, so words and images are chosen with care. Which are chosen, and to what effect?

We know that broadcasters tend to write their stories around what these organizations offer, and if they are not offered images, they will not report, or will minimize, an international story. Studies of television newsrooms have reported that the availability of visual images is an important factor in determining whether a foreign news story is included in a newscast (Cohen et al., 1996; Golding & Elliott, 1979; Helland, 1995; Molina, 1990; Rodriguez, 1996; Schlesinger, 1987).

Despite claims to the contrary by news agencies and some academic analyses, this study maintains that news images themselves convey meanings that cannot be, or routinely are not, substantially altered by the end users of those images. It is for this reason that the images of the world distributed by television news agencies are crucial determinants of popular perceptions. They may influence national and regional identities as well, especially if one's region is dependent on agency coverage due to the poverty of local media.

Television news agency impact is therefore dependent upon the influence of the portions of television newscasts to which the agencies contribute—primarily the visual component of international stories. After decades of study, there remains little consensus as to whether the messages conveyed by television news lie mostly in the auditory narrative or mostly in the visual (often agency provided) elements (Adams, 1982; Grabe, 1994; Graber, 1990; Grimes, 1990; Kozol, 1989). Tuchman (1978) observed that much of the literature of television news analysis, "naively suppose that news film captures reality without imposing its own rules" (p. 107). We must recognize the potential of agency images, sounds, and information to influence audience reception of a news story.

The agencies aggressively promote their ability to provide a "balanced," "objective," and "raw" view of the world, which permits any broadcaster to attach any "spin." They generally admit, however, that their newsfeeds concentrate upon news of the industrialized world. News managers explain that this is because these countries established them and (mostly) pay for them. Some argue, "news is news," and these countries are simply the most newsworthy. Several prominent news agency executives tell of how they have seen their pictures used one way by Israeli television, and another way by Arab broadcasters; and some academic analysts have faithfully repeated such assertions as proof that every broadcaster tells a different story with the material provided by news agencies. The claim of balance and objectivity has served the agencies in the promotion of their product and their growth.

This study complicates, and perhaps contradicts, the notion that infinite re-interpretations of television source material are either possible or likely. There is typically little variation among broadcasters in how agency visual and textual information is used to describe news events, and it seems common for highly subjective and interpretive (that is, ideological) aspects of news agency output to be reproduced in the news narratives of broadcasters around the world.

This quantitative and qualitative analysis of television news agency output indicates a number of textual consistencies between the product provided by the agencies and the product provided to audiences by broadcasters. Whether deemed themes, frames, or "ways of seeing" (Dahlgren & Chakrapani, 1982), a relatively small set of narratives and narrative devices are readily identified.

THE NEWS AGENCY FRAME

Hjarvard (1995a) previously identified key frames in the influential publicly funded Eurovison TV news exchange mechanism. He found the major theme of Eurovision and news agency news coverage to be "change in power" and reported that, in their Eurovision stories, television agencies focused almost exclusively on war, terrorism, diplomacy, and government. As other studies have found (e.g., Larson, 1984) a small number of countries receive heavy coverage, and most countries of the world receive little coverage. Yet news agencies represent themselves as global services covering the world for the world. The countries most dependent upon them—typically the smallest and poorest—are the most likely to be ignored, except occasionally in cases of extreme disaster.

Some general characteristics of the output of the three (at the time of this study) video agencies are revealed through content analysis. This involved the coding of most of their output for September 7 and 8, 1995, as part of a larger international news flow study, "Foreign News and International News Flow in the 1990s" (Sreberny, 1995). The major satellite news feeds from the agencies to broadcasters around the world were recorded and analyzed (with the generous cooperation of Reuters, WTN, and AP).

Agency stories averaged just over 2 minutes in length, ranging from 38 seconds to 5 minutes and 45 seconds. Of the total 256 stories, about one third were primarily concerned with issues of domestic or international conflict (n = 75, 29%). The main topic of a further one fourth was domestic or international politics (n = 59, 22%). These themes are explained by the traditional news agency and Eurovision (Hjarvard, 1995b) focus on strife, in this case including the breaking story of riots in Tahiti, and the ongoing story of war in Bosnia. The countries deemed by coders to be the most important in agency stories were most frequently the United States and Bosnia, each accounting for 12% of stories. The dominant type of main actor in the coded news agency stories was a state official or "nation" (n = 97, 38%).

The majority of agency stories during this period were about French nuclear testing and related protests (yet the war in Bosnia was the most common story among the broadcasters examined). Thirty-eight agency stories were about NATO bombing in Bosnia. A cross tabulation demonstrated that each of the three agencies were giving roughly equal coverage to these major stories. The causes of such a standardized television news agency agenda are explained in part by the following influences identified through analysis of agency production (Paterson, 1996):

- the similarity of extramedia factors influencing news production
- the similarity of news production routines
- competitive pressure to duplicate coverage by other agencies
- a universal focus on standard frames of news coverage deemed acceptable to clients

Before returning to the content study, I provide some additional observations about agency news framing based on the ethnographic observation and interviews over several months of 1995, which form the major portion of my news agency research. Schlesinger (1980) wrote that the ethnographic observations of moments of crisis in the television newsroom are revealing for their insights into how journalists revise their framing of news. In an agency the frames are so self-evident (and the types of stories so few) that such need for revision is rare.

For example, the standard visual grammar for the telling of an ex-Yugoslavia war story was so routine that many hours before an important turning point in the war—the fall of the city of Knin to Croatian troops—actually happened and any pictures had been shot, a WTN journalist confidently told me,

> The story today is the offensive (to capture) Knin, so we want (video of) the flag above Knin—that will be *the* picture—we want to have Croatian troops in Knin securing the place; you want to have the Krijina Serbs surrendering, retreating, or whatever, battle tanks burning, and that sort of thing, to tell the story.

The world is especially dependent on television news agencies for coverage of the developing world; the type of coverage most commonly critiqued as too distorted and too infrequent (e.g., Dahlgren & Chakrapani, 1982; Morales,1984; Paterson, 1992; Ramaprasad, 1993; Ungar & Gergen, 1991). The analysis of news production, however, rarely addresses such critiques. Textual analysis, and to a more limited extent, content analysis, can identify the existence of such frames, but only production ethnography can identify the causes of their reproduction.

For most agency staff, even those most frequently involved in scripting, the pictures are "the thing." Strong pictures arriving in a satellite feed evoke comment from throughout the newsroom; editors become almost giddy at the prospect of including them in their feeds. Comments like

"They're fantastic pictures" abound. A string of second rate pictures sours everyone's mood. A WTN editor deplored "talking head" video and would strive to use any other available shots to illustrate a story, remarking, "It's pathetic. People don't want all those talking heads. It's so boring."

As Rodriguez (1996) and others noted, television journalists often determine a story is a story on the basis of the availability of exciting or dramatic images to illustrate it. Television news agency workers are very much aware that such images make their product more valuable to clients. One WTN manager felt that the newsroom strives to balance "boring" video of diplomatic meetings with more exciting pictures whenever possible:

> It makes for extremely dull television a lot of the time. And we're always under a constant sort of self examination to try and have a limit to that kind of picture or at least have it balanced with fighting, or whatever. So if you've got your Brussels NATO conference and you can cut it with good pictures of aircraft taking off from aircraft carriers and people being shot up in Bosnia . . .

I frequently witnessed discussion about the preparation of outgoing stories which demonstrates this. Whenever related action pictures are available an effort is made to include them, especially where the main subject of the story involves unexciting pictures. If everyone involved in the production of an agency story implicitly understands how the raw footage and information arriving from the field are to be assembled, that assembly can happen faster and with fewer instructions or negotiations between news workers. Agency newsrooms would not function without a considerable shared understanding of narrative formulas for all kinds of agency stories. Seeking standard representational frames is more than a shared view of the news; it is a highly functional news production routine (Tuchman, 1978, p. 125).

One of the world's most famous news photographers, the late Mohamed Amin, described for me his experience of trying to convince his London VisNews (later Reuters) editors to use his African stories over the years, describing the representational frames traditionally sought by those editors:

> I have a lot of grievances with the decision makers, not necessarily with Reuters Television, but all of them. Because I think they live in a different world. They live in a completely different environment. They don't understand Africa. All they want out of Africa is death, blood, famine, corruption, and all that. We've got plenty of that in Africa—there's no shortage of that. But we've also got a hell of a lot of other stuff in Africa which is much more important to the continent than just the various wars that go on. I'm not suggesting for a second that these wars should not be covered—they have to be covered.

They're quite crucial in terms of the news coverage, but we should look at other stories as well.

A lack of familiarity with non-Western cultures negatively influences coverage of developing countries. Measurement of such influence is especially elusive, but examples emerged during my research. By way of illustration, while I was in the Reuters Television newsroom a story about the peace process in Angola arrived via satellite from the Reuters' Africa Bureau in Nairobi. Much of the tape contained footage of a traditional celebration. The Output Editor commented in disgust, "That's an entertainment story, isn't it? Six minutes, a bit of music, a bit of drums . . ." He deemed it to be improper illustration for a political story (according to the preferred news frames) and ordered old file footage of Jonas Savimbi attending meetings from the company archives to illustrate the story in place of the current footage.

CONNECTING SOURCES AND BROADCASTS

A comparative content analysis of newscasts from around the world during the study period (see Appendix) suggests a heavier dependence on television news agencies than the literature traditionally indicates. Coders visually searched for images provided to broadcasters by television news agencies in a two-day sample of television newscasts from around the world. Findings demonstrate a heavy reliance on the agencies and indications that decisions made by television news agency journalists significantly influence what international stories are told, what prominence they are given, and how they are told. 27 newscasts from 10 countries were compared with 10 hours of "raw" material fed to these broadcasters by satellite.[1] In all of those newscasts there were 185 nonlocal stories, 87 (47%) of which coders could ascertain contained images provided by television news agencies[2] (see Appendix).

---

[1]There is no way of knowing which news agency satellite feeds are received by or used by which broadcasters; this researcher has only partial information on the (normally confidential) subscription agreements between the agencies and the broadcasters.

[2]This study is a first attempt at such analysis. Many problems limit its generalizability and validity. For example, our sample of agency output included only what the agencies offered and included their major client feeds, but did not include everything these companies produced on the given days, nor would it have included agency material from days other than the ones studied. The detection of agency footage in broadcasts relied on the memory of the graduate student coders, and the careful, but ultimately imperfect, visual matching of agency images with newscast images. The amount of agency material found in newscasts is probably far lower than the actual, given these problems. The fact that an image was distributed internationally by a television news agency does not mean that it originated with that agency, but I have attempted to identify images not produced by the agencies and account for these.

Editing

Comparative analysis of story editing indicates a greater degree of news agency influence upon the local newscast's visual text than some studies have suggested. By not extensively re-editing agency material or adding images from other sources, broadcasters are allowing the news agencies to tell the story through their own arrangement of the pictures. Nonlocal narratives, and story frames, are therefore substantially dictated by the visual text created by a London news agency such as Reuters. Whether one accepts the editing process as highly or minimally influential in determining the meanings conveyed to the viewer, the fact that editing decisions are substantially made not by broadcasters, but by the few London based agencies, is a previously unrevealed and potentially crucial factor in the construction of international political discourse.

This practice is common among broadcasters worldwide. About 61%, or 53 of 87 news stories that could clearly be identified as containing television news agency footage, contained a substantial series of images edited by the news agency, not the broadcaster. Interestingly, these were stories produced by small broadcasters like Estonian TV or Future TV (Lebanon) *and* by large broadcasters, like CNN or Channel Four (UK).[3] Such minimal re-editing of agency product is a rational and efficient use by broadcasters of the costly services provided by the agencies, but it indicates a far higher reliance on the editorial decisions made by the agencies than has previously been revealed (or than the industry cares to acknowledge).

For example, the Finnish state broadcaster, YLE, on September 7, 1995, did their first international story about rioting in Tahiti. Most of this 146-second story contained footage from Reuters Television. In the YLE story large portions, including all the pictures in the first 30 seconds, was the edited visual text provided by Reuters in the story they fed to broadcasters. The images chosen and the manner in which they are connected tells a story of an angry mob invading an airport tarmac, viciously engaging lightly armed police in battle, and then looting the airport.

Finally, it is important to note that this study addresses the visual component of these newscasts only; in further analysis we will attempt to identify the extent to which information sent to broadcasters in textual and aural form also influences story construction. Participant observation and interviews with broadcasters suggest that when news agency video is used in a broadcaster's story, the television news agency is frequently also the main source, or the only source, for the aural narrative the broadcaster attaches to the pictures. Normally, this information comes from a written "script" which is transmitted by agencies directly to the computers in client newsrooms (detailed in Paterson, 1996).

[3]In some cases, the indication of heavy or total use of agency edits is the result of the broadcaster stringing together two or more extended sequences from different agency feeds.

YLE chose not to extensively re-edit agency material or add images from other sources, either of which might have changed the framing of this story. The YLE narrative *must* then be largely dictated by the visual text created by Reuters. The choice of a broadcaster to rely so heavily upon a news agency's telling of an important international story contradicts the argument alluded to earlier that global stories are substantially localized, or "domesticated," by local broadcasters—that there is indeed no "global" story.

The Run-Down

As London television news agencies prepare to satellite each new feed to client broadcasters throughout the day, agency "output editors" chose which stories go on the feed they are responsible for, and decide their "running order" or "line-up"—the sequence in which stories will be transmitted. There is considerable pressure from agency managers in regard to the important stories of the day, and which, therefore, should come first and last in the newsfeed. A typical passing comment from a news manager to a output editor regarding their story lineup came as a rebuke in the form of a question: ". . . you haven't put the China story on? I'd have thought for the 'A' (feed)" (referring to an afternoon trans-Atlantic feed). Output editors stray from the guidance of managers at their peril. At WTN, the news services manager, most directly responsible for output and most likely to shepherd the decisions of output editors, is also the person responsible for newsroom assignments and scheduling—a dominant form of punishment and reward for agency news workers.

The importance of the running order of news agency feeds cannot be overemphasized. For many broadcasters around the world, the priority that news agencies give stories, as indicated by their feed line-up and the amount of time given each story by the agencies substantially affect the story selection, running order, and time given to stories in the broadcaster's newscast. Preliminary agency run-down decisions come to broadcasters well in advance of the feed of pictures, leading broadcasters to plan their newscasts based largely upon the implicit agency promise that the first stories in the agency line-up will be the most newsworthy and the most visually interesting. Helland (1995) observed this phenomenon at the Norwegian commercial broadcaster, International News. He wrote:

> Because of the central position of the feeds in the news production apparatus, their content was obviously a determining factor in what news stories were selected to be carried in the news programs. The perceived quality of the feed sequences was also important for the running order of the news. Further-

TABLE 20.1
Importance of Story

	Comparison of Agency Line-Up With Broadcaster Line-Up		
Topic	Total number of agency stories on this topic (out of 256)	Average prominence given in agency feed line-ups to topic[1]	Average prominence given in newscast line-ups to topic[2]
Bosnia	48	HIGH, MID	5.6
Tahiti	37	HIGH	6.7
Beijing[3]	10	LOW	11.4
Lyon Bomb	8	MIDDLE	8

[1]For the purposes of this chart, HIGH prominence means that that the topic most frequently occurred in the first third of the news feed, MID means within the middle third, and LOW means in the last third. Agency feeds cover eight topics on average.

[2]Indicates distance from the first story in the newscast (i.e., the Lyon bombing was, on average, the eighth story in the newscasts examined).

[3]The final days of the Beijing U.N. Women's Conference.

more, the selection of the headline-stories was made with reference to the perceived news-worthiness of the available news pictures. (pp. 165–166)

If broadcasters often report a story only because they have news pictures to illustrate it, the importance of the international television news agency production process is especially apparent with small broadcasters who have no news gathering apparatus of their own, and choose to rely entirely on agency wholesale product to create their newscasts (an increasingly common trend among new commercial broadcasters worldwide).

Direct comparison of agency decisions on story importance with those of broadcasters is difficult. However, this study indicates some correlation between the two for the top stories of the day. Table 20.1 indicates the prominence given the top stories by the agencies as a whole (summarized here, given the complexity of this data), related to the average position of the story in all of the newscasts which carried it. Of course, in many newscasts, local news stories come first in the line-up. For example, the Bosnia story had high prominence in agency feed line-ups, and the highest prominence in the various newscasts examined, averaging between the fifth and sixth (5.6) story from the start of the newscast.

Differences Between Types of Broadcasters

On large, ongoing stories the wealthiest broadcasters will strive to avoid complete dependence on agency material, but smaller broadcasters, with little or no international news gathering capability of their own, typically demonstrate complete dependence on agency coverage.[4] For example, when antinuclear protests in Tahiti turned to violent demonstrations against French colonial rule, larger broadcasters could draw from the best agency coverage *and* coverage provided by videographers working directly for them or an allied network. (The important role of company alliances in television newsgathering is described by Paterson, 1996, Tunstall, 1992, and Wiener, 1992.)

NHK, the world's wealthiest public network, took only 54% of their coverage from agencies on the first day of the rioting; CNN took just 22%. In each case, these broadcasters have used the agencies to supplement coverage provided by their own videographers or allied companies. But smaller broadcasters could not similarly draw from such a diverse range of sources. Typically, we found that for smaller broadcasters, 80% or more of nonlocal coverage came from the agencies. It is probable that the remaining 20% may be accounted for as agency material we did not identify or material from other international sources to which the small broadcaster had access. Table 20.2 summarizes the differences in agency dependence for large and small broadcasters. Numbers represent the percentage of the broadcaster's story we could determine originated with an agency.

CONCLUSIONS

Although globalization trends suggest substantial growth of television news channels at the local, regional, and global levels, the sources for international television news—the television news agencies—remain a highly concentrated few. Recent trends suggest further homogenization of international news, despite the increase in news channels. For example, with substantial cutbacks to their own news operation, in 1993 Britain's ITN began exclusively using the international footage of its new shareholder, Reuters. Thus Reuters was supplying international news to every major British television newscast (BBC, ITN, and Sky)—virtually giving the British television viewer just one ideological window on much of the world.[5]

Why posit a homogeneous and hegemonic impact to news sources which seem so driven by competition and product differentiation? As Herman and Chomsky (1988) noted:

---

[4]The exception, of course, would be stories which are proximate to the smaller broadcaster, when they may be expected to invest in coverage of their own. Examples we encountered included heavy coverage by TVNZ of New Zealand of the French nuclear testing in the South Pacific, and heavy use of non-agency visuals for Middle-East coverage by a Lebanese commercial broadcaster.

[5]*Broadcast*, May 28, 1993; Westcott (1995) confirms that "Reuters now supplies news to all of the major UK broadcasters" (p. 22). The BBC has continued to draw international coverage from their own extensive resources and WTN and eventually added APTV.

TABLE 20.2
Percentage of Agency Footage in Major Stories

Broadcaster	Tahiti Day 1	Tahiti Day 2	Average Agency Use Over Both Days	Balkans Day 1	Balkans Day 2	Average Agency Use Over Both Days	China Day 1	China Day 2	Average Agency Use Over Both Days
CNN	22	NC	22	9	No Data	9	NC	NC	
BBC	35	27	31	24	0	12	NC	NC	
ABC (US)	58	NC	58	40	0	20	0	NC	0
NHK	54	100	77	NC	21	21	NC	NC	
Average agency usage for large broadcasters (by story)	47			16			0		
Cyprus	79	No Data	79	90	No Data	90	100	No Data	100
Finland	81	NC	81	100	0	50	NC	NC	
Lebanon	53	100	76	100	27	63	34	82	58
Estonia	NC	NC		NC	NC		100	NC	100
Average agency usage for small broadcasters (by story)	79			84			90		

Notes. 1. Numbers are percentages. Each daily percentage represents *seconds of identifiable news agency footage/total seconds of footage* used by that broadcaster to tell that story.

2. NC indicates broadcaster did not cover this story on this day.

It is much more difficult to see a propaganda system at work where the media are private and formal ownership is absent. This is especially true where the media actively compete, periodically attack and expose corporate and government malfeasance, and aggressively portray themselves as spokesmen for free speech and the general community interest. (p. 1)

The dominance of a few powerful media alliances in the provision of international news product means that news, in both print and electronic form, from much of the world, is now determined and provided by what is essentially a single editorial perspective—that of a small number of culturally homogeneous news workers in just two similar and occasionally allied Anglo-American news organizations based in London (APTN and Reuters).

Global television news production and distribution has become a fairly minor commodity subset of the cultural production of a few highly diversified transnational conglomerates. This is certainly the case at Reuters, where news is just 10% or less of the company's business; it is arguably true of Associated Press, which despite its claims to operate as a not-for-profit cooperative in service to member companies, increasingly acts like any other multinational communications firm. My extended ethnographic research with television news agencies demonstrated that they are more inclined to treat major corporations and Western governments as acceptable sources (of information or video images) than institutions from developing countries, and that management and news processing structures are designed not to insulate journalists' decisions from commercial considerations but to insure that such considerations prevail at all levels of news production.

Television news coverage of the developing world is likely to diminish and become increasingly more homogeneous. Globally, television news is also being seen less as a special case—a form of television that provides a needed sociopolitical function—than as just another transnational cultural commodity. The increasing control of global news production and flow by a decreasing number of institutions suggests a variety of dangers, as posited by Smith (1990), Bagdikian (1992), and others. The cultural product of the international television news agencies serves to perpetuate a Western hegemony hostile to developing nations. The diverse "marketplace of ideas" news would ideally represent is diminished. News agency dominance in international news provision in online media compounds the problem.

There are indications that through much of modern society, television news is playing an ever increasing role as the vehicle for essential civil discourse, the public sphere. Habermas (1989) summarized this as "a domain of our social life in which such a thing as public opinion can be formed" (p. 231). Hjarvard (1993) has theorized the potential development of a (useful) pan-European public sphere resulting from the increased influence of pan-

European television news services and the decreasing influence of national news.

There is no reason not to extend this argument globally. The globalization of television news is producing an international public sphere, but one dominated by mainstream Anglo-American ideologies conveyed in the texts of internationally distributed television news. Hallin (1994) raised the specter of an "international public sphere," but similarly noted that most countries are excluded from any political dialogues it entails (see also Venturelli, 1993).

The perception of a single, valid, and globally appropriate view of news is so pervasive among international television news agency workers and among broadcast journalists worldwide that cultural relevance (Duarte & Straubhaar, 1996) matters little in global television news distribution. And equality of information flow is similarly immaterial—for as long as the pictures of the world's news arrive each day from people with *the* shared understanding of news, its means of production and distribution are irrelevant technicalities.

This study demonstrates that the frames placed around international news stories by television news agencies (as determined by their production and distribution decisions and processes) do carry through to the stories that are broadcast and to the construction of newscasts, especially in the case of smaller broadcasters, which are highly dependent on agency product. Despite the increasing number of news services, ownership is highly concentrated, and broadcasters are becoming increasingly dependent upon just two news providers to supply the international images they use on the air. These images influence the framing of international television news stories.

Key elements of the news texts to which audiences are exposed (the texts from which we learn so much about our world) are effectively predetermined by a core group of journalists in London and, to a lesser extent, their operatives worldwide. As the corporatization of journalism increasingly demands cheaper newsgathering, the influence of agencies will increase. Consequently, the framing of news agency stories—in terms of importance, emphasis, and innumerable subtleties—must increasingly influence, if not determine, the framing of stories ultimately broadcast.

ACKNOWLEDGMENTS

Earlier versions of this chapter were presented to the 1997 USC conference on Media Framing and the 1998 meeting of the International Association for Media and Communication Research in Glasgow. The author is indebted to the companies and journalists who permitted extensive research into their news operations, to Georgia State University and the University of Texas for their support of this research, and to principal coder Andrea Thomas.

APPENDIX: STUDY DATA SET

Videotapes of the primary global satellite news feeds for September 7 and September 8, 1995 were provided courtesy of Reuters Television, Worldwide Television News, and Associated Press Television.

Coders used the major early evening television newscasts from the following broadcasters. The author is indebted to several researchers participating in the "Foreign News and International News Flow in the 1990s" international news flow study for providing videotapes.

Cyprus (one day only); Estonia: AK; Finland: MTV3, YLE; Germany: ARD Tagesschau; Greece: Mega Channel (one day only); Japan: NHK7, TV Asahi; Lebanon: Future TV; New Zealand: One Network News; United Kingdom: BBC 9 O'clock News, Channel 4 News, ITN News At Ten; USA: ABC, World News Tonight, CNN International World News (one day only).

REFERENCES

Adams, W. (1982). *Television coverage of international affairs.* Norwood, NJ: Ablex.

Bagdikian, B. (1992). *The media monopoly* (4th ed.). Boston : Beacon Press.

Behr, R. L., & Iyengar, S. (1985). Television news, real-world cues, and changes in the public agenda. *Public Opinion Quarterly, 49,* 38–57.

Boyd-Barrett, O., & Thussu, K. (1992). *Contra-flow in global news.* London: John Libbey.

Broadcast (1993). *Sky seeks co-op deals as route to expansion.* London, May 28, p. 1.

Broadcasting and Cable (1993). Special Report—News Services: *Filling Changing Needs and Niches.* May 31, 27–44.

Cohen, A., Levy, M., Roeh, I., & Gurevitch, M. (1996). *Global newsrooms, local audiences: A study of the Eurovision news exchange.* London: John Libbey.

Dahlgren, P., & Chakrapani, S. (1982). The developing nation on TV news: Western ways of seeing the other. In W. Adams (Ed.), *Television coverage of international affairs* (pp. 45–65). Norwood, NJ: Ablex.

Duarte, L. G., & Straubhaar, J. (1996, May). *Cultural proximity, class and the emergence of satellite TV services in Latin America.* Paper presented to the International Communications Association annual meeting, Chicago.

Fenby, J. (1986). *The International News Services. A Twentieth Century Fund Report.* New York: Schocken.

Foote, J. (1995). Structure and marketing of global television news. *Journal of Broadcasting and Electronic Media, 39*(1), 127–133.

Friedland, L. (1992). Covering the world: International television news services. Paper for the Twentieth Century Fund.

Fuller, C. (1995). Elbowing for news room. *TV World,* October, 63–66.

Gans, H. (1980). *Deciding what's news.* New York: Vintage.

Golding, P., & Elliott, P. (1979). *Making the news.* New York: Longman.

Gonzenbach, W., Arant, M., & Stevenson, R. (1991, August). *The world of U.S. network television news: Eighteen years of foreign news coverage.* Paper presented to the Association for Education on Journalism and Mass Communications meeting, Boston.

Grabe, M. (1994, August). South African Broadcasting Corporation coverage of the 1987 and 1989 elections: The matter of visual bias. Paper presented to the Association for Education on Journalism and Mass Communications meeting, Atlanta.

Graber, D. (1990). Seeing is remembering: How visuals contribute to learning from television news. *Journal of Communication, 40*(3), 134–151.

Grimes, T. (1990). Encoding TV news messages into memory. *Journalism Quarterly, 67*(4), 757–766.

Gurevitch, M., Levy, M., & Roeh, I. (1991). The global newsroom: Convergences and diversities in the globalization of television news. In P. Dahlgren & C. Sparks (Eds.), *Communications and citizenship: Journalism and the public sphere in the new media age* (pp. 195–215). London: Routledge.

Habermas, J. (1989). *On society and politics: A reader.* S. Seidman (Ed.), Boston: Beacon Press.

Hallin, D. C. (1994). *We keep America on top of the world: Television journalism and the public sphere.* Routledge: London.

Helland, K. (1995). *Public service and commercial news.* Unpublished doctoral dissertation, Norway, University of Bergen.

Herman, E., & Chomsky, N. (1988). *Manufacturing consent.* New York: Pantheon.

Hjarvard, S. (1993). Pan-European television news: Towards a European political public sphere. In P. Drummond, R. Paterson, & J. Willis (Eds.), *National identity and Europe. The television revolution.* London: British Film Institute.

Hjarvard, S. (1995a). *Internationale TV-nyheder. En historisk analyse af det europeiske system for udveksling af internationale TV-nyheder* [International television news: An historical analysis of the European system for the exchange of International television news]. Unpublished doctoral dissertation, Copenhagen.

Hjarvard, S. (1995b). Eurovision news in a competitive marketplace. *EBU Diffusion,* Autumn.

Johnston, C. B. (1995). *Winning the global TV news game.* Boston: Focal Press.

Kozol, W. (1989). Representations of race in network news coverage of South Africa. In G. Burns & R. Thompson (Eds.), *Television studies: Textual analysis* (pp. 165–182). New York: Praeger.

Larson, J. (1984). *Television's window on the world: International affairs coverage on the U.S. networks.* Norwood, NJ: Ablex.

Molina, G. G. (1990). *The production of Mexican television news: The supremacy of corporate rationale.* Unpublished doctoral dissertation, Leicester University.

Morales, W. Q. (1984). Latin America on network TV. *Journalism Quarterly, 61*(1), 157–160.

Ogundimu, F. (1992, November). Media coverage, issue salience, and knowledge of Africa in a midwestern university. Paper presented to the African Studies Association meeting, Seattle.

Paterson, C. (1992). Television news from the frontline states. In B. Hawk (Ed.), *Africa's media image* (pp. 176–191). New York: Praeger.

Paterson, C. (1996). *News production at worldwide television news (WTN): An analysis of television news agency coverage of developing countries.* Unpublished doctoral dissertation, University of Texas at Austin.

Paterson, C. (1997). Television news agency coverage of international conflict. *Journal of International Communication, 4*(1), 50–62.

Putnis, P. (1996). Producing overseas news for Australian television. *Australian Journal of Communication, 23*(3), 1–21.

Ramaprasad, J. (1993). Content, geography, concentration, and consonance in foreign news coverage of ABC, NBC, and CBS. *International Communications Bulletin, 28*(1–2), 10–14.

Rodriguez, A. (1996). Made in the USA: The production of the noticiero univision. *Critical Studies in Mass Communication, 13*(1), 59–82.

Schiller, H. (1991). Not yet the post-imperialist era. *Critical Studies in Mass Communication, 8*, 13–28.

Schlesinger, P. (1980). Between sociology and journalism. In H. Christian (Ed.), *Sociology of the press and journalism.* Keele, England: University of Keele.

Schlesinger, P. (1987). *Putting 'reality' together: BBC News* (2nd ed.). London: Routledge.

Smith, A. (1990). Media globalism in the age of consumer sovereignty. *Gannett Center Journal, 8*(4), 1–16.

Sreberny, A. (1995). International news flow in the post-cold war world: Mapping the news and the news producers. *Electronic Journal of Communication, 5*(2&3).

Tuchman, G. (1978). *Making news: A study in the construction of reality.* New York: Free Press.

Tunstall, J. (1992). Europe as world news leader. *Journal of Communication, 42*(3).

Ungar, S. J., & Gergen, D. (1991). *Africa and the American media.* Occasional paper for the Freedom Forum Media Studies Center, New York: Columbia University.

Venturelli, S. (1993). Democracy as fiction in the transnational public sphere. *Media Development, 4.*

Westcott, T. (1995). Getting mighty crowded. *Television Business International*, November, 18–22.

Wiener, R. (1992). *Live from Baghdad: Gathering news at ground zero.* New York: Doubleday.

Epilogue—Framing at the Horizon: A Retrospective Assessment

Oscar H. Gandy, Jr.

Funny thing about the horizon. No matter how far or how fast you walk toward it, it never gets any closer. Indeed, as we are often reminded, if we walk toward the horizon long enough, we eventually arrive back at the point from which we began our journey. Along the way, however, we often have a sense of making progress because the landscape appears to have changed so dramatically.

The scholars who have contributed to this volume have helped to mark our apparent progress by means of the trees, orchards, hills, and mountain ranges that they have chosen as markers, or goals that they have defined as being both essential, and within our reach. Along the way, we've taken some notice of landmarks that I feel are particularly important as markers of our progress: (a) We have come closer to a definition of what we mean by framing as a paradigm through which to study communication; (b) we have noted similarities and differences between framing and agenda setting as research programs that have particular relevance to the study of mass media effects; (c) we have examined a number of distinct frames that have come to dominate both media content and public discourse regarding issues of critical concern; and (d) we have also explored some of the ways in which differences in experience, socialization, motivation, knowledge, skill, responsibility, and the like, help to predict which frames will succeed in reinforcing, or even transforming individual knowledge, attitudes, or behavior. At one level, this seems like quite a lot. But from a more critical perspective, we ought to recognize that there are several blindspots or lacunae in our thinking about framing.

In this chapter I call your attention to the ways in which our authors come closer to, but still stop short of, our desired goal, that of establishing the place of framing research at the core of communications study. After establishing an initial framework, I discuss some critical differences between scholars at the level of theory and method. Some of these differences are illustrated quite clearly in the case studies included in this volume. After noting these, we turn our attention to some of the shifts in the framing resources that have become available to communicators in the information environment that has been transformed so dramatically by developments in networked computing. I finish with an appeal for a doubling of our efforts.

A FRAMEWORK FOR REFLECTION

In thinking about the ground we have covered, as well as the insights we have apparently missed by following a different path, or succumbing to some momentary distraction, I have been reminded of an earlier assessment made by Chaffee in 1977. Reflecting at that time on the nature of scholarship in mass communication, Chaffee suggested that we might understand our approach to the study of media effects by organizing our knowledge into categories defined by an 18-cell matrix. In describing this matrix, Chaffee suggested that media scholars have tended to distinguish between different kinds of effects. First, there were those that are determined by nature of the medium (its physical or structural characteristics, or the nature of the contexts in which it was used). Second, there were those effects that might be determined by exposure to specific media content. The engagement with framing and its effects by the contributors to this volume can be similarly divided, especially if we understand broad categories of frames, like "episodic" and "thematic" (Iyengar, 1991) or "strategy" and "issue" as being essentially content free, stylistic or format classifications (Cappella & Jamieson, 1997).

Chaffee's matrix included two additional dimensions along which our knowledge of media effects might be assessed. One dimension, which still seems to dominate our thinking about framing, is that which characterizes effects as being primarily cognitive or affective (attitudinal), rather than behavioral. The final dimension Chaffee identified is one that emphasizes differences in the level or scale of effect. Media (and communication) effects can be observed and evaluated at individual, interpersonal, or institutional (perhaps, societal or cultural) levels of analysis. Then, as now, our emphasis on framing effects as a subset of media effects more generally seems to have been focused primarily within an extremely limited number of cells: the effects of media frames on individual attitudes.

This characterization is not intended to ignore the important theoretical and empirical work that has been focused on attempting to understand the mechanisms that operate at the level of cognition. This important work has led us to examine how frames are implicated in the priming or activation of memories, which are themselves embedded in complex networks of schemata (Cappella & Jamieson, 1997).

My characterization of what we have and have not accomplished is also not intended to give short shrift to the body of interpretive work that attempts to go below the surface level of texts. Such work seeks to find the deeper structural connections between frames that operate, perhaps at the level of an ideological core (Deacon, Pickering, Golding & Murdock, 1999; Stillar, 1998). And I certainly don't intend for us to ignore the important work that builds on Gamson (1992), and others who have been extending social movement theory through a focus on the promotion of issue frames (Obershall, 1993). There is much to appreciate in the work of scholars who have examined how movement sponsored frames become aligned with and amplify other political frames (Morris & Meuller, 1992).

To a great extent, neither Chaffee's matrix nor the authors we have included in this volume have taken us very far "outside the box." There has not been much of an effort to examine the origins of frames, or the factors that determine which frames will dominate the various channels of communication through which they flow. Work that examines the strategic use of particular frames does not fit well within the matrix that Chaffee describes because he, and the field, have tended to treat media content and media system characteristics as given. We rarely make either content or form the dependent variables in our theoretical models, hypotheses, or research questions. As a result, with the exception of Pan and Kosicki's and Hertog and McLeod's efforts within this volume, very few of us attempt to identify those factors that influence how framing strategies develop, diffuse, and may ultimately become parts of the information environment.

As Rogers and Dearing (1988) noted in their review of agenda-setting research, studies that focus on the influences on media content are quite rare, and thus I am not surprised that very little framing research goes beyond describing and, on occasion, comparing the frames that different media seem to prefer. Dunwoody and Griffin (1997) called for greater attention to be paid to understanding the macrosocial influences on news construction. This is work that pushes the boundaries of the traditional concept of community pluralism. Their work makes it clear that the competitive status of media markets is only one of the many social, institutional, and structural influences that help to determine which frames will be preferred by institutional communicators. In my own work, for example, I have attempted to examine some of the structural influences in newspaper markets that influence the selection of frames for understanding the differences in social risks faced by Whites and African Americans (Gandy, Kopp, Hands, Frazer, & Phillips, 1997; Goshorn & Gandy, 1995).

I think it unfortunate that there has been so little effort applied toward following the lead of the Northwestern University group that studied investigative journalism (Protess, Cook, Doppelt, Ettema, Gordon, Leff, & Miller, 1991). It is important for us to explore the nature and extent to which coalitions or partnerships that develop between journalists and politicians help to frame investigative reports as well as the policy reforms that follow.

Understanding framing in the context of what the organizers of the South Carolina conference called "the new media environment" also seems to me to require some knowledge of how the development and diffusion of new media systems unfolds. It seems important for us to understand how the emergence of the networked computer is governed by a set of influences that mark a particular moment in time. Long wave theorists like Carlotta Perez have described these influences in terms of their "harmonic complementarity" (Hall & Preston, 1988). James Beniger (1986) has discussed the same process in terms of a "control revolution," through which the development and diffusion of innovations in communication reflects a chain of responses to different crises of control.

Engagement with these system level, macrostructural approaches would allow us to engage theoretical concerns about shifts in culture, and shifts in the popular spirit, that are reflected in a variety of communicative forms, from headlines to popular songs. Here I refer to the cycles of pessimism and optimism that on occasion bear only a distant relationship to objective indicators of the quality of life or the concrete social experiences of the masses of people. The "doing better, but feeling worse" mentality that overtakes a nation from time to time, may be attributed to the character of media competition that leads editors to favor bad news and hard times. Cappella and Jamieson (1997) argued that there is a link between the news media's use of strategic frames and the rise of cynicism among the American public. What they have not helped us to understand is the routine pressures are that lead the press to rely so heavily on such frames, even when opportunities to do otherwise abound.

This is in part the challenge that Durham sets before us in his chapter 6. A journalistic practice informed by an emergent postmodern sensibility might seek to attract and maintain the attention of its audience, not through sensationalist despair, but through the kinds of cognitive stimulation that a multitude of possibilities might produce. Durham's idealized postmodern openness may in fact come to characterize the "news" in the multidimensional hypertext environment that Pavlik and Fredin describe in their chapters.

CRITICAL DIFFERENCES AND MEANINGFUL DISTINCTIONS

Because our understanding of the nature of frames involves some consideration of the roles that conceptual frameworks may play in struggles over power and position, we did well in this volume to reflect some of the struggle taking place within our own field. Specifically, I refer to the unsettled relations between framing and agenda setting as theoretical paradigms. McCombs and Ghanem (chap. 2, this volume) describe relations between the perspectives as closely aligned and compatible, if not indistinguishable, at a fundamental core. On the basis of this assessment they invite an accelerated convergence of interests and effort around the identification of the *attributes* of communications that matter in the public sphere. On the other hand, Maher (chap. 3, this volume) was committed to sharpening the conceptual distinctions between the concept of frames and framing preferred by those most closely identified with this emerging paradigm, and how the process would be understood in the context of an "agenda-of-attributes" perspective.

Reflecting an awareness of the paradox of horizons, McCombs and Ghanem find irony in what they see as a return within media studies to an emphasis on attitudes and cognition. This irony is based in the fact that agenda setting emerged as an alternative to the assumption of "limited effects" that dominated thinking about mass communication in the 1940s and 1950s. Although the agenda-setting hypothesis assumes that the "pictures in our heads" are equivalent—especially when they are defined as "issues," and therefore appropriately comparable in terms of salience—it is not at all clear that this assumption is warranted. Indeed, much of what we have learned about framing suggests that the same event or related issue is understood quite differently depending upon the frames used to define it. Maher's analysis helps to make the implications of this distinction clear, as does the "pizza experiment" that Nelson and Willey describe in chapter 15.

We also observed that parallels between the agenda-setting and framing traditions of scholarship do not extend to a consideration of the resources that are available to actors that enable them to influence the understanding of issues. In addition, by exploring the conceptual links that exist between framing and systems theories, Maher underscores the importance of the *relationship* as a critical component of both analytic traditions. It is the relationships among elements in a message, as well as the relationships between those elements and sponsors' strategic interests that help to explain the emergence of particular frames. Agenda setting has traditionally taken the distribution of issues, events, and arguments that appear in the press as given, whereas the origins of frames, and the factors that determine their survival or decline, should be at the core of framing research.

Concerns About Methodology

Becker's (1982) assessment of the initial and subsequent body of research into the agenda-setting process is especially critical of the use of aggregate level measures of an effect that is discussed primarily as occurring at the individual level. Becker suggested that claims of an individual impact required the comparison of newspaper agendas with individual agendas. It would be fair to say that similar problems have to be addressed if we are to understand the ways in which framing affects social being at individual, interpersonal, and higher levels of aggregation.

Becker was also critical of the ways in which the relevant "variables" had been defined in much of the early work on agenda setting. Salience, or issue importance, is not a unitary concept, and the ways in which respondents might be asked to assess it can produce quite different rankings. Issues can be seen to be personally important, or they can be seen as being important to "people like me." As we have come to recognize in recent years, identification with social groups is the product of a complex of influences, and the salience of personal attributes, such as race, or gender will vary considerably among individuals (Cornell & Hartmann, 1998). Cues imbedded within a survey question or the context of research may prime or activate one or more of an individual's identities, which will then be used as a reference or guide in responding to an inquiry about the relative importance of issues or events. Such responses will be quite different from those generated when subjects are asked to evaluate the importance, or implications of these concerns for the nation as a whole. Recent work on what has been defined as a "third person effect" (Hoffner et al., 1999) as well as that which examines the nature of in-group and out-group distinctions in social perception (Sniderman, Piazza, & Kendrick, 1991) underscore the importance of being clear about exactly whose impressions are being described.

Along these lines, Tankard (chap. 4, this volume) emphasized some of the difficulty involved identifying and distinguishing between the frames that appear in the media. The difficulties, both methodological and conceptual, are the problems of reliability and validity that are especially troublesome in the analysis of media texts and political discourse. The problems of achieving and assessing the reliability of content analyses continue to limit our ability to understand the production, distribution, and reception of symbolic frames (Deacon et al., 1999; Riffe, Lacy, & Fico, 1998; Stillar, 1998). Even as the more tangible character of computer mediated communication makes the discourse of ordinary folks more readily available for analysis, not even computer automation overcomes the problems of meaningful classification, as Mabry (chap. 20) has shown in his chapter.

Because of the great complexity of issue frames, their identification tends be rather subjective. Although the discursive terrain of a particular issue may include a wide variety of distinct frames, Tankard also suggests that each frame may be marked or distinguished on the basis of the presence of specific keywords, catchphrases, and images. However, the fact that acceptable levels of reliability are achieved only when lists of frames are collapsed into two (e.g., support vs. opposition) suggests paradoxically that much of the meaningful insights that a framing perspective might ultimately provide is threatened by the demands of scientific precision (Deacon et al., 1999).

We see some signs of progress in the frame mapping methodology described by Miller and Riechert (chap. 5, this volume). Their use of multidimensional scaling and cluster analysis techniques may be understood as a way of standardizing and then automating some of the techniques used by more qualitative analysts. Still, the problem of interpretation remains. Miller and Riechert suggest, for example, the need to distinguish between the naïve constructions of ordinary folk, and the more sophisticated constructions of elites and political operatives.

Much work and considerable effort will be required if we are to understand much more about the life of frames and the nature of the competitive struggle between sources and sponsors, or advocates of particular frames. Domke and his colleagues have begun to make use of a sophisticated computer-analysis program to derive a number of novel insights into the relationships between media frames and elite political strategy (Domke, Watts, Shah, & Fan, 1999). Framing analyses have most often been used to illustrate the existence of bias within the media. This study helps us to understand the appearance of such claims within the mainstream press. Claims of liberal media bias have been reported with increasing frequency in the presidential elections of 1988, 1992, and 1996. Domke and his colleagues observed that conservative claims of liberal media bias were more likely to appear when Republican candidates were receiving rather favorable coverage in the press. Because such coverage indicates that conservatives and their allies were able to exercise greater control over their party's media image, it made sense for them to push their advantage by challenging the press. Thus, claims of bias were being used strategically to maintain the flow of positive stories about Republican candidates.

We might understand this finding as being consistent with the notion of a "Spiral of Opportunity" that Miller and Reichert explore in this volume. Especially important in their chapter is their emphasis on the rise and fall of frames within the life span of an issue. This historical process can be understood from a number of perspectives that emphasize conflict, assume progress toward equilibrium, or seek to identify the complementary linkages between systems that evidence a cyclical pattern (Baumgartner & Jones, 1993). Hertog and McLeod's chapter 7 provides explicit guidance, in addition to being a first-rate example of the way framing analysis might proceed. Going beyond the text to include other cultural artifacts, as well as the individualized expressions of frame sponsors and activists, increases the possibility that the "life of frames" will come to make sense within theories that are continually being tested against the flow of history.

Concern About Meaning

It is not clear that progress in the analysis of framing can be guided solely by research traditions that depend primarily on the analysis of symbolic materials. Although Gerbner talks about the power of media as being inherent in the nature of the stories that are repeatedly told, the content analyses at the heart of cultivation research are almost never about stories (Gerbner, 1998). The analyses are about acts of violence. They are about characters and their attributes. *Stories* are far more complex; they involve plots and subplots, each of which may make a statement about persons, institutions, and relationships. As Gerbner describes the method of content analysis appropriate for the identification of symbolic functions, four categories of content are generally produced by questions asked of the media text. These are questions about *existence* (which ought to mean absence, as well as presence), *priority or importance, evaluative assessments,* and *relationships between elements identified in response to the first question.*

Although there are more labor-intensive methods of content analysis that use the sentence, the evaluative assertion, or even the dramatic scene as the primary unit of analysis, most of the analyses invoked in support of cultivation effects are focused at the level of the television program. At this level of aggregation, the probability of saying anything useful about the relations between characters, acts, circumstances, and outcomes is really quite low. The same applies to the analysis of frames. If our analysis of frames is governed by an assumption that frames have a structuring influence on the meanings derived from a text, our analytical design has to incorporate a theory of meaning, interpretation, or sense-making. The contributions made by Osgood, Suci, and Tannenbaum (1957) to our understanding of the multiple dimensions of meaning ought not be ignored. Among the many insights to be derived from reflection on the nature of the semantic differential technique is the way in which particular attributes of "objects" may be emphasized, while others are ignored.

McCombs and Ghanem's contribution to this volume has emphasized the salience or importance of issues (or policy objects) in part because salience, or relative importance, is what rank-order correlation assumes to matter. On the other hand, the semantic differential technique emphasizes opposition, or difference, rather than priority. Recall that the use of the technique involves the selection of a number of bipolar adjectives, differentiated in seven intervals (Darnell, 1970). Although the results are never entirely independent of the adjectives selected, a three-factor structure usually emerges from the assessment of numerous attitude objects. Whereas there are many possible dimensions to be found, the use of this particular technique reveals the nearly universal reliance on evaluation (good–bad), potency (strong–weak), and activity (fast–slow) as core aspects of meaning. As a technique, the semantic differential, like Rokeach's (1968) value sort makes it possible to characterize populations in terms of shared meanings. It also makes it easy to identify differences among subgroups, as well as to predict and explain changes in meaning over time, or in response to experimental manipulations. In addition, the semantic differential technique is complexly relational, rather than a simple rank order of objects or attributes. Attitude objects can be located in a multidimensional semantic space.

Part of the challenge we face in linking the meaning of objects to the political realm, where *issues* become the focus of political talk, is to understand how particular attitude objects (persons, members of groups) come to be characterized and differentiated in semantic space. For example, we might note that affirmative action, as an issue of public concern, is understood, and supported or opposed, in part because of the ways in which beneficiaries and victims are framed. Kinder and Sanders (1996), for example, suggested that construction of African Americans as victims, deserving of assistance, was changed over time, perhaps in response to coverage of militant nationalists and the civil disorder that swept across the nation's cities. The more recent framing of affirmative action as a "zero-sum conflict of interest between whites and blacks" (Entman, 1998) both supports, and is supported by, the construction of African Americans as undeserving.

CASE STUDIES

The special character and contribution of recent framing research is reflected in several of the case studies we have included in this volume. Each makes considerable progress toward addressing the concerns raised by Reese, Pan and Kosicki, and Maher in their chapters.

If we understand framing as a strategic device useful for attracting audience attention and then controlling its movement through the narrative, then there is special value in observing the use of particular devices in the telling of particular stories. Indeed, following the suggestions of Miller and Reichart, we might take note of the ways in which the primacy or popularity of framing devices changes over the life of a story or public issue.

For example, Dickerson (chap. 8, this volume) makes use of an expanded notion of an episodic frame (Iyengar, 1991) to illustrate the use of different framing techniques in ways that we might expect to produce markedly different "understandings" of objectively similar stories. Dickerson's analysis takes due note of the departure from journalistic framing traditions that characterized the *New York Times'* construction of Leonard Jeffries. Her approach is similar to that taken by McManus (1994) in explaining the departure of television news portrayals from the ideals of journalism in the public interest. McManus places the departures he observes in the context of a theory of economic rationality. Dickerson, on the other hand, explains the *Times'* departures as a function of the constraints that are inherent in the nature of racial and ethnic group identity, ideology, or world view. Framing analyses that seek to explain *departures* from the routine have the potential to develop more useful theoretical insights than those that merely describe the commonplace. Such studies help identify some of the hidden constraints that operate within media systems.

Among the more unusual departures that we have examined are those rare occasions when the press turns its attention inward and reflects on its own role as part of the story. Zoch's chapter 11 calls our attention to the variety of ways in which members of the press can shape public awareness of the industrial technology behind the news they consume each day. An awareness that the news is constructed, rather than merely gathered and transmitted, is bound to affect the way news is consumed by its audience. Zoch actually found only one frame that might be read as potentially critical of the press—that which compared the coverage of the Smith trial as being another example of the "media circus" that accompanied the trial of O. J. Simpson.

Wiggins (chap. 12, this volume) interpreted *The State's* coverage of a lesbian wedding as though it were just another routine story about a romantic and spiritual union. Here again, a news story departs from the journalistic routine. This time it was not journalists that called for reflection, it was the readers. Letters to the editor provided an insight into the way readers of the story responded to what they saw as an unusual and inappropriate framing. The letters provided access to the kinds of frames that opponents and defenders of same-sex marriage use in their own discursive engagement with the underlying issue. Contrary to the findings reported by Miller and Reichert in which the use of particular frames could be predicted from the identification of the source, Wiggins found that the use of religious references did not distinguish supporters from opponents. The readers of *The State* are part of the cultural environment in which framing takes place. Many of the published letters, experienced as a tangible and palpably negative response to the publication of the story, helped to change the way this particular newspaper would frame its stories in the future. In the short term, the letters actually generated a published apology. Wiggins also describes actions that we might understand as a long-term act of contrition on the part of the paper. A follow-up study would no doubt find that the willingness of *The State* to risk the use of nonstandard frames in the realm of religious belief had been greatly reduced by the response of its readership.

Chapter 14 by Shah, Domke, and Wackman takes another approach. Their study exemplifies an increasing number of experimental efforts that are extending the boundaries of our knowledge of framing effects. Such studies explore how journalistic frames help to shape political views. As the authors suggest, there are critical distinctions to be made among the competing rationales and justifications that are presented by political elites for supporting a public policy or a political candidate. Similar distinctions have been made between moral or ethical justifications on the one hand, and more materialist concerns on the other. Napoli (1999) for example, described the shifting emphasis in policy discourse at the Federal Communications Commission between 1965–1998 as a move away from a concern with democratic ideals, and toward a concern with efficiency and consumer satisfaction as a justification for regulatory policy. Such a shift in policy discourse may reflect a shift in elite discourse as represented in the press. What Shah and his colleagues demonstrate is that voters, and presumably policymakers, can have their evaluation of policies or candidates shaped by the use of frames that suggest markedly different evaluative criteria.

FRAMING RESOURCES AND THE NEW MEDIA ENVIRONMENT

It is clear that we think about frames and framing techniques as strategic resources used by all communicators. These are resources that are used purposively to direct attention and then to guide the processing of information so that a preferred reading of the facts comes to dominate public understanding. We have noted that there are a variety of techniques available to journalists and their editors to foreground, as well as to distance themselves from, or to question the legitimacy of, claims made by participants in some ongoing debate. Among these framing techniques is the use of "quotes" around classifications of individuals in order to signal that a particular "professor" may be something less than the title implies (van Dijk, 1991).

Differences in tone, style, and pace can also be considered as framing resources because of the ways in which they convey information to the audience about how the information is to be interpreted or assessed (Kosicki, 1993). The subtle but powerful cues that the skillful orator brings into play at different moments during a speech do more than signal to an audience that an important point is about to be made. As Entman (1993) reminds us, frames also "call attention to some aspects of reality while obscuring other elements" even though those elements may be included within the field of vision (p. 55). Here we might include the resources of the magician, the stage director, or even the photographer who makes use of levels, planes, light, and texture to direct the eyes of the observer toward some things and away from others.

Reese's case study, which begins this volume, provides a well-developed example of a path we might take to look beyond traditional media to see other ways in which framing may occur through the strategic deployment of symbolic resources. The organization of public spaces like museums has been identified by Schiller (1989) as a prime example of corporate domination of public expression. Schiller suggests that "corporate sponsorship of museum exhibitions leads inevitably, as does advertiser-supported television, to self-censorship"—what we would recognize as the avoidance of particular frameworks for understanding history, culture, and social issues (p. 94). Reese's observation, that one of the primary frames of the Newseum is the denial of ideological structures or frames in news, makes precisely this point.

We have assumed that the resources available to communicators, and those relied upon by members of the audience, will somehow change in the new media environment. It seems almost certain that we will observe changes in the *ways* in which stories are told, even if the fundamental plots involving the conflict between good and evil remains. This too is part of the paradox of the horizon.

New Media Environments

It seems clear that for some the "new media environment" is a conceptual frame that includes images of networked computers, as well as a host of other converging sources of information that software-controlled digital networks will bring to a set-top box (Baldwin, McVoy, & Steinfield, 1996). Many assume this new media environment will be characterized by an almost unlimited variety of frames, accessible at will. If this revolution happens at all, meaningful access to this staggering variety would only be possible with the assistance of intelligent agents, or semiautonomous search engines, performing their classification functions somewhere in the background, behind a curtain of implicit but unwarranted faith (Gandy, 1993). Whether user frames will, as a matter of course, be modified by "sponsor" frames is as yet undetermined, but this is an aspect of the new media environment that bears close watching.

First, this new media environment will be characterized by increasing individualization. By this I mean more than the segmentation and targeting the marketers talk about (Turow, 1997). I mean that the context in which media content will be acquired and consumed will also become increasingly individual, rather than social. Changes in consumption patterns will come to reflect some the changes that have taken place in the character of the American household this century. Schement (1995) noted the continuing decline in the size of the American household from an average of around 5.5 persons in 1850 to around 2.5 in 1990. Within those households, evidence suggests that more and more media consumption occurs in relatively private spaces, such as bedrooms, kitchens, and offices, rather than being limited to the common family room. More importantly, the number of single-person households has increased to a point where 24 million households, or 25% of American households, are now composed of solitary individuals. Persons living alone tend to be heavy users of communications media. These isolates are not only "bowling alone" more these days (Putnam, 1995), but they are also reading, listening, and viewing alone much of the time as well.

If we now add to this trend the evidence that individuals in this new media environment are choosing rather than settling for media content because there are more specialized channels available (Webster, 1989), the importance of frames looms larger still. If we assume that the *variety* of frames available within specialized channels is less than that available in more general or mass appeal channels, then we might assume further that individuals will, on the average, be exposed to less variety in the frames they consume (Neuman, 1991). This might also mean that in the future, as consumers' tastes and preferences continue to be shaped by past exposure to media (Kubey & Csikszentmihalyi, 1990; Turow, 1997), their exposure to competing frames will become more limited still.

It is not just the new media that are changing, of course. Engel's chapter 17 reveals the ways in which the rapidly evolving world of digital media and hypertext is involved in the transformation of the traditional print media. This is a process that Engel associates with the generation of a new "rhetoric of the page" appropriate to the particularly fluid structure of "pages" within the domain of the World Wide Web. We understand that the visual layout of the traditional page serves the same sorts of functions that we have associated with rhetorical frames. Yet, the vastly more complex terrain that is engaged in a hypertext environment disrupts and discards the tried and true methods of visual organization that have evolved in the print environment. Engel's analysis of advertisements in three magazines, that are likely to be read by users of the Internet, points out the connections or bridges between the two media that have emerged in recent years. Among the innovations and transformations in framing techniques that Engel observes are the visual cues that are used to invite readers (surfers) in, and then guide their movement around the pages or "sites." The "connections" between elements on a printed page bear only the slightest resemblance to the connections enabled by a hypertext link, but the similarity in function is inescapable.

More importantly, perhaps, in terms of the social impact that we expect to flow from exposure, or engagement with networks, webs, or structures of meaning, changes in framing techniques are expected to generate changes in the patterns of exposure to "objects" within those frames. We recall that the Cultivation Hypothesis relies on an assumption of substantial homogeneity of content across program types and genre (Gerbner, 1998). Such an assumption supports the use of a rather imprecise measure of exposure such as hours of *television* viewed during the average week. It is difficult to maintain such an assumption, however, in the face of increases in the number of media channels that allow for individuals to pursue more specialized media diets (Tapper, 1995; Webster, 1989). The great cost involved in producing a content analysis of television content in a multichannel environment has severely limited the efforts of scholars to describe it (Whitney, Wartella, Lasorsa, & Danielson, 1999). In the absence of comprehensive descriptions of content that are updated periodically it becomes more difficult to evaluate the assumption of relative homogeneity across and within channels. Yet, the increasing emphasis within media industries on audience segmentation and targeting would lead one to expect increasing differentiation between more specialized channels (Turow, 1997).

In fact, changes in the nature of the Internet, and the ways in which hypertext structures are organized and explored, suggests that we would observe even greater variation in the ways in which individuals will encounter particular symbolic frames. Information providers on the Internet make use of a variety of techniques to identify, profile, and then provide specialized or individualized content to users of the World Wide Web. Although the success of "push" technology seems likely to fall short of its original hype, the effort to transform an electronic yellow pages or magazine rack into a more familiar source-controlled medium, also seems to presage a decline in the variety of frames that individuals will be exposed to (Shapiro & Varian, 1997).

This is a circumstance that raises, once again, the spectre of manipulative strategic communication. The ability of communicators to take advantage of transaction-generated personal information in order to deliver sponsored "packages" (Gamson, 1992) of information, organized in frames that resonate with the cultural themes common to individuals as members of identifiable groups, is an aspect of social control (Lindbloom, 1990). This is the basis of my concern with panoptic surveillance (Gandy, 1993), and its role in support of strategic communication (Gandy, 1982, 1996). This increased specialization, segmentation, or narrowcasting, might also mean, therefore, that as a nation we are exposed to fewer frames in common. Certainly this tendency, if correct, has implications for the character of the political process, and what we understand as the function of the public sphere (Carey, 1995; Katz, 1996). Carey suggests that public opinion depends on our ability to see our lives as part of a public community, rather than one that is more narrowly defined by race, class, gender, or interests in consuming.

What Fredin and Pavlik also help us to understand through their chapters are the ways in which the electronic journalist as author may shape the variety and distribution of symbolic frames. Fredin and Pavlik both express the hope that hypermedia will be developed in ways that invite and reward efforts by individuals to "read between the lines" or "outside the box" that routine news frames impose. Both authors assume a level of social commitment among journalists, or authors of hyperstories, that would seem incompatible with the bottom-line pressures being felt by many within the traditional news industry (McChesney, 1999). Yet, Fredin's engagement with the nature of hyperstories supports an optimistic view. He imagines the consumer of news as an active, creative investigator, who will be motivated by the rewards (flow) that come from navigating the informational web that such stories might provide. One possibility that Fredin entertains is the chance that hyperstories may provide more easily accessible bridges across the "boundaries" between fact and opinion, which we currently assume divides the news from the editorial section of the traditional newspaper. Arguments—which in Fredin's view are the product of particular combinations of facts, values, ideas, and assumptions—might be marked and organized in hyperstories in ways that reveal their underlying connections. Both Fredin and Pavlik recognize that providing alternative frames, and even glossaries of frames with hyperstories multiplies the level of necessary investment in the production of news (and editorial comment).

Mabry's chapter examines framing within the Internet environment, although he does not actually engage what we would ordinarily think of as mass media. Instead, Mabry explores the nature of computer-mediated communication (CMC) in discussion groups and forums. These are increasingly the primary sites of discursive interaction or political deliberation for the politically engaged. We might expect these deliberations to determine the extent to which elite frames derived from traditional mass media will dominate or even survive in recognizable fashion. The discussion groups that Mabry examine differ from those used by Gamson to demonstrate the capacity of "ordinary folk" to engage in high level discussion of contemporary issues (Gamson, 1992). Mabry's "groups" were naturally occurring, rather than constructed for the purposes of study. The interaction among members of these groups was electronically mediated and relied on typed messages. Among the unique features of the medium is the ability of participants or "members" of these groups to "cut-and-paste" parts of other participants' statements as framing elements in a discursive strategy. Mabry observes an interaction between group objective and message framing types. He concludes that the technology facilitates the use of more complex message strategies which enhance the cohesiveness of groups.

Although the nature of discursive interactions seems likely to change, the subjects of that political talk may also be changed in important ways. Our assumptions about the ways social, cultural, and economic influences determine the centrality of particular frames have to be re-examined in the context of an increasingly integrated global media market (Herman & McChesney, 1997). Critical scholars tend to assume that the effect of globalization is bound to be homogenization, or a reduction in cultural diversity. Bantimaroudis and Ban (chap. 9, this volume) fully expected to observe differences in the ways in which *The New York Times* and *The Guardian* would cover the turmoil in Somalia, given what had been assumed to be differences in European and American perspectives. Yet their content analysis revealed striking similarity in the frames used by these newspapers. We have to ask what might be the nature of the constraint that invites the use of framing labels like "warlords" and "factions" so consistently throughout the life of the story.

Paterson's chapter 20 on the global market for television news is especially relevant in this regard. Concentration within the industry that supplies the raw materials making up the core of "foreign news" for stations around the globe would generally be assumed to produce greater homogeneity in the frames used to tell the stories of the day. I find in Paterson's analysis a remarkable extension of the observations made by Paul Hirsch in his updating of the classic gatekeeping study of David Manning White. Recall that White's wire service editor ("Mr. Gates") was described as making autonomous choices about which stories would be published and which would be rejected, presumably on the basis of some idiosyncratic rules and personal preferences (White, 1950). Hirsch (1977) observed that despite the apparent freedom (and power) exercised by this editor "the types and proportions of news stories supplied by the wire services and the types and proportions chosen for the subscribing paper were *virtually identical*" (p. 22). Similarly, and contrary to the claims made by some agency executives and by some academics who favor an assumption of polysemic construction, Paterson finds remarkably little variation in the use of visual images to reproduce ideologically structured frames.

The Visual Domain

More image-based studies argue strongly in support of the need to remember that this new media environment will be entirely more visual than the dominant media of the past. Scholarly emphasis on framing, with rare exceptions, has focused on the analysis of language in textual form. We have tended to ignore the visual. Although Iyengar's work on framing has tended to focus on television rather than print, the details of that analysis suggest that the approach used to characterize media frames relied most heavily on the analysis of transcripts of the spoken word (Iyengar, 1991). Yet, as Graber (1990) reminded us, visuals are extremely important as determinants of what we learn from television. Messaris (1997) emphasized the use of visual devices within print and television advertising, and it would be unrealistic, if not naive, for us to assume that these techniques are not also used by those who capture, select, and organize the images that play a central role in the presentation of the news.

Graber's (1990) analysis of the visual themes, or frames, in numerous news stories revealed that those themes were far more memorable than the themes expressed verbally. Graber reported that three kinds of visual themes were especially important: closeups of familiar people, like presidents, or popes; unfamiliar people in unusual, or exotic circumstances; and unfamiliar people who got to speak and express their views. Although Graber suggests that the audience for television news has been conditioned to rely upon the verbal framing as conveying the "essence of the story" (p. 152), it is not at all clear that everyone accepts this lesson, or that text always dominates other channels within an audiovisual display.

It is also likely that learned conventions for the interpretation of visual frames will be overcome in the context of new media. Barnhurst (1994) described the history of photojournalism and the ways in which pictures became defined as another category of content within the American newspaper. Perhaps in the same way that researchers are evaluating the impact of episodic vs. thematic, or issue vs. strategic frames, the detail vs. the emotional focus of the images that are so central to the new media certainly need to be addressed.

Pictures differed from text because of the ways in which the picture could provide both facts or details as well as emotion. Although we note in Zoch's chapter the ways in which print journalists attempt to capture the visual impact of an army of journalists and their satellite vans, and snarls of cabling, we are reminded of the greater attention that was paid to the "blooper tapes" of behind-the-scenes mishaps that underscore the impression of a comedy of errors.

Barnhurst and others have also called our attention to the ways graphics, like bar charts, are being used to present thematic content. The use of charts to distort relationships seems especially likely to accompany thematically framed stories where the use of statistics is so common (Mauro, 1992). In addition to charts and photographs, the many other framing resources available to the communicator, including color, and position within the borders of pages and screens, ought to be included within our study of frames. Maps are among the more powerful, but undertheorized, visual resources that can be used to frame our understanding of people and their communities. The development of sophisticated Geographic Information Systems (GIS) increases the number of social actors who are using maps to shape discussions about social issues. At the same time, communication scholars have lagged far beyond cultural geographers in examining the ways in which maps can distort the impressions that we have of relationships defined in spatial terms (Goss, 1995; Monmonier, 1991; Pickles, 1995).

The relative power of images versus text as framing resources is a question that is also raised by the work of Gilens (1996). Gilens examined the photographs accompanying stories about poverty in the nation's leading newsweeklies, as well as the pictures of persons accompanying 50 network television news stories between 1988 and 1992. African Americans made up 62% of the poor people who were featured in the magazines, more than twice their actual proportion of 29% in the U.S. population. A slightly higher proportion, 65%, of the poor people included in television stories were identifiable as African American. According to Gilens, framing the story about poverty as a story about Blacks will prompt *fewer* Whites to characterize poverty as important than if they are shown a story that uses images of Whites to illustrate the same story.

Of course, the decision about which images to use to reinforce a story frame is not so easily made. Back in 1978, Turow discussed the ways in which casting for television reflected dominant views about what was normal and, by inference, what would be noticed as unusual. Casting for television sought to achieve a kind a visual balance that would not distract the viewers' attention from the story because they were wondering about what that African American was doing behind the surgical mask (Turow, 1978). By the same logic, the photo editors interviewed by Gilens (1996) based their selection of images of African Americans on their sense of "what the poor should look like" (p. 535). For these editors, poverty has a black face, and to represent poverty in some other way would require a compelling reason, such as that which might be provided by a particularly moving and sympathetic image of an elderly White man. The fact that television relies so heavily on familiar stereotypes to present and reinforce the intended message should certainly spark our interest if we are concerned about the influence of media on race relations and public policy that engages questions of race. Devine (1989) demonstrated how easily racial stereotypes can be activated, even in persons who are actively striving to oppose racial oppression. The activation of racial stereotypes, even in an unrelated story, affects the kinds of attributions of responsibility that will be made (Power, Murphey, & Coover, 1996).

Messaris and Abraham's chapter 13 provides additional justification for examining the use of visuals as framing resources in the news (and, I would suggest, in other media forms). Among the many insights that this piece contributes to our thinking about the nature of framing and framing effects, is that visual propositions may more easily bypass, or overcome, the cognitive barriers that may temper the impact of frames delivered through words. Although Cappella and Jamieson observed a more powerful framing effect associated with print rather than television news, they did not characterize the images in the news as either being consistent with, or distractions from, the "strategy" frames delivered verbally (Cappella & Jamieson, 1997). What Messaris and Abraham argue is that the power of the visual frame is inherent in its being "taken for granted," as analogs of that which they represent.

What Messaris and Abraham also suggest, and Paterson confirms, is that news frames are standardized and that it is common practice to "stage" scenes in order to produce the readily acceptable and widely expected images consistent with those frames. Even if images are not staged, they unquestionably have to be "selected," and that selection is constrained by more than news standards. Messaris and Abraham argue that the use of visuals facilitates the delivery of more subtle racial cues that might otherwise be edited out by producers concerned about a hostile audience response. In addition, Messaris and Abraham identify and classify several types of visual cues that are consistently used to "racialize" stories about social problems. Their classificatory scheme should prove useful to those of us who are concerned with our ability to reliably and accurately identify the entire array of framing resources that used to shape our understanding and our expectations of those we will encounter along the way to the future.

MOVING ONWARD FROM HERE

Although there are important differences and distinctions among the scholars we have brought together in this volume, I think it fair to say that each of us share a common concern with the role that framing plays in the distribution of life chances. While some may prefer to think about framing in terms of power and influence, and the nature of the inequalities and asymmetries that such a perspective assumes, others think it more than enough to be able to describe the ways in which frames rise and fall in importance over time. Whereas some are driven to understand more clearly what there is in human nature that makes individuals so susceptible to the influence of realistic images, others are more concerned to understand the differences in our response to frames that are somehow associated with our membership in socially defined communities or groups.

Although we have made some progress in understanding the role that framing plays in the modern public sphere, we have really just begun to imagine the nature of framing in a computer mediated environment. Here too we find differences in the assumptions and concerns that motivate our research. On the one hand, there are those of us who feel that a network environment with unimaginable bandwidth and unlimited access all but eliminates the possibility of domination or control by elites. Others are far less sanguine. For them, the evidence of a centripetal force is more compelling.

Critical scholars, especially political economists, have been taken to task for their failure to pay sufficient attention to the role that culture plays in the modulation of media effects (Livingstone, 1998). There are some signs that we have taken notice (Wasko & Hagen, 2000). The contributions from Pan and Kosicki and Hertog and McLeod suggest that some genuine progress is being made in this regard. It will be especially important for us to explore how globalization increases the rate at which imported frames will confront traditional ways of making sense of the world. We have been reminded of the importance of media frames to the development of social movements. Our emphasis on political discourse and frames within the news has led us to largely ignore the ways in which frames in the news echo or are reflected by frames that have become popular within media products design to entertain. The emphasis on "intertextuality" that is common within cultural studies may be combined with a concern about the homogenization of content that political economists attribute to mergers among media giants (McChesney, 1999; Schiller, 1999) to generate some testable hypotheses about what convergence might actually mean (Baldwin et al., 1996).

Although we may indeed learn more through experimental microanalysis about the ways in which particular frames affect cognitive responses, it also seems clear that our understanding of how social context and cultural difference intercede beyond the laboratory will depend on our willingness to pursue some of the analytical paths that ethnographic methods may provide. Although Mabry's investigation of the interactions among participants in online groups provide us with some insight into the nature of the complex interactions between frames and emotional responses, it seems that we are still far from being able to observe the ways in which the use of particular frames transforms the ecology of these groups. Perhaps a return to insights developed earlier through Bales' (1950) method for classifying group interaction may pay some unexpected dividends in our attempts to make sense of interactions in cyberspace. The fact that these interactions produce data trails that are more readily accessible than other sorts of interactions increases the opportunity for their observation and analysis. At the same time, increasing awareness of the troublesome ways in which this information may be put to use (Lessig, 1999) increases the likelihood that social norms, technical barriers, and legal restraints may limit the access of researchers to this data.

I began this chapter by talking about the journey. I have tended to equate progress with movement toward the horizon. Unlike most journeys, however, we have no destination in mind. There is no "emerald city" or "holy grail" just beyond the horizon. Instead, it is the journey itself that provides the reward. Engagement in the analysis of frames, their origins, and the quality of the experience they enable is justified on the basis of the contribution that this perspective provides to our understanding of where we are and where we have been. It may be too much to ask that it also provide some guidance as to whether we ought to turn left or right at the horizon.

REFERENCES

Baldwin, T., McVoy, D. S., & Steinfield, C. (1996). *Convergence. Integrating media, information & communication.* Thousand Oaks, CA: Sage.

Bales, R. F. (1950). *Interaction process analysis.* Reading, MA: Addison-Wesley.

Barnhurst, K. G. (1994). *Seeing the newspaper.* New York: St. Martin's Press.

Baumgartner, F., & Jones, B. (1993). *Agendas and instability in American politics.* Chicago: University of Chicago Press.

Becker, L. (1982). The mass media and citizen assessment of issue importance. A reflection on agenda-setting research. In D. C. Whitney, E. Wartella, & S. Windahl (Eds.), *Mass communication review yearbook* (Vol. 3, pp. 521–536). Beverly Hills, CA: Sage.

Beniger, J. (1986). *The control revolution. Technological and economic origins of the information society.* Cambridge, MA: Harvard University Press.

Cappella, J., & Jamieson, K. (1997). *Spiral of cynicism. The press and the public good.* New York: Oxford University Press.

Carey, J. (1995). The press, public opinion, and public discourse. In T. Glasser & C. Salmon (Eds.), *Public opinion and the communication of consent* (pp. 373–402). New York: Guilford Press.

Chaffee, S. (1977). Mass media effects: New research perspectives. In D. Lerner & L. Nelson (Eds.), *Communication research: A half-century appraisal* (pp. 210–241). Honolulu: University Press of Hawaii.

Cornell, S., & Hartmann, D. (1998). *Ethnicity and race. Making identities in a changing world.* Thousand Oaks, CA: Pine Forge Press.

Darnell, D. (1970). Semantic differentiation. In P. Emmert & W. Brooks (Eds.), *Methods of research in communication* (pp. 181–196). Boston, MA: Houghton Mifflin.

Deacon, D., Pickering, M., Golding, P., & Murdock, G. (1999). *Researching communications. A practical guide to methods in media and cultural analysis.* London: Arnold.

Devine, P. (1989). Stereotype and prejudice: Their automatic and controlled components. *Journal of Personality and Social Psychology, 56,* 5–18.

Dijk, T. van (1991). *Racism and the press.* London: Routledge.

Domke, D., Watts, M., Shah, D., & Fan, D. (1999). The politics of conservative elites and the 'liberal media' argument. *Journal of Communication, 49*(4), 35–58.

Dunwoody, S., & Griffin, R. (1999). Structural pluralism and media accounts of risk. In D. Demers & K. Viswanath (Eds.), *Mass media, social control, and social change: A macrosocial perspective* (pp. 139–158). Ames, IA: Iowa State University Press.

Entman, R. (1993). Framing: Toward a clarification of a fractured paradigm. *Journal of Communication, 43*(4), 51–58.

Entman, R. (1998). Manufacturing discord: Media in the affirmative action debate. In R. Noll & M. Price (Eds.), *A communications cornucopia: Markle Foundation essays on information policy* (pp. 39–71). Washington, DC: The Brookings Institution.

Gamson, W. (1992). *Talking politics.* New York: Cambridge University Press.

Gandy, O. (1982). *Beyond agenda setting. Information subsidies and public policy.* Norwood, NJ: Ablex.

Gandy, O. (1993). *The panoptic sort. A political economy of personal information.* Boulder, CO: Westview.

Gandy, O. (1996). Coming to terms with the panoptic sort. In D. Lyons & E. Zuriek (Eds.), *New technology, surveillance and social control* (pp. 132–155). Minneapolis: University of Minnesota Press.

Gandy, O., Kopp, K., Hands, T., Frazer, K., & Phillips, D. (1997). Race and risk: Factors affecting the framing of stories about inequality, discrimination, and just plain bad luck. *Public Opinion Quarterly, 61*(1), 158–182.

Gerbner, G. (1998). Cultivation analysis: An overview. *Mass Communication & Society, 1*(3/4), 175–194.

Gilens, M. (1996). Race and poverty in America. Public misperceptions and the American news media. *Public Opinion Quarterly, 60*(4), 515–541.

Goshorn, K., & Gandy, O. (1995). Race, risk and responsibility: Editorial constraint in the framing of risk. *Journal of Communication, 45*(2), 133–151.

Goss, J. (1995). "We know who you are and we know where you live.": The instrumental rationality of geodemographic systems. *Economic Geography, 71*(2), 171.

Graber, D. (1990). Seeing is remembering: How visuals contribute to learning from television news. *Journal of Communication, 40*(3), 134–155.

Hall, P., & Preston, P. (1988). *The carrier wave: New information technology and the geography of innovation. 1846-2003.* London: Unwin-Hyman.

Herman, E., & McChesney, R. (1997). *The global media. The new missionaries of global capitalism.* London: Cassell.

Hirsch, P. (1977). Occupational, organizational, and institutional models in mass media research: Toward an integrated framework. In P. Hirsch, P. Miller, & F. G. Kline (Eds.), *Strategies for communication research* (Vol. 6, pp. 13–42). Beverly Hills, CA: Sage.

Hirsch, P., & Thompson, T. (1994). The stock market as audience: The impact of public ownership on newspapers. In J. Ettema & D. C. Whitney (Eds.), *Audiencemaking: How the media create the audience* (pp. 142–158). Thousand Oaks, CA: Sage.

Hoffner, C., Buchannan, M., Anderson, J., Hubbs, L., Kamigaki, S., Kowalczyk, L., Pastorek, A., Plotkin, R., & Silberg, K. (1999). Support for censorship of television violence. The role of the third person effect and news exposure. *Communication Research, 26*(6), 726–742.

Iyengar, S. (1991). *Is anyone responsible? How television frames political issues.* Chicago: University of Chicago Press.

Katz, E. (1996). And deliver us from segmentation. *The ANNALS of the American Academy of Political and Social Science, 546*(July), 22–33.

Kinder, D., & Sanders, L. (1996). *Divided by color. Racial politics and democratic ideals.* Chicago: University of Chicago Press.

Kosicki, G. (1993). Problems and opportunities in agenda-setting research. *Journal of Communication, 43*(2), 100–127.

Kubey, R., & Csikszentmihalyi, M. (1990). *Television and the quality of life: How viewing shapes everyday experience.* Hillsdale, NJ: Lawrence Erlbaum Associates.

Lessig, L. (1999). *Code and other laws of cyberspace.* New York: Basic Books.

Lindbloom, C. (1990). *Inquiry and change: The troubled attempt to understand and shape society.* New Haven, CT: Yale University Press.

Livingstone, S. (1998). Audience research a the crossroads. The "implied audience" in media and cultural theory. *The European Journal of Cultural Studies, 1*(2), 161–178.

Mauro, J. (1992). *Statistical deception at work.* Hillsdale, NJ: Lawrence Erlbaum Associates.

McChesney, R. (1999). Will the Internet set us free?, *Rich media, poor democracy: Communications politics in dubious times* (pp. 119–185). Urbana: University of Illinois Press.

McManus, J. (1994). *Market-driven journalism. Let the citizen beware?* Thousand Oaks, CA: Sage.

Messaris, P. (1997). *Visual persuasion. The role of images in advertising.* Thousand Oaks, CA: Sage.

Monmonier, M. (1991). *How to lie with maps.* Chicago: University of Chicago Press.

Morris, A., & Meuller, C. (Eds.). (1992). *Frontiers in social movement theory.* New Haven, CT: Yale University Press.

Napoli, P. (1999). The marketplace of ideas metaphor in communications regulation. *Journal of Communication, 49*(4), 151–169.

Neuman, W. (1991). *The future of the mass audience.* New York: Cambridge University Press.

Obershall, A. (1993). *Social movements. Ideologies, interests & identities.* New Brunswick, NJ: Transaction.

Osgood, C., Suci, G., & Tannenbaum, P. (1957). *The measurement of meaning.* Urbana: University of Illinois Press.

Pickles, J. (Ed.). (1995). *Ground truth: The social implications of geographic information systems.* New York: Guilford Press.

Power, J. G., Murphey, S., & Coover, G. (1996). Priming prejudice. How stereotypes and counter-stereotypes influence attribution of responsibility and credibility among ingroups and out-groups. *Human Communication Research, 23*(1), 36–58.

Protess, D., Cook, F., Doppelt, J., Ettema, J., Gordon, M., Leff, D., & Miller, P. (1991). *The journalism of outrage. Investigative reporting and agenda building in America.* New York: Guilford Press.

Putnam, R. (1995). Bowling alone. America's declining social capital. *Journal of Democracy, 6*(1), 65–78.

Riffe, D., Lacy, S., & Fico, F. (1998). *Analyzing media messages. Using quantitative content analysis in research.* Mahwah, NJ: Lawrence Erlbaum Associates.

Rogers, E., & Dearing, J. (1988). Agenda-setting research: Where has it been, where is it going? In J. Anderson (Ed.), *Communication yearbook* (Vol. 11, pp. 555–594). Beverly Hills, CA: Sage.

Rokeach, M. (1968). *Beliefs, attitudes and values.* San Francisco, CA: Jossey-Bass.

Schement, J. (1995). Divergence amid convergence: The evolving information environment of the home. In Institute for Information Studies (Ed.), *Crossroads on the information highway. Convergence and diversity in communication technology* (pp. 135–160). Queenstown, MD: Aspen Institute.

Schiller, D. (1999). *Digital capitalism. Networking the global market system.* Cambridge, MA: MIT Press.

Schiller, H. (1989). *Culture, Inc. The corporate takeover of public expression.* New York: Oxford University Press.

Shapiro, C., & Varian, H. (1999). *Information rules. A strategic guide to the network economy.* Boston: Harvard Business School Press.

Sniderman, P., Piazza, T., & Kendrick, A. (1991). Ideology and issue persuasibility: Dynamics of racial policy attitudes. In P. Sniderman, R. Brody, & P. Tetlock (Eds.), *Reasoning and choice. Explorations in political psychology* (pp. 223–243). New York: Cambridge University Press.

Stillar, G. (1998). *Analyzing everyday texts. Discourse, rhetoric, and social perspectives.* Thousand Oaks, CA: Sage.

Tapper, J. (1995). The ecology of cultivation: A conceptual model for cultivation research. *Communication Theory, 5*(1), 36–57.

Turow, J. (1978). Casting for television. The anatomy of social typing. *Journal of Communication, 28*(4), 18–24.

Turow, J. (1997). *Breaking up America. Advertisers and the new media world.* Chicago: University of Chicago Press.

Warlaumont, H. (1997). Appropriating reality. Consumers' perceptions of schema-inconsistent advertising. *Journalism and Mass Communication Quarterly, 74*(1), 39–54.

Wasko, J., & Hagen, I. (Eds.). (2000). *Consuming audiences? : Production and reception in media research.* Cresskill, NJ: Hampton Press.

Webster, J. (1989). Television audience behavior: Patterns of exposure in the new media environment. In J. Salvaggio & J. Bryant (Eds.), *Media use in the information age: Emerging patterns of adoption and consumer use* (pp. 197–216). Hillsdale, NJ: Lawrence Erlbaum Associates.

White, D. M. (1950). The gatekeeper: A case study in the selection of news. *Journalism Quarterly, 27*(4), 383–390.

Whitney, D. C., Wartella, E., Lasorsa, D., & Danielson, W. (1999). Monitoring 'reality' television: The National Television Violence Study. In K. Nordenstreng & M. Griffin (Eds.), *International media monitoring* (pp. 367–386). Cresskill, NJ: Hampton Press.

Contributors

Linus Abraham did his doctoral work at Annenberg School of Communication, University of Pennsylvania. He is an assistant professor of Visual Communication, Cultural Studies, and Electronic Media Production at the Greenlee School of Journalism and Communication, Iowa State University. His research interests include the structure, interpretation, and social functions of visual media; cultural construction of ethnicity/race in the media; and critical cultural approaches to mass media.

Hyun Ban is now a full-time lecturer in the Department of Mass Communication and Journalism at the University of Incheon, Korea. He received a doctoral degree in journalism at the University of Texas at Austin. His research has focused on online journalism, new media, journalism framing, and news credibility.

Philemon Bantimaroudis is currently a lecturer in the Department of Cultural Technology and Communication of the University of the Aegean in Mytilene, Greece. He also taught at Northern Michigan University following doctoral study at the University of Texas at Austin. His research, which focuses on issues related to culture and media, as well as international and political communication, has appeared in various journals including *Communication Research* and *The Harvard International Journal of Press/Politics.*

Donna L. Dickerson is Professor of Journalism and Dean of the College of Arts and Sciences at the University of Texas at Tyler. Her research and teaching interests include media law, First Amendment theory, reporting of minorities, and media history. Her most recent book, co-authored with Robert Trager of the University of Colorado, is *Freedom of Expression in the 21st Century,* published by Pine Forge Press. Dr. Dickerson served eight years as Director of the School of Mass Communications at the University of South Florida and Interim Dean of the Graduate School at USF for three years.

David Domke is an assistant professor in the School of Communications at the University of Washington, having joined the faculty in 1998 after receiving his PhD from the University of Minnesota. His research interests include individual values and cognition, media framing and priming, and the interaction of elites and the press in social change. He received the Ralph Nafziger-David Manning White Award in 1997 for the outstanding dissertation in the field of mass communication, an award given by the Association for Education in Journalism and Mass Communication, and his research has been published in a wide number of journals in communications and political science.

Frank D. Durham is an assistant professor in the School of Journalism and Mass Communication at the University of Iowa. His research focuses on developing critical sociological perspectives of the media.

Eric Paul Engel has an academic background in communication and has conducted research on online writing: Linear Textuality vs. Hypertextuality. He has worked in a number of new media positions.

Eric S. Fredin is an associate professor in the School of Journalism and Communication at Ohio State University. He has also taught at Indiana University. He received his PhD from the University of Michigan in 1980 and prior to that worked as a reporter. His interests include the design and psychology of hypermedia as well as psychological effects of the news media. Publications include the Journalism and Mass Communication Monograph *Rethinking the News Story for the Internet: Hyperstory Prototypes and a Model of the User.*

Ross Stuart Fuglsang is an assistant professor in the Department of Mass Communication at Morningside College, Sioux City, Iowa. His dissertation, *Motorcycle Menace: Media Genres and the Construction of a Deviant Subculture,* completed his doctoral program at The University of Iowa in 1997.

William A. Gamson is a professor of Sociology and co-directs the Media Research and Action Project at Boston College. He is the author of *Talking Politics* (1992) and *The Strategy of Social Protest* (2nd ed., 1990) among other books and articles on political discourse, the mass media and social movements. He is a past president of the American Sociological Association.

Oscar H. Gandy, Jr. is the Herbert I. Schiller Term Professor at the Annenberg School for Communication at the University of Pennsylvania. He is the author of *Communication and Race, The Panoptic Sort,* and *Beyond Agenda Setting.* Since earning his PhD at Stanford University in 1976, he has focused his research and teaching in the areas of privacy, public policy formation, and communications and race relations, and has published in excess of 75 articles and book chapters in these areas.

Salma I. Ghanem is an assistant professor at the University of Texas at Pan American, where she also serves as Journalism Area Head. She earned her PhD degree from the University of Texas at Austin in 1996. Her areas of research interest include agenda setting, framing, social issues and the media, and Hispanics and the media. She is the recipient of the Outstanding Faculty Award for Professional achievement in 1998. Dr. Ghanem served as a Communication Specialist for Scott and White Hospital in Temple, Texas, and as a Press and Information Officer for the Egyptian Mission to the United Nations in New York.

August E. Grant (PhD, Annenberg School, University of Southern California) is a consultant on consumer adoption and use of new technologies and mass media. After spending nine years with the Department of Radio-Television-Film at the University of Texas at Austin he was founding Director of the Center for Mass Communication Research at the University of South Carolina. He has written numerous articles and conference papers dealing with adoption and use of emerging communication technologies, broadband services, audience behavior, and theories of new media. He is the editor of the *Communication Technology Update* (now in its seventh edition), a semiannual review of the latest developments in communication technologies.

James K. Hertog is associate professor of Journalism and Telecommunications at the University of Kentucky, where he has taught for 11 years. He received his doctorate in mass communication theory and research from the University of Minnesota in 1990. He has published a number of articles and book chapters on political communication with an emphasis on the portrayal of alternative voices in the media. Current research includes the study of press coverage of minor political parties and protest groups and the communication strategies of business groups attempting to influence public policy.

Gerald M. Kosicki (PhD, Mass Communications, 1987, University of Wisconsin-Madison) is Director of the Center for Survey Research in the College of Social and Behavioral Sciences at The Ohio State University. He is also an associate professor in the OSU School of Journalism and Communication. His research has focused on political communication and various aspects of public opinion, particularly on priming and framing of public issues.

Edward A. Mabry is associate professor of communication, University of Wisconsin-Milwaukee. His research and teaching focuses on group and organizational studies with an emphasis on mediated communication.

T. Michael Maher is associate professor of communication at the University of Louisiana-Lafayette. His research has centered on agenda setting and media framing of environmental issues, particularly population and biodiversity loss. He has also written book chapters on journalism history, and has contributed articles to *Quill, Editor & Publisher,* and *SEJournal,* the newsletter of the Society of Environmental Journalists. His PhD is from the University of Texas.

Maxwell McCombs holds the Jesse H. Jones Centennial Chair in Communication at the University of Texas. A fellow of the International Communication Association, past president of the World Association for Public Opinion Research, and recipient of the Deutschmann Award, McCombs has lectured recently on agenda-setting theory in Australia, Chile, France, Germany, Spain, Turkey, and Taiwan. His book on agenda-setting theory, *The Emergence of American Political Issues,* co-authored with Donald Shaw, was cited by *Journalism & Mass Communication Quarterly* as one of the "significant journalism and communication books" of the 20th century. His PhD is from Stanford University.

Douglas M. McLeod is an associate professor of Journalism and Mass Communication at the University of Wisconsin. His research focuses on media coverage of protest groups, the role of the media in social conflicts, and mass-mediated messages as forms of social control. He teaches courses on mass media and society, strategic communication, mass communication theory and research methods. He received his PhD from the University of Minnesota.

Paul Messaris is a professor at the Annenberg School for Communication, University of Pennsylvania. He teaches visual communication and is involved in the development and administration of a new major in Digital Media Design, which deals with the use of computers in the creation and modification of visual images. He is the author of *Visual Literacy: Image, Mind, and Reality* (1994; winner of the National Communication Association's Diamond Anniversary Book Award) and *Visual Persuasion: The Use of Images in Advertising* (1997).

M. Mark Miller is a professor in the School of Journalism and Public Relations at the University of Tennessee. A former newspaper reporter and editor, he holds the doctorate from the Michigan State University. His research focuses on the forces shaping news, news and public opinion formation, and environmental risk communication. He is the author of VBPro, a computer program for content analysis. He is a Fellow of the Midwest Association for Public Opinion Research.

Thomas E. Nelson is associate professor of Political Science at The Ohio State University in Columbus. He received his PhD in Social Psychology at the University of Michigan in 1992 and has been at Ohio State ever since, where he teaches in the Political Psychology program. He has served as Co-director of the Summer Institute in Political Psychology, and for the last two years he has been Director of the Political Research Laboratory. Besides political communication, his research concerns public opinion on racial issues and cognitive models of political attitudes.

Zhongdang Pan has taught at a number of institutions since receiving his PhD in 1990, including the University of Pennsylvania, the Chinese University of Hong Kong, Cornell University, and the University of Michigan. His research focuses on social and cognitive effects of media in the process of public deliberation and media reforms in the People's Republic of China. He has published numerous articles and book chapters and a co-authored book, *To See Ourselves* (Westview). His second co-authored book, *Global Media Spectacle,* will be published by SUNY Press.

Chris A. Paterson is an assistant professor of Media Studies at the University of San Francisco. Following doctoral study at the University of Texas at Austin, he also taught at the Centre for Mass Communication Research at the University of Leicester, in England, and at Georgia State University in Atlanta. His research concerns television journalism, news agencies, and the flow of international news.

John V. Pavlik is professor of Journalism and Executive Director of the Center for New Media at Columbia University. Pavlik's research examines the impact of new media on journalism and society. His articles have appeared in *New Media & Society, Media Ethics, Television Quarterly, Media Studies Journal, Columbia Journalism Review, Nieman Reports* and elsewhere. He is author of *New Media Technology: Cultural and Commercial Perspectives* and co-editor with Frederick Williams of *The People's Right to Know: Media, Democracy and the Information Highway* and with Everette E. Dennis of *Demystifying Media Technology.* He is contributing editor for the *Online Journalism Review.*

Stephen D. Reese has been on the University of Texas journalism faculty—most recently as G. B. Dealey Professor and Director—since 1982, following doctoral study at the University of Wisconsin at Madison. His research has focused on a wide range of issues concerning media effects and press performance, as published in numerous book chapters and articles. He is co-author with Pamela Shoemaker of *Mediating the Message: Theories of Influence on Mass Media Content,* now in its 2nd edition and named by *Journalism & Mass Communication Quarterly* as one of the "significant journalism and communication books" of the century.

Bonnie Parnell Riechert joined the University of Tennessee journalism and public relations faculty in 1999, following graduate study at the University of Georgia and the University of Tennessee. Her research addresses topics including news media framing and policy agenda development, news coverage of science and environmental issues, journalist-source relationship, political communications, and quantitative methods for framing analysis of text. She is co-author with Mark Miller of chapters in *Environmental Risks and the Media and Theory, Method, and Practice of Computer Content Analysis.*

Dhavan V. Shah is an assistant professor of journalism and mass communication and political science at the University of Wisconsin-Madison, where he joined the faculty in 1998 after receiving his PhD from the University of Minnesota. His research centers on the psychology of political communication, with particular emphasis on the role of media framing and cueing in political information processing and the influence of mass communication on civic engagement. He received the Ralph Nafziger-David Manning White Award in 2000 for the outstanding dissertation in the field of mass communication, an award given by the Association for Education in Journalism and Mass Communication.

James W. Tankard, Jr., has been on the faculty of the School of Journalism at the University of Texas for 29 years, after teaching at the University of Wisconsin and Temple University. He has published research articles on information graphics, science communication, and computer-assisted reporting. He is the co-author with Werner J. Severin of *Communication Theories: Origins, Methods and Uses in the Mass Media,* now in its fifth edition.

Daniel B. Wackman is a professor in the School of Journalism and Mass Communication at the University of Minnesota, where he joined the faculty in 1971 after receiving his PhD from the University of Wisconsin at Madison. At Minnesota, he was Director of the Research Division for twelve years and Director of the School for six years. His research has focused on political communication, advertising and consumer socialization, electronic commerce, and interpersonal communication, and he has published in a variety of academic journals and books. He received the Harold L. Nelson Award for Contributions to Journalism Education from the University of Wisconsin-Madison School of Journalism and Mass Communication in 2001.

Ernest L. Wiggins has been on the faculty of the University of South Carolina College of Journalism and Mass Communications since 1993, after ten years as a reporter and editor at *The State* and *Columbia Record* newspapers. His teaching and research interests include media ethics, minorities and the press and community journalism.

Elaine A. Willey is a PhD candidate in political science at The Ohio State University. Her research interests include political psychology, mass political behavior, and legislative politics.

Lynn M. Zoch joined the faculty of the College of Journalism and Mass Communications, University of South Carolina in 1993. Zoch is currently the College's director of the masters degree programs, and was previously the director of the College's Center for Mass Communications Research. She has a PhD in Public Communication from Syracuse University. Her research has focused on a wide range of issues including the roles of public relations practitioners, wome as news sources, crisis communication, and reaching undereducated audience She is the author of thirteen published book chapters, articles, and reviews and has presented her work at national and international conferences.

Author Index

Ghanem, S. 2, 8, 10, 31, 36, 38n, 62, 70, 71, 76, 77, 80, 81, 84, 88, 90, 93, 94, 100n, 101, 106, 177, 183, 196, 359, 362
Gibson, J., 251, 265
Gibson, J. O., 289, 292
Giddens, A., 129, 131, 132
Gieber, W., 123, 135
Gilbert, D. T., 272, 292
Gilens, M., 372, 376
Giroux, H., 22, 30
Gitlin, T., 11, 14, 16, 30, 36, 37n, 40, 42, 43, 49, 62, 87, 93, 99, 109, 114, 121, 123, 126, 135
Gladwell, M., 289, 292
Glasgow Media Group, 16, 123
Globerson, T., 275, 293
Goffman, E., 7, 11, 30, 37, 60, 62, 87, 90, 93, 98, 105, 125, 135, 208, 213, 214, 246, 265
Golding, P., 339, 352, 357, 375
Golonka, S., 288, 291
Gombrich, E. H., 216, 226
Gomery, D., 197, 205
Goodwin, C., 50, 65
Goodman, N., 216, 226, 276, 292
Gordon, M., 358, 377
Goshorn, K., 12, 30, 358, 376
Goss, J., 372, 376
Gossett, T., 172, 173
Govier, T., 326, 335
Grabe, M., 339, 352
Graber, D., 39, 63, 69, 81, 84, 94, 99, 105, 209, 214, 270, 282, 292, 339, 352, 371, 376
Gramsci, A., 126, 135
Gray, H., 223, 226
Gray, J., 168, 173
Green, D. P., 229, 231, 241, 250, 265
Greenhouse, L., 254, 265
Greenstein, R., 287, 292
Greenwald, A. G., 230, 241
Griffin, R., 357, 375
Grimes, T., 339, 352
Gripsrud, J., 197, 205
Grodsky, S., 297, 298, 308

Gross, D. S., 128, 136
Gross, K., 254, 265
Grube, J. W., 250, 266
Gurevitch, M., 40, 43, 61, 338, 351, 352
Guthrie, K. K., 230, 241

H

Habermas, J., 27, 63, 128, 130, 136, 350, 352
Hackett, R. A., 9, 30, 96, 97, 102, 105, 144, 156, 161
Hagen, I., 374, 378
Haider-Markel, D. P., 228, 239, 241
Hall, A., 86, 87, 93
Hall, B., 51, 63
Hall, P., 358, 376
Hall, S., 11, 30, 144, 161, 220, 226
Hallahan, K., 108, 121
Hallin, D., 109, 121, 350, 352
Halpern, R., 288, 292
Hamil, R., 270, 282, 292
Hands, T., 358, 376
Haraway, D., 22, 30
Hart-Davison, B., 298, 299, 308
Hartley, J., 40, 63, 220, 226
Hartmann, D., 360, 375
Hassett, M., 298, 299, 303, 308
Hastie, R., 231, 242
Hayes, C., 170, 173
Heith, D., 50, 65
Helco, H., 52, 53, 54, 63
Helland, K., 339, 346, 352
Hendrickson, L., 10, 31, 70, 81, 90, 94, 100n, 101, 102, 103, 105, 106
Hennessey, B. A., 276, 292
Herek, G. M., 230, 241
Herman, E., 349, 352, 370, 376
Herr, T., 288, 292
Hershey, A. M., 288, 292
Herstein, J. A., 231, 241
Hertog, J., 3, 11, 30, 63, 145, 151, 152, 157, 159, 161, 362, 374
Hertsgaard, M., 47, 63
Herzog, D., 40, 63

Subject Index

A

Accessibility, 38, 255, 256, 258-260, 262, 263
Activation (of memories), 38, 357
Affirmative action, 169, 248, 249, 255, 256, 363
Agenda setting, 2, 8, 9, 18, 38, 41, 67-74, 76-79, 83-92, 101, 108, 196, 245, 355, 357, 359, 360
Agenda building, 108, 111
Associative network, 38
Attribute(s), 18, 38, 68, 71-79, 85, 86, 89, 91, 92, 196, 231, 238, 249, 296, 327, 359, 360, 362, 363
Attribute agenda setting, 68-70, 72, 73, 76-79
Attribute salience, 69, 85, 91, 196
Attribution, 144, 168, 170, 229, 240, 372
Audience segmentation, 368

B

Bandwidth, 374
Bias(es), 9, 12, 18, 26, 27, 96, 97, 104, 155, 172, 211, 247, 361
Business communication, 295

C

Capitalism, 134, 249, 315
Case study, 139, 356
Catchphrase(s), 199, 282, 284, 285, 290, 361
Categorization, 252, 253, 258, 264, 277
Causal modeling analysis, 239

Causal reasoning, 87, 88, 89
Causality, 91, 219
Civic journalism, 97, 135, *see also* Public journalism
Civil rights, 211, 232
Claimsmaker(s), 110, 112
Cluster analysis, 114, 116, 117, 361
Cognition, 11, 239, 252, 307, 357, 359
Cognitive miser(s), 237, 255, 263
Cognitive psychology, 84, 87, 92
Collective action(s), 39-42, 49
Collective action frames, 246
Colloquialism, 328
Compelling arguments, 77
Computer-assisted content analysis, 108, 117, 120
Computer mediated communication (CMC), 6, 324-326, 329, 335, 360, 369
Computer networks, 269, 270
Connectivity, 5, 295, 296, 301-308
Conservatism, 211, 254
Continuity, 5, 295, 296, 301-308
Construct, 270
Constructionist (view), 16
Content analysis, 4, 8, 76, 78, 102-104, 114-116, 119, 229, 245, 329, 340, 341, 343, 360, 362, 368, 370
Credibility, 135, 172, 259, 299, 300, 317, 320
Cultivation, 362, 368
Cultural studies, 9, 374
Cyberspace, 5, 296, 305-308, 374

D

Decision frames, 246, 247